not ANGELS, BUT ANGLICANS

D1586483

Oldest? St Martin's Church,
Canterbury, believed to be
the oldest church in England
in continuous use.
*Photo © A. F. Kersting*

# NOT ANGELS, BUT ANGLICANS

## A HISTORY OF CHRISTIANITY IN THE BRITISH ISLES

*Consulting Editor: Henry Chadwick*
*Commissioning Editor: Allison Ward*

Published in association with the *Church Times*

CANTERBURY
PRESS
Norwich

COPYRIGHT
TEXT: © 2000 by the authors and in this compilation
© 2000 by the *Church Times*
ILLUSTRATIONS: © 2000 as credited

First published in 2000 by The Canterbury Press Norwich
(a publishing imprint of Hymns Ancient & Modern Limited
a registered charity)
St Mary's Works, St Mary's Plain,
Norwich, Norfolk NR3 3BH

British Library Cataloguing in Publication Data

A catalogue record for this book is available
from the British Library

ISBN 1-85311-352-2

Design by Vera Brice.
Typesetting by the *Church Times*, 33 Upper Street, London N1 0PN

Printed and bound in Great Britain by The Bath Press

SCM-Canterbury Press
Hymns Ancient and Modern Ltd,
St Mary's Works, St Mary's Plain,
Norwich NR3 3BH

# CONTENTS

Contributors    vii

List of colour plates    xi

Foreword by Paul Handley    xiii

Preface
*The Route from Galilee* by **Henry Chadwick**    1

Chapter 1
*From Rome to Augustine: Britain before 597* by **Paul Cavill & Michael Jackson**    9

Chapter 2
*'A dangerous, wearisome and uncertain journey'* by **Paul Cavill**    17

Chapter 3
*To Whitby for Easter: Wilfrid's Triumph* by **David Rollason**    25

Chapter 4
*Rape, Pillage and Exaggeration* by **Catherine Cubitt**    33

Chapter 5
*Apocalypse Then (AD 1000)* by **Simon Keynes**    41

Chapter 6
*The Norman Arrow Finds a Ready Target* by **Giles Gasper**    49

Chapter 7
*Monasticism in Britain* by **Benjamin Thompson, Gillian Evans & J. Wyn Evans**    59

Chapter 8
*101 Uses for a Dead Archbishop* by **Brenda Bolton**    69

Chapter 9
*War Against the Infidels - and Other Christians* by **Jonathan Riley-Smith & Alan Borg**    77

Chapter 10
*Crying 'God for Harry! England and St George!'* by **Norman Tanner**    87

Chapter 11
*Living in Heaven and Hell* by **Peter Heath**    95

Chapter 12
*1400: The Laity Begin to Take Control* by **Barrie Dobson**    105

Chapter 13
*How Luther's Vision Sundered a Continent* by **Euan Cameron**    115

Chapter 14
*The Reform That Wouldn't Stop* by **Margaret Bowker**    125

Chapter 15
*Of Ceremonies, Why Some Be Abolished* by **Diarmaid MacCulloch** 135

Chapter 16
*Anti-Papist, Anti-Puritan* by **Patrick Collinson & Rowan Williams** 143

Chapter 17
*The Settlement That Took Time to Settle* by **Judith Maltby & Kenneth Stevenson** 153

Chapter 18
*How the Old Church Grew Its Backbone* by **Judith Maltby & Kenneth Stevenson** 161

Chapter 19
*Becoming High and Mighty* by **Jonathan Clark** 169

Chapter 20
*The Moderate Men in Charge* by **Stephen Taylor** 179

Chapter 21
*The Man the Church of England Couldn't Contain* by **Henry Rack** 187

Chapter 22
*When One Revival Led to Another* by **Jeremy Morris, Arthur Burns & Frances Knight** 195

Chapter 23
*All Things That Give Sound* by **Richard Watson, Ian Bradley & Glyn Paflin** 203

Chapter 24
*When the Faith was Set Free* by **Edward Norman & David Edwards** 213

Chapter 25
*Scholars, Slums and Socialists* by **Jeremy Morris & Hugh Macleod** 223

Chapter 26
*Imperial England's Long Hand-over* by **William Jacob** 233

Chapter 27
*Looking, Learning and Leading from the Pews* by **Nicholas Orme & Ian Bradley** 243

Chapter 28
*Marching Forth with the Banner of Christ Unfurled* by **John Wolffe & Michael Perham** 255

Chapter 29
*Zeal for Reform as Numbers Slide* by **David Edwards & Grace Davie** 263

Chapter 30
*Into the New Millennium* by **John Bowker** 275

Further Reading 287

Index of proper names 297

# CONTRIBUTORS

**Brenda Bolton** read history at the University of Leeds, undertaking research with John Le Patourel. For many years she taught history in the University of London, specialising in ecclesiastical history and the pontificate of Innocent III. She has been a Leverhulme Senior Research Fellow and Visiting Professor in Italy and Denmark. She is the Secretary of the Commission Internationale d'Histoire Ecclésiastique Comparée. She is now engaged full-time in research, writing and guest lecturing internationally.

**Alan Borg** has been Director of the Victoria & Albert Museum, London, since 1995, and was previously Director of the Imperial War Museum from 1982. Trained as a historian and art historian, he specialises in the Romanesque period and in the art and architecture of the Crusades.

**John Bowker** is a Fellow of Gresham College in London, and Adjunct Professor at North Carolina State University. He was Professor of Religious Studies at Lancaster University before returning to Cambridge, where he was Fellow and Dean of Chapel at Trinity College until he had to retire through ill-health. Of his many books, *The Meanings of Death* was awarded the biennial HarperCollins Prize in 1993, and *The Complete Bible Handbook* received the Benjamin Franklin award for the best religious book in 1999.

**Margaret Bowker** was formerly a lecturer in history at the University of Cambridge, and Reader in History at the University of Lancaster.

**Ian Bradley** is Senior Lecturer in Practical Theology in the School of Divinity at St Andrews University. A minister in the Church of Scotland, he is the former head of religious broadcasting for BBC Scotland and a regular broadcaster and contributor to newspapers and magazines. He is the author of more than 20 books, the most recent of which are *Abide With Me: The World of Victorian Hymns*, *The Penguin Book of Carols*, *Celtic Christianity: Making Myths and Chasing Dreams* and *Colonies of Heaven: Celtic Models for Today's Church*. He is currently working on books exploring the spiritual dimension of monarchy and the theology of the musical.

**Arthur Burns** is Lecturer in Modern British History at King's College, London. He is the author of *The Diocesan Revival in the Church of England c.1800-1870*. He is currently one of the three directors of *The Clergy of the Church of England Database 1540-1835* and is also one of the editors of a new history of St Paul's Cathedral to be published in 2004. He is Treasurer of the Church of England Record Society.

**Euan Cameron** is Professor of Early Modern History at the University of Newcastle upon Tyne, and was previously a junior fellow of All Souls College, Oxford. He has written several books and articles, including *The European Reformation*, and *Early Modern Europe: An Oxford History*, and was advisory editor of *The German Reformation: Essential Readings*, edited by Scott Dixon.

**Paul Cavill** teaches Old English and is Research Officer for the English Place-Name Society in the School of English Studies at the University of Nottingham. He has published widely in academic journals, and his two most recent books are *Maxims in Old English Poetry* and *Anglo-Saxon Christianity*.

**Henry Chadwick** is Emeritus Regius Professor of Divinity at Cambridge. He was Regius Professor of Divinity in Oxford (1959-1969), Dean of Christ Church, Oxford (1969-1979), and Master of Peterhouse, Cambridge (1987-1993). He holds honorary doctorates from Yale, Chicago and Harvard Universities, and was a member of ARCIC from 1970 until 1990. Among his publications are *The Early Church* and *Augustine's Confessions*.

**Jonathan Clark** is Hall Distinguished Professor of British History at the University of Kansas. His writings on the history of religion include *The Language of Liberty 1660-1832* and *English Society 1660-1832*.

**Patrick Collinson** is Regius Professor of Modern History Emeritus in the University of Cambridge, and a Fellow of Trinity College. Many of his publications relate to the Reformation, the Elizabethan Church and Elizabethan Puritanism.

**Catherine Cubitt** teaches early medieval history at the University of York, and has published extensively on the Anglo-Saxon Church.

**Grace Davie** is Reader in the Sociology of Religion, University of Exeter, and the author of *Religion in Britain since 1945* and *Religion in Modern Europe: a Memory Mutates*.

**Barrie Dobson** retired as Professor of Medieval History at the University of Cambridge in 1999. He had held this chair since 1988, after 24 years (1964-1988) during which he taught medieval history at the then new University of York. He has written on many aspects of late-medieval English economic, social and church history, and made a particular study of the practice of the religious life within the three cathedral communities of Canterbury, York and Durham.

**David Edwards** is a former Dean of Norwich and Provost of Southwark, and author of a number of books on church history. These include *Christian England*, in three volumes, and *Christianity: The First Two Thousand Years*.

**Gillian Evans** lectures in history and theology at the University of Cambridge. Her books include *Anselm and Talking About God, Anselm and a New Generation, Old Arts and New Theology, The Mind of St Bernard of Clairvaux, Alan of Lille, Augustine on Evil, The Anselm Concordance, The Logic and Language of the Bible* (2 volumes), *The Thought of Gregory the Great, Problems of Authority in the Reformation Debates, Philosophy and Theology in the Middle Ages, The Church and the Churches, Method in Ecumenical Theology, The Reception of the Faith, Calling Academia to Account, The Medieval Epistemology of Error* and *Discipline and Justice in the Church of England*.

**J. Wyn Evans** has been Dean of St Davids since 1994. Before that he was Head of Theology and Religious Studies at Trinity College, Carmarthen. His initial degree was in archaeology, and he is a Fellow of both the Society of Antiquaries and the Royal Historical Society, and a member of the Cambrian Archaeological Association, the Society for Church Archaeology and the Ancient Monuments Society; and he serves on the Executive Committee of the Friends of Friendless Churches. He has lectured and published in the area of the history of the early Church in Wales.

**Giles Gasper** read modern history at Christ Church, Oxford. At present he is Junior Research Fellow at Wolfson College, Oxford, and is completing a doctorate on Anselm. His article "Anselm's *Cur Deus Homo* and Athanasius's *De Incarnatione*: Some Questions of Comparison" was published in *Studia Anselmiana*.

**Peter Heath**, formerly Reader in History at the University of Hull, is the author of *Church and Realm 1272-1461* and *The English Parish Clergy on the Eve of the Reformation*.

**Michael Jackson** is Rector of St Fin Barre's Union of Parishes in the united dioceses of Cork, Cloyne & Ross, Ireland, Dean of Cork and Chaplain of University College, Cork.

**William Jacob** is Archdeacon of Charing Cross in the diocese of London, and editor of *Theology*.

**Simon Keynes** is Elrington and Bosworth Professor of Anglo-Saxon in the University of Cambridge, and a Fellow of Trinity College.

**Frances Knight** is Senior Lecturer in Modern Church History at the University of Wales, Lampeter, and is Director of the MTh programme in Church History.

**Diarmaid MacCulloch** is Professor of the History of the Church in the University of Oxford, and Fellow of St Cross College. His biography of Thomas Cranmer won the Whitbread Biography Prize and the Duff Cooper and James Tait Black prizes. His most recent book is *Tudor Church Militant: Edward VI and the Protestant Reformation*.

**Judith Maltby** is Chaplain and Fellow of Corpus Christi College, Oxford, and the author of *Prayer Book and People in Elizabethan and Early Stuart England*. She is currently writing a book on the Church of England in the 1640s-50s.

**Hugh McLeod** is Professor of Church History at Birmingham University. His books include *Secularisation in Western Europe 1848-1914, Religion and the People of Western Europe 1789-1989, Religion and Society in England 1850-1914* and *Piety and Poverty: Working Class Religion in Berlin, London and New York 1870-1914.*

**Jeremy Morris** is Vice-Principal of Westcott House, Cambridge. He teaches and writes on modern church history and Anglican theology.

**Edward Norman** is Chancellor of York Minster, Emeritus Fellow of Peterhouse College, Cambridge, and a weekly columnist in the *Daily Telegraph.*

**Nicholas Orme** is Professor of History at Exeter University. His next book, *Medieval Children*, will be published in 2001.

**Glyn Paflin** is Assistant Editor of the *Church Times.*

**Michael Perham** is Dean of Derby. He is a member of the Archbishops' Council and the Liturgical Commission, and a lecturer and writer on Christian worship.

**Henry Rack** is a Methodist minister who read modern history at Oxford and theology at Cambridge. After working in churches and theological colleges he lectured in Manchester University, retiring in 1994 as Bishop Fraser Senior Lecturer in Ecclesiastical History. He is the author of *Reasonable Enthusiast: John Wesley and the Rise of Methodism.*

**Jonathan Riley-Smith** is Dixie Professor of Ecclesiastical History in the University of Cambridge. He has published widely on the crusades, and is a Knight of Malta and a Knight of St John.

**David Rollason** is Professor of History at the University of Durham, which he joined in 1977. He is known for his work on the early medieval cult of saints, and his research currently focuses on early medieval Northumbria and 12th-century history-writing in northern England.

**Kenneth Stevenson** is the Bishop of Portsmouth and a member of the Doctrine Commission. He is the author of a number of books on historical theology, including the 17th-century divines.

**Norman Tanner** SJ is University Research Lecturer, Oxford University, and editor of *Decrees of the Ecumenical Councils.*

**Stephen Taylor** is Reader in Eighteenth-Century History at the University of Reading. He has written widely on 18th-century religion, most notably *The Church of England, c.1688-c.1833: From Toleration to Tractarianism*, ed. with John Walsh and Colin Haydon. At present, he is joint director (with Ken Fincham and Arthur Burns) of *The Clergy of the Church of England Database 1540-1835.*

**Benjamin Thompson** is Fellow and Tutor at Somerville College, and University Lecturer in Medieval History. He is the editor of *Monasteries and Society in Medieval Britain*, Harlaxton Medieval Studies VI.

**J. R. Watson** is Research Professor of English, University of Durham, and author of *The English Hymn.* He was a member of the Archbishops' Commission on Church Music, and of the Committee to produce a new edition of *Hymns Ancient and Modern.*

**Rowan Williams**, Bishop of Monmouth and Archbishop of Wales, was formerly Lady Margaret Professor of Divinity at Oxford.

**John Wolffe** is Head of the Religious Studies Department at the Open University, and the author and editor of several books on 19th- and 20th-century British religious history. His latest book is *Great Deaths: Grieving, Religion and Nationhood in Victorian and Edwardian Britain.*

# LIST OF COLOUR PLATES

*The Book of Kells*: the opening word of St Luke's Gospel, in Trinity College, Dublin.

Pope Gregory, from a manuscript in Bibliotecca Casanatense, Rome.

Viking treasure found near Cuerdale Hall, Preston.

The ruins of Whitby Abbey, Yorkshire.

Harold crowned by Stigand, detail from Britain's Bayeux Tapestry.

Becket's murder and burial depicted on the Limoges reliquary.

*Between pp. 18 and 19*

Joseph Chauncy, Prior of the Knights Hospitallers (1273-80), kneeling at the feet of St John the Baptist; from a late-13th century Hospitaller missal.

The Campion Hall triptych, a 14th- or 15th-century travelling altar.

*The Seven Deadly Sins* by Hieronymus Bosch (1450-1516); oil on wood.

Erasmus, 1523, by Hans Holbein the Younger.

Henry VIII by Holbein.

*Between pp. 82 and 83*

Queen Elizabeth I at prayer: from Queen Elizabeth's Prayer Book (1569).

A 17th-century font cover in St Clement's, Terrington.

John Evelyn, the 17th-century diarist, by Robert Walker.

Portrait of John Wesley by an unknown artist (1789).

*Between pp. 146 and 147*

John Keble, by George Richmond (1863).

Hannah More, by Henry W. Pickersgill (1822).

*Matrimonial infelicities or Mr State and his wife Church*, June 1829, possibly by Seymour.

The gallery minstrels in *The Village Choir* by Thomas Webster (1800-1886).

*Charles Darwin showing an ape how alike the pair of them are* (unnamed artist, 1874).

Sixteenth-century pews, carved with sacred and domestic symbols, in St Nonna's, Altarnun, Cornwall.

William Temple, Archbishop of Canterbury, by Philip de Laszlo (1934).

Women priested in England in 1994.

*Between pp. 242 and 243*

# FOREWORD

Despite subscribing to a historical faith, Christians in the West have ambivalent feelings about their Church's past. They worship in ancient buildings, for the most part, using a liturgy that is even older than the oldest of the buildings, led by ordained ministers who wear vestments that date back further still. And, of course, the precepts by which Christians attempt to live can be traced, through Christ, to the historic teachings of the Israelite tribe. But in many churches, none of this matters. It is possible to be a follower of Christ in the 21st century without any reference to the previous generations of followers. The interests and problems of today are fully occupying, and Christianity, the living faith, can be reforged so that it relates to these alone. And all it takes, to follow this new Christianity, is to be studiously incurious about your surroundings: the architecture, the language used to describe God, the hymnody, the existence of different denominations, the ownership of the churches, the new-fangledness of women priests, the relations with the state — and the philosophical, political and cultural influences that have turned Christianity over the centuries into the set of beliefs presented to us now.

Incurious, or just too busy. The idea for the Not Angels, but Anglicans project came from our weekly efforts at the *Church Times* to tell people what is new in the Church. There always is something new, and next week, we know, there will be something newer. In this way, we, too, are part of the forward rush, in which, somehow, nobody ever has time to learn from the mistakes (and solutions) of the past. For this reason, we decided to take stock, and ask the foremost scholars and historians of our time to tell us the story of the Church's past. The result ran weekly in the *Church Times* between October 1999 and April 2000; and the letters we received from readers throughout the series told us not only of the high quality of the writing (which we knew, anyway) but also how valuable people found it.

Seeing all the material together in book-form, I am surprised to find myself encouraged. Time and again, the actions and motives of the Church's leaders have been fascinatingly reprehensible. One cannot imagine choosing such a vessel to hold the ancient teachings about purity and holiness. And yet the Church has survived, and each generation, for all its faults, has added something glorious to the Christian enterprise. And so now I look afresh at the Church of today, and expect simultaneously nothing and much.

Paul Handley, editor of the *Church Times*

# THE ROUTE FROM GALILEE

*Henry Chadwick*

*People who have lost their memory can be a problem to themselves and to those close to them. So, too, Christians do well to know where they have come from, and how they have got here.*

Christian beginnings are located in a group of neighbouring Galilean villages in a disturbed province of the Roman empire, where the Hebrew religious tradition had deep reverence for the instruction given through the law and the prophets. There, a carpenter's son received a divine calling to invite fellow-Jews to penitence and inner reform in view of the imminence of the rule of God. He was seen to fulfil the prophets' expectation of one "anointed" (i.e. Messiah) coming to save God's people.

The Gospels present varied portraits on a broadly shared canvas and frame. In all of them Jesus gathered round him a special community of disciples and an inner circle of "apostles", i.e. missionaries commissioned to proclaim God's kingdom to be now at hand; in Jesus something greater than the preaching of Jonah or the wisdom of Solomon was here.

This gospel was directed not primarily to the rich and successful, but rather to the poor, to "the people of the land" for whom the precise rules of Pharisees particular about ritual purity were actually impracticable in the day's labour.

Some Pharisees felt a bond to the impassioned seriousness of Jesus. Luke (13.31) records friendly Pharisees warning Jesus against Herod. The sharp criticism in Matthew 23 reflects the rivalry between Christian Jews and observant Pharisees after the fall of Jerusalem to the Roman legions in AD 70, with the destruction of the temple and the ending of sacrifices.

Jesus's teaching challenged ordinary morality. The Beatitudes of Matthew 5 defy the assumptions of this world. Disciples are to love their enemies. They are not to judge if they do not wish to be judged. They cannot serve both God and money. Because of the urgency of the gospel of the imminent kingdom of God, even the call to a family funeral has no priority. If we forgive those who injure us, our heavenly Father will forgive us.

It is a catalogue of costly obstacles. The gate is narrow and the way is hard that leads to life.

The Good Shepherd: wall-painting in the catacombs of St Priscilla, Rome.
*Photo © André Held*

The message of Jesus and the large following riveted by it clearly alarmed not only Herod, but the ruling classes generally, especially the Sadducees. The mission charge in Matthew 10, sending out disciples to preach the gospel, foresaw unpleasant opposition, with divided households and social conflicts. Roman governors of Judaea regarded claimants to be Messiah as inherently seditious. Pontius Pilate was persuaded that to avert serious disorders he needed to have Jesus executed by the exemplary deterrence of public crucifixion, a method of killing which prolonged the preliminary torture as long as possible.

Jesus's disciples became convinced that the tomb had been found awe-inspiringly empty; that his presence was still with them as they studied the Hebrew scriptures and prayed (Luke 24); that they had a list, headed by Simon Peter, of those to whom the risen Lord had appeared (1 Corinthians 15). The disciples were ready to sacrifice their lives for the proclamation of the gospel.

At an early stage, the community experienced disagreement about the universality or particularity of the gospel. Was the coming of Messiah (in Greek, "Christ") momentous only for ethnic Jews, for the "sons of Abraham"? Or could God raise up sons of Abraham among those hitherto outside the divine commonwealth, the Gentiles? Could the deaf hear and the dumb speak?

If the message about Jesus was proclaimed to Gentiles and there were converts, must they keep the Mosaic law? There were "liberal" or reform synagogues in the Gentile world where there was grave debate about the obligation of Gentile adherents to the synagogue to be circumcised, a rite which Gentile society regarded as unedifying, or to abstain from eating pork, which Gentile society regarded as bizarre.

The momentous consequence of the conversion and mission of Paul was to win the consent of the pillar apostles at Jerusalem to the terms on which he was evangelising Gentiles; that is, they acknowledged Jesus to be Lord, but were not asked to be circumcised or to keep sabbaths and Jewish feasts. However, the Passover was intimately associated with the time of Jesus's Passion, and so continued to be observed, at first on the same date as the synagogue, probably by all communities of the Pauline mission, later on the first Sunday following full moon after the spring equinox.

Nevertheless, the doctrine of justification by faith in Christ, not by keeping the Mosaic law, inevitably implied a separation sooner or later of church from synagogue. Christian Jewish communities in the second century admired Paul's heroism, but had serious doubts about this breach. For a long time (a few centuries) there were Gentile Christians who upset bishops (not rabbis) by worshipping both with the synagogue on Saturday and with the church on Sunday.

A related issue was the status of the Hebrew scriptures, generally available in Greek in the Septuagint version made in Alexandria in the third and second centuries BC to help Jews who were so far hellenised that they could not understand Hebrew. Some Gentile believers understood the gospel of Jesus to entail a complete and drastic break not only with Judaism, but with the law and the prophets.

But in the epistle to the Churches in Galatia in central Asia Minor, Paul contended that the law provided an education up to the coming of Christ, like a servant conducting the heir safely to Christ's school.

Alternatively, the Old Testament provided types or foreshadowing images of the gospel. Circumcision was a model for baptism, a renunciation and a gift by which the believer was incorporated in the society of the people of God. The great thanksgiving, or *eucharistia* as the Greek Christians called it, derived its central images from the Passover, and therefore the theme of redemption from a bondage in "Egypt", at the price of a sacrificial lamb. The crucifixion of Jesus was understood by Paul and others as the sacrifice atoning for the sins of the world.

Baptised believers shared in a memorial offering of consecrated broken bread and poured-out wine, symbols by which the reality of this offering was ritually re-enacted. Forms of prayer used in the synagogue liturgy at Passover were echoed in Christian prayers at the feast that the Anglo-Saxons were to call Easter after the name of an old Saxon goddess of spring.

The post-apostolic Churches were faced with hostility from city mobs and government officials, sharp criticism from pagan philosophers who feared a religious revolution scornful of the classical literary heritage, considerable tension with the local synagogues in certain places, and, internally, problems of both schism and heresy. Schismatics wanted to have nothing to do with the great majority Church; heretics were people ambitious to stay inside and to be granted "citizenship rights", but with an agenda painful to the main body. In the disorder of the time, bishops, as linchpins of the structure, made a decisive contribution to survival and coherence.

On ethical issues, Christians were generally agreed. Love of God and neighbour, or the Golden Rule, was primary, which in practice asked for chastity; respect for duties to family and society; not confusing ends and means; truth-telling, notably in commerce; hospitality; peace and justice; aversion to killing, including abortion, and especially to torture, capital punishment and gladiatorial combat (intoxicating to ancient people); restraint in food, drink and sex; no compromise with idolatry; using wealth and property for the common good; never treating fellow humans as chattels.

How important the Greek-speaking Gentile Churches were to the formation of Christian vocabulary can be seen from one simple fact: almost all the major technical terms of Christianity are untranslated transliterations (little modified) of Greek words: church (*kyriakon*), catholic, evangelical, baptism, eucharist, bishop, presbyter, deacon, prophet, charism, chrism, synod, canon, Bible, mystery, and others.

Some perennial problems beset the early Churches. They believed in only one God and rejected polytheism; yet they believed God uniquely present in Jesus the Christ. Already in the letters of Paul (2 Corinthians 13,14), or in the baptismal command at the end of Matthew's Gospel, they were speaking of God in triadic terms. How to reconcile that with monotheism? Alternative explanations were either to affirm that Son and Father were identical in being (as in the Nicene creed of 325), or to suggest that, as mediator between the supreme Father and this lower world, the Son was divine at a lower level of being.

The second line made critical minds ask if divine power less than that of the supreme Father, especially if belonging to the created order, could redeem.

Then there was the problem of human nature. Is humanity so far gone from original righteousness that redemption is more omnipotence than grace — more power than love — or are men and women so capable of heroic goodness that, in actuality redemption, beyond occasional help perhaps, is superfluous? The greatest controversies internal to the Church of the Fathers turned on three issues: the Trinity and the incarnation; the estimate of human nature; and the nature of redemption. These issues are alive today.

## Expansion and controversy

The rapidity with which the faith spread through the Roman Empire astounded the Christians themselves. Rome had crushed piracy in the Mediterranean, built military roads, constructed fine houses with central heating, and by the first century of our era was controlling not only the Celts of Gaul, later taken over by the Germanic Franks and called Francia, but also Spain, and then the Britons of Britannia. Before the end of the second century, Tertullian in north Africa was writing of Christianity having penetrated even to parts of Britain not yet colonised by Rome.

Until the fourth century we do not know much about Christians in Britain, and even then we have only fragmentary information. The archaeologist's spade can tell us more here than literary texts. At Lullingstone in Kent or Silchester, or Water Newton near Peterborough, or Hinton St Mary in Dorset, there were believers, some of whom possessed fine silver with Christian markings. It is likely enough that among the soldiers manning Hadrian's Wall there was the occasional Christian.

Detailed: believed to be the first factual portrait of the crucifixion, about AD400. *Photo © British Museum*

The martyrdom of St Alban is of uncertain date, but in the fifth century pilgrims were going to a shrine in his memory which had been in existence for some considerable time. In August 314, three British bishops went to Arles to sort out a schism on a moral issue in the churches of north Africa. They came from York, London, and (probably) Colchester.

Three bishops from Britain were also among the numerous bishops attending the large council at Rimini on the Adriatic coast of Italy in 359. We hear about these three only because they were too poor to pay their travel costs, and preferred to accept the emperor's reimbursement than an offer from episcopal colleagues.

In the 380s, a Christian from Britain settled in Rome and influenced society by his writings and by his call for a moral spring-cleaning in a society notorious among pagans for its laxity. He wrote a commentary on Paul's letters, which has survived, and other works especially insisting on human responsibility to make right choices between the evil and the good. He was to be the earliest surviving British writer, and was named Pelagius.

He felt unhappy with the gloomy view of human nature associated with the great north-African bishop Augustine of Hippo, who could end a magnificent portrait of human achievements by observing that nothing receives more concentrated pursuit than mendacity.

Was it thinkable that God could give ethical commands that lay beyond the power of humanity to carry out? To tell people that, since the Fall, the only freedom left was a capacity to do evil, and that only an overwhelming injection of divine grace made goodness possible — this seemed to Pelagius enervating and exaggerated in its pessimism.

Most problematic of all was Augustine's theme that original sin had been transmitted to everyone since Adam's fall. This was particularly apparent in the egotism and obsession with sex, unalloyed delight before the fall, often a source of pain and selfishness now. Pelagius's writings and influence continued to command sympathy in Britain and Ireland for a long time after his death. Like modern liberation theologians, he thought altruism possible.

Early in the fifth century, the impact of Germanic invasions caused a crisis of survival for the Roman Empire in the West. Alaric's Goths caused havoc in the Balkans and then in Italy, capturing Rome in 410, though they stayed only three days pillaging the city. Army units were called from Britain to help in the defence of Gaul and of the heart of the Western Empire.

Roman imperial administration in Britain dwindled to nothing, and left a vacuum for Saxons, Jutes and Angles to fill. The Angles were to change the name from Britannia to England, while the Saxons left their name on Sussex, Essex, and Wessex, or south, east and west repectively. They were pagan, and the original Britons did not appreciate their presence.

Among the Britons, however, Christianity continued, so that when in 597 the monk Augustine arrived from Pope Gregory the Great to evangelise the Angles of Kent, he found British bishops in the land, and even a shrine to an old saint at Canterbury.

Bede at Jarrow, writing early in the eighth century, thought the Church the one social cement capable of binding together the different tribes of England with its surrounding groups of Celts in Scotland, Wales, and Ireland.

It is hard to overestimate how much the Church in England owed to Bede's devotion and scholarship. He was conscious, as the old Britons and even the Irish at that time were not, of the importance to English Christians of being close to their brethren on the Continent. It is almost as if he could foresee and fear England, Scotland, Wales and Ireland having predominantly distinct religious allegiances. But he justly valued the Irish achievement of Iona, Lindisfarne and Aidan in evangelising Saxon England.

Before long, the Church of England could send out two heroes: Willibrord as a missionary to the Low Countries, and Boniface to evangelise Germany. Boniface had particularly close support from the see of Rome, which in that age played a notable missionary role.

The closeness of the link to the Continent made possible Westminster Abbey and the coming from Normandy to Canterbury of both Lanfranc and Anselm (an Italian from Aosta and the greatest philosophical mind to whom England can lay reasonable claim). The intellectual renaissance that such men represented was an export from France.

Admittedly, the English in the medieval age could not produce a mind to rival that of Peter Abelard's Héloïse. But she would have been an extraordinary phenomenon in any century. At least 14th-century England saw the emergence of John Wycliffe, Master of Balliol College, Oxford, a trenchant critic of the secularity of contemporary Christians; two world-class poets in Langland and Chaucer, both profoundly concerned about the religious scene; and spiritual writers such as Richard Rolle, Walter Hilton and Julian of Norwich.

Nevertheless, medieval kings of England came to want to be masters in their land, and did not wish the churches of England to be so dominated by the see of Rome. Hence the notorious statute of *praemunire*. This was not unique to England. French monarchs wanted a country that was Catholic, but not too Roman. The 15th-century councils at Constance and Basel were conciliar in thinking about the Church, and were uncongenial to Pope Eugenius IV (1431-47).

Eugenius therefore decided to strengthen his power by working for union between Rome and Greek Orthodoxy. By not asking too much he achieved a lot at the council of Florence; but the union was rejected by Greeks at home in Constantinople, who thought the Turks' conquest of their city in 1453 a divine judgement on a false ecumenism. The Western sack of their city in 1204 was unforgettable.

The Eastern Churches' rejection of papal universal jurisdiction directly influenced Henry VIII. Was the Reformation a kind of nemesis for the excessive claims of the medieval papal monarchy? Greek and Russian Orthodox minds have been tempted to think so. Until the ecumenical contacts of the present time, Roman Catholics and Eastern Orthodox Churches have had an uneasy relationship. Though it is unthinkable now, as late as 1919 the Vatican did not want Constantinople to pass into Russian hands, lest Justinian's great Church of Holy Wisdom should once more have an Orthodox liturgy; its being a mosque seemed preferable.

The upheaval of the Reformation was much less revolutionary in England than on the Continent. This was partly because of Erasmus's influence. Angered by his divorce proceedings, Henry VIII did not want the Pope, but would have no change in the Latin mass. Cranmer was too conservative for radical Puritans, who found his Prayer Books and especially his Ordinal too Catholic in content. The Thirty-Nine Articles of 1571 recognised the Pope as Catholic Bishop of Rome, but denied papal jurisdiction in England. His writ could run in Italy. There was no suggestion that by virtue of his office he might be Antichrist. There would be Puritans for whom that was insufficient, as it was for the Westminster Confession. And if one did not believe the papacy Antichrist, how could separation from Rome be defended?

When Elizabeth I succeeded Mary, the then Pope sent legates to express hope that she would keep the Church of England as it had been under Mary; they imprudently added that the daughter of Anne Boleyn could not be recognised as legitimate. This would have helped the Queen's decision.

The disputes of the 16th century wearied people. The 17th-century reaction produced two antithetical schools. The first saw all revealed theology as contentious, natural theology (God, providence, free will, immortality) as reconciling.

The second sidelined theology as dry intellectualism, whereas true religion should be about scripture and devotion, a religion of the heart rather than of the head. The faith which is a condition of justification then too easily becomes feeling. The problem was not confined to this country, but is apparent in continental Catholicism.

The 17th-century reaction against high Calvinism is paralleled by the troubled reception of Jansenist high Augustinianism.

Differing programmes continue to arise in the Church's story, partly from old questions — for instance about Catholic continuity, the primacy of the ancient Bible, and liberal openness to culture — but more from a secularity that has made God meaningless to a society hungry for power, wealth, honour and sex. Yet there certainly remains an inward yearning for a reality beyond these things, a reality seen in Jesus of Nazareth and his community.

A historian of the early Church, writing in the fifth century, ended his story by observing that it was one of controversy. He felt confident that there would be no further controversies, and therefore no more church history to write. Augustine of Hippo was ready to concede that conflict would occur, but he asked that it should always be conducted in charity and humility, in that to love God is to love his Church.

# FROM ROME TO AUGUSTINE: BRITAIN BEFORE 597

*Paul Cavill*

*With the coming of the warriors, Christianity discovered its militancy. We plot the persistence of faith on the mainland, and the success of the Church among the Celts.*

## Roman Britain to Anglo-Saxon England

Faced by wave after wave of Germanic invaders, Rome withdrew her last legions from Britain in the early fifth century. The legions left behind a relatively thinly populated land, civilised and Christian at least in parts, with an excellent defensive infrastructure, but without the means to make walls and roads effective against the marauding Picts.

According to the British monk Gildas, the British king Vortigern and his counsellors decided to hire heathen Germanic mercenaries from the north-western European seaboard to keep their enemies at bay. Gildas, with the benefit of hindsight and grim experience, saw the idea as a terrible mistake. But Saxons had been trading and raiding and serving as legionaries in Britain for centuries, so it was not unnatural to see them as possible allies.

Around the middle of the fifth century, an army of Germanic warriors under the leadership of Hengist and Horsa was invited to defend the Britons. Disputes arose between the British and their hired army, and, fully aware of the weakness of the Britons, the Saxons brought over their friends and families to such an extent that the homeland of the Angles in the area of modern Schleswig-Holstein was reportedly still depopulated three centuries later.

There are lurid accounts of the depredations of the Angles, Saxons and Jutes in Gildas and Bede (who saw them as God's judgement on the morally lax Britons), and more detailed accounts of their movements in the *Anglo-Saxon Chronicle*. By the end of the sixth century, the heathen Anglo-Saxons were in possession of much of what is now England and lowland Scotland, with most of the rather embittered Christian Britons forced into Wales and the south-west and north-west of England.

## Early Anglo-Saxons

In comparison with the Romano-British, the Anglo-Saxons were primitive in many ways. They did not read or write, build in stone, or have much concept of personal cleanliness. While scholarship and Christianity were flourishing in Ireland, the Anglo-Saxons were

# Roman beginnings

Cryptic references by Bede and Tertullian date the start of Christianity in Britain to the late second century. This is probable, but unverifiable. We are on firmer ground with St Alban, whose martyrdom is most likely to have occurred between 210 and 300. There have been attempts to explain him away as a Christian appropriation of elements from an earlier pagan cult; but the shrine appeared quickly. Two bishops from Gaul were said to have visited it in 429. Bede, writing in the late 720s, tells of a church on the site of the martyrdom "where sick folk are healed, and frequent miracles take place to this day".

Bede also tells St Alban's story, as he received it, including the detail about the executioners: the first baulked and was beheaded with Alban, the second lost his eyes.

In the centuries ahead, the British needed the example of a selfless martyrdom, surrounded by miraculous occurrences, to strengthen their resolve against invading war parties.

Illustration from a 13th-century *Life of St Alban* by Matthew Paris. *Photo © by kind permission of Trinity College, Dublin*

establishing their landholdings, settling new land, and above all, fighting. Kings and chieftains maintained their authority by keeping large bodies of retainers, who were lavishly rewarded from the booty gained in battle.

Their social system was driven by constant warfare, feeding ideals of personal heroism: bravery, loyalty, and aggression. When they were not fighting the Britons or the Picts, they fought each other. Blood feud was the main way of resolving inter-familial conflicts. Their gods were gods of war and fertility; their personal adornments were weapons and armour.

## Heathenism

We know little about Anglo-Saxon heathenism, but it was probably undogmatic, being polytheistic. Rædwald, King of East Anglia in the early seventh century, felt able to have altars to both Christ and his heathen gods. Churches were not specifically targeted by heathen conquerors: place-names containing *eccles* refer to places with surviving pre-Saxon churches. Sacrifices were made principally when cattle were killed off for the winter, and the religion was geared to the seasons. Burial practices varied, but rich graves such as the early seventh-century royal burial at Sutton Hoo, often associated with King Rædwald, suggest that there was some notion of a life after death in which a king would need his weapons, money, food and tableware.

## English, not Scandinavian

Heathenism and runic magic continue to fascinate the modern mind. To fill the gaps in our knowledge of the details of Anglo-Saxon heathen practice, many writers have borrowed details from Scandinavian mythology preserved in records five centuries or more later than the heyday of Anglo-Saxon heathenism.

The one-eyed, rune-casting valkyrie-and-raven-accompanied, Valhalla-inhabiting warmonger Odin, and the red-bearded, hammer-wielding, giant-fighting Thor are Scandinavian. There is no shred of literary evidence from Anglo-Saxon England that Woden and Thunor (the English forms of the names of the deities) had these characteristics. Nor do the day-names Tuesday, Wednesday, Thursday and Friday have any cultic significance: they simply reflect the correspondence of Tiw and Mars, Woden and Mercury, Thunor and Jupiter, Frig and Venus in learned Latin.

## A pagan observer

The Christian Church did not choose to record details of heathenism, seeing it as, at best, historical ignorance and, at worst, damnable error. We have to turn to an earlier pagan writer for details.

# Beowulf: Christian poet's tale of heathen ancestors

*Beowulf* survives in an Anglo-Saxon manuscript of the late tenth century, but the poem is about a warrior king from sixth-century Scandinavia. The poem makes reference to several datable wars and skirmishes of that time. The story concerns the hero Beowulf, who travels from his homeland in the south of Sweden to Denmark to help the ageing king Hrothgar, who has been beset for 12 years by a man-eating monster, Grendel. Beowulf defeats Grendel and then Grendel's mother.

Fifty years pass. Beowulf becomes king and is himself attacked by an enraged dragon. He takes 11 men with him to fight the dragon, and is fatally wounded. Ten of his men run away, and only one, his kinsman Wiglaf, remains to help him dispatch the dragon.

Armour: boar-crested helmet as mentioned in *Beowulf*. The Benty Grange Helmet. *Photo © Sheffield Galleries and Museums Trust*

The Grendel stories are based on well known folk-tale types, but the Grendels are also given a genealogy which rationalises their existence in the Christian scheme of things: they are descended from Cain, and are water monsters, so did not perish in the Flood. The dragon-fight borrows as much from early Christian saints' lives as it does from Germanic dragon legends. The main characters are remarkably pious, giving thanks to God, seeing his providence in things that happen, and being helped by him to overcome evil adversaries.

The poet portrays good and well-intentioned heathens, people with whom his audience might have sympathy, people for whom heathenism was a historical misfortune rather than a divine judgement. His approach to the heathen past is almost unique in Anglo-Saxon England. The poet asks the question, giving no dogmatic answer, "Can our righteous heathen ancestors not be saved?"

The Roman writer Tacitus, who observed Germanic tribes in their continental homelands at the end of the first century AD, noted that their sacred places were woods and groves. This is strikingly corroborated by English place-names, some of which contain the element *leah*, "wood, clearing", with the name of a deity.

The modern names Wensley, Thundersley and Tuesley represent original groves sacred to Woden, Thunor and Tiw; and there are several names like Willey (Surrey), which refers to a grove with a heathen shrine, and Harrow, which refers to a heathen grove or shrine.

Other landscape features, particularly open land and hills, are associated with heathen deities, and some harrow-names have a tribal name associated with them. What went on in these places has to be left to the imagination, though sacrifices of cattle and functions of a social and legal kind are likely to have gone on, and many sources mention idols and images of the gods as being found in shrines.

The more picturesque details of heathen practice recorded by Tacitus, including divination and human sacrifice, are difficult to confirm from Anglo-Saxon sources.

## Continuities

There were continuities between Christianity and heathenism. At a personal level, the intense loyalty which underpinned the ethic of the warrior band equally underpinned the relationship between the convert and Christ. Cognitively, all the biblical imagery of the Christian life as warfare must have had a striking immediacy for those habituated to the use of weapons and armour.

In terms of custom, Anglo-Saxon Christianity consciously adopted the seasonal cycle of religious festivals. And, exploiting that sense of sacred space which is evident in the place-names, churches are not uncommonly to be found built on ancient religious sites of both heathen and pre-Saxon Christian origin, or near mounds where assemblies were held.

The Christian world, just as much as the heathen world, was populated by a whole range of spiritual beings. The Anglo-Saxons borrowed the Latin words *giant* and *devil*, but only to add to a bewildering array of fiends, wights, elves and dragons. It seems likely that ordinary people did not quite know the difference between those which were theologically approved and those which were not, and dark places, pits, ponds and mounds were thought to be inhabited by these generally unpleasant creatures, and named after them.

A repeated denunciation in Christian writings throughout the early Middle Ages is against those who make offerings at stones, wells and trees, and it is possible that the better sort of spirit was thought to inhabit these.

Large numbers of charms of all kinds survive from Anglo-Saxon England, using herbs, rituals, prayers and mumbo-jumbo indiscriminately in the attempt to gain some therapeutic or material end (a cure for dropsy, return of lost cattle, productive land). Woden has a walk-on part as a healer in one of these, but many (including the one with Woden in it) incorporate bits of the Latin liturgy and prayers to Christ, Mary or the saints. The fear of disease and deprivation often made people, Christian or heathen, so desperate they would try anything.

The heathen gods soon passed into legend, but superstition lingered long in folk belief and social custom.

# THROUGH THE MIST

*Michael Jackson*

The early history of Christianity in Ireland and in what we have long referred to as "the Celtic Church" is shrouded in a heavy mist of

# St Patrick

St Patrick's *Confession* and *Letter to Coroticus* tell us his inner story. The earliest manuscripts are from the ninth-century *Book of Armagh*, and represent a vested interest in underwriting the supremacy of Patrick among early Irish bishops in order to underpin the claims of the Armagh church to jurisdiction and rents.

Patrick has been confused with Palladius, and the two episcopates interwoven in order to present Patrick as the first Bishop of the Irish. However, Patrick, from northern Britain, seems to have returned to the Ireland of his captivity as a bishop probably in the early 460s. He was determined to be a missionary bishop. His detractors tried to rein him in by charging him with dereliction of his duties.

The passionate commitment of Patrick to his new land comes through towards the end of his *Confession*. He cares deeply for the Irish, those nobodies from nowhere: "Therefore, let God never permit me to lose the people that he has won in the ends of the earth."

Patrick: stained glass by Catherine O'Brien, 1925, Dublin.
*Photo © David Lawrence*

hagiography and ideology. We need to understand the context and the agenda of those who crafted Christianity in the first centuries if we are to discern the achievements of the pioneers in mission in regions "beyond which", it was said, "there is no one".

Behind the Ireland of Patrick lies a period of sustained Christian settlement in Europe, made possible by the administrative structure of the Roman Empire. Behind the Iona of Columba lies a network of sea routes as sophisticated as Spaghetti Junction or Heathrow Airport.

There also lies a period of turbulent restructuring of Irish society in the wake of the collapse of the Roman Empire. Although Ireland seems to have lain outside the scope of the Roman invasion, it none the less experienced substantial Roman influence. Changes in the rural economy of the fifth century were driven by the introduction from the Roman Empire of a plough which made possible the cultivation of heavy soil, together with the water-mill.

Changes were also occurring in the fabric of society. Plundering expeditions to Roman Britain in the late fourth and fifth centuries brought an enforced cohesion to a society hitherto characterised by large, sprawling tribal nations.

The new machinery of war came home to roost when the source of Roman plunder in Britain ran dry. In order to fuel the needs of a style of life which had rubbed off from the now dismembered wealth of

# CHRONOLOGY

*It is often difficult to be precise about dates for this early period*

**AD 98** Tacitus writes *Germania*, his anthropological and moral study of the Germanic heathens in the Roman Empire. These were the ancestors of the Anglo-Saxons

**200** Christianity had penetrated Britain, according to Eusebius

**Third century** Roman forts are built on the southern coast, called "the Saxon shore", to defend it against pirates, suggesting that the Saxons are settled there; or, more likely, the pirates are Saxons

**314** Three bishops — London, York and possibly Lincoln or Colchester — attend Council of Arles

**325** Council of Nicaea produces an agreed Creed

**410** "Rome fell to the Goths and thereafter Roman rule came to an end in Britain" (Bede)

**415** Suggested date of Patrick's birth, perhaps in the Carlisle region.

**423-32** Prosper of Aquitaine seeks to eradicate Pelagianism from Britain

**449** Hengist and Horsa, Germanic mercenaries, are invited to Britain by Vortigern, and land at Ebbsfleet, Kent

**455** Hengist and Horsa fight against Vortigern at Aylesford, Kent. Horsa is killed, but Hengist gains the kingdom

*c.***493** Death of Patrick

**495** Cerdic and Cynric, founders of the West Saxon dynasty of King Alfred, land in Britain and fight against the Britons

**519** Cerdic becomes king

*c.***521** Birth of Columba

*c.***521-8** King Hygelac of the Geats, a historical figure who appears in the poem *Beowulf*, dies in a battle in Frisia. This event is recorded by the Frankish Christian historian Gregory of Tours in his *History of the Franks*. In the poem, Beowulf becomes king of the Geats shortly afterwards

*Continued opposite*

# St Columba and Iona

With St Columba, we move into a different arena from St Patrick's in the evolving Celtic Church.

His own family belonged to one of the dynasties which began to emerge around the time of the coming of Christianity to Ireland, the Ui Neill lineage of the Cenel Conaill. His own persona owes much to the ecclesiastical revolution in north-east Ireland. It is no accident that the full flowering of Iona coincides with the successive reigns of three strong kings from Columba's kin (AD 628-658); and such a link can again be traced in the 11th century.

The island of Iona, where he founded his monastery after leaving Ireland in AD 563, is not on the edge of the then world, but strategically placed on the most important sea routes leading to the centre of Pictish power. Set in territory of the Irish-speaking Dal Riata, it was at the heart of multi-cultural northern Britain.

From the Columban foundation at Iona, the monastic urge to "wander for God" resulted in a flowering of monastic mission in Europe in the time of Columbanus and beyond.

History went full circle. The Irish, who had been frog-marched into the collapsing imperial ecclesiastical edifice, in time attempted to re-Christianise the areas of lost empire in Europe. Yet the Viking threat to Iona resulted in the Columban community moving to Kells in Co. Meath in 807, and bringing with it the literary treasures of the island monastery.

Prayer and devotion, learning, art and poetry are central to our picture of Columba's Iona. So also is his management institute of kingship and diplomacy. But the monastery combines the individual withdrawal (anchoritic) and the community (coenobitic) models of monasticism intrinsic to its origins in the fourth-century Eastern Church. Columba broke the rules every bit as much as did Patrick. He was a pioneer in equipping his monks for pastoral mission abroad although *The Penitential of Finian* (alias Fin Barre) forbids monks from engaging in pastoral work.

The library and literary output of Iona together give us a window on the preoccupations of the monastery. The Bible and Apocrypha are there.

There emerges subtly but clearly a devotion to Columba the founder. The cult of Mary is clearly important, in the image of Mother and Child, so reminiscent of the *Book of Kells*, on two eight-century crosses, and in the Cantemus. The underpinning of devotion to Mary by Pope Sergius I (d. AD 701) points us to the way in which Iona was in the mainstream of the very early medieval Church, and seriously challenges the idea of a Celtic Church that went it alone in an odd and cavalier way.

Roman Britain, the warlords plundered their own country in the late fifth and early sixth centuries.

The time of social restructuring coincided with the organisation of the Christian Church in Ireland. It is not surprising that Patrick should represent to future generations something essential in Irish Christianity, no matter how larded the history may be with legend.

The overlapping of Church and state in the post-Constantinian settlement left the Church in Britain and Gaul with an off-the-peg metropolitan and diocesan system.

The heresy of Pelagianism — which has been caricatured as self-service salvation — caused widespread alarm in Gaul. Prosper of Aquitaine's *Chronicle* for AD 429 records that Agricola was spreading Pelagianism in Britain. The Council of Ephesus in AD 431 condemned many Pelagians. This was a green light to Gaul to clean up Britain and, by extension, Ireland doctrinally, by restoring orthodoxy. The appointment of Palladius as Bishop of the Irish in the same year brought Ireland for the first time into the ambit of institutional Christianity.

But the responsibility of a bishop was specifically towards Christian communities already in existence. Of these, there clearly was a number in Ireland, with the human traffic in trade and slavery from Britain during the fourth and fifth centuries, as attested by the capture of Patrick himself.

In taking root in Ireland, Christianity took two paths. One was the assimilation of the pagan pantheon into the galaxy of Christian saints: for example, Gobnet, the pre-Christian patron of iron-workers, becomes, under the Christian dispensation in Munster, St Gobnet of Ballyvourney, Co. Cork.

The other was confrontation with the indigenous religion. This approach emphasised God's power over the elements of nature, particularly the sun.

It deliberately built churches, under various bishops, on sites with a commanding and confrontational view of ancient hilltops associated with pre-Christian kingship: Dunsthaughlin (Secundinus's church), just north of modern-day Dublin, opposite Tara; and Armagh (Patrick's church), opposite Emhain Macha.

## CHRONOLOGY

*Continued*

**c.540** The monk Gildas writes his diatribe *The Ruin of Britain*

**560** Æthelberht, the first English king to be converted, becomes king of Kent

**563** Columba builds the monastery of Iona as a base for mission to the Picts

**590** Gregory the Great becomes Pope

**596** Augustine's mission to England sets out

**597** Death of Columba

**623** Death of Fin Barre

**c.625** The Sutton Hoo ship burial

**731** Bede writes his *Ecclesiastical History of the English People*

**806** Vikings raid Iona

**807-814** Vigorous building programme at Kells, where the Columban community re-establishes itself

**891** The first edition of the *Anglo-Saxon Chronicle* is published under King Alfred

**c.1000** The only existing manuscript of *Beowulf* is written

# 'A DANGEROUS, WEARISOME AND UNCERTAIN JOURNEY'

*Paul Cavill*

*Bede tells the tale of the earliest missions to England; from Gregory's vision to the integration of Augustine and his fellow travellers into Anglo-Saxon culture.*

As they made the perilous trek north and west over the Alps and through the provinces of Gaul in the year 596, it was not the dangers of the journey that preoccupied Augustine and his forty companions. After all, Gaul had its churches and saints, scholars and monasteries, culture and peace, as well as dangers on the way. Pope Gregory's writ ran here, as the Roman imperial writ had done before. No, it was the prospect of arrival in a barbarian land, England, where there was no living Church, and where the language was unknown and unpronounceable.

What they knew of the people was unappetising: they fought each other and sold their captives as slaves, they were heathen, they were uncivilised, they knew no pope. The unarmed embassy from Rome would be helpless. Certainly, as they thought about it, they saw their mission as hopeless: wouldn't they be better employed teaching their own people rather than trying to convert others? And this whole idea of mission *was* rather a new thing. They decided to beg off, and Augustine trekked back to Rome to try to change Pope Gregory's mind.

Pope Gregory's mind was not to be changed. He had long cherished the desire to convert the peoples of England, and although he was unable to go himself, he was determined that the mission should succeed. So, with much fear and trembling, in the late summer of AD 596, Augustine again left Rome to complete the commission, and early the following year he arrived in Thanet to greet King Æthelberht of Kent.

The King granted the monks a base in Canterbury and permission to preach in his lands. From here, and later reinforced by more missionaries from Rome, they set out to convert, establish bishoprics, and bring all the benefits of the gospel to the people. Augustine kept in close touch with Gregory by letter, and in 601 was made Archbishop.

## Disputes with the Welsh Church

The mission needed reinforcement: with the best will in the world, a

Preacher: St Aidan, Holy Island, Northumberland. *Photo © Leslie Garland Picture Library*

# Gregory the Great: scholar with a pastoral heart

Gregory not only initiated the conversion of the Anglo-Saxons, but he imbued Anglo-Saxon Christianity with his temperament. The letters that passed between Augustine and Gregory show the Pope's deep humanity and concern for the spiritual well-being of both missionaries and converts.

He recommends Augustine to be aware of the habits of the people, and to use them in spiritual formation: if the people are used to sacrifices at sacred places, let these places be consecrated to God, and Christian feasts take the place of heathen rituals.

He is also concerned that the success of the mission, welcome though it is, should not lead Augustine into pride.

Gregory never visited England, yet his memory was held dear. The earliest biography of him was written at Whitby, and it is there, as well as in Bede, that the story of Gregory seeing Anglo-Saxon slaves in the market-place is told. When Gregory puns, calling the slave boys "not Angles but angels", not from Deira (part of Northumbria), but to be rescued from God's wrath (*de ira* in Latin), and says that Ælle, the name of their king, echoes the Alleluia to God in the future, he shows not only wit, but also a profound optimism about the mission of the Church and the potential of the people. Often ill, and beset with complex diplomatic problems, Gregory never lost his vision.

He was a scholar without pretension, and with a pastoral heart. His *Dialogues* manages to be not only one of the best examples of early medieval hagiography, especially the material on the life of St Benedict, but also genuinely a dialogue in which questions are raised and answered.

Gregory's *Pastoral Care* was one of the books that King Alfred thought important enough to be translated into English. It sets out first and foremost the character of the pastor, and then gives helpful advice on how to deal with people according to their needs and dispositions. His *Homilies on the Gospels* are echoed again and again in Old English literature, and constitute a very accessible medieval theology.

Pragmatic, tolerant, evangelical, pastoral, scholarly and optimistic: such was Gregory's temperament. And such has been the temperament of the English Church, at its best, ever since.

small band of monks, struggling with the language, could hardly cover all the ground.

Augustine looked for help, and asked the British bishops from the west to get involved. Confident in his own authority, he suggested that they might like to submit to him and to Rome, and adjust their practices to suit, as well as take the heavy responsibility of preaching to their long-standing enemies.

Despite lengthy and repeated discussions, the two sides never reached agreement on either of those two main points. Help in the mission to England was to come only long after Augustine's death, and from Ireland, a Celtic Christian island at some remove from the bloody conquest of British lands that continued even alongside the Christian mission well into the seventh century.

## Early gains

Early in Augustine's mission, King Æthelberht was converted, and he had influence over much of the south of England, which he used to encourage the growth of the Church. Later, in 627, King Edwin of Northumbria, with far-reaching influence over the north of England,

The Book of Kells: the opening word of St Luke's Gospel. *Photo © reproduced by kind permission of Trinity College, Dublin*

Pope Gregory, from a manuscript in Biblioteca Casanatense, Rome. *Photo © by courtesy of the Italian Ministry of Culture*

Viking loot?: treasure found near Cuerdale Hall, Preston. Detail from *The Oxford Illustrated History of the Vikings*, ed. P. Sawyer, 1997. *Photo © British Museum*

Monument: the ruins of Whitby Abbey, Yorkshire. *Photo © D. Houghton; reproduced by permission of the Leslie Garland Picture Library*

Harold acclaimed (detail from Britain's Bayeux Tapestry): sources do not agree as to who crowned him. Normans say Stigand (shown). *Photo © Reading Museum and Archive Service (Reading Borough Council)*

Cult: Becket's murder and burial depicted on a late 12th-century Limoges reliquary
*Photo © V & A Picture Library*

also received baptism from Paulinus, one of the Roman missionary reinforcements.

The East Anglian king, Sigeberht, was baptised in Gaul, and enlisted the help of the Burgundian Felix in the conversion of his kingdom. The Mercian Midlands, however, ruled for a long time by the firmly heathen Penda (reigned 632-654), took longer to reach. So did the forested and impenetrable areas of Sussex, Hampshire and Wight. And in the early years, the hold of the Church was tenuous: Eadbald, son of Æthelberht, returned to heathenism, as did the Northumbrian kings Eanfrith and Osric, successors to Edwin.

## The Iona-Lindisfarne mission

Out of the chaos of the Northumbrian wars during the early seventh century emerges Oswald.

Oswald, who was son of King Æthelfrith, Edwin's predecessor, had fled to the Irish monastery at Iona because of the habit kings had of killing off any possible contenders for the throne. There he became a Christian, and, returning to Northumbria with a small band in 633, he defeated Cædwalla, the Welsh king who had seen off Kings Edwin, Eanfrith and Osric, and who had devastated the land.

Established as king, Oswald sent to Iona for a missionary bishop, and in 634 Aidan and a company of monks arrived to preach in Northumbria. They made their base on Lindisfarne, and their gentle and selfless influence made for a rapid and effective growth of Christianity. Bede tells memorable stories of Aidan and Oswald travelling the country, Aidan preaching and Oswald translating.

## Monasteries

Despite plague, war and apostasy, the progress of the conversion was inexorable. Sees were founded, bishops consecrated, and monasteries proliferated.

Some monasteries emerged into fame: Bede's twin monasteries of Monkwearmouth and Jarrow; the "double" monastery of Whitby, housing both men and women separately, under the royal Abbess Hilda. Many more have been lost, and we know some only by name, and not by location; others have in all probability disappeared from the record altogether.

Exquisite: Canterbury pendant, early seventh century. *Photo © Collection Canterbury Museums*

Bede's tomb, Durham. *Photo © Alan Curtis, reproduced by permission of the Leslie Garland Picture Library*

# Bede on King Edwin's Council

A nobleman speaks. "It appears to me, O King, that the present life of man on earth, in comparison with that time which is unknown to us, is like this. You are sitting at the feast with your noblemen and warriors in wintertime. A good fire is burning on the hearth in the middle of the hall, and all inside is warm, while outside the winter storms of rain and snow are raging.

"A sparrow flies swiftly through the hall. It comes in at one door and quickly flies out through the other. For the time it is inside, the storm and wintry tempest cannot touch it, but after the briefest moment of quiet, it vanishes from your sight. It flies out of the winter storm and quickly into it again. So this human life appears for a short time: of what is to follow, and what went before, we are completely ignorant. So if this new doctrine gives us more certain information, it seems right that we should follow it."

Other elders and counsellors of the king said the same things by divine prompting. . .

The King publicly allowed Paulinus to preach the gospel, and, renouncing idolatry, professed faith in Christ. When he enquired of their high priest who should be the first to desecrate the altars and shrines of the idols, together with the surrounding enclosures, Coifi answered, "I will. For who more properly can destroy those things which I foolishly worshipped and so set an example to all? . . ."

And immediately, despising his vain superstitions, he asked the King to give him weapons and a stallion. And mounting the horse, he set out to destroy the idols. It was not allowed for a high priest of their religion to carry weapons or to ride on anything but a mare. So with a sword belted round his waist and carrying a spear in his hand, he mounted the King's stallion and set off to where the idols were.

The ordinary people who saw him thought he was mad. But, without hesitation, as soon as he reached the shrine he desecrated it by throwing into it the spear which he carried. And rejoicing greatly in the knowledge of the worship of the true God, he ordered his companions to destroy and burn down the shrine and all the enclosures.

**From Bede's** *Ecclesiastical History*, II, 13; **translation (and that in facing panel) from Paul Cavill,** *Anglo-Saxon Christianity* **(Fount, 1999).** *Reproduced by kind permission of HarperCollins Publishers Ltd*

## A bishop to admire: Bede on St Aidan

He had zeal for peace and love, self-restraint and humility. He overcame anger and greed, he despised pride and vainglory. He devoted himself to keeping as well as teaching the heavenly commandments; he was expert in reading and vigils. He used his authority as a priest to stand against the proud and powerful, and his kindness to comfort the sick and defend and relieve the poor. To put it briefly, so far as can be ascertained from those who knew him, he took care to overlook nothing of all that is written in the commands of the Evangelists, apostles and prophets, but tried with all his power to carry them out. These things I greatly love and admire about Bishop Aidan.

*Ecclesiastical History, III, 17*

But it was predominantly the monks who effected the conversion in this early period, providing preaching, teaching, hospital, hotel and orphanage facilities, as well as counsel for kings. Monasteries were not cut off from the world: Augustine, Wilfrid, Hilda and Aidan were politicians, whether they liked it or not, and, indeed, whether they were suited to it or not.

## Cultural change

In the wake of the conversion and establishment of Christianity came many material changes.

The exquisite craftsmanship of the Anglo-Saxons, originally lavished on personal adornments and weapons, was now equally lavished on manuscripts, stone sculpture, building and ecclesiastical furniture. The cross becomes a dominant decorative motif, whether on jewellery (such as the Canterbury pendant or St Cuthbert's cross) or on stone memorial slabs or preaching crosses. A new kind of music was introduced, as was representational art for church walls, and the use of glass.

Access to Latin learning brought science of a kind, reading, writing, grammar, and metrics, the Latin Classical authors, the Bible and the Fathers. The Augustine Gospels still used at the consecration of an archbishop are of sixth-century Italian work, and both text and illustration are copied in later Anglo-Saxon manuscripts.

At Malmesbury in the mid-seventh century, the future bishop Aldhelm (639-709) learnt such fluency and virtuosity in Latin that the prose and poetic versions of his treatise in praise of virginity still defeat all but the most proficient linguists.

## Why the missions succeeded

The story above, with the added detail about material and cultural developments, is widely accepted as what really happened in the conversion of England. But it tells us little about what factors led to the success of the Christian missions.

At the time of the conversion, the Anglo-Saxons were settled, relatively cultured, and had good contacts with the rest of Europe and beyond. King Æthelberht was married to a Frankish princess, and the Sutton Hoo grave goods have glass, silverware and other pieces ultimately from the Mediterranean and the Near East. These argue diplomatic and trade contacts far beyond English shores.

The Christian missionaries would not, then, have been instantly impressive, nor have given the impression of being super-intelligent aliens.

## Similarities

The missionaries very likely presented a complex mixture of similarities and contrasts, the familiar and the strange, to the Anglo-Saxons.

Augustine and his companions approached King Æthelberht singing and carrying a silver cross and a picture of Christ. King Æthelberht received them in the open air for fear of magic. It would have been obvious that the missionaries were of the priestly type, carrying no weapons, and singing; the silver cross and picture proclaimed power.

Monastic organisation with a single person in authority was not very much different from the warrior band, demanding loyalty and obedience, and often the absence of women. Christianity itself would not have been utterly unknown to Æthelberht and Edwin, both of whom had Christian wives, and both of whom would have seen its monuments or its practice.

## Differences

It was possibly the differences between what they were familiar with and what the missionaries brought that struck the ordinary people most powerfully. The sweetness of the message the monks taught should not be underestimated: news of a powerful creator God who loves rather than demands, and hope for a better life after this brief struggle (for such it was) must have been welcome.

The example of saintly lives and institutions devoted to pastoral care involving both the physical and the spiritual must also have been powerful. The pharmacopoeia of the monks was not very much different from that of the pre-Christian Anglo-Saxons, but, administered by characters such as Aidan or Cuthbert, it would have been hard to resist.

The Church also offered an alternative, neither easy nor safe, but an alternative nevertheless, to the habitual warfare and feud that afflicted normal Anglo-Saxon life. One of the patterns of archaeological finds from Anglo-Saxon England which have puzzled scholars is the apparent increase of deposits of single weapons in rivers around the time of the conversion.

This has often been seen as a heathen resurgence. But we know that missionaries baptised mostly in rivers, and that, on entering the monastic life, Cuthbert, for example, handed over his horse and spear, "for", Bede tells us, "he had not yet put off his secular habit."

The notion that a man might go into baptism in his warrior regalia and emerge to be clothed in the regalia of a soldier of Christ, and leave behind his weapons, has imaginative power, and offers a plausible explanation for the finds.

## A Christian society

The converted kings did their best to bring Christianity quickly within the customs and traditions of the Anglo-Saxons. In an illiterate society such as Anglo-Saxon England was and very largely remained, custom is law, and law is custom.

King Æthelberht's laws are preserved in a late manuscript, and they set down the customary penalties for offences: the very first law decrees compensation for theft or damage to property belonging to the Church, and down through the clerical orders; then the text proceeds with offences against the king, and other social orders.

Similarly, the *Anglo-Saxon Chronicle* in the early years records only the most basic information: this king died, another fought against the Welsh, another succeeded to the throne.

After the conversion, details of bishops' deaths and consecrations are added to this information, and religious conquests are added to details of land conquests. So the Church was quickly naturalised, at least in the higher echelons of society.

## Confusion

A couple of comments in Bede's works suggest that ordinary folk did not always understand what was going on.

In the *Life of Cuthbert*, Bede relates an incident where monks on rafts at the mouth of the Tyne are in difficulties. The crowd on the shore jeer at them because they are different, and, as one says to Cuthbert, "they have taken away the old ways of worship, and nobody knows how the new worship should be carried out."

This story relates to a time before 651 when Cuthbert became a monk. The story of the destruction of the shrine at Goodmanham after Edwin's council, and datable to 627, suggests one way in which "the old ways of worship" were taken away; and there must have been a span of time when people were in the dark about what was happening as far as the state religion was concerned.

# CHRONOLOGY

*c.*575-79 Gregory sees the English youths, and asks if he may be allowed to evangelise the English

596 Pope Gregory sends Augustine on his mission

597 Augustine arrives in Kent and is permitted to preach

601 Pope Gregory makes Augustine Archbishop of Canterbury, and sends helpers for the mission, including Paulinus, who preaches to King Edwin in Northumbria

604 Gregory dies

*c.*604-9 Augustine dies

616 King Æthelberht of Kent dies, and his son reverts to heathenism

617 Edwin becomes king of Northumbria. He is married to Æthelburgh, Christian daughter of King Æthelberht of Kent, and allows Paulinus to preach. During his reign, Oswald and Oswiu (sons of his predecessor) flee to Iona and become Christians

627 King Edwin is baptised on Easter Day, and Hilda, future Abbess of Whitby, with him

633 Edwin is defeated by King Penda of Mercia and Cædwalla, British king in North Wales. In the year following, two Northumbrian kings are killed

634 Oswald returns to Northumbria from Iona and, raising the standard of the Cross, defeats Cædwalla at the battle of Heavenfield

634-5 Oswald asks for a missionary bishop from Iona to preach in Northumbria. He gives Aidan land on Lindisfarne for a monastery

642 Penda of Mercia kills Oswald at the battle of Maserfeld. Relics of Oswald reputedly work miracles

654-5 Death of Penda. His son Peada is Christian, having married the Christian daughter of King Oswiu of Northumbria, Oswald's successor

*c.*704-14 A monk of Whitby writes the first *Life* of St Gregory the Great

## Settlement

The death in 654 of the heathen King Penda of Mercia signalled the effective end of organised opposition to Christianity. Most of the Anglo-Saxon aristocracy was at least nominally Christian, and the infra-structure of court and Church was in place to give Christianity the opportunity to consolidate.

Some developments which would aid that were still to come: an adequate number of bishops, a properly educated clergy, and a parish system, among them. Already brewing, however, was an acrimonious controversy which divided Christians according to their allegiance to the two main missions, the Celtic and the Roman: the Easter controversy, which led to the Council of Whitby.

# TO WHITBY FOR EASTER: WILFRID'S TRIUMPH

*David Rollason*

*The Synod of Whitby has gone down in history as the clash between two Christian cultures. But was it?*

Was the Synod of Whitby of 664 a momentous event in the history of the English Church, or a routine meeting held to resolve technical issues of the functioning of the Church in the Anglo-Saxon kingdom of Northumbria?

Has its importance been blown up out of all proportion by modern historians and indeed by the near-contemporaries who described it — Stephen, priest of Ripon, whose hero Wilfrid (d. 709), future Bishop of York, was a leading light of the synod, and Bede (d. 735), who became the foremost authority in Europe on the problems of fixing the date of Easter, and who naturally regarded a synod devoted to that topic as of epoch-making significance?

To answer these questions, we need to go back to the history of the conversion of Northumbria. The mission of Augustine had converted Kent in the years after 597; but, although Paulinus, a member of that mission, had succeeded in converting Northumbria, this was only temporary, and, after a short revival of paganism, King Oswald invited Aidan from Iona, the Irish monastery established in the Hebrides, to come to Northumbria.

He founded the church of Lindisfarne (Holy Island) in 635, and from this Northumbria was evangelised again, under strong Irish influence and with Bishops of Lindisfarne (Aidan himself, then Finan and Colman) who were from Iona. What led to the Synod of Whitby was the fact that the church of Iona had a method of calculating the date of Easter which was different from that employed by the Church in the south of England and on the continent, and which it passed on to Northumbria.

A particular circumstance was the marriage of Oswald's successor Oswiu to Edwin's daughter, who had been brought up in Kent and whose household adhered to the southern method, whereas Oswiu followed that of Iona. The result, Bede tells us, was that the King might be celebrating Easter Sunday, while the Queen was still observing Palm Sunday, such were the variations produced by the use of two methods for fixing the date of Easter.

Aidan and Hilda: a window by Christopher Whall, produced in 1901 for Gloucester Cathedral.
*Photo © Sonia Halliday and Laura Lushington*

## Synod convened

Clearly, there was much acrimony, which affected Christians generally. "The dispute", wrote Bede, "naturally troubled the minds and hearts of many people who feared that, though they had received the name of Christian, they were running or had run in vain."

There was another rift at the heart of the royal family, between Oswiu and his son Alhfrith. Alhfrith had been taught by Wilfrid, future Bishop of York, who had by this time studied the teachings of the Church in Rome and at Lyons in what was then Gaul, and who therefore opposed the Easter calculation of the clergy from Iona, to which Oswiu adhered.

So the synod was called, and Oswiu himself presided over it, with Alhfrith also present. On the one side were Colman, the Irish Bishop of Lindisfarne, and his Irish clergy, supported by the saintly Abbess Hilda of Whitby, and the equally saintly Bishop Cedd, who was at this time Bishop of the East Saxons, but was another product of Lindisfarne.

The other side was led by a visitor from the south, Agilbert, who was Bishop of the West Saxons, although he came from Gaul. With him were Wilfrid, whom Alhfrith had made Abbot of Ripon; a Kentish priest, Romanus, who had come to Northumbria with Oswiu's queen; and James, a deacon who had come to Northumbria with the ill-fated mission of Paulinus in the late 620s, and must now have been very elderly. Agilbert also had a priest called Agatho, about whom nothing is known.

Bede and Stephen allow us to watch the synod as it unfolded. King Oswiu began by stressing the importance of unity, and then invited Colman to speak, which he did to the effect that the method of keeping Easter which he observed was that of the apostle John.

Oswiu then asked Agilbert to speak, but he deferred to Wilfrid, who

# St Wilfrid: 'Roman' or 'Celtic'?

Wilfrid (d. 709), then Abbot of Ripon, was the successful protagonist at the Synod of Whitby (664). He is often regarded as a representative of the traditions of the Roman Church in the seventh century, and indeed credited with introducing them into Northumbria in opposition to the "Celtic" or Irish traditions represented by the Church of Lindisfarne and its founder Aidan.

After becoming a monk at Lindisfarne in his youth, Wilfrid had indeed travelled to Rome, which impressed him greatly, and where he learned about the calculation of Easter. And it was to Rome that he repeatedly appealed when his later career brought him into conflict with the Northumbrian kings.

Wilfrid was unquestionably a very ambitious churchman, becoming Bishop of York soon after the Synod of Whitby. He had himself consecrated in Gaul at Compiègne, where he was "borne into the oratory aloft on a golden throne by nine bishops". Jealous of the landed possessions of his churches, he also patronised at least one Gospel book written in gold on purple parchment, and he built churches at his two most important monasteries of Hexham and Ripon, the magnificence of which still finds some echo in their crypts, which are all that survive of the architecture that he patronised.

But to categorise Wilfrid as "Roman" is to ignore the influence of the Church of Gaul on him. He spent three years in Lyons after his first visit to Rome, and

Echoing: St Wilfrid's Crypt, Hexham Abbey, Northumbria. *Photo © Hexham Abbey*

his consecration in Gaul was, Bede says, according to Gaulish traditions. In this sense, the term "Roman" applied to Wilfrid is an over-simplification.

Some aspects of Wilfrid's career even look rather Irish in character. Although he became Bishop of York, he seems mostly to have worked through a network — a confederation — of monasteries, of which he was the head. Their abbots and abbesses even willed their possessions to him, and his biographer Stephen calls them his "kingdom of churches".

That "kingdom" transcended political boundaries. We find Wilfrid active not only in Northumbria, but also in Mercia, Sussex, and Kent. Such confederations of monasteries were characteristic of Irish church organisation, a notable example being the confederation centred on Iona itself, so that in this respect Wilfrid looks more Irish than "Roman". His career in the Church had, after all, begun at Lindisfarne, the monastery founded from Iona; and in Gaul, too, he had probably been exposed to Irish influence, for the Irish missionary Columbanus, who had founded highly influential monasteries there and in northern Italy, had had a major impact on the Gaulish Church, including Jouarre, the monastery with which Wilfrid's partner at the Synod of Whitby, Agilbert, was associated.

However useful labels like "Roman" and "Celtic" and even "Irish" may be, they can over-simplify and distort our view of the past — and never more than in the complexities of church life in the remote period we have been discussing.

# Dating Easter: a centuries-long conundrum

The claims of the two disputants at the Synod of Whitby — Colman, the Irish Bishop of Lindisfarne, and Wilfrid, the young Abbot of Ripon, who had been trained on the Continent and at Rome — were false. The apostle John had most certainly not used the method of dating Easter recommended by Colman, and St Peter had had no inkling of that successfully urged on the synod by Wilfrid; nor indeed was the latter used as universally in the later seventh century, as Wilfrid claimed.

The technical arguments deployed at the synod, however, were indeed those which the Church had wrestled with since at least the third century. The problem was rooted in the very origins of Christianity. Easter was, of course, tied to the Jewish Passover (the Last Supper in the Gospel account), which was a feast fixed by the lunar rather than the solar calendar.

Following the account of the first Passover in Exodus, Passover was to be celebrated at the first full moon of the Hebrew month of Nisan, the first month of the Jewish calendar. This was taken by Christian churchmen to be the first full moon after the spring equinox, so that, since Easter had to fall on a Sunday, the rules were clear: Easter must be the first Sunday after the first full moon after the spring equinox. But when was the spring equinox?

Some churchmen stuck to 25 March, the date fixed by the Julian calendar in 46 BC, but the Council of Nicaea (AD 325) defined it as 21 March (in fact, of course, it was moving earlier with time, because the solar year is slightly less than 365.25 days, so that insertion of a whole day every leap year produces this effect), and other churchmen followed this, although some also favoured 22 March.

This had in itself the potential to cause variations in Easter dating of up to a lunar month, but there was another related problem: in what period in the lunar month was it appropriate to celebrate Easter?

This problem of the Easter "term" was much discussed at Whitby. Dionysius Exiguus, drawing on the traditions of the Alexandrian Church, specified 15-21 of the lunar month, and this was what Wilfrid favoured and Bede adopted; but Victorius of Aquitaine had opted for 16-22, and Colman's method took 14-20. Again, the scope for variant dating of Easter was considerable, at least in certain years.

Even if you had solved the problem of the spring equinox and the Easter term, you could not just wait for the vernal equinox, observe the next full moon, and then celebrate Easter the following Sunday, because you had to have begun the observance of Lent.

Prediction required the correlation of lunar months with the solar calendar. Since neither solar years nor lunar months have whole numbers of days, this involved complex corrections by the insertion of days in both the lunar and solar calendar, and in the end it required construction of Easter tables which were necessarily artificial.

This too was much discussed at Whitby. Colman's party favoured an 84-year cycle, but Wilfrid — and Dionysius Exiguus before him — favoured a 19-year cycle, after which the same Easter dates would recur. It was this cycle which won the day, and had in fact been used by Victorius of Aquitaine. He had projected 28 such cycles to make a great Easter table showing the dates of Easter over a period of 532 years.

Bede, in adopting this method and applying Anno Domini dates to it, not only defined for the future the Church's method for the calculation of Easter, but also played a major part in establishing Anno Domini dating as the normal system of dating in Western Europe.

could explain the matter better in English. Wilfrid asserted that the Easter he and his party observed was universally celebrated in Rome, Italy, Gaul, Africa, Asia, Egypt, Greece, and "throughout the whole world", except for Colman and his Church and "their accomplices in obstinacy", the Picts and the Britons, that is, the inhabitants of north and west Britain.

Colman countered by invoking the practice of the apostle John, but Wilfrid responded with a lecture on the history of fixing the date of Easter, showing that John's practice derived from the earliest phase of the Church, when Jewish customs were still favoured.

## St Peter the key

In desperation — or so Bede makes it appear — Colman referred to the authority of the third-century writer Anatolius of Laodicea (Wilfrid hit back at once with the accusation that Colman did not in fact follow that sage), and then to the saintliness of Columba (d. 597), the founder of Iona, and his successors. Wilfrid effectively shed doubt on their standing — "the Lord will answer that he never knew them" — and then played his trump card. The Easter calculation that he favoured was that of St Peter, he claimed, to whom were given the keys of the kingdom of heaven.

King Oswiu asked Colman to confirm that Christ had indeed given the keys to Peter and, when he had done so, the king declared for Wilfrid's side of the case, for "Peter is the doorkeeper, and I will not contradict him."

Holy table: Bede's 19-year Easter cycle, in the 12th-century MS Hunter 85. *Photo © reproduced with permission from Glasgow University Library, Special Collections Department*

The immediate result of the synod's decision was that Bishop Colman "saw that his teachings were rejected and his principles despised", and taking — rather pathetically — part of the bones of Aidan and those who wished to come with him, including a number of English, he withdrew to Ireland, eventually founding the monastery of Mayo.

After the brief pontificate of Tuda, a man from southern Ireland, Wilfrid was made Bishop of York (which now replaced Lindisfarne as the Northumbrian episcopal see). There were to be no more bishops of Northumbria from Iona, or indeed from Ireland; so the relationship inaugurated by Aidan was ended. But to see the Synod of Whitby as marking the end of Irish influence in the Northumbrian, or indeed the English, Church is quite wrong. Bede himself was deeply influenced by Irish scholarship, especially in his own work on Easter calculation, as were his contemporary Aldhelm of Malmesbury (d. 709/10), and the King of Northumbria in his youth, Aldfrith (685-705).

Equally misconceived is the often repeated view that the Synod of Whitby marked the victory of the "Roman" Church over the "Celtic" Church, for the terms themselves are misleading. There was no homogeneous "Celtic" Church, for there were substantial differences in the organisation and practices of the Churches of Ireland, Wales, the south-west of England, and Pictland; nor does "Roman Church" mean a great deal in this context, for the situation was much more complex.

The Irish monk Columbanus (d. 615) and his companions had founded monasteries such as Luxeuil and Bobbio on the Continent half a century or so before, so that the Gaulish Church (from which Agilbert came, and from which Wilfrid drew many of his ideas) was itself under Irish influence. By the same token, the Church in Ireland was much more open to continental influence, including that of the Church of Rome itself, than Wilfrid's harsh words about the Irish and their neighbours living in the "remotest islands of the ocean" would suggest.

Irish churchmen were masters of the most sophisticated Christian Latin scholarship of the age, and in the particular area of Easter-calculation the southern Irish had already in 620 sought and adopted the advice of the Pope.

## Bede's opportunity

So what was the Synod of Whitby about? Our two contemporary writers are absolutely clear: it was about "the proper time for celebrating Easter". Bede adds that there was also discussion of "the tonsure in the shape of a crown" and "other matters of ecclesiastical discipline", evidently not important enough to be specified.

This does not mean, however, that the synod was about mere technicalities. The form of the tonsure was itself a major issue, for it really mattered that those who had abased themselves for the Church by shaving their heads should be assured that they had done so in the correct way, especially in view of the claim that the tonsure in the form of a crown was that of St Peter.

But it was the Easter controversy that was, as Bede and Stephen state, the real driving force. The problem was a very complex one, and the Church had made several attempts to resolve it. In one sense, the Synod of Whitby was just another attempt, successful in bringing the Northumbrian church into line with the practice of the Continent —

to be followed in the 680s by the conversion of northern Ireland to that practice, and in 716 of Iona itself.

But in another sense it was just as important as Bede and Stephen regarded it. For its real result was to open the way for Bede's own work on Easter calculation and the study of time ("compute" as the scholars of the period called it).

At the synod, Wilfrid had advocated the work of an Egyptian living in Rome in the sixth century, Dionysius Exiguus, whose work on Easter was superior to that of Victorius of Aquitaine. Bede developed and further improved Dionysius's work in his book *On the Reckoning of Time*, which definitively established the Church's method of dating Easter, and made Bede the acknowledged master of *computus* in the Western Church.

The Synod of Whitby was thus a turning-point in the history of the Church, not because it broke the links between England and Ireland, not because it resolved some great clash between "Celtic" and "Roman", but because it began the process by which one of the greatest scholars of the Middle Ages at last established the rules for fixing the date of the Church's greatest festival — and did so from a remote monastery in the valley of the River Tyne.

## CHRONOLOGY

**563** Arrival of Columba in Scotland
**631** Synod of Mag Lene in southern Ireland
**635** Foundation of monastery of Lindisfarne
**664** Synod of Whitby
**669** Appointment of Theodore as Archbishop of Canterbury
**709** Death of Wilfrid
**716** Iona adopts Roman Easter
**735** Death of Bede
**793** Viking attack on Lindisfarne
**804** Death of Alcuin

# RAPE, PILLAGE AND EXAGGERATION

*Catherine Cubitt*

*Catastrophe or continuity? We assess the Viking impact on the Church, the reforms of Alfred, and the development of monasticism.*

On hearing the news of the Viking raid on the monastery of Lindisfarne, a contemporary churchman, Alcuin of York, wrote: "The calamity of your tribulation saddens me greatly every day . . . when the pagans desecrated the sanctuaries of God, and poured out the blood of saints around the altar, laid waste the house of our hope, trampled on the bodies of saints in the temple of God, like dung in the street. What can we say except lament in our soul with you. . ."

Alcuin's words paint a vivid picture of the horror felt by contemporaries at the pagan attack on one of the holiest of all England's sanctuaries, the violation of the shrine of St Cuthbert, and the butchering of his community; they bring home to us the shock of the first Viking raids.

But Alcuin's words are a deliberate echo of St Augustine's response to the sack of Rome, a learned rhetorical device. Should they nevertheless be read at face value, or is our perception of the impact of the Northmen hopelessly exaggerated by the hysterical reaction of the churchmen, our only informants? The scholarly world is divided on the impact of the Scandinavian raids, and indeed the evidence is ambiguous.

On the one hand, there is the sombre record of the *Anglo-Saxon Chronicle*, which reports the increasing severity of the Viking incursions.

Regular annual raiding started in the 830s, and in 865 the scale of Viking operations greatly increased when a Viking army invaded England, to be followed in 871 by another large force. These forces did not return to their homelands for the winter, but remained encamped in England. Their purpose was no longer the easy collection of booty, but the conquest of the kingdoms of Anglo-Saxon England.

These went down like nine-pins. Northumbria in 867 was the first to go, then East Anglia in 869, and finally most of the Midlands kingdom of Mercia in 874-7.

Only Wessex was able to resist conquest, holding out under its king, Alfred the Great. But Wessex's fate also hung in the balance, and it was

Viking spoil: detail from the Codex Aureus (MS A 135), a mid-8th-century English Gospel book. *Photo © Stockholm Royal Library*

The kingdoms: line shows limit Danelaw, *c.* 880. *Photo © Oxford University Press 1997. Reprinted from the* Oxford Illustrated History of the Vikings, *edited by Peter Sawyer (1997) by permission of Oxford University Press*

a great victory in 878 at Edington in Wiltshire that saved the kingdom from Viking conquest. Alfred's victory was sealed by a treaty with the invaders and the baptism of their leader, Guthrum. This agreement partitioned England between between the Viking-ruled region of the Danelaw and the southern states governed by the Kings of Wessex.

Gradually, in the course of the tenth century, the Danelaw itself was brought under West Saxon control, and the Viking rulers and their kingdoms defeated.

## Archaeological evidence

The *Chronicle*'s terse account can be fleshed out with archaeological evidence. For example, it records the establishment of a Viking camp at the monastery of Repton, Derbyshire, in 874.

Repton was a major monastery under royal patronage, which had functioned as the mausoleum for members of one branch of the ruling family of Mercia, the kingdom in which it was situated. Its Anglo-Saxon chancel and crypt still survive, but the community who had prayed there for centuries did not, either fleeing in advance of the Vikings or facing probable death at their hands.

The church became part of the fortifications of the Viking camp, near which a great pagan mass burial of the Viking battle dead was made.

No trace remains of the gold and silver treasure which once must have adorned the church, nor of any Gospel books used in the church's services. We can glimpse what these could have been like from the Gospel book from Canterbury, whose inscription records that it was stolen from the Vikings by an Anglo-Saxon nobleman and given to Christ Church, Canterbury.

One can set against this rather anecdotal evidence of destruction and loot more substantive facts. In the Danelaw, only the episcopal sees of Lindisfarne survived without any disruption in the succession of bishops, and the community of Lindisfarne migrated with bones of their patron saint, Cuthbert, to Chester-le-Street in 883, and eventually to Durham.

The sees of Hexham, Leicester and Dunwich disappear totally. Moreover, almost no records survive from the pre-Viking era from the churches in their territory. In contrast to the southern churches, where reasonably rich documentation survives, no property charters are preserved from any church or monastery in the Danelaw, and only a few manuscripts from churches, like that of Lindisfarne, which were able to survive the Viking raids.

This near-total obliteration of manuscripts and documents from areas under Viking control suggests that the monasteries and cathedral churches in which they were housed were destroyed.

## A more complex picture

But the impact of the Vikings is less simple than this appears. Our picture of complete destruction must be modified. It is clear, for example, that within a couple of generations the pagan Vikings discarded their native religion and silently integrated themselves into the Christian community.

By the early tenth century, the sons and grandsons of the invaders were occupying high places in the church hierarchy as bishops and archbishops. No written records survive of this conversion, but it could not have happened unless the Vikings had left the infrastructure of pastoral care within their territories intact.

Sculpture alone witnesses the mingling of Viking and Christian. This can be seen in the Middleton cross, which sports a Viking warrior, perhaps its patron. Other crosses were decorated with pagan and Christian scenes.

Documentary evidence also records the continuing existence of small monastic communities or local churches. Moreover, the debilitation of the early Anglo-Saxon dioceses in the Danelaw was clearly exacerbated by West Saxon neglect, since the new English rulers of the Danelaw did nothing in the tenth century to restore defunct sees, but simply amalgamated them with the surviving ones. The see of Dorchester, for example, stretched into East Anglia and far north into Yorkshire to absorb the old bishoprics of Leicester and Lindsey.

## Change and decay?

Part of the problem in assessing the impact of the Vikings on the Church is the stark contrast which tends to be drawn between the golden age of Bede and Bishop Wilfrid, when monasteries and learning flourished, and the dark days of the ninth and early tenth centuries, which were characterised by communities not of monks, but of clergy, and which were castigated by the later Benedictine reformers of the tenth century as corrupt and loose-living.

The truth must lie somewhere in between: the great monasteries such as Bede's house at Wearmouth-Jarrow were few and far between, and many Anglo-Saxon monasteries were probably small communities of a few members of the clergy. Thus the predominance of such monasteries in the post-Viking age may not be because the Vikings had

Viking and Christian: stone cross with warrior from St Andrew's, Middleton. *Photo © Peter Harris*

destroyed "proper" monasticism, but because many were simply the continuation of pre-Viking-age houses.

## The Alfredian reforms

One oft-cited piece of evidence for Viking destruction is the account of Alfred the Great himself, who meditated on the woeful state of his contemporary Church, reflecting on its lack of Latin learning.

He wrote that "there were very few men . . . [south] of the Humber who could understand their divine services in Latin or even translate a single letter from Latin into English. . . I recollected how, before everything was ransacked and burned, the churches throughout England stood filled with treasures and books. . ."

Again, the situation was probably more complex than Alfred seems to imply. Documents from late-ninth-century Canterbury, long before the worst attacks of the Vikings, show knowledge of Latin already badly in decline. Alfred himself, in his efforts to revive learning in Wessex, brought in scholars from the see of Worcester, situated on the edge of the southern Danelaw and a still lively intellectual centre.

Alfred wrote these words himself at the start of his campaign to restore the Church and learning in his kingdom. His actions were prompted by his belief, probably widely shared by his contemporaries, that their humiliating defeats at the hands of the pagan Norsemen and the near total destruction of the Anglo-Saxon kingdoms reflected divine vengeance for the sins of the Anglo-Saxon people. The survival of his kingdom depended as much on prayer and right belief as on armies and weapons.

Alfred embarked on a campaign to educate his people in Christian teaching. The crucible of his efforts was the circle of scholars that he assembled at court; and the main instruments of his policy were the bishops. Alfred and his scholarly advisers produced a series of translations from Latin into Old English of "certain books most necessary for all men to know", as the King himself wrote.

The first of these translations was the *Pastoral Care* of England's own evangelist, Pope Gregory the Great. This was a handbook for bishops, one of the most popular works of the early Middle Ages. Alfred was not alone in finding its lessons not confined to the religious, but in seeing it as a guide for all those in responsibility. This and other translations were circulated to the bishops of Alfred's kingdom for the education of lay boys in their cathedral schools.

Alfred's innovation was not the idea of educational reform (the Emperor Charlemagne had done something on a much larger scale almost a century earlier), but his desire that laymen should be actively educated to read and write in the vernacular, and should have access to translations of key religious texts like the *Pastoral Care* and also the

Psalms. Alfred set up a school at court at which not only his own sons but also other lay boys could be taught.

However, the focus of the Alfredian reforms was on bishops, schools, and the correction of the laity, not on monastic revival. The King saw his bishops as the channel for his educational reforms, and he also sought to improve standards of Latin among the clergy.

Unlike the Emperor Charlemagne, Alfred did not use the monasteries of his kingdom to implement his intellectual revival, and his reign does not see a great flourishing of monasteries. Alfred himself founded two religious communities, a house for nuns at Shaftesbury, and a monastery at Athelney in thanksgiving for his victory there; but his lead does not seem to have been followed by his nobility.

Alfred's church reforms were limited both in ambition and in geographical range, and did not extend beyond the areas under his control. He may have reinvigorated his Church by his urgent sense of the need for moral reform in society, but there is little evidence for a lively monastic culture. Indeed, at the monastery of Abingdon, he was remembered as a despoiler of their property.

## Jury is still out

This makes our verdict on the impact of the Viking raids on the Church complex and contingent. The Vikings undoubtedly destroyed many monasteries and many centres of learning, but they were not responsible for everything which historians have deemed corrupt or decayed in the ninth- and early-tenth-century Church.

Monasteries certainly declined from their flowering in the age of Bede, but this may not be solely the result of Viking devastation, but may also reflect a shift in the balance of the religious life, where monasteries became less favoured by the nobility for endowment.

Certainly Alfred did not make the revival of the monasteries a major part of his religious programme, and his successors on the West Saxon throne who brought the Danelaw under their control were not anxious to revive defunct sees. The monasteries and churches of England had to wait until the tenth century and the reign of King Edgar for reform and patronage on a large scale.

## Anglo-Saxon monasticism

The conversion of England in the sixth and seventh centuries was followed in the late-seventh and eighth centuries by a flowering of the monastic life under the patronage of kings and the nobility.

As David Rollason has stressed, in this, England was part of a wider movement, initiated on the Continent by the Irish monk Columbanus, under whose influence important Frankish nobles founded many monasteries. Columbanian monasticism was marked by a number of distinctive features: the use of the Benedictine Rule, but adapted for the use of the individual house, and the foundation of "double houses", joint communities of monks and nuns governed by a single abbess.

The most famous Anglo-Saxon example is Whitby, whose abbess Hilda played an important part in the synod held at her own monastery. Whitby was a powerhouse of learning, producing the cowherd poet Cædmon and five bishops, and was a centre of religious and political power. Founded by King Oswiu, it was governed by his kin, and housed the graves of his kindred and the martyred king, St Edwin.

Royal foundations such as Whitby buttressed royal power not only through their prayer and prestige, but also through their landed wealth. The nobility, too, founded monasteries which were closely aligned to the interests of their family, usually placed in the hands of their female kindred.

Monastic land had a special and protected status in Anglo-Saxon England, and it enjoyed freedom from the usual demands of royal service, such as the provision of soldiers. Nobles were therefore keen to convert their property to religious use by using it to endow monasteries. The result, ironically, was that they thus effectively ensured that the land remained within the family's control, since it could not be alienated from the house, which remained in the kindred's control through the imposition of a family member as abbot or abbess.

It might be cynical to regard these communities as simply "tax-dodge houses", because their founders were also keen to ensure that they and their families would be commemorated in prayer after death. However, it is plain that the system was open to abuse.

Bede voiced his complaints in an unusually unrestrained letter to the Archbishop of York, demanding that any such houses should be annexed to proper monasteries in order to endow more dioceses for pastoral care. He described how laymen "give money to kings, and under the pretext of founding monasteries buy lands on which they may more freely devote themselves to lust. . . And thus, having usurped for themselves estates and villages and being henceforward free from divine as well as human service, they gratify their desires alone. . . The very same men are now occupied with wives and the procreation of children, now rising from their beds perform with assiduous attention what should be done within the precincts of monasteries." He regarded houses of this kind as completely fraudulent.

Bede's judgement was conditioned by his own community of Wearmouth-Jarrow, the leading Anglo-Saxon monastery of its day, and he may have been excessively critical of houses with less ascetic standards, and prone to exaggeration. By the eighth century, a great variety of monasteries existed in England: major houses endowed by kings and great nobles, centres of book-production and learning, such as Bede's own house of Wearmouth-Jarrow (a double foundation, but of men this time); much smaller communities, often of women, in the control of a noble family; and tiny establishments of a few men, probably members of the clergy rather than monks.

It has been argued that all such establishments took part in pastoral care and had their own jurisdictional regions; but the evidence is ambiguous, and scholarly debate rages. It does appear that many monasteries were involved in the cure of souls, possibly simply on their monastic estates, and that when the parish system developed these houses became part of it, and the centres of very large territories.

Each of these houses seems to have followed its own rule, often probably a customised version of the Rule of St Benedict. For example, Bede proudly reports of his own community that its rule was put together by its founder from those followed in 17 houses in England and on the Continent. None the less, his writings also show that the Benedictine Rule was a large constituent.

There is also a question of the nature of these communities. Were they monastic or clerical? Many, I suggest, were probably houses of clerics upon whom the duty of pastoral care would naturally fall. It may even be that by the ninth century these houses outnumbered the more strictly monastic, particularly as in the course of the eighth century bishops were active in bringing the monasteries in their dioceses under their control.

Monasteries were the backbone of the religious life of Anglo-Saxon England, acting as educational centres, providing liturgical services for the laity, and meeting their needs for intercessory prayer. They left a lasting imprint on the landscape of England; the limits of their estates and territories often survive in parish boundaries. Some, such as Wearmouth-Jarrow and Whitby, could rival continental houses in their wealth and learning, while others operated on a humbler scale, meeting the needs of the local nobility.

**CHRONOLOGY**

**735** Death of Bede
**793** Viking sack of Lindisfarne
**794** Viking sack of Jarrow
**800** Charlemagne crowned Holy Roman Emperor
**802** Viking sack of Iona
**848** Birth of Alfred
**871** Accession of Alfred the Great
**878** Battle of Edington
**892** King Alfred translates Gregory's *Pastoral Care*
**899** Death of King Alfred
**943** Dunstan becomes Abbot of Glastonbury
**954** Eric Bloodaxe, last Viking King of York, driven out — completion of the West Saxon conquest of the Danelaw

# APOCALYPSE THEN (AD 1000)

*Simon Keynes*

*The first millennium AD closed under King Æthelred the Unready, amid expectations of the end of the world — but, with the Vikings at hand, fact overtook speculation.*

## On good authority

In June 601, Pope Gregory the Great apprised Æthelberht, King of Kent, of a particular reason why he should encourage the English people to adopt Christianity: "Besides, we would wish your majesty to know that the end of the world is at hand, as we learn from the words of Almighty God in the holy scriptures. As the end of the world approaches, many things threaten which have never happened before. These are changes in the sky and terrors from the heavens, unseasonable tempests, wars, famine, pestilence, and earthquakes in divers places. Not all these things will come about in our days, but they will all follow after our days."

King Æthelberht would doubtless have been impressed by the Pope's cosmic ultimatum, and was moved, therefore, to give much-needed support and protection to Augustine and his fellow missionaries.

A few years later, in the kingdom of the Northumbrians, one of King Edwin's chief men famously likened the life of man (in his pagan state) to the flight of a sparrow through a hall, coming from the cold unknown into the warmth, and then going out again into the cold unknown; the point being, of course, that he was impressed by the superiority of Christian teaching in such matters.

The rhetoric of the Last Days was certainly compelling, as much for what it promised as for what it threatened, and we may imagine that it always exerted a strong influence on the faithful. Those who entered Bede's church at Monkwearmouth, in the late seventh century, would have seen the north wall decorated with scenes from St John's vision of the apocalypse, including a representation of the Last Judgement; but unfortunately the English seem to have left the visualisation of the Last Days largely to their own imaginations, and little survives from the gallery of Anglo-Saxon art which can be set beside (for example) a manuscript as fine as the mid-13th-century Trinity Apocalypse, or the set of woodcuts published by Dürer as the end of the world approached in 1498.

Most people would have relied on readings from the Bible to tell

Focal point: the ruins of Crowland Abbey. *Photo © Barry Davies* them how to recognise the coming of the end, and what awaited them thereafter. The disciples had asked Jesus, as he sat upon the Mount of Olives: "when shall these things be? and what shall be the sign of thy coming, and of the end of the world?" They were told how they would hear of wars, and rumours of wars, though the end was not yet. "For nation shall rise against nation, and kingdom against kingdom: and there shall be famines, and pestilences, and earthquakes in divers places" (Matthew 24; Mark 13; Luke 21).

Many must have been familiar, moreover, with St John's statement that Satan would be loosed from his chains after a thousand years (Revelation 20), even if it would have been difficult for them to know what construction to put on it.

It became a commonplace of Christian teaching, however, that the "sixth age" of the world, in which we live, extended from the Nativity to the coming of Antichrist; and although the official line had long been that the end of the sixth age was known only to God, there were texts on the subject which stated quite explicitly that the sixth age would extend for a period of 999 or 1000 years.

## Millennial apprehensions

There is no good evidence, in England, of any kind of mass hysteria as the millennium approached. Yet a draftsman of charters issued in the name of King Edgar, in the 960s, invoked the imminence of the world's end as a pretext for an act of giving; and, in much the same vein, the author of a vernacular homily expounded his view that the end was nigh, pointing out that the greater part of the sixth age had already passed, in as much as he was writing in the year 971.

We need not doubt, therefore, that in the 990s at least some of the God-fearing people in England would have been getting distinctly apprehensive.

The Anglo-Saxon Church in the last quarter of the tenth century was well organised, well staffed, and well integrated into the fabric of the nascent kingdom of the English. The archbishops and bishops took their respective places in the ecclesiastical hierarchy, and played their appointed roles in the routine of local administration, presiding with the ealdorman at meetings of the shire court, and superintending pastoral care at the parish level.

There were religious communities of one kind and another through-out the land, observing rules or practices that doubtless varied from place to place. Within this wider and more permissive context, the hardline monastic reform movement which had gathered momentum in the 960s, and which had gained some sense of direction in the 970s, was making its impact in the spread of newly founded or reformed houses throughout southern England, creating new opportunities for the development of learning and culture, and in various ways advancing the social and political interests of the newly unified kingdom.

The houses scattered throughout Wessex and Mercia, such as Glastonbury, Bath, Malmesbury, Abingdon, Pershore, St Albans, and Westminster, were united in their adherence to the Rule of St Benedict and in their loyalty to the king, and soon became the focal points of localised identities. Much the same applied in the fenlands, where ancient houses such as Ely, Peterborough, and Crowland were reformed or refounded, to be joined by newly established houses at Ramsey, Thorney, and elsewhere.

Lay men and women contributed much to the process, by gifts of land and treasure, generally in the hope of eternal reward; and in the late tenth century a few of the more prominent thegns were themselves moved to establish religious houses for the good of their souls.

## Men of influence

Many of the first generation of the reformers, including St Dunstan, St Æthelwold, and St Oswald, had died by the mid-990s; but there were others trained with them or under them who now held high office, and who can be seen in some instances to have exerted an important influence in affairs of state.

Their names do not trip lightly off the tongue; but in their day Ælfric, Archbishop of Canterbury (995-1005), (St) Ælfheah, Bishop of Winchester (984-1005), (St) Wulfsige, Bishop of Sherborne (993-1002), Lyfing, Bishop of Wells (998-1013), Aelfweard, Abbot of Glastonbury (975-1009), Ælfsige, Abbot of the New Minster, Winchester (988-1007), and Wulfgar, Abbot of Abingdon (990-1016), were prominent among the movers and shakers of Æthelred's regime.

All of them participated in the regular meetings of the king's councillors, and many of them enjoyed a share of the grants of lands and privileges which came from the king. Yet the most closely approachable figures in the English Church at the turn of the century were the four scholars who are known to us from their own writings.

Two had been pupils of St Æthelwold at the Old Minster, Winchester. Ælfric of Cerne, in Dorset, later Abbot of Eynsham, was active in the 990s, and in the first decade of the 11th century, and has long been renowned as the author of a large number of vernacular homilies, saints' *Lives*, and other improving or educational works.

Wulfstan of Winchester, who wrote mainly in Latin, was also active in the 990s, and is renowned as the author of a long poem on St Swithun and as the author of the earliest and most important *Life* of St Æthelwold.

The two other scholars of the same period appear to have been trained in the fenland abbeys of eastern England. Byrhtferth, monk of

Ramsey, was an expert in all matters to do with ecclesiastical computation, and has been identified, on stylistic grounds, as the author of major works of history and hagiography (including a *Life* of St Oswald).

Wulfstan was Bishop of London from 996 to 1002, and, on becoming Archbishop of York (1002-23), held for a while the bishopric of Worcester (1002-16); his origins are unknown, but the fact that he was buried at Ely Abbey, in the fens, might be held to suggest an original connection with that region.

Wulfstan was active as a homilist in the late tenth and early 11th centuries, culminating with his famous "Sermon of the Wolf to the English", first preached in 1014; from about 1008, he had also drafted legislation for King Æthelred, and subsequently did the same for King Cnut.

The writings of these men are matched by the extraordinarily high standards of book-production represented by the finer manuscripts written and decorated during this period, while elaborate building works, such as the decorated tower of the New Minster, Winchester, dedicated in the 980s, suggest that architects and church-wrights were not lagging very far behind. In short, the Church was flourishing, and there was much for it to do.

## Plague and war

The Anglo-Saxon equivalent of Y2K, known in its own day as M, fell just over half-way through the long and troubled reign of King Æthelred the Unready (978–1016). An event which might have been interpreted by some as one of the signs of impending doom was registered in the *Anglo-Saxon Chronicle*, for 986: "In this year the great murrain first occurred in England." The wording suggests that this occurrence of plague was regarded in retrospect as the first of a sequence of similar calamities.

More serious, however, was the renewal of Viking activity in England, which contemporaries would have regarded with good reason as another portent of cosmic closure.

After the trials and tribulations of the reign of Alfred the Great (871–99), the English had earned a rest from external invasion, and used the time well to rebuild the fabric of their society, their culture, and their kingdom. The raids resumed, however, in the 980s, and soon got worse. In 991 a large Viking fleet arrived in the south-east, and set about its grisly business: ravaging the countryside, overcoming local resistance, extorting money in return for peace, but presently transforming itself into a force hired to protect the English against other raiders, until it finally turned against its employers and reverted to its former ways.

To read the account of the activities of this force in England, from

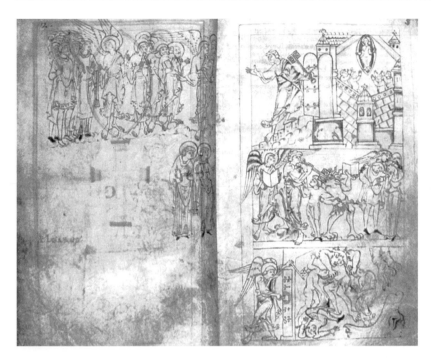

## The Last Judgement

A representation of the Last Judgement, from the *Liber Vitae* of the New Minster (later Hyde Abbey), Winchester. In the upper register, St Peter shows the way to the heavenly kingdom; in the middle, St Peter and the Devil fight each other for the soul of a little boy; in the lower register, an angel locks up the door of hell, depicted as a mouth devouring the damned.

The *Liber Vitae* of a religious community contained the names of the members and friends of the community in question, in the form of a visitors' book. The names which accumulated in the book were read out in the course of the daily service, in the hope of ensuring that they would be entered in the Book of Life, to be opened in God's presence at the time of the Last Judgement (Revelation 20.12).

The *Liber Vitae* of the New Minster, Winchester, contains the names of members and friends of the community from its reform in 964 to the time of the production of the manuscript in 1031. The manuscript was used for its intended purposes thenceforth until the dissolution of Hyde Abbey in April 1539, testifying in a remarkable way to the continuity of religious practice for a period of more than 500 years. It is now one of the treasures of the British Library (MS Stowe 944). *Photo © by permission of the British Library*

991 to 1005, is to realise how much the English suffered from its unwanted attentions, and how the chronicler despaired of the measures undertaken by King Æthelred's government: "And ever, as things should have been moving, they were the more delayed from one hour to the next, and ever they let their enemies' force increase, and ever the English retreated inland and the Danes continually followed; and then in the end it effected nothing — the naval expedition or the land expedition — except the oppression of the people and the waste of money and the encouragement of their enemies."

This was in 999; and it may be that the reality disposed of any need for apocalyptic fantasies. The Viking army was eventually driven from England by another pestilence in 1005, though it was not long before it came back.

In accordance with standard Anglo-Saxon attitudes, the Viking invasions which took place in Æthelred's reign would have been regarded by many as a form of divine punishment for the sins of the English people, giving churchmen a good pretext for urging the people to pay their tithes and mend their errant ways.

## Works, saints and relics

The powers of persuasion at the command of these churchmen may have been enough to encourage a positive response, from the king and from the people at large. The question arises, however, whether the impending millennium helped in any way to concentrate the collective

## *Agnus Dei* coinage

A silver penny of the *Agnus Dei* type, issued in the name of King Æthelred the Unready in 1009. On the obverse, the king's head (used in all other types of the period) was replaced by the Lamb of God; on the reverse, the usual cruciform design was replaced by the Dove, symbol of the Holy Spirit. Only 15 specimens survive, suggesting that the type was current for a very short period, and had been issued for a special purpose — probably in response to the Viking invasion of that year.

*Photo © British Museum*

---

# CHRONOLOGY

**975** King Edgar (the Peaceable) dies. Succession disputed between supporters of Edward and Æthelred, his sons; Edward became king

**978** Edward, King of the English, killed by his political opponents at Corfe Castle, in Dorset; succeeded by his half-brother, Æthelred (the Unready)

**979** Body of Edward (the Martyr) miraculously revealed. Coronation of King Æthelred

**980** Resumption of Viking raids

**984** Death of Æthelwold, Bishop of Winchester (963–84)

**988** Death of Dunstan, Archbishop of Canterbury (959–88)

**991** Large Viking army arrives at Folkestone, and makes its way round coast to Maldon. Battle of Maldon

*Continued opposite*

---

mind, and made everyone more than usually aware of the need to do good in the sight of God, and to honour the saints who could intercede on their behalf at the Last Judgement.

In dedicating his "First Series" of homilies to Archbishop Sigeric (990-4), Ælfric stressed the need for good teaching, "especially in this age, which is the ending of this world". It is interesting to observe, therefore, that there are signs of a quickening, in the 990s, of precisely those kinds of activity which were calculated to earn divine favour.

King Æthelred broke free from the influence of those who had influenced his actions in the earlier years of his reign, and gave his ear to a different party, better disposed towards the interests of the Church. He was moved (or prevailed upon) to confirm or to renew earlier grants of lands and privileges to particular churches, or to grant them lands and privileges which they had not enjoyed before.

The institutions which benefited in this way during the 990s included Abingdon Abbey (993, 999), the see of Cornwall (994), Wilton Abbey (994), Muchelney Abbey (995), the see of Rochester (995, 998), St Albans Abbey (996), the Old Minster, Winchester (996, 997), the see of Sherborne (998), and doubtless several others whose charters have not chanced to survive.

It is no less striking that there was an increased incidence, in the 990s, of the various practices associated with the development of the cults of saints. The earliest *Lives* of the three leading exponents of monastic reform — St Æthelwold (d. 984), St Dunstan (d. 988), and St Oswald (d. 992) — were written *c.* 1000, as if the need was suddenly felt for the intercession of some English saints.

The churches themselves owed their separate identities to a combination of factors: not only the circumstances of their original foundation, and the connections of present patrons, but also the associations of those known to have been buried there, and the vitality or efficacy of the cults of those saints whose relics were known to be there. A healthy rivalry arose between neighbouring churches, as they vied with each other in accumulating relics of saints who could be relied upon to protect the interests of the public, and thereby to promote their own.

Moreover, there was an increased incidence in the ceremonial translation of holy relics from a lesser to a greater place, or from a less important part of a church to a more conspicuous location. St Cuthbert at Durham in 995, St Æthelwold at Winchester in 996, and St Edith at Wilton in 997 were among the saints whose relics are known to have been translated in the late tenth century; to which one might add St Edward at Shaftesbury in 1001, St Oswald at Worcester in 1002, and St Ivo at Ramsey, also in 1002.

All this in combination represents a significant change from the

980s, and seems to reflect an intensification of religious fervour among the English; and although no explicit connection is made between activities of such a kind and the impending millennium, one is left wondering whether the connection had existed at the back of the minds of those in positions of influence and power.

## Against the heathen

The world did not end in the year 1000. Yet if some breathed a sigh of relief, others would have been more concerned with the continuing struggle against the Viking invaders. The strength of anti-Danish feeling among the English is demonstrated by the Massacre of St Brice's Day, in 1002. A few years later, in the summer of 1009, a pan-Scandinavian force known to contemporaries as Thorkell's Army arrived at Sandwich, and brought the people to their knees.

The King and his councillors instituted an extraordinary programme of public prayer, for the three days before Michaelmas: the people were to process barefoot to church, the votive mass "Against the Heathen" was to be said in religious houses throughout the land, and all were to sing the psalm "Why, O Lord, are they multiplied?" There was even a special issue of coinage, invoking the Lamb of God and the Holy Spirit, apparently timed to coincide with the programme of prayer.

Alas, it was all to no avail. Swein Forkbeard and his son Cnut invaded England on their own account in 1013-16, and finished off the job. As for the Last Days, the official line remained that only God knew when the sixth age of the world would reach its end.

There was nothing, therefore, to prevent Archbishop Wulfstan, in the midst of crisis in 1014, from repeating the ultimatum deployed more than 400 years earlier by Pope Gregory the Great. "*Leofan men. . .*", "Beloved men, realise what is true: this world is in haste and the end approaches; and therefore in the world things go from bad to worse, and so it must of necessity deteriorate greatly on account of the people's sins before the coming of Antichrist, and indeed it will then be dreadful and terrible far and wide throughout the world."

For Archbishop Wulfstan, the Vikings were the sons of Gog and Magog, and their invasion of England a sign of impending doom; while, for the English themselves, the Vikings were quite unpleasant enough as they were. Churchmen had learnt, however, as some already knew, that it was better always to insist upon the imminence of the end than to predict its occurrence in a particular year.

## CHRONOLOGY

*Continued*

**992** Death of Oswald, Archbishop of York (971–92)

**994** Tribute of 16,000 pounds paid to the Vikings; army now a mercenary force, hired by the English to protect the kingdom against other enemies

**997** Viking army resumed its hostile activities

**1000** Viking army went to Normandy in the summer, and remained there until its return to England in 1001

**1002** Tribute of 24,000 pounds paid to the Vikings. Massacre of the Danes in England, on St Brice's Day, on instructions of King Æthelred

**1005** Famine throughout England. Viking army forced to return to Denmark

**1006** Invasion of England by a "great fleet", apparently under leadership of Tostig. Tribute of 36,000 pounds paid to the Vikings in 1007

**1009** Invasion of England by an "immense raiding army", under Thorkell the Tall

**1011** Archbishop Ælfheah taken prisoner at Canterbury

**1012** Archbishop Ælfheah put to death at Greenwich. Tribute of 48,000 pounds paid to the Vikings

**1013** Invasion of England by a force under Swein Forkbeard, king of the Danes, leading to its conquest. Æthelred was forced to take refuge in Normandy, but returns to England following Swein's death in 1014

**1015** Invasion of England by a force under Cnut, son of Swein Forkbeard and brother of Harold, King of the Danes

**1016** Death of King Æthelred; succeeded by his eldest surviving son, Edmund (Ironside). Further activities of Danish army in England, leading to a division of the kingdom between Edmund Ironside and Cnut. Death of King Edmund, and accession of Cnut

# THE NORMAN ARROW FINDS A READY TARGET

*1066: has the distinction between Norman control-freaks and Saxon creatives been overdone?*

## Giles Gasper

The year 1066 is accepted as a pivotal date in British or, perhaps more accurately, English history. Before it, at least as far as the English are concerned, lies the rulership of Anglo-Saxons; after it, that of the Norman kings.

They can come to represent a contrast between the old and the modern, the good-natured, long-whiskered, real-ale-appreciating thegns and housecarls succumbing before the tide of brutally efficient, close-cropped, frenchified Normans — characterisations familiar enough. Clearly, though, changes did accompany the Norman conquest of England in the 30 or 40 years after 1066, the conquest of Wales and Scotland belonging to the succeeding generation.

As regards the Church, the conquest appears to have caused and inspired wholesale reorganisation and reorientation. By 1093, the date of the elevation of Anselm, Abbot of Bec, to the archbishopric of Canterbury, there remained only one Anglo-Saxon bishop, Wulfstan II of Worcester, and no Anglo-Saxon abbots. Most of their replacements, although not all, were Norman. An identifiable change of personnel had taken place.

With the Normans, the story goes, come the long arms of papal government and interest, and reform of the decadent Old English Church. Lord Lytton in his *Harold, Last of the Anglo-Saxon Kings* (1848) has Harold advised by a Norse pagan priestess.

Nothing so exciting outside fiction: archdeacons made their appearance; the clergy were brought into line with the standards expected by Rome; and soaring cathedrals were erected. The English Church was now governed and guided by Norman masters.

## Monastic historians

One aspect of the Norman conquest which affects greatly how this episode is interpreted was an upsurgence in historical writing from the 1070s. Within this writing grew a celebration and exploration of the Anglo-Saxon Church and its achievements.

Centred in monasteries, which were not only the repositories of

Norman strength: the Tower of London; the White Tower, from the south. *Photo © A. F. Kersting* learning, but also, because occupied by English men and women, repositories of English memory and tradition, the assertions of these authors have exercised considerable influence. Leading lights in the process include Eadmer and Osbern of Canterbury, Colman and John of Worcester, the monks at Peterborough, and the half-English Orderic Vitalis, who spent most of his life, as child and adult, at the Norman monastery of St Évroul.

The testimony of these writers is extraordinarily valuable as source material, but we should be aware that already it represents an interpretation of the past. The monastic way of life and the assumptions it involved permeate the work they produced, and we risk seeing the Norman conquest exclusively from a monk's-eye view. Moreover, part of the purpose of these writers was to explain why events transpired as they did, a task naturally affected by their context.

Third, but not least, these sources were composed after the conquest, in the late 11th and early 12th centuries, a period in which church reform had spread across Western Christendom. We should be wary lest the desires and aspirations of those later years are written up in the record of the past. The record of the Norman conquest is one of detailed interpretative threads.

## Orderic Vitalis

Orderic Vitalis exemplifies a number of these traits. Most celebrated for his *Ecclesiastical History*, written between the 1110s and the 1140s, and surviving in only two manuscripts, Orderic made the following observations on the English Church:

"King William was justly renowned for his reforming zeal; in particular he always loved the true religion in churchmen for on this the peace and prosperity of the world depend. . . The Normans found the English a rustic and nearly illiterate people, although they had once been fully instructed in the best customs by the Roman pontiffs. . . After the destruction of the monasteries regular life was undermined, and canonical discipline was not restored until the time of the Normans. Indeed for a long time previously monasticism had been declining on that side of the Channel, and monks differed very little from seculars in their way of life. They wore no habit and took no vows; they indulged in feasting and private property and countless foul transgressions."

Reform and true religion are associated with William I. Left to their own devices, the English could not reform themselves, despite their Roman pedigree — the mission of St Augustine. Orderic's monastic point of view emerges; the tenth-century "Reformation" of monastic life is recalled as a golden age of religious life from which there was catastrophic decline.

# A question of primacy

Near the beginning of his archiepiscopate Lanfranc wrote to Pope Alexander II describing himself as "a novice Englishman, virtually ignorant as yet of English affairs, except for what I have learned at second hand".

When it came to his ecclesiastical colleagues, however, there was no doubt about whose knowledge of English affairs was deeper. In a memorandum on the primacy of Canterbury, included within Lanfranc's correspondence, Thomas, Archbishop of York, is recorded as objecting in 1070 to the profession of obedience and oath of loyalty to Canterbury demanded by Lanfranc.

The memorandum notes that "He acted in this way from ignorance rather than from a proud and obstinate spirit. For he was a newcomer, with no experience whatsoever of English usage, and he placed more confidence in the advice of flatterers than was right and proper."

Thomas did not understand, apparently, the ancient privileges accorded to Canterbury; privileges which Lanfranc was able to persuade William I were genuine, backed up by, as the memorandum puts it, "the English who already understood the matter". In fact, Thomas probably understood far too well the strained nature of the privileges so claimed.

Lanfranc claimed primacy for Canterbury over the whole of Britain, the ecclesiastical equivalent of William the Conqueror's claims to rule as *rex britanniae* and even *basileus* of Britain, echoing the pretensions of tenth-century Saxon rulers.

Lanfranc pursued this design to the limit, claiming authority over the other archdiocese, of York. What is more, he asserted the claims of Canterbury as historically grounded and justified.

In fact, the case was difficult to establish in so clear-cut a fashion, no such claims having been made by Anglo-Saxon archbishops. Bede's account of the Gregorian provisions for the rule of the Church of England in the first place refers to the Bishops of London and York, not Canterbury, and secondly refers to a transferable primacy depending on the relative seniority of the two archbishops.

Lanfranc, whose early training probably had been in secular law at Pavia, and who later turned to canon law, managed to force his interpretation of affairs through, gaining a personal submission from his Archbishops of York, though failing to enshrine the claims in perpetuity.

Claims for the primacy of Canterbury did become enshrined, however, at Canterbury itself, emerging as part of the heritage of St Augustine, to be defended at all costs.

Eadmer, one of the leading lights in the promotion of Canterbury's position, wrote of Lanfranc: "Then what pains he took to uphold the dignity of the Church of Canterbury! Abetted by some of the other bishops, Thomas, Archbishop of York, who had only recently become an English subject, tried hard to humiliate the Church of Canterbury with a view to the glorification of his own Church."

Canterbury provided itself with as much material as possible for the defence of its position. The translation of St Augustine's relics in 1091 provided the occasion for new *Lives* of St Augustine and his successors, *Lives* which emphasised the primacy. Finally, and there is still some debate on the matter of the date — whether in the late 11th century or in the 1120s — documents supporting the Canterbury case were forged.

The local aspect to the primacy dispute is revealed neatly in the fact that it was the neighbour of Christ Church, Canterbury, St Augustine's, which produced the most virulent opposition and criticism.

Lanfranc's great design was faithfully adopted by his successors, notably Anselm, who took their charge to defend the rights of St Augustine seriously. The tide of events was turning, and Canterbury's claims when presented before the Papal Court were deemed insufficient, many of the monks blaming Anselm in particular for having failed them.

The Norman conquest had ushered in a resurgence of Canterbury's claim to be the mother church of the British Isles, but also an age in which custom alone, without written proof, was no longer enough to support it.

Orderic's image perhaps draws rather too freely on the conditions prevailing at the time of writing. The position of the English Church in the mid-11th century was not so bleak as Orderic implies; nor was it so very different to the situation on the Continent.

Professor Frank Barlow described the Western Church at large in this period as "a Church without a mainstream". In this respect, the English Church was not especially more insular or peculiar than anywhere else. Its attitudes and activity might be similarly described; decadent it certainly was not. Abuses of clerical regulations did occur, spectacularly in the case of Stigand, Archbishop of Canterbury (1052-1070), who was a pluralist to rival Thomas Wolsey; but such behaviour was unusual, and hardly confined to the English.

Church reform — the call for better practice of organised religious life and worship — became a widespread phenomenon in the West throughout these years, and was not simply the prerogative of the Norman Duchy. As Orderic himself tells us, monastic revival in Normandy itself hardly got off the ground until the 1030s, and was a process continually evolving throughout the years of the conquest.

Ecclesiastical influence during this period is not simply a question of isolating cause and effect, of, for example, the Normans upon the English, but rather a search for multifarious contacts. The Anglo-Saxon Church was much influenced by developments in Germany, as, for example, in its knowledge of the canonical Rule of St Chrodegang of Metz.

In this manner, attitudes towards church reform, the celibacy of the clergy, and the better practice of Christian Rules were not so behind the times in the English Church. Without the Norman conquest, there would probably have been movement towards them, anyway.

## Norman and English saints

Norman reaction to English saints offers insight into this state of affairs. Previous scholarship tended to emphasise the negative response of Norman invaders to Old English saints and shrines. Lanfranc, Archbishop of Canterbury (1070-1089), originally from north Italy and a close adviser to William I, was viewed as prominent in this response. Under his instruction a purge of the Anglo-Saxon calendar of saints took place, and his grave doubts over the sanctity of Elphege, one of his predecessors at Canterbury (d. 1012), formed the basis of an important theological debate with Anselm over the question of justice and truth.

Lanfranc's attitude was apparently mirrored by Paul, Abbot of St Albans, who removed the bodies of Anglo-Saxon abbots from the monastery church. In both cases, though the significance has been over-played.

Lanfranc's liturgical alterations to the calendar in no way constitute

Cathedral and fortress: Durham.
*Photo © Claughton Photography*

a purge; and, in the case of Abbot Paul's action, there is no suggestion that the bodies he removed from the church were regarded as saints by the Anglo-Saxon community at St Albans.

In fact, Norman abbots and high ecclesiastics tended to support and promote the saints of the monastic houses under their charge. The sanctity of corporate traditions was an ingrained element in church life across the board.

It is an element that illuminates the relationship between the English Church and Rome. A distinction could and should be made between calls for reform of clerical and monastic life, and the assertions of control of such matters by the Church at Rome. Neither Lanfranc nor his successor Anselm had any intention of surrendering the rights of St Augustine to those of St Peter. Norman control of the upper echelons of the English Church did not go hand in glove with dramatically increased papal involvement in the ruling of the Church of England. Where that influence is detected, it is better considered as part of a general growth in the power and attraction of the papal court at Rome.

# Theologian at Canterbury

Anselm, Archbishop of Canterbury (1093-1109), is one of the few medieval theologians who are well-known. A doctor of the Church, "The Magnificent Doctor", he had an original and highly disciplined theological mind.

From the *Proslogion* which deals with the so-called ontological argument, that is, the existence of God in being, to *Cur Deus Homo* (Why the God-Man), perhaps the finest medieval treatise on the incarnation and atoning work of Christ, Anselm deals with the great questions of Christian doctrine.

These are not treated as academic subjects divorced from the rest of the Christian experience. Anselm recognises the limitations of the human mind; for him, the beginning and end of theology is a recognition of this mortal state in silent and wondering prayer.

It was the joy experienced by Anselm in his prayerful theology and theological prayer which inspired him to communicate it to others. Christian thinking was a necessary duty, and to be approached with due seriousness of purpose, but not as an arid theology; rather it was part of the joyful, living faith.

Anselm was famous within his lifetime for his talk, as a preacher and more informally. In *Cur Deus Homo* he remarks: "Not only the learned, but also many unlearned persons interest themselves in this inquiry and seek its solution. Therefore, since many desire to consider this subject, and, though it seems very difficult in the investigation, it is yet plain to all in the solution, and attractive for the value and beauty of the reasoning; . . . I will take pains to disclose to inquirers what God has seen fit to lay open to me."

The effect of Anselm's words was electrifying, both to intimate and larger audiences. Eadmer, an English monk of Canterbury, Anselm's self-appointed biographer, recorded his impressions of Anselm preaching in England: ". . . in his usual way he showed himself cheerful and approachable to everyone. . . He adapted his words to every class of men, so that his hearers declared that nothing could have been spoken more appropriate to their station."

Eadmer elaborates on this approach: "and when we say that he admonished, or instructed, or taught these things, he did it not as others are wont to teach, but far differently; he set forth each point with familiar examples in daily life, supporting them with the evidence of solid reason, and leaving them in the minds of his hearers, stripped of all ambiguity."

## Majestic new cathedrals

Veneration of Anglo-Saxon saints may lie behind one of the most famous of Norman introductions to England in the wake of the conquest, that is, architectural innovation, and, in its ecclesiastical form, majestic and enormous cathedrals.

Cathedrals and other church buildings provide a visible and lasting sign of the conquest. That said, not much of the post-conquest building programme survives intact today. Present-day cathedrals and churches often reflect building of the late 12th century and after. But enough survives — the interior of Gloucester Cathedral, for example — to gain impressions of the size of these new constructions, an area in which archaeology triumphs, and we do have a number of literary accounts.

Castle and cathedral stand together, literally so at Durham, in signifying the extent and permanence of Norman domination. It should be recalled, though, that many were built as fitting monuments to the

# What the clergy did with their wives

St Wulfstan. *Photo © Malvern Priory, from* The Ancient Windows of Great Malvern Priory Church *by L. A. Hamand*

In 1071, as part of the purge of Anglo-Saxon bishops, Leofric of Lichfield resigned his bishopric, having openly acknowledged his wife and children and refused to disavow them. Insistence on clerical celibacy, one of the watchwords of papal reform from the 1050s, provided the grounds for Leofric's removal. Clerical marriage tells us much about the nature of the conquest of England: it was not a peculiarly English problem addressed only by conquering Normans, and is an issue affected by the interpretation of the succeeding generation.

Orderic Vitalis recorded a violent incident at the Rouen synod of 1072, part of the drive by the Archbishop of Rouen, John of Avranches, against the married clergy.

John, Archbishop 1067-1079, was "continuously striving to separate immoral priests from their mistresses: on one occasion when he forbade them to keep their concubines he was stoned out of the synod, and fled exclaiming with a loud voice: 'O God, the heathen are come into thine inheritance.'[Psalm 79.1]"

Orderic is our only source for this episode. By the time he was writing, in the 1110s and early 1120s, attitudes to the issue of married clerics had hardened considerably, and John's policy sits more comfortably with the approach of later years. John had received information that Lanfranc had criticised the action taken. Lanfranc wrote to John in about 1075, reassuring him that this was far from the case; indeed, he, Lanfranc, had been inspired by John to formulate his own provisions against married clerics.

But, on closer examination, Lanfranc's prohibitions are not so stringent. They affect only canons, and so not the lower orders of priests. Also, those who give up their prebendal income do not have to abandon their wives.

Lanfranc's more moderate approach on this issue is demonstrated again by comparison with the record of Wulfstan, Bishop of Worcester, in his vigorous campaign against married priests. According to his biography, Wulfstan abhorred the sin of sexual incontinence, and brought married priests "under one edict, commanding them to renounce their fleshly desires or their churches. "If they loved chastity, they might remain and be welcome: if they were the servants of bodily pleasure, they must go forth in disgrace. Some there were who chose to go without their churches rather than their women: and of these some wandered about until they starved: others sought and at last found some other provision."

Once more this source is a generation later than the events it describes. A *Life of Wulfstan* had been written in Old English by his protégé Colman. This work, now lost, formed the basis for William of Malmesbury's Latin *Life of Wulfstan*, written in the 1120s. The description of the aggression directed to married clergy perhaps owes something to the prevailing ethos of the 1120s.

The starvation of the unfortunate sexual incontinents should be compared with Lanfranc's injunction to Bishop Herfast of Thetford regarding a married deacon, that the man should be fed and supported, and under no circumstances starve. Already by the 1120s, the effects of the Norman Conquest were being historically manipulated and interpreted.

saints of the churches they replaced. Canterbury and its neighbour St Augustine's Abbey were associated with the apostle of England; Worcester — where the "Norman" cathedral was built by an Anglo-Saxon, Wulfstan — with St Oswald; Durham with St Cuthbert; Bury St Edmunds with King Edmund the Martyr.

English saints provided the inspiration for the great programme of Norman buildings in England; but the influence of the English may have gone further than that. It may well be the case that the Norman style of building, far from being an import to England, had in fact been exported to Normandy from England.

Jumièges Abbey in Normandy is one of the architectural seed-beds of Norman Romanesque architecture. Robert Champart, Abbot of Jumièges, in 1037 went on to become Bishop of London and Archbishop of Canterbury, but was banished from England in 1052. During his time in England, work began on the royal Abbey of Westminster, inspired perhaps by German architectural practice, many of whose features figure also at Jumièges. It now appears likely that the line of architectural allegiance runs from Westminster to Jumièges rather than the other way round.

Romanesque architecture was not, then, a direct consequence of the conquest. Recent archaeological work at Worcester might suggest that the size of the Anglo-Saxon cathedral replaced in the 1080s by Bishop Wulfstan's new church was considerable, putting the lie to the idea that Anglo-Saxons could not build big. The reason why Anglo-Saxon cathedrals appear less frequently is by virtue of the fact that they were built over.

## English dough and Norman leaven

The Norman conquest as a whole, and in respect to the Church, did have profound and lasting effects, and it would not do to negate them.

Sir Richard Southern has written of the Normans that "they came to England at a time when the country was wavering between a closer approach to, or a wider alienation from, the culture and organisation of Latin Europe, and they settled the question in favour of the first alternative for the rest of the Middle Ages."

The nature of the effects lies perhaps more in this encouragement and enlivening of latent tendencies than in a strict dichotomy between old-fashioned Anglo-Saxons and pace-making Normans.

The combination of English dough and Norman leaven proved to be potent, as the conquest by the English of Wales and Scotland revealed. That the invaders of Wales, Scotland and at a later date Ireland were known as such points to another aspect of the conquest, the relatively small number of incursive Normans, and their essential taking-over of pre-existing structures rather than the development of new mechanisms of government. If this was the case with secular government, so, too, with the Church. It would have been surprising if the Normans had, in fact, completely reorganised the English Church. Our sources do not tend to offer much insight into the history of popular Christian practice, but the indications are that the changes were not as great an upheaval as might at first be thought. English retreated before Latin as the language of scholarly discourse and as the benchmark of literacy, but the fact that we are writing and speaking in English nowadays relates directly to a tenacious survival from the conquest of English at the parish level.

It is a survival perhaps mirrored more widely in religious life. The Norman invasion of the English Church coincided with the development of attitudes towards reform among the higher clergy. It should be viewed with a wider perspective, and seen in the context of changes across Christendom encapsulated in the fact that it was presided over by two Italians, Lanfranc and Anselm.

## CHRONOLOGY

**1066** Battle of Hastings
**1070** Consecration of Lanfranc as Archbishop of Canterbury
**1073** Election of Pope Gregory VII
**1085** Death of Pope Gregory VII
**1087** Death of William the Conqueror; accession of William II (Rufus)
**1089** Death of Lanfranc
**1093** Consecration of Anselm as Archbishop of Canterbury
**1095** Death of Wulfstan, Bishop of Worcester
**1100** Death of William II; accession of Henry I
**1109** Death of Anselm

# MONASTICISM IN BRITAIN

*We focus on some key figures of medieval monasticism, and look at how the religious orders were torn between the sacred and the secular.*

*Benjamin Thompson*

The vocation to live the Christian life under vows, according to a Rule, can take a range of different forms, from the hermits in the desert to canons and friars providing active ministry. In the middle of this spectrum is the monastery for monks or nuns living in common, represented most obviously by the Benedictines.

All these different ways of life involve rejecting the "world" in some way, whether society itself or worldly standards and morals. Yet the religious life also depends on society, most obviously for recruits and for the material means of support. Monasticism is thus characterised by a constant tension between world-rejection and assimilation into the world, between isolation and integration. As such, it presents a microcosm of the problem of the whole Church, of living in the "world" according to non-worldly standards.

For much of the early Middle Ages, monks and monasteries were leaders of the Church, which compromised their isolation. Even the tenth-century reform in England, which introduced stricter observance along continental Benedictine lines, paradoxically created a strong connection between monasteries and royal government.

## Benedictine heyday

The Norman Conquest demonstrated forcefully the dependence of ecclesiastical institutions on secular powers. The English monasteries lost lands and rights in the upheaval of the new tenurial settlement, and had to accommodate themselves to the new regime; they accepted Norman abbots (the best route to recovery, as for instance at St Albans), and an even stronger dose of royal lordship, seen in the quotas of up to 60 knights they owed to the royal army, finding land for whom involved further alienation of their property.

Nevertheless, the Normans arrived at a propitious moment for monasticism. The black monks (Benedictines) were in their heyday, under the leadership of Cluny, with its emphasis on never-ending liturgical intercession for Christian society as a whole and benefactors in particular.

Heyday: Benedict and the Benedictines, a window in Norwich by Moira Forsyth (1964). *Photo © Sonia Halliday and Laura Lushington*

# Why seek the religious life?

## Gillian Evans

Why should someone want to become a monk or nun? Often in the early centuries there was no choice. Infants were given to monasteries as child oblates, and simply grew up in the house. But in the late 11th century there was a change of fashion, and adults in middle life began to "get a vocation".

One monk, Guibert of Nogent, who wrote his own life story, described how knights, with their children grown up, would make an agreement with their wives, and both would enter the religious life. There was a similar turning to monastic life in old age among retired academics in the 12th century.

But that did not mean that to become a monk or nun was simply to enter a retirement home. Conversion was a decision with consequences. It had many of the features of the classic conversion experience, the growing sense that this was the will of God, the period of resistance to having one's life turned upside-down, then capitulation and the great sense of peace.

Society valued monks and nuns because they performed a valuable service. Monks and nuns prayed on behalf of those too busy to pray much on their own account; and their life of holiness was taken to make their prayer especially effective.

There were also practical benefits in having a monastic community near a village. When he was still at Bec, Anselm wrote letters in which he mentions a *medicus* (physician) among the brothers. England produced several leading figures in setting demanding standards for the living of monastic life.

# Anselm

Anselm of Bec and Canterbury (1033-1109) was an Italian who left his home as a young man to go in search of higher education. He wandered for three years in northern France until he settled at the new monastery of Bec as a student of Lanfranc, who was running a famous school there and attracting the sons of the local nobility.

Once he had had a taste of it, Anselm found himself drawn to the monastic life. But he was faced with a dilemma. If he stayed at Bec, he could go on being an active student. If he went elsewhere, the best place would be the strict, reformed monastery of Cluny, where he would have little time for study.

He chose Bec. This was a period when the would-be "academic" did not yet have universities to go to. Anselm took over in due course from Lanfranc as chief "schoolmaster" at Bec. He taught his pupils to think like philosophers by beginning from what they already understood, and proceeding by clear reasoning until they understood what before they had simply believed. The context was always spiritual, and although some of Anselm's arguments — especially his ontological proof of the existence of God — have been long-lived, they remain essentially products of the monastic life.

Not all his writing was theological. He is also the author of a series of prayers and meditations, which were immensely attractive to readers throughout the Middle Ages because they were designed for private, not liturgical, prayer. Anselm encouraged the user to take them as starting-points for independent spiritual journeys.

Lanfranc had become Archbishop of Canterbury; and in 1093 an unwilling Anselm followed him into that office. Although Anselm found himself forced into conflict with two successive kings, and went twice into exile, he always strove to continue to live the monastic life to which he had dedicated himself as a young man.

# Ailred of Rievaulx

Ailred (1109-67), son of a parish priest of Hexham, grew up at the court of the King of Scotland, but about 1133 he felt called to become a Cistercian monk at Rievaulx. He prospered in the order, and became Abbot of Revesby in 1143, and Abbot of Rievaulx in 1147.

Ailred had none of Anselm's formal education, and in his day that was a more conspicuous lack, for now there were beginning to be "schools" in which a high level of scholarship could be achieved. Ailred learned by reading the Fathers. His writings reflect that background. He wrote a book about the soul in which there is a strong influence of Augustine's thinking on the same subject.

But Ailred had ideas of his own. He puzzles over the way in which it is possible to hold in one's head a picture of a city the size of London, although London would not fit into anyone's skull. His chief interests lay in the emotional and affective texture of the daily living of the monastic life. He wrote a "mirror of love" (*Speculum caritatis*) and a book, *On Spiritual Friendship*, in which he explores the special form of a monastic friendship in which the two human friends always have Christ with them as a third.

# Gilbert of Sempringham

Gilbert of Sempringham (*c.* 1083-1189) saw a practical need to be met: that of his female parishioners wanting to commit themselves to the religious life. Seven women of his parish of Sempringham formed a community under his guidance, and began to live under the Cistercian system, using the Rule of St Benedict (as all Cistercians did).

Gilbert's bishop supported the venture. Groups of lay sisters and lay brothers were brought together to sustain the life of the community. In 1139, a second house followed the first, and then another.

But these communities of women remained anomalous, and when Gilbert went to Cîteaux in 1148 to try to arrange for his communities of nuns to be properly recognised as Cistercians, he was refused. He therefore made arrangements for them to be under the supervision of Augustinian canons. In 1148 Gilbert gained papal approbation of this uniquely English new order.

Scholar: an image of Anselm made by the monks of the Abbaye Notre Dame du Bec. *Reproduced with kind permission of the Dean and Chapter, Canterbury*

Expanding aristocracies all over Europe were giving some of their new wealth to monks. The conquerors gave plenty from their windfalls in England to monasteries in France, such as William I's twin-foundations at Caen, and the Abbey of Bec.

The Normans also quickly imported their native monasticism into England by founding new monasteries colonised by French monks, beginning with the Conqueror's memorial to Hastings, Battle Abbey. Cluny sent monks in 1077 for William de Warenne to establish a priory at his castle at Lewes, and many other lords founded new houses on their baronies.

Thus ecclesiastical foundations reflected worldly success: a monastery was a complement to a castle, both for its spiritual combat of intercession for the founders' souls, and for the impressive statement of lordship which its buildings made.

## New religious orders

The Benedictine monopoly was on the point of being broken, however, by different types of monasticism. The papal reform of the mid-11th century inspired a revival of the canonical ideal of members of the clergy living a stricter life under vows. A letter of St Augustine provided the basis for a rule, and from the end of the 11th century small groups of canons established themselves, often in towns, to live the common life, perhaps to care for the sick and travellers, and to supplement the ministry of the as yet inadequately structured Church.

Another reforming impulse moved in the opposite direction, to revive a more eremitical monasticism, encouraged by increasing criticism of the black monks' liturgical over-emphasis and secularism. From the later 11th century, many monks left traditional monasteries in search of a stricter regime on the margins of society; monks of St Mary's Abbey, York, headed west into the Yorkshire Dales, and in 1132 established Fountains Abbey under the aegis of the most successful of such new orders, St Bernard's Cistercians.

The Cistercians' ascetic way of life was framed by St Benedict's prescribed day, divided equally between common liturgy, private prayer or spiritual reading, and manual labour — the latter elements largely neglected by the black monks. But its harshness could also be tempered by warm spirituality, such as that of Ailred of Rievaulx, with his emphasis on monastic friendship.

The 12th century therefore opened up many opportunities to those wishing to pursue the religious life, both in terms of numbers (there were nearly 20,000 religious in the 13th century), and of different types of vocation.

Even stricter than the Cistercians were the Carthusians, who lived as individual hermits, but round a common cloister. Other new orders adopted the canonical life, but with stricter customs, like the Premonstratensians and the men of the only English order, the Gilbertines. The military orders, Templars and Hospitallers, enabled knights to fulfil their belligerent vocation, but in the service of the crusades and under religious vows.

Many orders found places for people from lower ranks of society than the traditional aristocratic monks; men with little education could become Cistercian lay brothers.

Women in particular benefited from the new diversity, since nuns in the early Middle Ages had been few and aristocratic. Perhaps this reflected the new, more human-centred — even feminine — spirituality, evident in the greater prominence of the Virgin and the efflorescence of her miracle-stories.

Groups of women attempting to live in common, or as anchorites, are glimpsed in the early 12th century (such as Christina of Markyate, whose determination to maintain her chastity inspired a biography), and from about the 1130s around 150 nunneries were founded to house them.

## The pull of worldliness

Yet, however the religious conceived themselves as leaving the world — whether physically or morally — escape could only be partial.

The Cistercians' retreat to the margin quickly made them rich, as, with exquisite timing, they caught the tide of European economic expansion, cultivating new lands and using the fells for enormous sheep-runs. Moreover, their reputation for unworldliness attracted benefactors in the political turmoil of Stephen's reign, since giving disputed land to the religious prevented opponents' controlling it.

Far from taking the initiative in leaving the world, monks were pawns in its power-politics. The success of canons and nuns was also based partly on their ability to meet secular needs. Since their priories were smaller and involved a less elaborate lifestyle, they provided a cheaper alternative to the Benedictines; lesser land-holders (knights) were able to found them. Nearly 350 canonries were founded in the 12th and 13th centuries.

These forces gradually transformed the monastic orders. In the 13th century, spiritual leadership passed to the friars, with their unique mixture of active ministry in towns and rejection of landed endowment in favour of mendicant begging.

The monasteries' role within the Church was also diminished by the gradual success of the parish in delivering ministry to the vast bulk of the population. Even intercession for souls was increasingly provided by "secular" (non-regular) clergy.

Among monks and nuns, continued ascetic vitality was practised only

**CHRONOLOGY**

*c.* **943-70** Reform by Sts Dunstan, Æthelwold and Oswald, and King Edgar

*c.* **1070** Foundation of Battle Abbey by William the Conqueror (Benedictine)

**1077** Foundation of Lewes Priory, first Cluniac house

*c.* **1100** Establishment of St Botolph's, Colchester, as first Augustinian house

**1128** Foundation of Temple, London, for Templar Knights

**1132** Foundation of Fountains Abbey (Cistercian)

**1131-39** Foundation of Sempringham, double house for nuns and canons

**1143** Foundation of Newhouse (Premonstratensian)

**1215** Establishment of Benedictine and Augustinian provincial chapters at Fourth Lateran Council

**1221** Arrival of first friars

**1335-39** Reforms of Benedict XII

**1414** Statute formally dissolving alien priories

**1536-40** Dissolution of the monasteries

by a few hundred religious in the strictest orders, the Carthusians, Bridgettine nuns, and Franciscan Observants, especially under the patronage of Henrys V and VII. Periodic attempts to reform the major orders, notably in the 1330s, only show how expectations had been lowered, as the religious slipped into comfortable mediocrity, and increasing time was devoted to management.

## Towards the Dissolution

Nevertheless, religious houses remained in possession of great wealth in the later Middle Ages. They justified their existence by contributing to society in many different ways. Visitations show religious houses as integral parts of their local communities. The religious were out on business, running errands, or administering their estates (sometimes far-flung), or sometimes for the pleasures of wine and women. Equally, the cloister was filled with guests, pensioners, and armies of staff and servants.

The more, therefore, monasteries conceived of themselves as providing social services, the less they resembled earlier blueprints. In the early 16th century, conservatives such as John Fisher and the stricter orders urged reform, and in the later 1520s Wolsey almost implemented a plan which would have dissolved or combined 80 per cent of them.

As a result, the monasteries were caught between competing identities: their natural evolution was to secularise, but they were stuck with a monastic tradition which, although in itself not widely valued, imposed upon them expectations which most could not satisfy. This left them highly vulnerable to the cataclysm which engulfed them in the 1530s.

It could be said that the laity — who so often hold the whip hand in the Church's history — secularised the monasteries, then dissolved them for being secular. Yet even the Dissolution can be seen as a natural evolution: the monasteries had fulfilled their historic function, of leading the Church, and providing the basis for papal reform in the 11th century, which constructed the medieval Church.

Although that very process marginalised them, it also enabled some religious, briefly, to adopt a more separate monastic vocation away from the world. That enthusiasm for such asceticism on a wide scale was short-lived is no surprise; it may be the more noteworthy not that the monasteries were ultimately dissolved, but that they had played such an important part in the ecclesiastical and social history of these islands for so long.

# THE LEGACY OF THE WATERMEN

## *J. Wyn Evans*

*How Norse attacks recalled the Welsh to their noble past.*

The decades before and after the turn of the first millennium were difficult ones for the Welsh Church. In common with its sister Churches in these islands, it had suffered severely at the hands of Norse raiders, and was to suffer equally severely for another 80 years or so. Its life was disrupted; many of its churches were pillaged; and many of its clerical communities were displaced, moving from place to place, carrying with them the relics of their founders.

By this period, the Welsh Church had for several centuries been serving the people of the emergent Wales. Its general tenor appears to have been conservative and even isolationist.

As for the theological stance of the Welsh Church, the evidence is ambiguous, and although recent work has suggested an emphasis on creation and community, as far as can be seen, the Welsh Church appears to have shared the same orthodox stance as any other Church in early medieval Europe. It saw itself as being in communion with Rome as part of the Church universal. Its differences from the Anglo-Saxon Church were probably as much to do with feelings of resentment for the loss of the island of Britain as with any theological emphases.

At the turn of the 11th century, the Welsh Church seems to have been organised in bishoprics related to the secular divisions of the country, with a hierarchy of mother churches staffed by hereditary bodies of clerics, called *clasau*, which could be up to 24 in number and headed by an "abbot". Such communities could also possess a "doctor" who was presumably in charge of educating and training clerics; and a "*sacerdos*" or archpriest.

The mother churches appear to have been more collegiate than monastic; they appear to have exercised pastoral care over areas of considerable extent; and their members were, at a slightly later date, called *canonici*. The most prestigious of them were very wealthy indeed.

Despite this, these mother churches frequently claimed that they had been founded by the great, heroic and ascetic founders of the monastic movement of the sixth century.

It is true that Dewi (David), who had died at the end of the sixth century, had not been unique among that early and heroic generation of monastic founders in his asceticism. Others had lived on bread and water or, like Samson, slept leaning against the walls of their cells. There was a whole sect of "watermen" (and women) who, like Dewi, stood up to their necks in cold water for hours on end to subdue the flesh, though few had carried self-denial to the point where they had, as

Welsh remnant: Valle Crucis, a Cistercian abbey near Llangollen.
*Photo © A. F. Kersting*

Dewi had done, refused to allow their communities to use animals to till the fields, but made them place yokes on their own shoulders.

By the 11th century, such asceticism was a thing of the past, though its example was still potent. Rhigyfarch, son of Bishop Sulien of St Davids, when he came to write the *Life of Dewi* towards the end of that century, made a point of describing in detail the ascetic practices both of Dewi and his community.

But the *Lives* of such founders were written and preserved for another purpose: to emphasise the heroic quality of the saints' revenge on those who would deprive their successors of their possessions. It was to the possession of the relics of such saints that the *clas* communities looked to secure their title to lands and gifts, especially when such donations had been entered into the margins of the Gospel books laid on the altars of the founding saints; and it was maintained that when their churches were violated that it was the saints' own status that was at stake.

Such sanctions did not discourage the Norsemen — or others — from plundering and killing and destroying, however, and their raids served to recall the Welsh to their former fervour.

A particular Norse raid on Menevia (St Davids) struck a chord with contemporaries as far away as Ireland. The raid which occurred in 999 was no more intense than previous ones, though it did lead to the death of its bishop, Morgenau. Churchmen of the time and later saw his death as a judgement, for Morgenau had been the first to break the tradition of not eating meat which had characterised the community of Dewi at Menevia since the days of the founder himself.

Such resilience in the midst of disaster stood the Church well, as towards the end of the century increasing Norman interest    usually hostile — in the Welsh Church brought it unwillingly closer into the ambit of the reforming currents within the Church on the continent of Europe.

Not that there was much of a gap in time between the activities of the Norsemen and their successors, the Normans. In 1080, St Davids was again badly raided by Vikings, resulting in the death of Bishop Abraham. In 1081, however, William the Conqueror himself came to St Davids, ostensibly to pray, but certainly as a harbinger of change.

St Davids retained its status as an episcopal church and its patronage both of Norman lords and native princes. Many of its fellow mother churches either became the possessions of Norman Benedictine houses, abbey and priory churches themselves; or transformed themselves into houses of Augustinian canons. And many of the clerical families who had governed them became part of the new order.

# 101 USES FOR A DEAD ARCHBISHOP

*Brenda Bolton*

*How Becket's death and their conflicts with the papacy undermined the power of the crude and religiously ambivalent Plantagenets.*

In the period from 1100 to *c.* 1215, the Church in England was deeply affected by far-reaching changes, some specific to that country, but others occurring throughout Christendom.

No fewer than three Archbishops of Canterbury experienced long periods of exile: Anselm, between 1103 and 1107, then Thomas Becket from 1164 to 1170, and finally Stephen Langton twice, from 1206 to 1213 and again in 1215-18; while, in 1170, Becket had sacrificed his own life for his beliefs. In addition, between 1208 and 1213 the people of England suffered the disgrace and ignominy of the Pope's Interdict on the normal activities of their Church, while the king himself experienced the ultimate penalty of excommunication.

Behind these significant events was the underlying struggle of the Church for freedom from lay control, *libertas ecclesiae*. The outstanding issue for the papacy — the Church at its highest level — as it gradually reformed itself by throwing off royal or princely control, was to encourage properly conducted, canonical appointments throughout all levels of the hierarchy.

In this relevant century, the greatest changes occurred in the perception of the bishop's role in pastoral care. At the end of the period, the Fourth Lateran Council of 1215, summoned by Pope Innocent III (1198-1216), stressed the pastoral responsibilities of all of the clergy. The Council's distinctive approach, with its emphasis on preaching, confession and penance, was based on its understanding that many dioceses were large and scattered, and hence bishops needed the support of competent men to assist them.

Interestingly, in spite of previous differences which the English clergy may have had with the Pope, once decisions were agreed, they carried them through loyally. In the case of the Lateran Council, this applied not only to Stephen Langton, who had disagreed with Innocent III over Magna Carta, but also to his suffragans, such as Richard Poore of Salisbury and William de Blois of Worcester, whose implementation of the conciliar decrees was among the most rapid and thorough in Christendom.

Horrific act: the murder of Thomas Becket. Harl. 5102 f.32
*Photo © by permission of the British Library*

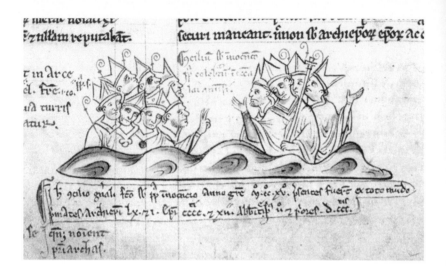

All at sea: the Fourth Lateran Council (1215), from the Chronicle of Matthew Paris (CCC MS16, f.43v). *Photo © Master & Fellows of Corpus Christi College, Cambridge*

Langton had acquired his theology in the 1180s from the School of Pastoral Theology headed by Peter the Chanter in Paris. As a teacher himself in Paris, Langton was influenced by the *vita apostolica*, or imitation of the apostolic life, yet he was also in the mainstream of English biblical scholarship. He not only championed the cause for which Becket had died, his reverence for ideals of liberty placing him squarely with the reformers; he also promoted a model, pastoral episcopate, with bishops henceforth free to concentrate on spiritual matters and the preaching of the faith.

The reign of Henry I (1100-35), King of England and Duke of Normandy, coincided with the so-called Investiture Contest, during which Anselm, Archbishop of Canterbury (1093-1109), retreated into exile for refusing to perform homage for his lands or to consecrate bishops whom Henry had already invested with their symbols of episcopal office. The statesmanlike compromise reached by Anselm on his return in 1107 allowed the King to receive the bishops' oaths of homage while the Archbishop retained the right of investiture.

## Many titles, one policy

Until Henry I's death in 1135, England formed part of an Anglo-Norman state whose absentee rulers were first and foremost Dukes of Normandy. From 1154 until the early 13th century, England was one among an extensive collection of lands stretching from the Pyrenees to Scotland. This territorial assemblage is now known as the Angevin Empire, although contemporaries would not have seen it as such; nor were its rulers ever deemed to be emperors. Henry II Plantagenet (1154-89) and his sons, Richard I, Coeur de Lion (1189-99), and John (1199-1216), were dynastic rulers with a variety of styles or titles — kings in England, counts in Anjou, Maine, Touraine and Poitou, and dukes in Normandy and Aquitaine — who pursued a unified policy towards the Church in all of their dominions.

The Plantagenets claimed the right to interfere in the election of bishops, prevent direct appeals to Rome, and end the clerical privilege of immunity from secular punishment, whether in Normandy, Anjou or elsewhere. Unfortunately for them, a famous dispute, occurring in England assumed a Europe-wide dimension. The cause of this dispute — a struggle to preserve the independence and freedom of the Church — became a matter of vital concern to every ecclesiastical province throughout Christendom. In England, the conflict is erroneously associated with the civil war of Stephen's reign (1135-54), a period in which the Church made considerable advances in England, through new monastic and canonical foundations which, by midcentury, had done much to revitalise the spiritual climate.

## Murder of Becket

This extension of papal jurisdiction has been regarded as a contributory motive for Becket's murder on 29 December 1170 before the high altar of his cathedral by four of Henry II's household knights. The impact of Becket's violent death caused such shock-waves that he became England's best-known saint and heroic martyr, and Canterbury was transformed into one of Europe's greatest pilgrimage centres.

No other English saint has been so widely venerated, nor has his shrine — nowadays a memorial plaque — at Canterbury ever been superseded as the goal of pilgrims everywhere.

The cult of this newest saint spread with remarkable rapidity. Before the end of the 12th century, Becket was depicted visually in mosaic in the cathedral of Montreale in Sicily; his feast was celebrated in Norwegian, Polish and Hungarian liturgies; he appeared in Castilian and Aragonese wall paintings; exquisite caskets in Limoges enamelwork were manufactured to hold his relics; and, by the 13th century, so-called Thomas sagas had begun to be composed in Iceland in his honour.

In England, as was to be expected, Becket celebrations increased in intensity, and his recorded miracles came to number more than 700.

The martyrdom of Becket, and Richard I's activities in taking the cross, disguise the Plantagenet conflict with the papacy. So far as the Church was concerned, something of a compromise was achieved when Richard, taken captive while returning from the Third Crusade, was nevertheless able to send letters to England successfully urging that his candidate, Hubert Walter, should be elected to Canterbury in 1193.

## King versus Pope

The conflict became more obviously serious with the election of Innocent III in 1198, and the formal accession of Richard's brother

# St Hugh — the bishop with bite

Hugh, elected to the see of Lincoln in 1186, was mourned on his death in 1200 as a zealous champion for the freedom of the Church and energetic pastor of his flock.

A Carthusian monk from Burgundy, Hugh was much in tune with ideas current in the Paris School of Pastoral Theology. As friend and spiritual adviser to all three Plantagenets, he came first to royal attention as Prior (1179-86) of the Charterhouse of Witham in Somerset, Henry II's own foundation.

Hugh's biographers, Adam of Eynsham and Gerald of Wales, provide unique eye-witness evidence of how ordinary churchgoers in the diocese at the turn of the 12th century regarded the highly successful 14-year reign of their bishop.

In the diocese of Lincoln, vacant for nearly 18 years before Hugh's arrival, much pastoral work was required. Hugh first attracted wise and learned assistants, not only from England, but also from the Continent, and established them in the cathedral chapter of Lincoln.

His pastoral duties were performed with tireless zeal and incredible staying-power. In particular, he is credited with actually dismounting from his horse to administer the sacrament of confirmation to children, so as not to scare them as he rode by. If some lay retainer chanced to cuff these children, Hugh's anger was terrible, and he even returned their blows. The faithful were clearly able to sympathise with Hugh's human weakness, for the Bishop possessed a hot temper which he did not always manage to control — even in the presence of Henry II himself.

Hugh was a great builder, responsible for creation of the new Angel Choir at Lincoln after the old Norman cathedral had been almost destroyed by a great earthquake on Palm Sunday, 1185. He was also a highly motivated collector of relics, which he kept for safety in a huge reliquary ring.

Some of these were acquired by dubious means, like the two fragments broken off when he bit into the arm bone of Mary Magdalene, the most prized possession of the Abbey of Fécamp, and ground away at it with his molars. What seems to us to have been a shocking act of impiety was warmly commended by his biographer as a saintly deed which served only to increase his reverence, and attracted the attention of his flock to whose church the relic was donated.

Hugh saw the needs of the people and concentrated on them. He was a people's bishop *par excellence*.

---

John in 1199. With Hubert Walter's death in 1205 a dispute broke out over his successor. The Canterbury monks supported their candidate; King John, another. Innocent III proposed a third, his former fellow student and Paris master, Stephen Langton.

When the King expelled the Canterbury monks and rejected "insolently and impudently" Innocent's nomination, the Pope warned John how dangerous it would be "for him to fight against God and the Church in this cause for which St Thomas, that glorious martyr and archbishop, recently shed his blood", reminding him that Henry and Richard, "your father and brother of illustrious memory, when they were kings of the English, abjured that evil custom."

In June 1207, Innocent personally consecrated Langton at Viterbo, and prepared to use sanctions against the King. John's defiance was met by a papal Interdict placed on England to take effect from 24 March 1208, followed by John's excommunication on 8 November 1209. The time-lapse indicates that neither Pope nor King thought the other serious. In February 1213, Langton, never before able to visit his

# Plays and Miracles

By the 12th century, England was organised into several thousand parishes, most presided over by clerics whose education and living standards were not far removed from those of their congregations.

There are many accounts of unintelligent sermonising to congregations who completely misunderstood what was involved in attendance at church. How, then, were the laity to be taught the rudiments of the faith?

One way was through the dramatisation of events in the lives of Christ and the saints and Old Testament prophets. The nativity and the Easter sepulchre were two such events which lent themselves to this medium of parish drama, being both didactic and devotional; and, although performed in Latin, their message came across clearly.

In St Albans, in the early 1100s, a play was composed dealing with the life of St Katherine of Alexandria. Although this play is now lost, its existence is known through a contemporary record of the fire which occurred among the props. The Cathedral Statutes of Hugh de Nonant, Bishop of Coventry and Lichfield (1188-98), show a Play of the Shepherds and two Easter plays being performed at Lichfield.

At Beverley Minster, around 1200, a resurrection play, performed "in words and actions of players", attracted a great crowd of people for a variety of motives, including "the desire to have their devotion awakened".

This play, staged outside, for it was summertime, attracted such a large crowd that shorter people had difficulty in seeing over the heads of taller ones. Two young boys climbed up into the triforium of the nave in order to see and hear better, but one fell down from a great height. His resuscitation was attributed to the local saint, John of Beverley.

Miracles were another means by which the devotion of the faithful could be aroused, helping to emphasise the worthiness of a particular candidate for canonisation.

To Becket are attributed more than 700 posthumous miracles, the largest collection for any medieval saint. Two Canterbury monks and contemporaries of the murdered archbishop, Benedict and William, gathered together miracle accounts within a few years of 1170. Relics of Becket's blood and the water used to wash the stones before the altar where he had died were found to possess special healing powers for blindness, leprosy and recovery from apparent death or difficult childbirth.

All shrines were popular, but that of Canterbury after 1170 exerted a national appeal to ordinary English lay men and women, serving to enhance their faith still further.

English province, was consulted about the preparation of detailed letters for John's deposition, but before this threat could be put into action, the King submitted, handing over the kingdoms of England and Ireland as papal fiefs, and promising to pay an annual tribute quite distinct from the usual Peter's Pence.

Subsequently, Innocent instructed Langton to return all the letters so that "they could be immediately torn to shreds or burned to ashes, so that no mischief can be started against the King."

Arrangements to lift the Interdict were slow and protracted, but, in November 1214, John granted a charter of free election to all bishoprics and abbacies in England. On Ash Wednesday, 4 March 1215, the king went even further and enlisted in the Fifth Crusade, thus ensuring for himself the protection to be afforded to crusaders. Soon

# Skin-deep Plantagenet piety

Henry II and his sons displayed attitudes to religion which alternately infuriated and bemused their contemporaries, the depth of their piety being hard to determine.

No Angevin king was specially noted for paying attention to the mass. Indeed, Henry II particularly enjoyed chatting and doodling throughout. All three kings were reluctant to take the eucharist once they had reached the age of discretion, and all swore crudely on the various parts of God's body.

In moments of crisis, they increased their piety and repentance, often taking out a form of "insurance" through their benefactions to religious houses. Henry II's public avowal at Avranches in 1172 of regret for Becket's murder was followed up by his foundations for monks at Witham and nuns at Amesbury, while John kept his promise to the Cistercians to build an abbey at Beaulieu, and requested that he should be buried in Worcester Cathedral between his favourite saints, Oswald and Wulfstan.

If their piety did often appear to be only skin-deep, the Angevins were certainly intrigued by prophecy. Both Richard and John were inclined to seek out alternatives to the norm. While at Messina in early 1191 on his way to the Holy Land, Richard heard of the prophetic powers of a certain Calabrian, Joachim of Fiore, then Cistercian Abbot of Corazzo.

The King had this holy man sent for, and Joachim explained for Richard the meaning of the seven-headed dragon of the Apocalypse 12 and 17, predicting that Saladin would finally lose the Holy Land in 1194. The meeting of king and prophet concluded with a deep discussion over the proper view of Antichrist, in which Richard joined fully in the debate.

John, in addition to contacting the particularly austere hermit, Robert of Knaresborough, was even accused of having flirted with the idea of turning to Islam. Like many of John's ideas, nothing came of it; other evidence suggests that he was conventionally devout and orthodox.

---

after, John faced a baronial revolt, which was supported by Langton and which produced the document known as the Great Charter (Magna Carta).

On 24 August 1215, Innocent announced his open condemnation of Magna Carta, declaring it to be "null and void of all validity for ever". He did so on the grounds of the threat to legal kingship and the serious danger to the whole crusade, having condemned Langton and the bishops as "accomplices, if not partners, in a wicked conspiracy".

On 4 November 1215, Innocent announced a sentence of suspension on the Archbishop of Canterbury, and even after this pope's death in July 1216, Langton continued to remain in exile. In May 1218, the new pope, Honorius III, finally allowed him to return to England, where he supported the regency of the young Henry III.

## Promoting the Becket cult

Langton's task was to promote the cult of his murdered predecessor. This he did by such original means that he anticipated by 80 years the first Roman Jubilee of 1300 declared by Boniface VIII.

The Jubilee of Canterbury was first celebrated in 1220, and Langton, with his affinity for his saintly predecessor, was its driving force. As a biblical scholar, he was well aware of the implications of Leviticus 25, when the 50th or jubilee year served to strengthen the faith, restore the

## How the Pope's sanctions hit the poor

The interdict on England and Wales imposed by Innocent III was deliberately aimed at convincing the King's subjects of the need to follow the papal will in recognising Langton's election to Canterbury. The sentence, designed to make the innocent suffer with the guilty, was a sweeping one — which, in effect, was calling for a general strike of the clergy.

John's feisty reply was to swear on God's teeth that if the Interdict was enforced, he would return all clerics to Rome with their noses slit and their eyes put out. While succeeding in depriving them of their property and driving them from the country, the King seems not to have carried out his threat of mutilation. The real sufferers were to be the faithful.

From mid-1208 to mid-1214, the laity lost all rights to the sacrament of the altar, marriage, confirmation, and Christian burial in consecrated ground. Church bells no longer tolled, while coffins, piled high in churchyards, awaited burial.

Less formal arrangements made good use of ditches, woods or swamps for this purpose. As with many sanctions, the desired outcome may not have been achieved, and those who suffered most were the weakest and least involved.

land to equilibrium, and renew the kingdom. Langton was aware that the year 1220 would be specially favourable for the translation of the body. It was a leap year, which had the full and perfect number of days.

Not only was 7 July, the day chosen for the translation, a Tuesday, and therefore one of Becket's "special Tuesdays", but the actual anniversary of the murder — on Tuesday 29 December 1170 — also happened to fall on a Tuesday in December 1220. A further coincidence which pleased Langton was that 7 July also marked the anniversary of Henry II's burial at Fontevrault. Several ghosts could therefore be laid to rest at once.

On his return from exile in 1218, Langton could well make the comparison between England and that other troubled land, the Israel of the Old Testament; hence the need for jubilee. Between 1218 and 1219, Langton proposed the translation or removal of Becket's body from his crypt tomb to the new chapel dominating the east end of Canterbury Cathedral.

To encourage pilgrims to go in person to visit the new shrine within a week of the feast, Pope Honorius III promised 40 days' remission of penance, meanwhile inviting them to contribute to the cost.

A great banquet was held to inaugurate the new bishop's palace, and confirmation made of an indulgence of one year and 40 days of remission annually. A new liturgical office, composed by Langton for the Feast of the Translation, was celebrated on 7 July 1221 at the first anniversary. The Jubilee of Canterbury was commemorated every 50 years down to 1470, only the final break between England and Rome in the 1530s ensuring the end of these English celebrations.

## CHRONOLOGY

**1107** Anselm's return from exile
**1140** Gratian's *Decretum* published at Bologna
**1152** Marriage of Henry of Anjou to Eleanor of Aquitaine
**1154** Election of Adrian IV, the first and only English pope
**1155** Becket as Chancellor
**1162** Becket elected Archbishop of Canterbury
**1164** Becket in exile
**1170** Becket's martyrdom
**1173** Canonisation of Becket
**1174** Great fire at Canterbury Cathedral
**1189** Death of Henry II
**1193** Captivity of Richard I
**1198** Election of Innocent III
**1199** Death of Richard I and succession of John
**1205** Death of Hubert Walter
**1207** Consecration of Stephen Langton
**1208** Interdict on England
**1209** John declared excommunicate
**1213** Peace agreed with Pope
**1215** Declaration of the Great Charter by the barons
**1215** Langton sent into exile
**1215** Fourth Lateran Council
**1218** Langton returns to Canterbury
**1220** The Jubilee of Canterbury

# WAR AGAINST THE INFIDELS – AND OTHER CHRISTIANS

*Jonathan Riley-Smith*

*Was the root of the crusades greed or piety? We examine the novel idea of a penitential war, and the consequences as it seized the imagination of Europe.*

England was closely involved in the crusading movement for four-and-a-half centuries, from the preaching of the First Crusade in 1095 to the Reformation.

Everyone of English stock has forebears who took part, or contributed financially, or listened to crusade sermons. That there was such lasting enthusiasm throughout Western Europe requires explanation, but many of the underlying issues remain controversial.

## Controversy 1: definition

Even after two centuries of academic research, historians are not in entire agreement about the nature of the subject on which they work.

Some maintain that any Christian religious war fought for God, or in the belief that its prosecution was furthering his intentions for mankind, is a crusade, while to a few the essence of crusading lies in a prophetic, eschatological, collective exaltation arising in the masses and expressing itself in movements like the Children's Crusade (1212) or the Crusade of the Shepherds (1251).

The vast majority define a crusade as a penitential war waged on Christ's behalf in defence of Christendom, for which each crusader made a vow, signified by the wearing of a cloth cross and rewarded with the grant of an indulgence. But, whereas some treat as authentic only the series of campaigns fought for the recovery of Jerusalem or in its defence, most are convinced that many others, proclaimed by the popes as crusades and fought by men (and women) who had taken crusade vows and enjoyed crusade privileges, were also authentic.

These crusades were launched in North Africa, Spain, the Baltic region — very popular with the English in the 14th century — Hungary, the Balkans and even Western Europe. Many were preached long after Jerusalem had faded from the scene, and the crusading movement is often described nowadays as lasting until the late 16th century, perhaps to the end of the 18th.

It would obviously be wrong to suppose that the Muslims were the crusaders' only enemies. Although they also provided the chief

Gone West: the Pala d'Oro, the high altar of St Mark's, Venice, partly made with spoils from Constantinople.
*Photo © Scala, Florence*

opposition in North Africa and Spain and, from the later 14th century onwards, in the Aegean and the Balkans, they soon came to share that role with Pagan Wends, Balts, and Lithuanians, with Shamanist Mongols, with Orthodox Russians and Greeks, with Cathar and Hussite heretics, and with Catholic political opponents of the papacy.

## Controversy 2: motivation

Everyone agrees that material and ideological motivations are not incompatible, and that any crusade must have included men with a wide variety of reasons for taking part; but most people outside the historical profession — and some within it — still hold to the view that crusaders were generally inspired by the prospect of profit.

They assume that crusading was a colonial enterprise, or that the early crusades were little more than large-scale plundering expeditions, or that they provided an economic safety valve, in that measures taken by land-owning families to prevent the subdivision of their estates had destabilised society, and had led to a surplus of young men with no prospects, for whom adventure, spoil and land overseas were attractions; a crusade was a good way for these men to reduce the burdens their families faced.

The material on which these explanations rest is so slight that they often look as if they are merely providing those who believe in them with an escape from the uncomfortable reality that ideological violence appealed to the public in the Middle Ages. There is such overwhelming evidence that crusading was a severe drain on the resources not only of the crusaders themselves, but also of their families, that materialism is no longer tenable as a generalisation.

In the last few years, a great deal of work has been done on the ideas, cerebral and popular, which underpinned crusading, and on the religious and social aspirations which helped to generate recruitment.

## Controversy 3: practice

It has always been held that, whatever their motivation, crusaders tended to behave abominably once they were in the field. But new work on one of the most notorious incidents of all, the sack of Jerusalem in July 1099, is leading some historians to question even this, at least with respect to crusades to the East.

It has been shown that the long-held belief that the Jewish community in Jerusalem was particularly targeted by the crusaders is a myth, and the figure for Muslim dead, which used to range from 10,000 to 70,000 on the basis of accounts written long after the event, has been revised downwards, because a contemporary Muslim source has been discovered which puts the number at 3000.

Three thousand men and women is still a large number of people, of course, but it is low enough to make one wonder why the Western eye-witnesses, who gloried in generalised descriptions of slaughter, felt the need to portray a bloodbath. Although all religious wars are horrible, the question arises whether the behaviour of the crusaders in the East can really be considered to have been worse than that of those fighting any war of this sort — the Thirty Years' War, for example.

And it may be that a distinction should be made between the behaviour of the crusaders in Europe itself, and their activities in the Levant. The European prologues to the Jerusalem crusades in the 12th and 13th centuries were certainly characterised by extremely violent outbreaks of anti-Judaism in France, Germany and England; in other words, focused persecution occurred in the preparations for an eastern crusade rather than in its course.

And the most unpleasant examples of loss of discipline and control on the march took place during crusades launched against fellow-Christians or heretics: the sacks of Constantinople in 1204 and of Béziers in 1209 spring to mind.

The fact is that holy war has a tendency, whatever the religion involved, to turn inwards and be directed against the members of the community which has generated it. It can be no coincidence that the less successful crusades became against external foes, the more regularly they were redirected internally.

## Theological context

The attraction of religious wars to Europeans can be explained only by challenging the widespread assumption that the Christian justification of violence has always been consistent. In fact, modern just-war theory — the idea that violence is an evil which can in certain situations be condoned as the lesser of evils — is relatively recent. The older war theory passed down to it the need for the criteria of legitimate authority, just cause and right intention, but rested on two foundations which have since been jettisoned: that violence can be employed on behalf of God (or Christ), and can even be directly authorised by him; and that it is a morally neutral force which draws whatever ethical colouring it has from the intentions of the perpetrators.

It was only in the 16th century that Christ's authority for the use of force came to be replaced by the Aristotelian idea of "the common good", the defence of which was the prerogative of every community, but which had to be justified in accordance with accepted earthly laws; while the borrowing from pacifism of the conviction that violence is intrinsically evil, rather than morally neutral, was probably an achievement of the peace movement which swept Europe and America after the Napoleonic Wars.

From the fourth to the 19th centuries, therefore, Christians thought

# Taking the cross: royal crusaders

A commitment to Christian crusading tended to run in families.

William the Conqueror's eldest son, Duke Robert II of Normandy, took part in the First Crusade. He was offered, and refused, the rulership of Jerusalem after its capture. His great-nephew, King Henry II of England, took the cross, but never went.

Henry's grandfather, Count Fulk of Anjou, had become King of Jerusalem through marriage, which meant that members of the royal house of Jerusalem

were Henry's cousins; and his sons Richard I and John both made the crusade vow. Richard was a hero of the Third Crusade, but John never went.

Neither did John's son, Henry III, although he had taken the cross; but Edward I crusaded to Palestine just before he inherited the throne from Henry. Throughout his reign he was almost obsessed with the needs of the Holy Land. Edward II took the cross and never went.

Edward III was the first English king since Stephen not to make a crusade vow. Neither did his grandson and heir Richard II, who was nevertheless an enthusiastic patron of crusading. His supplanter, Henry IV, had campaigned twice in the Baltic region with the Teutonic knights. Henry V wanted to crusade to Jerusalem before his early death.

Thenceforward, none of the Lancastrians, Yorkists or early Tudors took the cross, although the kings were sympathetic to the movement. It should be remembered that the Field of the Cloth of Gold, that theatrical encounter between Henry VIII and Francis I of France in June 1520, was concerned primarily with the preliminaries to a new crusade, to which Henry VIII was emotionally, even noisily, attached.

Churchwoman militant: Eleanor of Castile, who went crusading with her husband Edward I. During the 1270 crusade, legend has it that she saved his life by sucking poison from a wound. *Photo © Joe Whitlock Blundell*

about violence in quite different ways from ourselves. It must be stressed, however, that the crusade idea was almost unique. The cross was enjoined on men and women not as a service, but as a penance, the association of which with war had been made about a decade before the preaching of the First Crusade.

The idea of penitential war was unprecedented in Christian thought, and it was radical, because it is no exaggeration to say that summoning to war "for the remission (of all) sins" put the act of fighting on the same meritorious plane as prayer, works of mercy, and fasting.

It seems to me that we should be asking ourselves some serious questions. What was so potent in the Christian ideas of positive force, some of which, incidentally, were revived by the militant wing of the liberation movement in the 1960s? It is sentimental and unhistorical to portray Christianity as an unambiguously pacific religion. Modern just-war theory represents a relatively short-lived departure from a much more positive tradition.

Is that tradition the norm, and, if so, what should be done to prevent its revival? And what attracted Catholics, including saints like Bernard of Clairvaux, Thomas Aquinas, Brigid of Sweden, Catharine of Siena, John of Capistrano, even possibly Francis of Assisi, to the notion of a penitential war?

# CRUSADER BOOTY IS AT THE HEART OF THE RENAISSANCE

## *Alan Borg*

*Did the riches of the returning crusaders justify a holy war — even one so morally dubious as the Fourth Crusade?*

"The principle of the Crusades was a savage fanaticism . . . Each pilgrim was ambitious to return with his sacred spoils, the relics of Greece and Palestine; and each relic was preceded and followed by a train of miracles and visions. . . The active spirit of the Latins preyed on the vitals of their reason and religion; and if the ninth and tenth centuries were the times of darkness, the thirteenth and fourteenth were the age of absurdity and fable."

— Edward Gibbon, *Decline and Fall of the Roman Empire.*

Contrast this judgement with some visual imagery. Imagine yourself in Paris: cross the Seine, and stand inside the Sainte Chapelle. It is a jewelled casket of glittering glass, built by St Louis, king and crusader, to hold the crown of thorns that he had purchased in Constantinople in 1239. The sale was possible only because the Byzantine capital had fallen to the Christian crusaders from the west in 1204, yet the Sainte Chapelle is one of the glories of Western civilisation. No crusades, no Sainte Chapelle.

If we are to try to judge the success or failure of the crusades today, it should be in terms of how the movement influenced the development of society and civilisation in Christian Europe. This was ultimately more significant than the achievement of the crusading armies in the field.

## Not just the Holy Land

The crusades were fought to regain the Holy Land; but we must not forget that they were fought for other reasons and in other places as

Stronghold: Krak des Chevaliers, one of the key crusader castles in the Holy Land, and the site of many conflicts with the Muslims. *Photo © Museum of the Order of St John (St John Ambulance)*

well. One of the remarkable things about the crusading movement as a whole is the way the ideal of saving lands and peoples from heathen darkness remained in place, wherever the crusade took place.

In several areas, these holy wars proved to be highly effective in permanently rooting Christianity — in Sicily, Spain, and north-eastern Europe, for example. In some ways, the most successful crusades were the northern ones, which established Christian states in much of central Europe and Russia.

True faith inspired many to take part (among them Henry Bolingbroke, later Henry IV of England, who twice campaigned in Lithuania). Anyone who reads the sermons of those who preached the crusade in the first place, or dips into the chronicles of men who actually took part, cannot fail to appreciate the sincerity or the emotion of the enterprise.

Pope Urban II, speaking at Clermont in 1095, made clear the need and the rewards: "Stop hating one another, stop quarrelling, stop fighting... Undertake the journey to the Holy Sepulchre. Capture the land the heathen have seized, the land God gave to the children of Israel... Jerusalem, navel of the world, is now held captive by enemies ignorant of God and is made to serve their heathen ceremonies. So undertake the journey for the forgiveness of your sins, sure of a glory that never fades in the kingdom of heaven."

The First Crusade certainly did spring from pure if misguided motives, and most people took the cross in the genuine belief that this was a right and just Christian cause.

But, of course, it might also prove to be profitable, and it certainly

Act of faith: Joseph Chauncy, Prior of the Knights Hospitallers (1273-80), kneeling at the feet of St John the Baptist; from a late-13th-century Hospitaller missal. *Photo © by courtesy of Sotheby's Picture Library, London*

Playing around: *The Seven Deadly Sins* by Hieronymus Bosch (1450-1516); oil on wood in the Museo del Prado, Madrid. *Photo © AKG London*

Art for the holy eucharist: the Campion Hall triptych, a 14th- or 15th-century travelling altar. *By permission of the Society of Jesus/Photo © V & A Picture Library*

Humanist: Erasmus, 1523, by Hans Holbein the Younger. *Photo © private collection/Bridgeman Art Library*

Catholic reformer: Henry VIII by Holbein. *Photo © Board of Trustees of the National Museums and Galleries on Merseyside (Walker Art Gallery, Liverpool)*

provided a change from life that was all too often devoid of new opportunities. Nothing succeeds like success, and the relatively easy capture of Jerusalem must have convinced many that God favoured the enterprise. Traders and craftsmen followed in the wake of the crusaders themselves, and the quality of crusading art shines through the fragments.

The new Church of the Holy Sepulchre became the most important Christian shrine, and, with its pointed arches and ribbed vaults, can be seen as an important influence on the development of the Gothic style.

There is much evidence for cultural exchanges between Palestine and the West, and links with Jerusalem can be traced as far afield as Canterbury.

All this was to come to an end with the loss of Jerusalem after the Battle of Hattin in 1187. However, this too had significant cultural repercussions, since it led to the evolution of the great series of stone castles that were to form the last bastions of crusading power in the East. Krak des Chevaliers is as complete an expression of medieval ideals as any ecclesiastical monument (and, significantly, itself contains a very beautiful chapel).

## Attack on Byzantium

The Fourth Crusade was probably the most important of all for the transmission of cultural influences, if the most problematic in moral terms.

The attack on Constantinople in 1204 resulted in a celebrated act of pillage that neatly puts the "crusading question" in focus. Here, in the name of the crusade, one Christian tradition assaulted and totally defeated another. It has to be understood that many regarded the Greeks as a worse danger to the true faith than the infidels. According to Odo of Deuil, "they were not judged to be Christians, and the Franks considered killing them a matter of no importance."

Since soldiers back home in Europe spent much of their time fighting and killing people they did regard as fellow Christians, the attack on the Eastern empire probably seemed far less surprising or shocking to those who took part in it than it has to subsequent historians. For some others involved, especially the Venetians, there were practical and perhaps cynical motives for manipulating the events so that they led the crusaders to attack Byzantium.

None the less, unedifying as the spectacle may be to us, the outcome of the Fourth Crusade was of general benefit to the civilisation of Europe. Many objects, including books, icons, relics, and antiques came back with the crusaders. The building of the Sainte Chapelle has been mentioned, but to this we can add the enrichment of Venice, from the famous bronze horses outside St Mark's Cathedral to the Pala d'Oro

Early Gothic: the round nave of the Temple Church of St Mary, London. The rare circular form of the nave was favoured by the Templars in imitation of the Holy Sepulchre in Jerusalem. *Photo © Crown copyright. NMR*

within. Of course, some links existed before, but it is doubtful if the early Italian Renaissance would have taken the form it did without the fall of Constantinople in 1204. What price Cimabue and Giotto, not to mention Michelangelo and Raphael?

This is to challenge the traditional Byzantine view that the Fourth Crusade was an unmitigated disaster; but the truth is that, if the crusaders in 1204 had not looted so much from Constantinople (so ensuring its preservation in the West), it all would have disappeared when the city finally fell to the Turks in 1453.

Then the looting was every bit as violent as it was in 1204, and the destruction of buildings considerably greater. Byzantine civilisation was destroyed by the Turkish invasion, whereas the crusaders only interrupted it.

## To understand is to forgive?

As in all wars, there were countless cruelties, violations of people and property, and many atrocities committed on all sides. The chivalric ideal presented by Richard Coeur de Lion and Saladin was and is little more than a cosy myth. But, equally, there is no point in blaming the crusaders for what happened (or, in my view, for apologising for it retrospectively).

Without the crusades, European civilisation would have been much the poorer; and that provides more than sufficient reason for us to try to understand them.

# CHRONOLOGY

**1096-1102** The First Crusade (proclaimed 1095)

**1099** Jerusalem taken

**1120** Foundation of the Templars

**1120-25** Crusading concurrently in two theatres of war (Spain and Palestine) for the first time

**1135** Crusading proclaimed introspectively for the first time; against the enemies of the Pope in Italy

**1187** Jerusalem and most of Palestine taken by Saladin

**1189-92** The Third Crusade, one of the leaders of which was Richard I of England, reoccupies the Palestinian coast

**1199** Taxation of the Church introduced to subsidise crusading

**1204** Sack of Constantinople by the Fourth Crusade

**1209-29** The Albigensian Crusade: first major instance of crusading against heretics

**1229-1525** The Teutonic Knights in Prussia

**1291** Last outposts in Palestine fall to the Muslims

**1307-12** Trial and suppression of the Templars

**1307-1522** The Knights Hospitallers on Rhodes

**1332-34** The first crusade league

**1396** The Crusade of Nicopolis

**1420-21** The Hussite Crusades

**1492** Fall of Granada to Spanish crusaders

**1530-1798** The Knights Hospitallers on Malta

**1535, 1540, 1541** Crusades of Charles V to North Africa

**1571** Battle of Lepanto

**1588** The Armada

**1684-97** The Holy League begins the recovery of the Balkans

# CRYING 'GOD FOR HARRY! ENGLAND AND ST GEORGE!'

*Norman Tanner*

England took a full part in the flourishing culture of late-medieval Western Christendom, while doing battle for its national interests in Europe.

Throughout the four centuries before the Reformation, England was part of Western Christendom, and this was a basic framework for the Church of England.

In 1054, less than half a century earlier, the schism between the Eastern and Western Churches began with the mutual excommunications of the bishops of Constantinople and Rome. At the time, and for long after, most people assumed the schism would soon be healed, but, sadly, it has endured to this day. Soon after the end of our period, the Reformation began, producing divisions within the Western Church itself.

By Europe is meant here western and parts of central Europe. England's relations with Europe during this long time can be looked at in various ways. Two extremes, however, must be avoided.

On the one hand, it is wrong to see the English Church as simply a province of the Western Church with virtually no self-identity or autonomy or initiative of its own: as if England were merely reproducing, for the most part at a weaker level, what was going on elsewhere in Europe. This is a simplistic view, suggested by some Roman Catholic scholars of an earlier generation, mostly from continental Europe and not themselves English, which does no justice to the brilliance and creativity of the English Church in this period.

The other extreme is to suggest that the English Church was already virtually a national Church, going its own way and almost independent of the rest of Western Christendom.

## Relations with the papacy

The English Church's relations with the papacy may seem the obvious place to begin a study of England's place in Western Christendom. We shall start here, but with some hesitation. We have to be careful not to exaggerate the importance of the papacy at this time, nor to project the preoccupations of the Reformation and later periods back into the Middle Ages. Most people, for example, would probably have had little

Glories of art: panels from Bishop Despenser's retable, Norwich Cathedral. *Photo © Dean & Chapter, Norwich Cathedral*

Fearless critic: an illumination showing Robert Grosseteste, Bishop of Lincoln. *Photo © by permission of the British Library*

# A wigging for Pope Innocent IV

Robert Grosseteste (c. 1170-1253) is one of the most remarkable personalities of the English Church. Theologian, scientist, linguist, a pastoral and reform-minded priest, at the advanced age of more than 60 he was elected Bishop of the vast diocese of Lincoln, and spent the remaining 18 years of his life as an energetic and outspoken pastor.

What concerns us here is the dramatic visit he paid in 1250 to Pope Innocent IV, who was then residing in Lyons in France, in order to present to him a written denunciation of what he saw as the abuses of power by papal officials and by the pope himself, particularly their sale of church offices and the promotion of their families. Grosseteste's speech to the pope reached a climax:

"The papal see, the throne of God, the sun of the whole world . . . which should, like the sun, give light, life, nutrition, growth, preservation and beauty to the earth, has lost its proper functions, its *rationes causales*, the reason for its existence. It has been perverted, and it has become a source of perdition and destruction. He who bears the *persona* of Christ has divested himself of this *persona* and taken that of his earthly relatives and his own flesh and blood."

He went on almost to identify the pope with Antichrist, the "Son of Perdition", and then outlined his own pastoral vision with a further sideswipe at the pope and curia:

"The most divine and absolutely overriding art of saving souls must be given to those who understand the gospel of Christ as set forth in the Old and New Testaments, without the interference of those who understand only the subordinate arts of secular administration."

It is to the credit of Pope Innocent that he listened to Grosseteste, though he was annoyed, and does not seem to have changed his behaviour. The two men soon clashed again when the pope appointed his nephew to a canonry in Lincoln Cathedral, an appointment that Grosseteste fiercely resisted.

Grosseteste shows the extent to which robust criticism was acceptable in that age: how concern for the papacy could be combined with outspoken remarks.

idea of the name of the pope of the time, and no "picture" of him such as has been possible since the arrival of television and other mass media.

On the one hand, the tensions can be highlighted. Just before the beginning of the period, William the Conqueror was King, and Lanfranc was Archbishop of Canterbury. Both were devout men, who worked closely together, and while they supported many of the aims of the reforming papacy of the time, they strongly resisted those that seemed to encroach on the rights of the king in his government of the realm and of the Church.

Later, in the 14th century, when the papacy moved from Rome to Avignon in southern France, and when all the popes for some seventy years, 1307-1378, were Frenchmen, there was tension between England and what was seen as a "French papacy", especially because for most of the time England was at war with France, in the Hundred Years War, and the popes were seen as favouring France in this quarrel.

In the middle of the period lived Robert Grosseteste, Bishop of Lincoln: his remonstrations with Pope Innocent IV are discussed opposite.

On the other hand, Nicholas Breakspear of St Albans in Hertfordshire was elected pope as Hadrian IV in 1154. He was an able pope, whose reign was cut short by an early death. There seemed nothing unusual in electing an Englishman to the post, though in fact he was to be the only man from the British Isles ever to become pope.

Later, too, during the papal schism of 1378 to 1417 — when there were two claimants, and sometimes three, to the papacy — England was a strong supporter of the "Roman" pope against the Francophile claimant based in Avignon. And afterwards the English government was seen as an important ally of the popes in their struggles with a succession of church Councils about authority in the Church.

## Canon law

Historians have debated how far the law of the Church of England was already in the Middle Ages independent of the canon law of the Church of Rome. Frederick Maitland and William Stubbs began the debate in the late 19th century. Stubbs argued for a large measure of autonomy, pointing especially to the book on canon law entitled *Provinciale*, which was written by the Englishman William Lyndwood in the 15th century, and which seemed to Stubbs to prove an independent tradition of English canon law. Maitland, on the other hand, argued that *Provinciale* always pre-supposed the binding force of *Corpus Iuris Canonici*, the canon law of Western Christendom as a whole, and that English canon law was merely a set of by-laws or appendices to this basic law.

Maitland had the better of the argument, and his basic thesis about the recognition of *Corpus Iuris Canonici* in England proved to be right. On the other hand, he interpreted canon law in an overly legal or literal sense, as if it were a "code", somewhat similar to the Napoleonic Code of a later period. Hence, Stubbs's emphases on custom, and on a certain flexibility within the *Corpus*, so that it was open to a good measure of interpretation and adaptation within the English scene, were important insights, too.

The English Church was, for the most part, well able to manage its own affairs, and unwelcome interventions from outside were the exception, not the rule. This self-sufficiency in church law, as in other areas of church life, became more pronounced in the late Middle Ages, in the 14th and 15th centuries.

# 'Against the malice of the French'

The Council of Constance, which met from 1414 to 1418 for the dual purpose of healing the papal schism and reforming the Church, was organised according to "nations".

That is to say, the bishops and other members of the Council met and voted in their national groupings, and then the Council reached its collective decision by considering the votes of the individual nations.

Controversy raged about whether England should be considered a nation. At earlier Councils, at which this "national" arrangement had existed in embryonic form, Western Christendom was divided into four nations: French, Spanish, Italian and German. The last was a catch-all for the countries outside France, Spain and Italy, and included, besides Germany itself, the Slavic countries, Scandinavia and the British Isles.

The English delegation to the Council, which was high-powered and well organised, led by the Bishop of Salisbury and including four other bishops as well as the personal ambassadors of King Henry V, pushed hard for England to become a fifth nation, separate from Germany.

The Germans proved to be England's staunchest ally, perhaps happy to shed a difficult partner!

The chief opponents of the proposal were the French, who argued that England was too small to be considered a separate nation, and ought to continue to form part of the German nation. The changing fortunes in England's favour in the Hundred Years War, however, added weight to the English case: the Battle of Agincourt was fought in 1415, towards the beginning of the Council.

The English case prevailed. Indeed, the Anglo-German alliance, now comprising two of the five nations, endured throughout the Council and proved important for its eventual outcome.

The saga revealed some unpleasant sides of nationalism and ecclesiastical politics. Henry Chichele, the Archbishop of Canterbury, wrote to the Bishop of Salisbury and his colleagues congratulating them on defending English rights "against the malice of the French, who have always been our enemies", and urging unremitting vigilance "lest by their wiles they regain the control over the Church which they had in times past, and cunningly rob others of their rights."

## Continental Councils

Councils provide another example of England's relations with Western Christendom. Ecumenical Councils, such as Nicaea I and Chalcedon and others in the early Church, were regarded as impossible without the participation of the Eastern Church, so that "General Councils" were the highest and most authoritative church Councils in the medieval West. They were the European Parliament of the time.

Ten of them were held in various cities of Europe between 1123 and 1512-17: the five Lateran Councils in Rome, two in Lyons and one in Vienne in France, one in Constance in Germany, and one which began in Basel in Switzerland and ended in Florence in Italy.

There were representatives from the British Isles at almost all these General Councils, and — another sign of interest — some of the best contemporary accounts of their proceedings were written by English chroniclers. English bishops were particularly zealous in enforcing in their dioceses the decrees of the Fourth Lateran Council of 1215, which was the most thoroughgoing of the ten Councils with regard to reform of the Church.

On the other hand, English bishops were ready to defend the interests of their country when the occasion demanded, as happened most notably at the Council of Constance.

## Theology and learning

The British Isles played a full part in the development of Western theology. Anselm of Canterbury was the most brilliant mind of his age. He is often called the first "scholastic", inasmuch as he was the first medieval theologian to question the Christian religion systematically by reason, though he put it more gently in his famous description of theology as "faith seeking understanding" (*fides quaerens intellectum*). He proposed a proof of the existence of God, the "ontological argument", that still excites philosophers today.

Hell's teeth: the "Ladder of Salvation" wall-painting from Chaldon, Surrey.
*Photo © Mick Sharp*

Anselm spent the last part of his life in England, as Archbishop of Canterbury from 1093 until his death in 1109, yet he was a cosmopolitan European. He was born and brought up in Aosta in northern Italy and he spent many years as a monk at Bec in northern France: so that while he is known here as Anselm of Canterbury, in Italy he is known as Anselm of Aosta, and in France as Anselm of Bec.

John Duns Scotus (*c.* 1266-1308) and William of Ockham (*c.* 1285-1347) were also the leading thinkers of their time, and they, too, were European figures. The former, as his name indicates, was born in Scotland, possibly in the town of Duns: he became a Franciscan friar, and taught at both Oxford and Paris Universities, and at Cologne in Germany. Whereas Thomas Aquinas, his brilliant predecessor, had emphasised knowledge and reason, Scotus stressed more the importance of the will and of love.

William of Ockham, from Ockham in Surrey, where his shrine exists today in the parish church, also became a Franciscan friar and taught at both Oxford and Paris. During a second spell of teaching in Oxford, he ran into trouble with the chancellor of the university on account of his teaching, and as a result he was summoned to appear before the pope in Avignon.

He obeyed the summons, but, having spent some time in Avignon, and fearing the punishment that might befall him, he fled to Germany and spent the last 20 years of his life in Bavaria under the protection of Emperor Louis. At Oxford and Paris, Ockham wrote on philosophy and theology; in Germany, on political theory.

Ockham was a highly original thinker: his sharp mind gained the epithet "Ockham's razor". Analytical and critical, more positively, however, he strove to preserve the transcendence and freedom of God from any attempt to tie God down to our human categories and wishes: a Barthian before Karl Barth. He was the most influential thinker in Western Christendom, especially in university and academic circles, during the two centuries before the Reformation, more influential even that Aquinas or Scotus.

## Riches of art

The cathedrals, so well kept by the Church of England today, are the architectural glories of medieval England. The thousands of medieval parish churches that still survive are beautiful and fascinating, often exquisitely so, at a more intimate level.

At both levels, the architecture was influenced by developments on the Continent, Norman in the early period and Gothic later. Even so, the rich variety and distinctive local characteristics are obvious to any visitor. In England, particularly, there developed a national style in the later Middle Ages: English Perpendicular or Late English Gothic.

Much the same may be said of other aspects of the Church of England's artistic heritage from the Middle Ages, though this is often difficult to know for certain, because much religious art was destroyed after the Reformation.

There is the fine stained glass in York Minster, for example; or the murals in Chaldon Parish Church in Surrey, showing even Byzantine influences; or the Wilton diptych that portrays King Richard II before Mary, the saints and angels; or the five-panel retable now in Norwich Cathedral, depicting Christ's Passion, death and resurrection, seemingly a mixture of English and Flemish influences; or the 12th-century ivory cross or the 14th- or 15th-century travelling-altar in gold and enamel, preserved respectively in the Cloisters Museum in New York, and in the Victoria & Albert Museum, as the Campion Hall triptych, in London.

## Popular religion

The English Church was a community of remarkable energy and variety, especially in view of the much smaller population: just a tenth of what it is today, and with the large majority living in the countryside.

For many people, a primary identity in religion, as in other matters, was the locality: the village and the parish in the countryside, the parish or a street or a ward in the towns. In larger towns, such as Norwich or York, there could be as many as 50 parish churches; in London, much the largest city with perhaps 40,000 inhabitants in 1300, there were more than 100.

Guilds and confraternities, sometimes based on crafts and trades, sometimes on parish churches or religious houses, provided another identity for many people, especially in towns, providing a mixture of religious, social and economic functions and activities, including the drama of the mystery plays.

The diocese, with its bishop and cathedral (sometimes two), was another unit: 17 in England, five in Wales, separate hierarchies in Scotland and Ireland. But the diocese was largely an administrative unit. An area with which more people probably identified was the region: sometimes this coincided with a diocese. In some ways England was still a federation of regions, the Church of England a federation of regional churches: the north with its capital of York, East Anglia with Norwich, the Midlands, the West Country, the south-east with the national capital of London.

There were the liturgical rites of the regions: the Norwich rite, the Hereford rite, and the expanding Sarum (or Salisbury) rite. There also seem to have been noticeable regional variations in religious temperament, especially in the later Middle Ages: a more "high-church", almost Baroque, Christianity in East Anglia and the diocese of York; a more puritanical spirit in the south-east and the Midlands, with large Lollard communities in London, Coventry and Leicester.

At the popular level, too, it is remarkable how much Christians from the British Isles took an interest in the wider fortunes of Christianity. The crusades, however much we may now regret them as a false goal, were one aspect of this wider concern.

Pilgrimages abroad were another popular activity. There was a hostel in Rome, still surviving today as the English College, which was specifically for English pilgrims in the city. Margery Kempe, the redoubtable lady from King's Lynn in Norfolk, after she had borne 14 children, set out on a series of distant pilgrimages: to Jerusalem and Rome in 1413-15, to Santiago de Compostela in Spain in 1417-18, and to Norway, to Danzig in Prussia and back through Paris in 1434-5, when she was probably aged at least 60.

## CHRONOLOGY

**1054** East-West schism begins
**1095** First Crusade called by Pope Urban II
**1170** Martyrdom of Thomas Becket
**1215** Fourth Lateran Council
**1309-77** Papacy at Avignon
**1337-1453** Hundred Years War between England and France
**1347-50** Black Death plague
**1414-18** Council of Constance
**1453** Fall of Constantinople
**1492** Christopher Columbus reaches America

# LIVING IN HEAVEN AND HELL

*Peter Heath*

*They might have been unlettered, but 14th-century Christians had a clear view of life's duality. We trace the growth of popular spirituality.*

Purgatory — a kind of decontamination chamber scarcely less horrifying than hell — was the fate that confronted every Christian. Alleviation or abbreviation of the experience was naturally pursued by all means possible: by personal prayer, by commemorative masses, by invoking the prayers and merits of the Blessed Virgin and the saints, by procuring pardons or indulgences, and by alms or good works.

The abuses which ensued have long been notorious, and too often have tended to obscure from view more significant developments in the evolution of the English Church which are the concern of this survey.

In 1215 the Fourth Lateran Council stipulated that the laity should take communion at least once a year, at Easter, and confess before doing so. One result of this requirement was a flood of books and episcopal decrees to guide the priest on the nature and practice of confession, its theology and law as well as its human aspects.

In 1281 John Pecham, Archbishop of Canterbury, ordered the parish priest to preach to his flock four times a year on the basic Christian tenets: the Creeds, the Ten Commandments, the Pater Noster, the Seven Deadly Sins, the corporal acts of mercy, and so forth. More than 70 years later, in around 1356-7, Archbishop Thoresby of York published a similar digest, the so-called *Lay Folks' Catechism*, first in Latin and then in English, and rewarded with an indulgence parents who taught it to their children. In the Southern Province, Archbishop Islip soon afterwards issued a tract for his clergy.

These instructions were echoed in numerous other sermons by friars and parochial clergy, and although it is uncertain how many of the extant sermon texts were, in fact, declaimed to an audience, it is reasonable to suppose that at the least they were consulted by preachers for apposite arguments and details.

The fact that the *Fasciculus Morum*, a vast Latin homily on confession and all the myriad branches of the seven deadly sins, contains within it snatches of English verse seems to indicate its intended audience. Nor can there be any doubt, in view of the number of surviving manuscripts, that the sermons for Sundays and saints' days that John Mirk, an

Regal: St Patrick's, Patrington. Taken from *England's Thousand Best Churches* by Simon Jenkins. *Photo © Paul Barker/Country Life Picture Library*

Augustinian canon, compiled in around 1380 were given a wide hearing.

The laity were required to attend church on Sundays and feast days, but because of their want of Latin what they saw was more likely to command their attention than what they heard, except possibly when there was a sermon. Thus in the mass the highlight, which came to be regarded as the indispensable sight, was the elevation of the host, the very body of Christ. From the rest of the mass many absented themselves; others resorted to their own prayers or, we are told, to gossiping and unruliness.

On the rare occasions when the laity took communion, they did so in one kind only, the wafer but not the wine; at other times they shared the holy bread which was given in place of the consecrated wafer.

## Church building

The churches in which people worshipped continued to be re-fashioned and rebuilt throughout the century and across the land, often acquiring new aisles and chapels, as at Chesterfield for example, to accommodate chantries and guild altars.

If the distinctive Perpendicular glories of the next century were as yet only dimly glimpsed among the parish churches of the 14th, there were some exhilarating Decorated examples to rival any in the later style; not least among them is the church at Patrington, or "the Queen of Holderness" as it is known today.

The institution of the perpetual chantry, an endowment of one or more secular clergy to pray for the dead, which dates back at least to the 12th century, became a well established fashion in the early 14th century, even before the Black Death.

In fact, after 1349 the number of new foundations of this kind declined; instead there emerged religious fraternities — in effect, collective chantries — dedicated to individual saints, above all to the Blessed Virgin. Whereas we know of five in London before the Plague, more than 100 are detectable during the next 50 years. Beginning as local associations, some of them evolved into craft guilds, but they still retained the original obligations to bury the dead decently, pray for them, and dispense alms to the needy.

On a humbler level within the parishes, poorer parishioners were collaborating to support the maintenance of candles before revered images or altars in their church. Richer individuals bequeathed money to support a temporary chantry to sing masses or say obits over a period, varying from six months up to several years.

## The mysteries

The most spectacular of the guilds were those which sprang up to commemorate the feast of Corpus Christi. This feast, which fell in May or June, was instituted throughout the Church in order to promote and defend the doctrine of transubstantiation.

Already by 1326 such a guild is recorded at Louth, and four more emerged in England before 1349; but expansion accelerated after the Plague, and by 1388 there were more than 40.

On the feast day a great procession, representing all the crafts and ranks of a city or town, accompanied the host through the streets to the principal church for high mass. In effect, this procession was a public confession of faith as well as being a social, civic and secular celebration.

Soon associated with it were the mystery plays, each performed by one of the crafts or trades of the town, "mystery" being the word for trade or craft. The best known cycles — from Chester, York, Wakefield and N-Town (most probably in East Anglia) — cover the story of humankind from the Creation to Redemption and the Last Judgement. They are essentially about the saving love of Christ, and they are focused on the narrative of his life. Many single plays from other towns and villages on other topics, about Noah, and the Pater Noster, for example, are also known.

As befits a general audience, most of these plays tend to avoid theological subtleties, adopting instead an approach that is affective where it is not didactic or moralistic.

The veneration of saints and their relics and images figured prominently in the lives of the people. They attracted huge followings — during 1335 nearly 8000 pilgrims visited the shrine of St Hugh in Lincoln Cathedral — and pilgrim badges, denoting the shrines visited, were as eagerly collected as relics.

The curative powers of the saints and their artefacts encompassed all manner of physical as well as spiritual ailments; perhaps unsurprisingly, the most omnicompetent saint of all was the Blessed Virgin. Despite the distortions that often resulted, this enthusiasm for Christian heroes satisfied deep emotional and spiritual needs among all classes of people, from king to pauper.

## The contemplatives

Alongside these developments, the monastic ideal of a life devoted to prayer and contemplation continued to exert a profound influence upon the laity at large. Among the nobility, for example, the Scropes of Masham and the Nevilles patronised devout solitaries of all kinds — hermits, anchorites, and anchoresses. At a time when new monastic foundation had virtually ceased in England, members of the aristocracy were instrumental in establishing six houses of the Carthusian Order, renowned for the rigour of its austere and quasi-solitary life.

Corpus Christi: angels holding a monstrance with the host; Trinity MS B.11.11 f.197r.
*Photo © Master and Fellows of Trinity College, Cambridge*

The founders and benefactors of these houses demonstrated their esteem for the contemplative life that they themselves (like other lay-folk) could not undertake.

The life of contemplation was commended as the highest Christian vocation in a series of notable treatises from this period, usually written by religious or hermits for their fellows or nuns. Richard Rolle's *Fire of Love*, the anonymous *Cloud of Unknowing*, Walter Hilton's *Ladder of Perfection*, and *The Revelations of Divine Love* by Julian of Norwich represent a remarkable body of spiritual and devotional writings, of which they are merely the most outstanding.

Against this background, it is perhaps not so surprising to find a layman, Henry, Earl of Lancaster, writing in 1354 a work of spiritual and moral reflection entitled *Le Livre de Seyntz Medicines*, in which Christ is the physician called upon to cure the sickness inflicted by the seven deadly sins.

## Christian charity

"As water quenches fire, so alms deeds quench sin," the preacher declared: alms, along with fasting (abstinence to partner generosity), were the wings which bore up prayer to God, the listeners were assured. There is abundant evidence that people took alms, and the closely associated corporal works of mercy, seriously; the laity were, after all, constantly reminded, visually and orally, of the importance of alms, the suddenness of death, and the fate of misers.

Not only were the endowed prayers for the dead often linked to charitable institutions, such as schools and hospitals, but distributions to the poor, the sick, unmarried girls, and prisoners were commonplace in wills.

## Bible knowledge

Although doubts have sometimes been cast upon the role of the Bible in popular devotion at that time, its essential teachings were widely disseminated in the syllabuses instigated by Pecham, Thoresby and Islip.

Moreover, biblical learning and assumptions of general biblical knowledge suffuse the poetry of Chaucer and, above all, of the cleric William Langland, whose *Piers Plowman* has been likened to an encyclopaedia of theology and, for its depth and intensity, even compared with *The Divine Comedy*.

Perhaps more revealing, however, is Sir John Clanvowe's short devotional treatise, *The Two Ways*, which contrasts the broad way to hell with the narrow way to heaven, and buttresses the argument with accurate citations or recollections of the Psalms, Gospels and Epistles. Sir John, who died in 1391, was a soldier and courtier.

While fragments of the Bible, notably the Psalms, had long been available in English, it was only in the 1390s, after some 20 years of work, that Oxford scholars produced a readable English version of the whole. The impetus for this translation came partly from the needs of an increasingly literate laity; but another root — and one which led the Church to suspect, disown and ultimately ban the translation — was in the radical ideology of John Wycliffe.

The most celebrated Oxford academic of his time, Wycliffe was a systematic critic of the clergy, to such an extent that he distinguished between the invisible Church of the saved on the one hand, and the visible, corrupt institutional Church, headed by the pope or Antichrist, on the other. His conclusion from this was that authority and truth could be found only in the scriptures.

Sometimes regarded as Wycliffe's disciples, and tainted with guilt by association, the heretics known as Lollards were chiefly artisans, their families and a few minor clergy. They attacked clerical authority and greed, denounced images, often denied the real presence (as defined by the Church), and copied and read English versions of the scriptures among themselves. They shared with some more orthodox members of the Church an emphasis upon personal austerity, charity, and the study of the Bible; and even their criticisms (except of transubstantiation) were commonplace in sermons and literary works of the time.

By the end of the century a striking development in lay devotion was evident, the result both of the pastoral efforts stemming ultimately from the Fourth Lateran Council and of changes in society generally.

Before he died in 1396, Hilton had written *The Mixed Life* to encourage the laymen and women to combine their active secular life with one of prayer and contemplation.

The example of Clanvowe was soon to be eclipsed by the redoubtable Margery Kempe, burgess and widow from King's Lynn, whose dictated autobiography shows how vigorous, informed and thoughtful the spirituality of even the unlettered could be.

Widening enthusiasm for ascetics and their life of prayer, and for devotional writings and the scriptures, added new dimensions and depths to lay religion. The cruder elements outlined at the beginning of this survey were not expunged but transcended by an increasingly personal and ardent devotion to Jesus Christ.

# THE ANCHORESS ENCLOSED IN THE GOODNESS OF GOD

Unlike other key spiritual writings in 14th-century England, Dame Julian's *Revelations of Divine Love* is neither a practical manual for the would-be contemplative nor an effusive commendation of ecstatic prayer, but a thoughtful interpretation of 16 visions of Jesus which she had experienced.

She pondered on their meaning for nearly 20 years before she completed her full account of them in 1393, bringing to this task an intimate knowledge of the Bible, familiarity with earlier mystical writings, and a thorough command of all the classical rhetorical devices.

The result is, as one critic has written, a work distinguished by "a high concentration of thought together with a sparkling stylistic clarity".

That Julian, who was born in 1343, became a nun is inferred from her knowledge of the scriptures, theology and rhetoric, which only a woman who was a member of a religious order would have been likely to acquire, and only one whose exceptional talents attracted the attention of scholarly tutors.

She finished her life in around 1415 as an anchoress attached to the church of St Julian, in Norwich, where Margery Kempe, among many others, consulted her and received "good counsel".

In May 1373 she suffered a mysterious illness which incapacitated her for almost a week. It was then that she had the visions of Christ

All well: window in Julian's cell.
*Photo © by kind permission of the Vicar and PCC of Parmentergate Parish, Norwich*

which were to occupy her thoughts and prayers and fill the book for which she is celebrated.

In these visions, or "showings", she saw the Saviour at various stages of his Passion, and he spoke to her "without voice and without moving his lips", forming the words in her soul or intellect by spiritual sight.

The visions, she tells us, were full of "secrets", and "from the time of the showings, I desired often to understand what was Our Lord's meaning." While engaged in this endeavour, she had "inward teaching" and "received spiritual answers".

She was prompted to write her book "by charity to my fellow

"More nearer to us": cell doorway,
St Julian's, Norwich.
*Photo © Irene Ogden*

Christians that they might see and know what I saw so that it might comfort them", for these things were not shown to her because she was better and more loved of God than others, but because they were intended for the comfort of all.

Although even before her illness she had longed to identify with Christ and to suffer as he suffered, she at first dismissed the visions as mere feverish delirium — "raving" is her word — until a priest convinced her of their importance. Moreover, when Christ appeared to her she was not meekly passive, but questioned him closely about the nature of sin, the reasons for it and the consequences of it. However, although during her long years of meditation and prayer God slowly unveiled most of the secrets with which he had confronted her, he did not reveal all of them. Where she received no satisfactory answers she explicitly rests upon, and commends trust in, the teachings of the Church.

Since God is the creator of all things, he is as much in us as we are in him, "more nearer to us than our own soul, for he is the ground on which it stands"; "in fact nearer to us than tongue may tell or heart may think". With her unerring feel for the vivid and homely image, Julian tells us that "as the body is clad in clothes, and the flesh in skin, and the bones in flesh, and the heart in the body, so are we, soul and body, clad and enclosed in the goodness of God".

Puzzled by the paradox of why God allowed sin into the world, she is comforted by the realisation (or revelation) that sin, which she defines as "all that is not good", "makes us know ourselves and ask for mercy": it brings us to a recognition of our dependence on God and his love for us.

She refuses to blame God for her sin, "since he does not blame me for it". Rather does God our Father hold on to us "so tenderly when we sin", "our failing does not stop him loving us"; the repentant soul, as though released from a cruel prison, is met by our Lord "with friendly welcoming".

Once a sinner's soul is healed by penance, God views our sins not as wounds, but as honourable scars. "God loves us endlessly and we sin constantly."

No writer in that period so effectively countered the temptation to despair that assails the sinner. Strikingly comforting is her portrayal of God as the mother who feeds us with herself in the sacrament of the mass, and who "as our patient mother does not want us to flee away . . . but wants us to do as a child does. For when it is diseased and afraid, it runs quickly to its mother." And Holy Church is "our mother's breast".

Julian stresses not only God's love for us, but also God's need of our love for him. We show this by penance (the act of reconciliation), and particularly by prayer, which even in dry periods, when it feels forced and mechanical, is still "full pleasant" to God "though we think it of little use".

In a world where emotions were often extravagantly manifested, and in a Church sometimes too emphatic about the penalties of sin and the horrors of purgatory and hell, Julian's book conveys an air of composure and tranquil optimism. Her words focus intently on Christ's tender and encompassing love for us. "The soul which beholds the love of Jesus will not hate hell but mortal sins."

The sin that most concerns her is none of the seven deadly ones, but despair, for which she commends the sovereign remedy: God's unfailing love for each of us.

Her consoling message and trusting approach are summed up in the words addressed to her by Christ, that despite sin, which is necessary, "all shall be well".

## CHRONOLOGY

**c.1300-1349** Richard Rolle
**1307** Accession of Edward II
**1309-77** The Avignon exile of the papacy
**1327** Accession of Edward III
**c.1330-1385** John Wycliffe
**c.1330-1386** William Langland
**1337** Start of Hundred Years War with France
**c.1340-1400** Geoffrey Chaucer
**1343-c.1415** Julian of Norwich
**1348-49** Principal visit of plague (and also 1361-62, 1369, 1379, 1390-91)
**1373-c.1433** Margery Kempe
**1377** Accession of Richard II
**1378-1418** The Great Schism of the papacy
**1396** Death of Walter Hilton
**1399** Death of Richard II

# 1400: THE LAITY BEGIN TO TAKE CONTROL

*Barrie Dobson*

*For 100 years the Church kept its head down and most of its walls up. But how did it manage to stay calm during a time of political turmoil?*

Half a millennium later, the most striking feature of the history of *Ecclesia Anglicana* between the accession of Henry IV in 1399 and the first visit of Erasmus to the court of Henry VII exactly a century later seems to have been its ability to maintain a highly successful institutional resistance to social, intellectual and religious change.

In many ways, indeed, the 15th century is the most intriguing, precisely because it is the least dramatic, period in the entire history of the English Church.

Compared with the fiercely Evangelical radicalism preached by John Wycliffe and his Lollard followers shortly before 1400, and contrasted with the sweeping religious revolution to come at the hands of the English disciples of Martin Luther, the religious life of Lancastrian and Yorkist England was apparently as comparatively tranquil as its political history was turbulent and factious, especially between the 1450s and 1480s (the period of the Wars of the Roses).

## Conformity and dissent

Was that tranquillity deceptive? Were most Englishmen and Englishwomen content or not with the clerical establishment they sustained and the spiritual instruction they received during the century between 1400 and 1500?

Despite the strenuous efforts of many historians over many years to answer that particular question, it still remains obstinately open. More of a "police state" than is usually acknowledged, 15th-century England was a country in which it was often less dangerous to commit a murder than to speak one's mind — at least on doctrinal and other religious issues.

As it is, historians should perhaps be less confident than they usually are that most English parishioners were unquestioningly obedient in their attitudes towards the organised Church. By a paradox which seems fundamental to our understanding of 15th-century religion, the pastoral and evangelistic efforts of many late-medieval bishops and clergy had been so successful in making their parishioners

Royal chantry: King's College Chapel, Cambridge. *Photo © by kind permission of the Provost and Fellows of King's College, Cambridge* identify themselves with the life and teaching of Christ that many of them had become increasingly conscious of the discrepancy between spiritual ideal and ecclesiastical practice.

Accordingly, the largely successful persecution of the Lollards, especially after the enactment of the statute *De Heretico Comburendo* of 1401, and the absence of any great public ideological debates in England thereafter, did not prevent "many Englishmen, although good Christians, from having very varying opinions concerning religion".

Such at least was the judgement of an Italian visitor to England in 1497, who went on to declare — less plausibly — that "the English people all attend mass every day and say many Paternosters in public (the women carrying long rosaries in their hands). They always hear mass on Sunday in their parish churches, which is where they give their most liberal alms.

"For it is above all in the church treasuries that their riches are displayed; and there is not a parish church in the kingdom without crucifixes, candlesticks, censers, patens and silver cups worthy of a cathedral."

## The parish churches

In however transformed and sometimes truncated a form, the great majority of the parish churches of late-medieval England still survive as the greatest of all memorials — unrivalled in Western Europe — to the Christian devotion of our predecessors five centuries ago.

No one in 1500 could have conceived that within 50 years, as a result of a devastating "stripping of the altars" about which Dr Eamon Duffy has recently written with such eloquence, those churches were never going to be as impressive — or, indeed, quite as influential — again.

Not for nothing did the late Alexander Hamilton Thompson, still perhaps the greatest of all 20th-century historians of the institutions of the late-medieval English Church, once declare that "there is no period at which money was lavished so freely on English parish churches as in the 15th century."

Although between 1400 and 1500 nearly all of England's 9500 or so parish churches survived, often enlarged and more elaborately fitted (especially with stained glass) than ever before, almost no new parishes were created in the later Middle Ages. Fifteenth-century rectors and vicars therefore ministered to their flocks within a framework of parish boundaries which fossilised the practice of three or more centuries earlier.

Thus many of the older towns of medieval England found themselves progressively and seriously "over-churched" as a result of progressive demographic attrition during the century and more after the first onslaught of the Black Death in 1348-49. To take the most notorious example, according to a petition of its citizens to the Crown in 1442, no fewer than 17 of the parish churches of Winchester were then in a state of acute dilapidation.

Elsewhere, however, urban parish churches managed to survive their acute periods of financial crisis tolerably well, above all in London, where a staggering total of no fewer than 106 churches — within or very near the city walls — were still viable in the age of Henry VIII and Thomas Cromwell.

The plight of pauperised urban churches was, in any case, quite untypical of most regions of the English countryside, especially perhaps East Anglia and Somerset, where the great and often extravagant 15th-century towers and spires of village churches still dominate the landscape to this day.

In the words of the late Professor Postan, "What do the Perpendicular churches prove?" Although this famous question is by no means as easy to answer as is usually assumed, one obvious conclusion is hard to resist. The great majority of Englishmen who could afford to do so, whether wealthy county gentlemen, overseas merchants or prosperous town burgesses, seem to have cherished an almost obsessive ambition to adorn, to refurnish and if possible to rebuild their parish churches completely.

Not all the builders and benefactors of 15th-century parish churches were laymen. Shortly before his death in 1423, a comparatively obscure residentiary canon of York Minster, Thomas Parker, could afford to finance the complete reconstruction of his parish church of Bolton Percy in the most fashionable Perpendicular style.

Twenty years earlier, one of the richest bishops in the kingdom, Bishop Walter Skirlaw of Durham, financed the building of so lavish a church in his birthplace at Skirlaugh in the East Riding that, in his *Contrasts* of 1836, the younger Augustus Pugin chose it to demonstrate the superiority of medieval church architecture to that of the newly built St Pancras Chapel in Euston Road, London.

Most frequently, however, the new churches and church towers of the 15th century are memorials to the piety and enhanced sense of self-importance of county gentry and wool merchants.

A particularly instructive if unfamiliar example, because it preserves its contemporary fittings and stained glass almost entirely intact, is the exceptionally well preserved little church of Holme, north of Newark, rebuilt in 1485 by John Barton, stapler of Calais.

At a much more exalted level, Lavenham and Long Melford, the most spectacular of all Suffolk's many spectacular churches, owe their present appearance primarily to collaboration over many years between successive generations of local knights and local clothiers. As the inscription over the north porch of Long Melford still reminds us,

The tomb of Lady Margaret by Pietro Torrigiano. *Photo © Dean and Chapter of Westminster*

# Margaret Beaufort — lady of rare virtues

Lady Margaret Beaufort, Countess of Richmond and Derby (1443-1509), is best remembered as the mother of King Henry VII, in which capacity she was undoubtedly the most influential, as well as the best-documented, Englishwoman of the late 15th century.

In their recent study *The King's Mother*, Michael Jones and Malcolm Underwood have at last provided detailed confirmation that she was indeed — in the words of her first historian, Bernard Andre — "more firm and constant than the weakness of woman usually allows". Nor can there be any doubt that Lady Margaret owed her resilience to her early exploitation as an immensely valuable pawn on the aristocratic marriage market.

The daughter and heiress of John, Duke of Somerset, who died a year after her birth, she was married to four husbands in succession, namely John de la Pole (marriage dissolved in 1453), Edmund Tudor (the father of the future Henry VII, born in 1457), Henry Stafford (died 1471), and Thomas Stanley (died 1504).

None of her marriages seems to have been particularly successful in personal terms; but her very careful management of her extensive estates made her an even more benevolent patroness of spiritual causes than the many other devout queens (like Elizabeth Woodville) and ladies (like Margaret Lady Hungerford) of the 15th century.

Her most enduring religious foundations were both academic establishments in Cambridge, namely Christ's College (which was founded in 1505) and St John's College, well under way before her death in June 1509.

Her great partner in these enterprises was John Fisher, Bishop of Rochester, whose tribute to Lady Margaret's undoubtedly intense devotion is the most impressive she ever received: "I learned more of what leads to an upright life from her rare virtues than I ever taught her in return."

"Pray for ye sowlis of William Clopton, Margy his wife, and for the sowle of Alice Clopton, and for John Clopton and for alle thoo sowlis that ye seyd John is bounde to prey for."

## Chantries and obits

No one who reads the last wills and testaments — which begin to survive in great numbers during the 15th century — of late-medieval Englishmen and their wives and widows can be in any doubt of their intense obsession with the need to secure prayers by the living for the salvation of the souls of the faithful departed.

Since at least the mid-13th century, that obsession had found its greatest — if most expensive — fulfilment in the creation of a perpetual chantry, whereby the benefactor endowed one or more priest chaplains to sing masses daily for the souls of himself, his family and his ancestors for ever.

In Lancastrian and Yorkist England, enthusiasm for the perpetual chantry continued to be intense, even if — a most important point — perpetual chantries always need to be set against the background of a multiplicity of temporary chantry foundations, of which prayers and masses at the anniversary of one's death (the "obit") were the most common.

By the 15th century, the proliferation of chantries had in effect transformed the routines and indeed the physical structure of almost all the churches in the country. Even England's 19 cathedrals, although they continued to fulfil their primary purpose as the mother churches of their dioceses, were now honeycombed with private chantry foundations. By 1500 there were at least 56 perpetual chantries in York Minster, and possibly as many as 80 at St Paul's Cathedral.

More celebrated still were many of the exceptionally elaborate chantries to be found in the cathedral monastery of Canterbury, including those of the Black Prince as well as of the first King (Henry IV) and the first Archbishop of Canterbury (Thomas Arundel) of the 15th century.

However, it was within the parish churches of England that the multiplication of chantries had its most important effect. Many chantries were admittedly too poorly endowed even to survive; but not infrequently two, three or more chantry chaplains are to be found assisting rectors and vicars in the performance of their duties.

To a remarkable and not yet properly appreciated extent, the 15th-century parish church could sometimes become the centre of a team of priests and chaplains, capable of providing an impressive variety of educational and other — including musical — attractions for their parishioners.

More significantly still, by its very nature the private chantry or obit

# Kempe's spiritual jig

*The Booke of Margery Kempe* deserves its fame not only as the "first autobiography in the English language", but because it offers a unique and remarkably direct insight into the female spirituality of the 15th century.

Margery was the daughter (born c. 1373) of John Burnham, perhaps the richest citizen of King's Lynn, of which town he was mayor at least five times. She was married (c. 1394) to another burgess of Lynn, John Kempe, by whom she allegedly had 16 children.

It is, however, a comment on how little can be known about most English women of the period that she would remain in almost total obscurity were it not for the fortunate survival of her famous *Booke*. Only one copy of this survives, once in the possession of the Carthusian monastery of Mount Grace in Yorkshire, and only rediscovered among the library of the Butler-Bowden family in 1934.

As described and dictated by Margery, her turbulent travels and mystical experiences began when she experienced a series of visions after a period of mental breakdown. After taking a vow of chastity in 1413, she travelled to the Holy Land, her later pilgrimages including journeys to Compostela (1413) and even Norway and Danzig (1433), a few years before her death shortly after 1438.

Margery's claims to direct communion with Christ, and even more her liability to fits of loud sobbing and crying, especially in cathedrals, made her a controversial figure in her own day, as indeed ever since. Obviously not a typical burgess's daughter, she nevertheless expressed the devotional hopes and fears of her fellow Englishwomen with merciless honesty. "She kept her from crying for as long as she might, but at the last she broke out with a great cry and wonder sore."

represented the intrusion of lay, family interests within the ecclesiastical arena. The founders, descendants and patrons of chantries naturally had a vested interest in their prosperity, both spiritual and material. For this and other reasons, by 1500 there are increasing signs within the parish church itself not only of what the French historian Georges de Lagarde once called "*la naissance de l'esprit laïque*", but also of more and more administrative control by the laity.

## Chantry and academic colleges

In sharp contrast to the hundreds of poorly endowed one-chaplain parish chantries were the new chantry colleges of many priests, created as a result of a passionate wave of enthusiasm for such foundations among the kings, magnates and very richest merchants of Western Christendom in the 15th century.

Although nearly all the 900 or so long-established English monasteries, nunneries and friaries weathered the economic problems of the century reasonably well, it was this enthusiasm for chantry colleges which created what are still the most spectacular new buildings of the period, like Eton and King's College, Cambridge (a twin foundation by Henry VI from 1441 onwards), St George's Chapel, Windsor (reconstructed by Edward IV from 1474), and St Stephen's Chapel, Westminster Abbey, built in 1503-19.

If Richard III had won rather than lost the battle of Bosworth in 1485, there is little doubt that the greatest royal chantry chapel of all would have been at York Minster, where that short-lived monarch

Enriched: the Church of St Peter and St Paul, Lavenham, in Suffolk. *Photo © A. F. Kersting*

intended to found a college, presumably around his projected tomb, of no fewer than "100 prestes".

More important still, above all because they survived the Reformation, were those chantry foundations which took the form of academic colleges founded at Oxford and Cambridge. Although their primary practical purpose was to train the clerical bureaucrats who staffed the upper ranks of medieval Church and state, the universities of Oxford and Cambridge should themselves be interpreted as religious as much as educational establishments.

This was equally true of the new 15th-century university colleges, less likely to be founded by members of the royal family than by bishops: for example, Archbishop Henry Chichele in the case of All Souls College, Oxford (1438), and Bishop William Waynflete in that of Magdalen College, Oxford (1448).

Royal patronage of the two English universities, most conspicuously to be seen in King's College Chapel (not in fact completed until the reign of Henry VII), was in any case less evident at Oxford than in Cambridge. In the latter university, the number of academic colleges rose from seven to 16 between the foundation of God's House in 1439 and that of Trinity College in 1546. It was undoubtedly during the

Henry VI, a Tudor copy derived from an original portrait probably painted in the 1450s, after the king's first mental breakdown and before he was deposed by Edward IV in 1461; artist unknown. *Photo © by courtesy of the National Portrait Gallery, London*

course of the late 15th century that Cambridge — at long last — achieved an approximate parity in numbers, prestige and influence with Oxford.

Indeed, with the possible exception of Parliament, it could well be argued that the university colleges of Oxford and Cambridge were the greatest of all the 15th century's institutional legacies to the future of the English Church and state. However, until and indeed beyond 1500, the masters of both English universities remained remarkably resistant to the new-fangled learning of both Italian and North European "Renaissance humanism". It is no coincidence that when Sir Thomas More established his reputation as the first profoundly original English humanist, he did so when a London lawyer rather than a university clerk.

## The Crown and the Church

The execution on Tower Hill of Sir Thomas More in July 1535 exemplified in a peculiarly vengeful fashion a quite different and fundamental ecclesiastical theme: the English monarchy's supremacy over the English Church.

No doubt, the most alarming and totalitarian features of Henry VIII's attitude to his clergy owe much to that king's break with Rome and his own personal cantankerous temperament. However, it is essential to remember that the "absolutist" tendencies of the Reformation monarchy were firmly grounded in 15th-century precedents.

As early as 1408, at the Council of Pisa, Richard Ullerston, a fellow of Queen's College, Oxford, expressed an already widely held view that no ecclesiastical reform was possible in England "without the protection and strength of the prince, considering the weakness of priests". The increasing political weakness of the English clergy, and above all of their 17 bishops, did indeed become more and more evident during the course of the 15th century.

By contrast, all the six kings who ruled England between 1399 and 1500, although extremely different from one another as personalities, were alike in being not only genuinely devout, but also men with the highest conception of the spiritual significance of their office.

Whether waging God's battles against the French (Henry V in the late 1410s), deliberately attempting to be a priest-like king (Henry VI), or engaged in a strenuous attempt at the "reformation of the realm" (Henry VII), all the predecessors of Henry VIII had no doubt that they were chosen by God to be the potential spiritual redeemers of their kingdoms.

Was there indeed a more influential — more baneful — ideological legacy of the 15th century to the Reformation than the assumption (to quote the words of Edmund Dudley, one of Henry VII's closest and most unpopular councillors) that "the root of the love of God must chiefly grow out of our sovereign lord the King"?

In the last resort, Sir Thomas More himself was prepared to die for exactly the contrary opinion, not least because he believed that the imminent destruction of the traditional medieval English Church was less the result of its own inherent weaknesses than of the revolutionary preaching of a German heretic and the vagaries of the royal will. Whether Sir Thomas was right or wrong is likely to remain on the historian's agenda for as long as the 15th-century Church exerts its perennial fascination on us all.

## CHRONOLOGY

**1399-1461** The Lancastrian monarchy
**1401** Statute *De Heretico Comburendo*
**1413** The Oldcastle (Lollard) Revolt
**1414-15** Henry V founds Sheen and Syon Abbeys
**1440-41** Henry VI founds Eton, and King's College, Cambridge
**1461-85** The Yorkist monarchy
**1472** Consecration of York Minster
**1476** Caxton begins printing in Westminster
**1485-1509** The reign of Henry VII
**1488** Oxford University Divinity School completed
**1499** Erasmus's first visit to England

# HOW LUTHER'S VISION SUNDERED A CONTINENT

*Euan Cameron*

*The implications of Protestant teaching about justification by faith were tremendous: the medieval system appeared obsolete, and 'reforming' the Church became an exciting popular activity.*

The Reformation forms the great watershed in Western Europe's religious history in the past 1000 years. It divided the Latin Christian tradition into two strands with quite distinct visions of God.

In the Catholic tradition, God operated through a continuous, trustworthy and authentic Church. In the reformed or Protestant traditions, God acted directly, immediately and transcendently upon the individual soul.

These basic differences have ever since been reflected in different styles of worship, different modes of organising people's lives, and in different climates of intellectual debate. Why did such a chasm open up within the diverse, organic entity which was the late-medieval Church?

## Medieval abuses

There is no straightforward answer. Partly, medieval religion had assumed forms which serious, thinking people found increasingly hard to accept.

In the 13th century, it was argued that the more masses were said to help a given soul through purgatory, the more "*quanta*" of divine grace were assigned to that soul. By the 15th century, masses were bought for the dead in increasing arithmetical profusion, often in multiples of the "magic" number 30. So certain was this belief in the absolute quantitative value of the memorial mass, that the wealthiest founded perpetual chantries where priests would, in principle, sing masses for the founders or beneficiaries until the end of time. Some of the chapels thus created remain to this day in parish and collegiate churches.

The doctrine of Christ's presence in the transubstantiated elements of the eucharist had, by 1500, spawned miracle-stories and cults, like the indestructible and bleeding mass-wafers at the German shrines of Wilsnack and Sternberg. The Church had long since offered "indulgences" remitting penances due for sins committed, to reassure crusaders against the fear of sudden death. By the 1500s, however, "full confessional letters" made plenary absolution available for sale in a tailored, means-tested system.

Martin Luther, by Lucas Cranach, the Elder. *Photo © Bristol City Museum and Art Gallery, UK/Bridgeman Art Library*

At its most ambitious, the system of absolution claimed to extend its benefits beyond the grave. From 1476 onwards, papal indulgences were issued whereby it was hoped that the souls of the dead, contrite but suffering in purgatory, might be released from part or all of their torments. Since the purchaser of such an indulgence was not the same as its beneficiary, there was no obligation on the former to undertake any specific spiritual preparation before acquiring one.

## Luther's protest

When Martin Luther (1483-1546) wrote his 95 theses for disputing on the power of indulgences in late October 1517, he was attacking only the most prominent, dubious outgrowth of an overgrown system of transferable, negotiable "grace".

Already, scattered across Europe, knots of thinking Christian scholars could not believe that God mechanically rewarded the performance of ceremonial, ritual acts (though nothing was further from their minds than to challenge the system openly). Such "Christian humanists", whose most prominent but not most typical figure was Erasmus of Rotterdam (?1467-1536), felt that God must require moral goodness and personal commitment in a believer, rather than just ritual purity. They would form a responsive, though selective and critical, audience for Martin Luther.

After issuing his theses, Luther became notorious — and survived — partly through a set of unpredictable coincidences.

The Dominican friars stung by his rebukes howled for his burning so fiercely that they made themselves odious. The Pope, desperate to prevent the election of Charles of Burgundy and Spain to the Holy Roman Empire and the ensuing creation of a Habsburg super-monarchy, would not press too hard on Luther's prince, an elector of the Empire. The Italian theologians commissioned to write against Luther wrote so clumsily that Luther's respect for the papacy speedily evaporated. His pamphlets — which reached a peak of influence and cogency in 1520 — entered the public domain through a frantic ex-pansion in the printing and publishing business.

So, when Luther was called to appear before the Holy Roman Emperor Charles V (elected despite the pope) at the meeting of the German Reichstag at Worms in 1521, he was an academic celebrity threatened by intellectually and morally disreputable clerics, and protected by an aura of learning and fame.

He seems to have been bewildered by the flat request to acknowl-edge his books as his own, and to renounce the errors contained in them. Pausing to reflect for 24 hours, he gave a detailed but conclusive answer: there was nothing he could say to the proofs he had adduced from scripture for his claims. "His conscience was captive to the Word

of God." That (authentic) utterance is, across the intervening centuries, at least as resonant as the (spurious) "Here I stand: I can do no otherwise" fathered on Luther by later tradition.

Just over a century before, the Bohemian Jan Hus had been burned as a heretic notwithstanding an emperor's safe conduct. The Saxon Luther was too public a figure for such a sophistry to be allowed. He left Worms in safety at the end of April 1521, and was spirited away to protective custody in one of his prince's more out-of-the-way castles, while his tonsure grew out and his beard grew long in the manner of a nobleman's.

## Justification by faith

The man became famous before his words were fully grasped. So shocking were the implications of Luther's message, that it might have made fewer friends if fully understood. Preparing his lectures between 1513 and 1519, Luther had come upon a meaning for the Christian gospel which had never occurred to him before. Crucial parts of the

Calvin, pictured on his deathbed by a 19th-century French engraver. *Photo © Private Collection/Ken Walsh/Bridgeman Art Library*

New Testament could mean that God spontaneously, from simple mercy, and for Christ's sake, *forgives* people their faults *while they remain impure*.

As Luther himself wrote, while in his castle retreat of the Wartburg: "If you take mercy away from the godly, they are sinners, and really have sin, but it is not imputed to them because they believe and live under the reign of mercy."

Suddenly, it was no longer a struggle to become a purer, holier person through sacrament, prayer, and "habits of grace", as in the medieval Church. It was the blissful release of accepting that God is generous, and calls on everyone to believe and trust in the forgiveness which they are offered. Once so forgiven, the believer would strive fervently to live a godly life of study, prayer and neighbourly charity: but out of serene thankfulness, not anxious solicitude for a soul perched between heaven and hell.

Luther's discovery might just have eased a troubled conscience. However, Luther was a rigorous thinker and a brilliant communicator.

If God spontaneously forgave the impure, rather than purifying the guilty through ritual, then vast areas of the Christian religion as then practised were unnecessary, even fraudulent. Indulgences remitting penances, then monks' vows, private masses for souls, and "holy"' things, places, and people fell under the scythe of his logic. Worship became a matter of hearing the gospel, of having its meaning expounded by a competent specialist, of accepting its implications for one's spiritual state, and of giving thanks and praise to God.

The international machinery of the Catholic Church, distributing "grace" through ceremonially authenticated channels, became a needless deception. The "Church" meant simply the community of Christian people at prayer, organised in its social and political units. In one of his most famous pamphlets, *The Address to the Christian Nobility of the German Nation*, Luther translated the implications of his message into a programme for social reform and restructuring. No longer were the clergy to be a privileged class living by separate laws, within their communities, but not of them: pastors should be civic functionaries, like schoolmasters or midwives.

## Reforming ordinances

From the late 1520s, the implications of Luther's new vision of the Christian community were worked through in reforming ordinances, individual to each state and its circumstances. In practice this meant that city-states such as the free city of Nuremberg (in 1525-33), principalities like electoral Saxony (in 1525-42), and ultimately whole kingdoms like Denmark (in 1536-39) acquired new orders for church worship, new structures for the management of church affairs, and rules for poor relief and education. The point needs to be stressed: the Lutheran movement did not, initially, generate a "Lutheran Church" as an alternative over-arching structure to the Roman one. Rather, it created a plethora of state and community Churches, which reflected the diversity of the many political units within the German world.

How had such a sweeping, shattering insight gained acceptance? Luther did not lead a coherent movement. An inspirational writer, teacher and preacher, he had no control over what others made of his message. Initially, many intellectual clerics mistook his message for a more explicit version of Erasmus of Rotterdam's Christian humanism. Erasmus, after all, had attacked a religion of superficial ceremonies, spurious relics, self-righteous monasticism, and Aristotelian theology some years before Luther did, albeit for different reasons and from a different view of human nature.

Subsequently, such intellectuals could rediscover and reformulate Luther's general insight, with glosses and emphases of their own. Luther's personal foibles — a need for the sacraments physically to embody God's promises, a wish to educate people before changing their religious surroundings — were not shared by others such as Huldrych Zwingli (1484-1531), Martin Bucer (1491-1551), or John Calvin (1509-1564).

## Zwingli, Bucer and Calvin

Zwingli, the first of the great reformers of the Swiss Confederation, re-invented Luther's ideas on what may have been no more than a cursory reading. He brought to them his own highly rational, rigorous cast of mind.

Sacraments, symbols, and rituals could not, he argued, confine or embody divine power in any way: they were signs people gave to God of their devotion and their decisions.

Moreover, Zwingli did not think one could usefully preach against idolatry while "idolatrous" remnants of the old order remained in the Churches. So, in the "reformed" tradition of Switzerland and southern Germany, change in the physical appearance of the churches came sooner rather than later, with drama and abruptness, rather than gradually and patiently as in the north.

Luther, fatefully for the Reformation, found Zwingli's rationalism arrogant and his advanced techniques of scripture exegesis disrespectful to the sacred text. The discussions between them at Marburg in 1529 brought a measure of agreement, but no real unity. It was the task of the Alsatian Martin Bucer and the Picard John Calvin, through their long careers, to try to blend the insights of Luther and Zwingli into a spiritually satisfying whole.

Bucer worked for many years at Strasburg and ended his life at Cambridge. He was an inveterate temporiser and a loquacious, verbose exegete, who always seemed to believe that a few thousand extra words of explanation could resolve disagreements on every issue. His strength lay in a passionate belief in the value of the Christian community, which contrasted with Luther's vision of true Christians as individual souls isolated among the indifferent.

Bucer communicated this ideal to the young John Calvin at Strasbourg during 1538-41. Calvin, a tireless preacher, teacher, and author, transformed the minor episcopal city of Geneva into a religious metropolis. He contrived to combine Luther's profound reverence for scripture with Zwingli's robust reasonableness, and created a theology which was better articulated and arguably more profound than either of his predecessors'.

In the *Institution of the Christian Religion* (written and re-written between 1536 and 1559), he gave the Protestant tradition a theological manual of immense power and durability. To Germans he became the greatest threat to Luther's ascendancy; to Germanic Swiss, ironically, this Frenchman seemed at first to be the Lutherans' Trojan horse in the Zwinglian citadel.

## A giddying time

The Reformation, then, was never an ideologically uniform movement: it started as a chaotic mixture of loosely similar messages, then coalesced into several "confessions", fundamentally the Lutheran and the "reformed" (later known as the "Calvinist").

Political circumstances in Germany ensured that from 1555 to 1648 only adherents of the Lutheran Confession of Augsburg could formally enjoy the civil rights allowed to non-Catholics. This made the distinction between "Lutheran" and "Calvinist" one of great legal and political significance. In the later-16th and 17th century, it divided German states between the introverted and exclusivist Lutherans and the potentially "illegal", internationalist and militant Calvinists led by the Electors Palatine at Heidelberg.

Such "confessionalism" hardened lines of allegiance and hostility, and helped to provoke one of the most agonisingly drawn-out and destructive wars to afflict central Europe between 1618 and 1648.

Outside the Reformation proper, splinter-groups rejected basic premises of reformed belief, but exploited the disintegration of religious authority to branch out in their own directions: "Anabaptists", spiritualists, anti-Trinitarians, and others. After unsuccessful essays in sudden, fundamental reformation, these movements retreated into quietism in parts of the Netherlands, Moravia, and Poland.

To their own embarrassment, some reformed churchmen were

Rationalist temper: Zwingli, after Hans Asper. *Photo © National Gallery of Scotland, Edinburgh/ Bridgeman Art Library*

manoeuvred into defending "orthodoxy" (elements of the Christian faith and tradition shared by Catholic and Protestant) and attacking the "sectaries" almost like medieval inquisitors. Toleration was not, in those days, a virtue.

For the ordinary believer the early 1520s were a giddying time, full of alarming and enticing possibilities. Learned scholars vied for attention in readable, accessible pamphlets in the common tongue, and in competing sermons in the churches.

Lay men and women found a (temporary) voice, as printers lapped up almost any contribution to the ferment of debate. Pamphlets contrasted the honest, straight-thinking layman with the devious and hypocritical priest; former nuns wrote to justify leaving their monasteries; priests' mistresses justified becoming lawful wives.

During the great protest uprising in Germany in 1525 (the so-called Peasant War), it seemed that rural communal self-determination and the new idea of the lay Christian community might coalesce to re-shape the social and political order.

The leaders of the "Peasants" in southern Germany (actually a preacher and an urban furrier) demanded that congregations be allowed to elect their own pastors, and that common lands, woods, and rivers be restored to the community by the lords who had seized them. Such aspirations were speedily and bloodily crushed in a wave of punitive raids in the early summer of 1525.

Nevertheless, "reforming" one's community remained an exciting participatory activity. Whole towns such as Ulm, Esslingen, Biberach, Constance, or Heilbronn polled their citizens for their opinions around 1530, then resolved collectively to abolish the mass. In many places townspeople destroyed the "idols" no longer seen as holy, and seized charitable religious endowments to fund a rational system of welfare and education.

## Changes in church

How much changed for the ordinary lay person in church?

It would be easy to argue that the main Sunday service altered only gradually and slightly from the old parochial high mass. The usual medieval "observed mass", where no members of the laity communicated, was succeeded by the Protestant service, often loosely based on a medieval "ante-communion", where praise, reading and exposition of the scriptures, general confession, absolution, and intercessory prayer formed the standard elements.

The reformers would have wished to restore the ancient practice of frequent, even weekly, communion. However, centuries of infrequent communion, compounded by the medieval Church's insistence on detailed enumeration of sins in confession and specific penances before receiving the eucharist, had discouraged all but the most devout from anything more than a once- or twice-yearly reception.

On the other hand, the new rites broke down symbolic barriers between priest (or minister) and people. Vernacular languages were spoken throughout rather than Latin, and the priest no longer made a private act of communion from which the people were excluded.

The Lutheran tradition, from Martin Luther onwards, developed the medieval practice of singing verse hymns into a central act of worship. In the reformed confessions, metrical settings of the psalms served the same function: they became memorable, symbolic expressions of the solidarity of the congregation in worship. Anglicans cannot forget that the *Old Hundredth* stands securely in this tradition.

Music and singing replaced the participatory element lost when the versicles and responses were dropped from much Protestant worship. "Reformed" believers developed a special aversion to addressing God in stereotyped phrases rather than improvised prayer. When one group of English exiles insisted on saying the Prayer Book responses in the Frankfurt English Church in early 1555, a fateful rift opened up between those who had rejected these medieval remnants and those who still clung to them.

## Winnowing of medievalism

To the ordinary believer, more striking than the changes to Sunday worship was the ending of a range of extra religious ceremonies.

Abolishing the sacrificial private mass removed, at a stroke, an expensive proliferation of eucharists (and priests). Destroying pilgrimage shrines restored to central importance "baptism, the sacrament, preaching, and your neighbour", as Luther had urged in 1520. Devotional confraternities, special vows, cults of particular saints for particular reasons — all lost their rationale.

Lay people now faced the insecurities of life without the arsenal of helps, "sacramentals" like holy water, salt, or palms, which they had used to defend themselves, and their children, animals, and homes from natural and supernatural evils.

This winnowing-out of the medieval heritage would leave ordinary people psychologically exposed to the terrible judgements of a God from whom, they were told, they deserved nothing but punishment. On the other hand, new forms of voluntary devotion appeared: study groups and informal religious societies, "inner rings" of committed reformed Christians whose sense of solidarity and purpose would find expression in the Puritan social system in both the old world and the new.

Within a generation, the Protestant message gave its people an identity and a sense of place in salvation history. Accused of being

**CHRONOLOGY**

**1517** Luther writes 95 theses against indulgences
**1520** Luther's three major treatises published
**1521** Reichstag at Worms: Luther outlawed
**1525** Peasant War in Germany; debate between Erasmus and Luther; Luther's German mass issued; worship reformed at Zürich
**1529** Religious conference at Marburg between Swiss and German reformers
**1530** Reichstag at Augsburg; Lutheran confession issued
**1531** Death of Zwingli; Swiss Reformation stabilised
**1541** Church Ordinances issued for Geneva
**1546-7** Death of Luther; religious war in Germany
**1555** Reichstag at Augsburg; German Reformation formalised
**1564** Death of Calvin

old heretics (Waldenses, Lollards, Hussites) writ large, Protestant apologists like the Lutheran Flacius Illyricus or the reformed John Foxe replied that the "True Church" and Catholicism had parted company around the 11th century, and the gospel had survived underground, only to burst forth at the Reformation. Some incorporated the Reformation into the prophecies of the "unbinding of Satan" after a thousand years in chains, as foretold in Revelation 20.1-3.

The sense of being a chosen people, an "elect", carried risks as well as benefits. It could lead to a morbid introspection of one's own sins, or a fervent bigotry which sought to "cleanse" the world of pollutants (though neither attitude would have been endorsed by the leading reformers).

At best, the Reformation taught its people to stand humbly and without pretence before a sacrificially loving God, to strip away all aspirations to "holiness", and to accept that temporary human institutions cannot capture the divine promises in tangible form.

That message loses none of its poignancy at this juncture in history.

# THE REFORM THAT WOULDN'T STOP

*Margaret Bowker*

*King Henry VIII started out as Defender of the Faith — but then lust, greed and a strong court took over. We tell the story of the English Reformation.*

On 22 April 1509, when Henry VIII became King of England, the Venetian ambassador remarked how handsome he was, with his glowing auburn hair and splendid build. England had at its helm a king who would and could rival any potentate in Europe. He was seemingly tireless at jousting, hawking, wrestling and dancing, with a healthy appetite for eating and drinking.

Henry was a second son, and his brother's death in 1502 had made him the unexpected heir, facts that may well have contributed to his restless competitiveness and incessant appetites, which could be turned in unexpected directions, or on unsuspecting victims. The English Church was to be the beneficiary of this vain and unpredictable monarch, but also at times his victim.

## Flowering of religious thought

No one would have predicted any fundamental disagreements in the Church at the time of Henry's accession. He was devout and was ambitious to excel in piety as in all else. He was also the centre of a court that praised learning and the arts, even if it did not always promote them. In Oxford and Cambridge, colleges were founded, and, throughout England, schools established and churches refurbished.

When the internationally renowned scholar Erasmus of Rotterdam visited England in 1505, he found that there were Greek scholars — like Cuthbert Tunstall, William Grocyn and Thomas Linacre — as great as any in Europe, who befriended and stimulated him. There were also bishops who helped to finance his writing and who were promoting the reform of the Church, especially of the clergy. England, from being something of an intellectual backwater, was, by the time of Henry's accession, humming with life.

The centre of that life was religion, and it was flowering in many directions: John Colet, eventually Dean of St Paul's, held the University of Oxford enthralled with lectures on the Epistles of St Paul to the Romans and Corinthians in 1497-98. He attempted to explain to his audience what these letters were about, and, on his acceptance of the deanery, he tried to explain to the congregation what the Christian life really meant. Erasmus saw him as a rare example of godliness — and Erasmus was a discerning critic.

Colet was not a Greek scholar, but, by the time he refounded St Paul's School in London in 1509, Greek was in his curriculum, and his friend Richard Fox, who founded Corpus Christi College, Oxford, made it a compulsory subject there; both saw it as the tool to understanding the New Testament and other Christian classics.

## Impact of the printing press

Colet was not alone in seeking the depth and true meaning of the Christian message. The invention of printing in Europe, and the arrival in England of William Caxton's press in 1476 meant that books no longer had to be copied by hand, but could be, in his words, "begun on one day, and also finished in one day".

The dramatic impact of printing cannot be overstated. Not only did an ever-increasing number of books come from English presses, but books were imported from overseas. Many of the books were of a devotional character, and were aimed at teaching the faithful an understanding of faith greater than could be imparted by the repetition of well loved and well known rituals.

The press broke through the language barrier. People no longer needed to be pure Greek or Latin scholars. *The Fruyte of Redempcyon* (1514) states that it was written "for your ghostly comforte that understande no latyn". The laity were now encouraged to assist the clergy in explaining the faith. The local incumbents, who may sometimes have understood the Latin of the Gospels and the mass, were no longer the only evangelists.

But books raised inevitable questions, and these were debated widely. In England, such matters had previously been aired primarily in the comparative security and obscurity of the universities. John Wycliffe (1320-1384) had challenged accepted doctrine and had urged the need for a return to scripture, but the impact on the nation at large was limited.

When, however, Martin Luther (1483-1546) began to wrestle with his own conscience and with the questions of "what must I do to be saved?", and when he came to the conclusion that he must have faith in Christ, who alone could achieve that seeming impossibility, not only the news, but also the details, of his argument were published and disseminated all over Europe.

Not surprisingly, many other issues flooded in: should the Bible be in the vernacular for all to read — and perhaps to be misled by? Should the eucharist be in Latin? In what sense should Christ's words "This is my body" be understood? Was purgatory invented by priests to keep

# 'That men may know what they pray'

The Bible in English was not readily available in England on Henry's accession. In Spain, Germany and France, the Bible was read in the mother tongue.

In England there was hostility to it. In 1523 William Tyndale asked Cuthbert Tunstall, Bishop of London, for help with the necessary expense of translating and printing the New Testament. He was refused, and sought help abroad. By 1526, copies were available, and, by 1527, Robert Necton of Norwich was importing them by the dozen and then by the hundred. Anne Boleyn had a French Testament and probably a Tyndale, too. Thomas More wrote against Tyndale's translation in vitriolic terms, and a royal proclamation of 1530 forbade translations in English, French or Dutch, "printed beyond the sea", to be imported.

No proclamation could stem the tide, and by 1537 an English Bible, printed by Grafton and Whitchurch and known as Matthew's Bible, appeared (*illustrated left* © *British Library*). It was put together by John Rogers, using Tyndale's translation of the Pentateuch and the New Testament, and his drafts of the historical books, unfinished when he was arrested and burned. The rest was largely supplied by Coverdale. The royal injunctions of 1538 ordered its use in churches. With this advance went the publication of an authorised Primer in English, printed by Grafton in 1545. It contained prayer, graces and psalms. Its preface from the King echoed (or was it supplied by?) Thomas Cranmer.

The purpose was "that men may know what they pray, also with words lest things (that are) special good and principal, being enwrapped in ignorance of the words, should not perfectly come to the mind and to the intelligence of men". Once understanding replaced ignorance, the battle was on for the minds as well as the hearts of Englishmen.

people in fear? By 1521, Lutheran books were coming into England and were raising fears of dissension in the Church and of criticisms, not only of its doctrine and practice, but of its powers and privileges.

## Panic reaction

The senior bishops, with the full support of the King behind them, panicked. John Fisher took on the monumental task of refuting Luther, both in preaching at the ceremonial burning of Luther's works at St Paul's in 1521, and in publications that were circulated throughout Europe. But to burn books was not to extinguish the ideas that gave them birth; nor was there in England the power to call in all offending copies. Bishop Longland of Lincoln ordered a search in the University of Oxford for Luther's works, and he urged a look-out to be kept on the eastern seaboard for imported heretical literature. But all this simply gave lustre to forbidden fruit.

In the universities and in London, reading parties gathered in secret, and Luther was the talk of the town. Gradually he became much more than talk. In Cambridge, Thomas Bilney began to convert his fellow students, Hugh Latimer, Nicholas Ridley and Matthew Parker. In London, a group of "known men" met at night to read and exchange books, and to use their positions as City Company Mercers, Grocers and Drapers not only to import books, but to make contact with latter-day followers of John Wycliffe.

The people who were delighted by Luther's message were, many of them, the most devoted and serious men of faith. William Roper was one. Son-in-law to Thomas More and married to his beloved Margaret, he was resident in More's house. Yet he was to be found in Lutheran circles in London in the 1520s. His scrupulous Catholic piety turned to relief and joy as, like Luther, he learned to understand that salvation came through faith alone.

Outside the towns, loyalty to the time-honoured traditions of worship, the honouring of saints and the celebration of the liturgical year was still largely unaffected by the talk of the town in London, Bristol and Oxford. Indeed, the talk may have simply underlined the fundamental importance of faith. But for Tyndale, Barnes, Bilney, Latimer and an ever-increasing number of others, that faith had become detached from the scripture which gave rise to it.

But whether people followed a Lutheran or reformed understanding of Christianity or a Catholic one, they had roots in the same soil, the faith which had characterised the late 15th and early 16th centuries. Accordingly, whether England could have become a country of the Catholic Reformation, like Spain, rather than a Protestant one is a question to which there is no answer. Reformation in Europe in the 16th century rarely resulted in the overthrow of the established ecclesiastical order without the assent of the ruler; and in England that ruler was Henry VIII.

## Henry and Wolsey

Henry was aware that his title of "King of England" appeared puny beside that of his continental counterparts. He longed for a papal title, and wrote a tract (with help) against Luther in 1521, earning himself the title of Defender of the Faith.

At his side was Cardinal Thomas Wolsey. The Cardinal could exercise papal power in England, although the law required it to be with royal assent. Between the two of them, all seemed set fair for a Catholic Reformation. But the very forces which seemed to be promoting that outcome were in fact to wreck it.

Wolsey, a butcher's son who rose by his intellectual gifts through Magdalen College, Oxford, to the court, was not popular. By 1521, he was Lord Chancellor, Archbishop of York, and Cardinal. He was also *legatus a latere*, a legate at the elbow of the Pope, and possessed of his power. The highest temporal and spiritual offices were his — but by the gift of the King. His use of that power spared the King time and paperwork, and thus left him free to wrestle and joust, to hunt, wine and dine.

His Cardinal, far from promoting the asceticism preached by Colet and practised by Fisher, fathered illegitimate children, blatantly increased his wealth by multiplying his appointments, and placed his own coat of arms on everything: on his palace at Hampton Court, for example, and on his college at Oxford. He so displayed his power that the chroniclers described him as one whom "all men almost hated" — but that was in London, and he certainly had friends elsewhere.

With the dislike of the Cardinal went the dislike of the evils attributed to all the clergy (and for which Colet had chided them). Such criticisms were given public utterance in the printed works of Simon Fish and others.

The clergy were accused of ignorance, of neglecting their parishioners, of being too exact in their reckoning of their dues, and of failing in general to follow the Master they claimed to serve. All these complaints were grossly exaggerated, but they made good copy for ballad-writers and the scurrilous printers of London.

## The marriage question

Wolsey, however, for all his power, could not give the King the one thing he wanted: a male heir. Henry's marriage to his brother's widow had resulted in the birth of a daughter, Mary. By 1526, it was clear that his wife was unlikely to produce another child. How was Henry to produce a male heir?

He had thought of trying to legitimise an illegitimate son, but then he began to wonder whether he could replace his wife. There were a number of possible ways that could be pursued, all of which required a papal decision declaring his marriage null. Wolsey worked unceasingly on the problem, but not only was the case inherently difficult, the Pope was a pawn of the interested party, the Spanish relatives of Henry's queen.

In the event, before all the diplomatic and canonical avenues could be exhausted, the ever impatient Henry was sufficiently in love with Anne Boleyn to take matters into his own hands. He largely sidelined Wolsey, and put all his jousting energy into gaining a divorce.

His eye had been caught by Anne in 1525. Had she agreed to be his mistress, things might have been different. But by 1527, the King

Thomas Cromwell. *Photo © Private Collection/Ken Walsh/ Bridgeman Art Library*

intended marriage, and he began to use every means to gain his end, including, by 1529, dispensing with Wolsey, who, in October of that year, was found guilty of *praemunire* — in effect, the charge of serving another monarch at the expense of his own king.

By November 1530 Wolsey had died, on his way to his trial and almost certainly his disgrace. Among his last words were those of regret: "If I had served God as diligently as I have done the King, he would not have given me over in my grey hairs."

Henry, meanwhile, ever restless, had not got his divorce. All ways forward were attempted: the universities of Europe were canvassed for their views, and tentative moves were made to proceed without the Pope. To that end, the senior bishops and clergy, and thereafter the clergy in general, were threatened with *praemunire* for exercising judicial powers over the Church. To buy pardon, Convocation agreed that the King was "sole protector and supreme head" of the English Church. The addition of a caveat, "as far as the law of Christ allows", meant that even Fisher could accept this title; but what would be the consequence?

## Royal supremacy and Cranmer

In order to make the submission a reality, a former servant of Wolsey, Thomas Cromwell, became the King's right-hand man, and took on the drafting of the laws that would turn a grudgingly extorted supremacy into a political reality. It became more straightforward when death removed conservative bishops, notably the Archbishop of Canterbury, in August 1532.

The way became clear, not only for the King to break off negotiations with Rome and to cease to allow payments of any kind to go to Rome, but for him to have a new Archbishop who could declare his marriage null. Thus he could marry Anne and be recognised by Parliament as Supreme Head of the Church in 1534. He was also able to make sure that the succession to the throne lay with Anne's children.

In the space of four years, the party for the reform of the English Church, possibly along Lutheran lines, emerged to influence the court, and to reshape and transform the Church of England without reference to popes who might understand little of the bedroom politics that surrounded the English succession, or the weight of support for Lutheran ideas, if not in the country at large, certainly at court.

Central to the guiding of an autonomous English Church was the new Archbishop of Canterbury, Thomas Cranmer. He had become familiar with Luther's views in Cambridge and as an exponent of Henry's case in Italy and subsequently in Germany. He had witnessed the Protestant Reformation in practice in Nuremberg, and he had married the niece of a prominent reformer.

None of this can have adequately prepared him for the task ahead. In order to advance the cause of Protestant reform, he was asked to declare the King's marriage to his first wife null, to preside over the coronation of the new Queen, and to dissolve her marriage and hear her confession before her execution a mere three years later.

Thomas More and John Fisher were victims in 1535 of the need to enforce the line of succession through the recognition by oath of the supremacy of the King over the Church. How far the royal supremacy over the Church would cause any change in it was a debated question.

Henry, it seems, was largely conservative. He liked the Latin mass, he did not doubt that the sacrament was the Body of Christ, and he had none of the reformers' objections to "creeping to the cross" on Good Friday. Thomas Cromwell and Archbishop Cranmer had, and so had a number of English bishops. Debate was rife, and uncertainty was destructive.

## The bloodshed spreads

Attempts to clarify the doctrine of the independent Church appeared in the Ten Articles of 1536. These were certainly a move towards a new position: the practice of regarding saints as "more merciful than Christ" and of elaborately adorning their images was condemned. The status of holy days, intercession for the dead and some of the sacraments was in question.

Wolsey's woe: Hampton Court, acquired by King Henry, in an engraving from Havell's *History of the Thames*, 1793 by Joseph Farington. *Guildhall Library, Corporation of London. Photo © Bridgeman Art Library*

Dissolved: the ruins of Wenlock Priory. *Photo © Roy Morgan*

# End of the monasteries

Among the grievances advanced in December 1536, in the Pilgrimage of Grace, some touched on the monasteries. Cromwell's deputies visited them in 1535 and (with no relationship to the visitation findings) had begun to suppress them according to their value in the subsequent year. The pilgrims argued that "the abbeys in the north part gave great alms to poor men and laudably served God; in which parts, of late day, they had but small comfort by ghostly teaching."

The attack on the monasteries was scarcely a measure of reform. The indictment against them for the failure of some to keep to their vows can be supported by some evidence from successive bishops who visited. But the scale of Cromwell's findings suggests evidence careless of date, corroboration or geography.

There were severe failings in certain monasteries, and lethargy was apparent in others. The Augustinian house of Great Missenden in Buckinghamshire, in the 1520s, for instance, shocked the bishop: its canons wined and dined, might attend office if they were not too drunk, or might slip out to the women in the village. But these flagrant lapses were rare.

Whatever the faults, the religious were not past reformation. Their most telling advocates came from the new and more observant orders: the Bridgettines of Syon, the Carthusians, and the Observantine Franciscans. From them came a spiritual leadership and direction, resourced by books written to help religious and lay.

Among their members there were a number who refused the supremacy, and who were executed brutally. Not all religious took that line, and when offered capacities, or a pension, they quietly merged into lay society.

It was hoped by some reformers that the dissolution would yield money for education and pious purposes. It did not.

The questions were made more pressing by the visitation and destruction of monasteries in the same year. Whether or not parishioners understood the Ten Articles, they could hardly miss hearing the demolition squad at work on the lesser monasteries. Unrest was all too likely, and it occurred in the autumn of 1536.

The Lincolnshire rebellion of October 1536 was immediately followed by more serious risings in Yorkshire and then in Lancashire and Cumbria, known as the Pilgrimage of Grace. The reasons for the rebellions differed from place to place. The penalty was savage: few of the clergy or religious were spared, and many of the leaders were hanged in chains until they died.

The Act of Six Articles of 1539 tried to reverse any suggestion of radical reformation, but the fat was in the fire. The Bible in English was mandatory for all churches by 1541, but had had episcopal authority as early as 1537. Shrines were demolished between 1538 and 1540, and the laity learned fast that gifts to the Church were rapidly becoming Henry VIII's pocket money.

Henry died in 1547. He left the English Church "but half reformed". He left his son in the hands of Protestant uncles and tutors. Hope lay with Cranmer, who toiled in his study to provide England with an English Prayer Book; but although he had survived so far, he must have known that in the twists and turns of royal policy his life was in perpetual danger: a wrong move could put a tinder to all his liturgical drafts.

The cost had been heavy: Wolsey, Fisher, More, Anne Boleyn, Tyndale, Cromwell, and many, many others had been executed or burned. More and Cromwell (for opposing reasons) had presided over the torture of suspects to elicit confessions, and had stood quietly by as they were savagely executed.

Cranmer in the interests of policy did not remonstrate with Henry over Anne Boleyn. The weapons for reforming the faith were not love and charity: they were propaganda and execution. The English Reformation avoided outright war, but it did not avoid the shedding of blood.

## CHRONOLOGY

**1502** Death of Prince Arthur (Henry becomes heir apparent)
**1505** Second visit of Erasmus
**1509** Henry VIII accedes
**1521** Henry becomes Defender of the Faith
**1530** Death of Cardinal Wolsey
**1531** Thomas Cranmer appointed Archbishop of Canterbury
**1532-33** Henry marries Anne Boleyn
**1533** Henry's marriage to Catherine of Aragon annulled; birth of Princess Elizabeth
**1534** Act of Supremacy
**1535** Executions of John Fisher and Thomas More
**1536** Execution of Anne Boleyn; Ten Articles; dissolution of lesser monasteries; beginning of the Pilgrimage of Grace
**1538** Royal Injunction for English Bible in churches
**1539** Act of Six Articles; Act for the dissolution of the greater monasteries
**1540** Execution of Thomas Cromwell
**1544** English Litany published and authorised
**1547** Death of Henry VIII

THOMAS . CRANMER . B[...] . MARTIR .

# OF CEREMONIES, WHY SOME BE ABOLISHED

*The Reformation caught fire after Henry's death, and Mary's pyres could not consume it.*

*Diarmaid MacCulloch*

A decade of indecisive politicking around the ailing Henry VIII was suddenly resolved in late 1546 with the arrest of Thomas Howard, Duke of Norfolk, England's premier conservative peer.

Norfolk's son, the poet Earl of Surrey (who had caused the disaster by flaunting his royal blood), was beheaded; only Henry's death saved Norfolk from execution. The accession of a boy-King, Edward VI, left Protestant politicians in firm control, and power was swiftly diverted to Edward Seymour, created Duke of Somerset and Protector.

Somerset's overbearing tactlessness to other leading men, and a breakdown of public order in 1549, led to his overthrow; but his successor John Dudley, Earl of Warwick (later Duke of Northumberland), out-manoeuvred powerful conservatives to press on with Protestant policies up to 1553.

## The Protestant vision

Somerset was deeply committed to Protestantism. With his encouragement, Thomas Cranmer, the Archbishop of Canterbury, could speed the Reformation. This meant destroying what remained of the old devotional world. The 1547 Chantries Act allowed the Crown to seize all remaining chantries, explicitly because praying for souls in purgatory was a waste of time, purgatory and masses for the dead being "vain opinions" [i.e. pointless fantasies].

The clergy's special status was undermined by allowing them to marry, while a chief instrument of clerical control over lay consciences, regular confession of sin to a priest, was made optional.

Royal orders were put out to destroy all religious images. Hacking down statues, whitewashing over wall-paintings, attacking tomb inscriptions with prayers for the dead, all revived and extended Thomas Cromwell's campaign of vandalism.

Naturally, much old ceremonial was abolished, and with such visual assaults came an assault on conservative ears: the replacement of Latin services by a single set of English rites contained in the 1549 Prayer Book.

Cautious reformer, radical liturgist: Archbishop Thomas Cranmer. *Photo © by kind permission of His Grace the Archbishop of Canterbury*

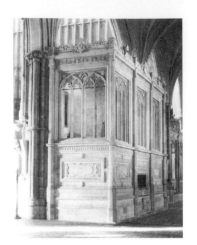

Last of the line: the chantry of
Bishop Stephen Gardiner in
Winchester Cathedral.
*Photo © John Hardacre/Dean and
Chapter of Winchester*

Much of this destructive programme implied a positive system to
replace it: a married clergy leading the people in a vernacular liturgy
that concentrated their minds on a single road to salvation through the
saving work of Christ on the cross. If people did not get the point of the
new liturgy, and if clergy did not have the heart or the capacity to
explain it in sermons, Cranmer had led a team producing 12 official
sermons (homilies) for non-preachers to read from the pulpit. These
explained the central themes of the Protestant view of salvation, and
other guidelines for Christian life and thought.

For many, especially in south-east England and London, this was a
message of liberty from ceremonial observance, and deeply exciting. It
seemed to herald an age of general change and reform, a notion that
Somerset expansively encouraged.

Cranmer was a cautious and quiet revolutionary. For 20 years he had
cultivated wide contacts with Evangelicals abroad, and he had a vision
of a new religious commonwealth in England and Wales to lead and
defend a new Western Christendom freed of Romish error.

The first fruit of his intentions took a very practical form: emergency
hospitality. In 1547 central European Protestantism was thrown into
disarray by defeat of the Protestant princes by the Holy Roman
Emperor, Charles V. Refugees flooded into England, providing
Cranmer with both welcome advice and unwelcome criticism. He
hoped (in the end in vain) to host a General Council of reformed
Churches, to outface the false General Council being held by the Pope
at Trent. With the Lutherans ceasing to take initiatives in continental
Protestantism, and Calvin's Geneva not yet in its later dominant
position, England had a good chance of taking the leading international role.

Cranmer thus thought on a heroically wide scale; yet he faced
multiple problems. He needed to complete an uncompromised
Reformation while not provoking desperate violence from the large
section of the nation at all social levels who had no sympathy with his
aims.

He also had to pursue international Protestant consensus in the face
of the inconvenient fact that England's chief ally, the Holy Roman
Emperor, was highly suspicious of Somerset's religious policy and
anxious about the steadfastly Catholic Princess Mary, his cousin and
Edward's half-sister. Cranmer's appreciation of the need for caution
baffled and infuriated both English Protestants home from continental
exile and continental reformers who had dealings with him.

## The reforms take hold

Nevertheless, 1550 was propitious for further reform. Dudley, now
unchallenged in government, negotiated an end to the war with France,

leaving him less dependent diplomatically on the Emperor. Although ordinary people may have found Somerset's changes more obvious and traumatic, now came more far-reaching theological consolidation of the new order. Altars were demolished in 1550, replaced by wooden tables, an act of discontinuity with the sacrifice of the mass. Cranmer published a new ordinal, carefully omitting any notion of a priest offering sacrifice and instead emphasising a role as pastor and teacher. Revised in some details in a Protestant direction, this formed part of the drastically revised Book of Common Prayer in 1552. In 1553 the doctrines of the Church of England were summarised in Forty-Two Articles.

But now time was running short. The Articles were never brought before the provincial Convocations, while a committee's draft work known as the *Reformatio Legum*, which would have ended the Church's dependence on medieval canon law and given it a reformed basis of discipline, remained a draft only, sabotaged by intervention from Northumberland himself.

Edwardian theologians never worked in a political vacuum; their efforts were compromised by the selfishness and greed of their allies in the regimes of both Somerset and Northumberland. Northumberland remains one of the most shadowy of Tudor statesmen, and, although there can be little doubt of his Protestant sympathies, his motives are dubious. The destruction of the old world meant further pickings for the nobility and money for the hard-pressed government: bishops and cathedral chapters had to surrender ancient estates on very unequal terms, and selling the chantries realised perhaps as much as a quarter of the previous windfall from monastic dissolutions.

Many chantry foundations had been associated with wider charitable purposes, including education. Despite a rash of refounded schools bearing the name of Edward VI, the short-term loss was considerable: literacy among those educated in the 1540s and 1550s fell back from levels achieved earlier, and it is difficult not to make a connection.

In the last months of Northumberland's regime, plans were going ahead to list and confiscate most bells and a wide range of church plate from parish churches. There was an unmistakable atmosphere of suspicion and separation between Protestant clergy and the leading men of government who were formulating such schemes: witness Northumberland's scuppering of canon-law reform.

Nevertheless, so far the local élites crucial to enforcing the Government's will had not been openly polarised, as they were to be under Mary and Elizabeth. Justices of the peace, and those whom the Government recommended as suitable for election as MPs, were a cross-section of positive supporters of reform alongside those who later remained Catholic sympathisers. Even the 1553 commissions to survey church goods, an acid test of a gentleman's willingness to collaborate with Northumberland, included a significant number of later religious conservatives.

Perhaps enough confusion reigned among the gentry to make it difficult to take the drastic step of openly opposing the Government's will; perhaps conservatives at this stage felt that they could best obstruct the Reformation by working from within. Conservative higher clergy generally seem to have seen the need for resistance before conservative lay magnates, but they remained isolated in their resistance.

## Mary miscalculates

In the winter of 1553, Edward VI (previously a healthy boy) contracted what was probably pneumonia. His rapid descent towards death spelt disaster for Protestantism: Mary, his designated heir, was notoriously a Catholic. Desperate, the young King and Northumberland determined to alter the succession to secure the revolution. That they did not succeed is one of the greatest surprises of 16th-century English politics. From London to York, Anglesey to Cornwall to Kilkenny, Jane Grey was proclaimed Queen; but in a remarkable *coup d'état* Mary supplanted her. Mary relied on a tightly knit group of Catholic gentry supporters, but the secret of her success was a much wider appeal to legitimism, and a careful avoidance of religious issues during the course of her rebellion.

Mary's triumph discredited leading Protestant churchmen, like Cranmer, who backed Queen Jane, leaving them with the taint of treachery, and giving the new Government good excuse to arrest them for treason even before restoring the old heresy laws.

However, the Queen's very success may have given a mistaken impression of her potential backing. Her legitimate claim to the throne rather than her religion had spread her support beyond Catholic sympathisers: now she found that, even among Catholics, her fervent wish to return England to papal obedience came as an unwelcome surprise. Moreover, she gained a mistaken impression of Protestant lack of steadfastness when Northumberland abjectly returned to Catholicism before his execution; not every Protestant was so easily led.

Her task was formidable: rebuilding the Church on the twin pillars of the old faith — traditional devotional practice and union with Western Christendom under the Pope — then convincing the population that the one pillar could not stand without the other. After Henry VIII had apparently proved the contrary, this would not be easy. In the brief time available, few among her advisers and officers could see that building the Catholic Church anew needed almost as much imagination and innovation as building a Protestant realm.

Vested interests in former church lands meant that those great

# The Prayer Books of Edward VI

Cranmer's agenda for religious revolution did not always coincide with Henry VIII's eccentric theology: his only English-language liturgical work that Henry allowed for public use was the Litany, substantially that still in the Prayer Book.

Under Edward, Cranmer made much more progress, and he brought his own agenda to creating an English liturgy. Along with most Protestant reformers (the main exception being Martin Luther), he no longer believed that eucharistic bread and wine physically became the body and blood of Christ. For Cranmer, Christ's body was in heaven; it was blasphemous to suppose that he could be elsewhere. Christ called faithful communicants up to him in heaven, rather than coming down to them himself in bodily form. If he was present in the communion, it was in spiritual form, a gift provided only for the chosen (the elect). This "spiritual presence" view of the eucharist underpinned Cranmer's remodelled Prayer Books.

Cranmer worked in stages. First, in 1548, he created an "Order of Communion" to be inserted in the old Latin mass, so that, at every eucharist, the people were exhorted to come forward and receive the consecrated bread and wine. Then, in 1549, came the first Prayer Book, the entire liturgy in English. The book attracted mixed reactions. In Devon and Cornwall, popular anger became full-scale rebellion, brutally repressed. Elsewhere, in eastern and southern England, there were widespread disturbances over a variety of other grievances, but the protesters gladly used the new book.

Thereafter, Cranmer and the Government were emboldened to go further. Cranmer was particularly annoyed that the more subtle conservatives, in particular Bishop Gardiner, said that the 1549 Book could be understood as expressing the old theology. Accordingly, by 1552, he had drastically revised the book.

The changes are most obvious in the communion service, but equally revolutionary was Cranmer's restructured funeral service. One of the great Reformation issues was the power the old Church claimed to exercise over death. In medieval theology, most people's fate was purgatory, not heaven or hell; the prayers of the living could shorten the time of those in purgatory. The reformers were determined to combat this compelling idea. The funeral service therefore needed to remove any notion that it might help the dead in any way.

Eamon Duffy has commented that: "The oddest feature of the 1552 rite is the disappearance of the corpse from it. . . At the moment of committal in 1552, the minister turns not towards the corpse, but away from it, to the living congregation around the grave." Cranmer's 1552 Book was used for less than a year before King Edward died. Elizabeth I restored it, hardly altered.

With further modifications, made in 1662 after Charles II had returned from civil-war exile, the Book achieved the form still in use. Not merely its shape but its language remains Cranmer's: a majestic, deliberately conservative English, avoiding pompous Latinisms, capable of being used by everyone in lifetimes of repetition. The most frequently performed text in the English tongue, it has shaped the destiny of the world's dominant language.

factories of traditional prayer, the monasteries and the chantries, were beyond recall after five years. For a start, Catholics held more church lands than Protestants. Papal obedience, the other pillar of the old system, was not a cause to arouse enthusiasm. Conservative bishops like Stephen Gardiner and Edmund Bonner, who had accepted Henry VIII's supreme headship of the Church, had been made to realise their mistake by the exercise of the same headship under Edward VI. Their renewed enthusiasm for the Pope made it easy for their Protestant opponents to taunt them, particularly in the case of Gardiner, whose 1535 defence of Henry VIII's proceedings in his book *De Vera Obedientia*, and his sneering attacks on the executed and saintly Bishop Fisher were difficult to explain away.

In theory, Mary could have submitted her realm to the Pope immediately; but the precedents of parliamentary involvement in two decades of sweeping religious change meant that this was not practical politics. While politicians and churchmen argued about giving land back to the Church, she was forced for 15 months to use the supreme headship, which she detested and considered a fiction, in order to take drastic action like depriving the Protestant bishops and married clergy.

## Undone by death

Meanwhile, Rome faced the facts of English politics about the confiscated church estates. Only in November 1554 did the new papal legate, Reginald Pole, reconcile England to Rome, and Parliament equip the Church to suppress heresy. Pole was not consecrated Archbishop of Canterbury until March 1556, after Archbishop Cranmer had been deprived and burnt for heresy.

After that, it was a tragic irony that the accession, in 1555, of a rabidly anti-Spanish pope, Paul IV, was followed by open warfare between Mary's husband, Philip of Spain, and the papacy. Pole was always a man vainly working against time; circumstances wasted the potential of a man who had been noted in his long Italian exile as one of the leading exponents of reform within the Roman Church.

Pole did begin moves that, with time, might have transformed the English Catholic Church beyond the understanding of his conservative cousin the Queen. His legatine synod, a body transcending the ancient ecclesiastical division of Canterbury and York, began examining and sorting out the chaos in the Church's remaining financial resources, and took a potentially highly significant step by planning seminaries in each cathedral city to train the clergy, a brand-new idea.

Pole's vision of the Church can be seen in orders to bishops to remain in their dioceses and restrain their style of living. It is noticeable that, of the new bishops appointed during Mary's reign, none was a career royal civil servant, and few had their primary training in canon law rather than theology, as had been so common in the Church before 1533. Indeed, the virtually unanimous and unprecedented refusal of Mary's bishops to co-operate with Elizabeth I showed that morale had returned to Catholicism.

Similarly, an active Catholic party formed among the gentry, an abiding legacy of the Marian regime to Elizabeth. This meant local polarisation, increased by the bitterness engendered by Mary's burn-

# Burnings that fired the imagination

Few people in the 16th century thought that it was a bad thing to burn heretics. (John Foxe was an exception.) We worry about the individual's agony and the affront to freedom of conscience; they worried about the damage done to society and the insult to God which heresy represented.

So Henry VIII burned heretics, some of them close friends of cautious Archbishop Cranmer. He also burned Friar John Forest (with a miraculous image as firewood), calling him a heretic for affirming traditional religion, although later Protestant regimes never again labelled Roman Catholicism as heresy.

Edward's regime was notably merciful to Catholics. Although it imprisoned and deprived conservative bishops, there was no mass persecution, apart from the political executions of the 1549 western rebels. Instead, two radicals died for heresy, as Dudley's Government (genuinely nervous of religious extremism) burned the unitarian activists Joan Bocher and George van Parris, and devoted much energy to searching out similar enthusiasts. This was ironical, because in 1547 Somerset had abolished the medieval heresy laws to protect Protestants; the renewed burnings were justified by the royal prerogative.

Mary's burnings of Protestants were a serious miscalculation. Bishop Gardiner had pressed for them, but Mary obstinately backed the continuing campaign when both he and the Queen's Spanish advisers saw that it was proving counter-productive. Of nearly 300 burnings, geographical distribution was patchy, with no more than three executions in Wales and only one in all English counties west of Salisbury. Even within dioceses heavily affected, there were concentrations in particular counties or specific areas — Suffolk in the Norwich diocese, Essex in the London diocese, or east Sussex in Chichester —

evidence that initiatives came primarily not from church officials but from lay magistrates, particularly those who subsequently remained Catholics under Elizabeth.

Protestant pamphleteering energy was already orchestrating popular indignation before any publication by John Foxe; the damage done to Protestantism by the Jane Grey fiasco was expunged, and divisions among the Edwardian Protestant leadership paled into insignificance when the former rivals, Bishops Ridley and Hooper, both died in the flames.

Cranmer's burning ought to have been the ultimate triumph for Mary's regime, but he made a last-minute withdrawal of his signed recantations, and ostentatiously placed his writing-hand first into the fire. Foxe's enormously influential and constantly revised book *Acts and Monuments* ("Foxe's Book of Martyrs") turned such sufferings into a struggle of heroism against evil that affected the English imagination for the next four centuries.

Flames of martyrdom: the burning of Thomas Cranmer. *Illustration from John Foxe's Acts and Monuments (1563). Photo © by permission of the British Library*

## CHRONOLOGY

**1547** Death of Henry VIII; accession of Edward VI. Edward Seymour Earl of Hertford becomes Duke of Somerset and Lord Protector

**1548** English Order of Communion stipulates that all communicate and receive in both kinds

**1549** First full English Prayer Book; rebellion in the West Country; commotions in south-east England. Somerset deposed; John Dudley Earl of Warwick leads Privy Council

**1550** Cranmer publishes ordinal. All stone altars destroyed

**1551** Somerset executed. Warwick becomes Duke of Northumberland

**1552** Second English Prayer Book

**1553** Death of Edward VI. Reign of Jane Grey; *coup* of Mary I

**1554** Mary marries Philip II of Spain. Papal obedience restored

**1556** Thomas Cranmer burnt at the stake; Reginald Pole becomes Archbishop of Canterbury

**1558** Death of Mary I and Cardinal Pole; accession of Elizabeth I

ings. The energy of certain JPs in promoting the burnings was a proof of the effectiveness of unprecedented purges of the justices' bench. This solid basis of support for Marian changes would have expanded in time.

The regime faced only one serious uprising, Wyatt's rebellion of 1554, and, despite prolonging it through incompetence and near-panic, did not have major difficulty in defeating it. Convinced Protestants among the gentry either fled abroad (a minority) or preserved their faith in a passive fashion, semi-conforming rather like their mirror image, "church papists", in later Protestant reigns.

After these beginnings, what was needed was time, not simply to restore structures administrative and architectural, but also to restore patterns of mind.

It would take education to restore meaning to the complex of traditional beliefs: new university colleges and schools. The Society of Jesus, in the first flush of its success and energy, would have galvanised what was begun; indeed, Pole and the Jesuit founder, Ignatius Loyola, had been on friendly terms. However, other preoccupations and ill-luck postponed the arrival of a Jesuit representative until a month before Pole's death.

Death was the greatest enemy of the struggle for Catholic restoration. Gardiner, Mary's ablest and most experienced minister, died in 1555. A great influenza epidemic of 1557-59 was crucial in weakening the Marian leadership, in which the generation that had grown to maturity before the schism of the 1530s was disproportionately represented: ageing bishops and justices of the peace were easy prey for the disease.

In the midst of this was the ultimate disaster of Mary's cancer, the cruel truth about her last hopes of a pregnancy to provide a Catholic heir. She and Cardinal Pole died within hours of each other.

# ANTI-PAPIST, ANTI-PURITAN

*Patrick Collinson*

*Elizabeth was conservative in religion, but her Church's leaders were iconoclasts. We assess the settlement.*

It is a persistent myth of Anglicanism, an "-ism" not given a name before the 19th century, that the Elizabethan Settlement of Religion established a Church of the *via media* (an expression associated, especially, with John Henry Newman). The notion is very Victorian, in its reaffirmation of a kind of Catholic churchmanship, its proudly insular exceptionalism, and in a kind of Hegelianism: Protestant thesis under Edward VI, Marian antithesis, Elizabethan synthesis.

Generations of theological students learned from standard manuals on the Thirty-Nine Articles that their Church taught something more "balanced" than the Lutheran doctrine of salvation by faith alone, although an informed glance at Cranmer's homily on salvation will find that that was exactly what it did teach.

But if "Anglicanism" was unheard of in the later 16th century, the Church of England was a local and political entity, a portion of the Church Universal with its own distinctive features and qualities, and, in an age marked by eloquent patriotism, it was possible to take some local pride in these.

Archbishop John Whitgift (1583-1604) could maintain, when circumstances warranted, that his Church was in no way beholden to Geneva, while, in the next generation, George Herbert extolled as "dear Mother" not the Church, but "the British Church": "A fine aspect in fit aray, Neither too mean, nor yet too gay." "Too gay" was "she on the hills", meaning Rome; "too mean" was "she in the valley", an almost naked Geneva.

But this was poetic rhetoric, against which to set words of Bishop Joseph Hall: "Blessed be God, there is no difference in any essential matter betwixt the Church of England and her sisters of the Reformation." Sisters meant Protestants of the Reformed, or, in vulgar parlance, Calvinist persuasion.

Much depended, of course, on what was meant by "essential matter". The reformed Church of England had its distinctive differences, notably the retention of an episcopal hierarchy and a relatively unreconstructed liturgy, although these features were not yet accorded the significance which would later attach to them, and were reckoned inessential, or, in the language of the time, "indifferent". Far from being a half-way house to or from Rome, the Elizabethan Church, in its clerical and representative leadership, held Rome to be absolutely false, Antichristian.

## The religion of Elizabethans

So the Church which Elizabeth built was not really a Church of the middle way, but, as it was deftly described at the time, "a constrained union of Papists and Protestants".

A. F. Pollard, the Gladstonian who once dominated Tudor historical studies, believed that under Elizabeth universal suffrage would have returned the pope. Although in the 16th century such matters were not put to the vote, more recent historians have good reason to doubt that Protestantism was yet popular, except in the sense that it recruited a cross-section of society, including representatives of those lower orders often referred to as "the people".

Most of the victims of the Marian burnings had been very ordinary people, of both sexes. But they were still in a minority, as people with strong religious convictions (as distinct from habits) usually are. The trick in making a Protestant settlement of religion stick was to sell it to that social majority for whom "religion" was part and parcel of good-neighbourhood, and of all the changing scenes of life; to make it as a instinctive as what Elizabethans remembered as "the old religion". It would take time.

Whether time would be given was one of those things which Elizabethans could not know. Mary had not been given time, and another change of religion was more likely than not. As an examination candidate once wrote, "Elizabeth never had a moment's peace because Mary Queen of Scots was always hoovering in the background." But at some point, the insomniac historian needs to start counting a minority of Catholics rather than a gaggle of Protestants in order to get to sleep.

Historians continue to disagree about when and where to place that alteration; but almost all agree that eventually it did happen. One of the most Catholic countries in Europe became, if not one of the most Protestant, the most virulently anti-Catholic.

## Elizabeth: an odd Protestant

Elizabeth's personal contribution to this process will always be debatable. She was reluctant to open windows in men's souls, and the windows of her own soul were heavily curtained. She was a Protestant by her birth, and by upbringing. But what kind of Protestant?

Hot Protestant spin-doctors constructed her not as a Protestant heroine, but as the chosen instrument of a Protestant God, who was made to say: "Love me and I will love you." If she were to "juggle" with God, "look for no more favour than Saul had showed to him."

That she was a woman laid her open to this kind of advice; and it was needed. She was thought not to take sufficiently seriously the threat posed to her state and her person by international Catholicism. This was a woman who still used the old Catholic oaths, "by the mass", "by God's body". She was attached to such religious symbols as the cross, which for Reformed Protestants was an odious idol; and she retained it in her own chapel.

Her dislike of preaching, except in small and controlled doses, made her a rather odd sort of Protestant, for Protestants believed that preaching was the "ordinary" means of salvation. Her second Archbishop of Canterbury, Edmund Grindal (1575-1583), could not stomach her views on this matter, and allowed himself to be sacked.

We probably owe to this odd Protestant the survival of our cathedrals and their music. For Protestants, there was really no alternative to Elizabeth; but, if there had been, her position would not have been as secure as it was.

## Protestants in power

The Queen and her religion was but one factor reshaping the religion of the English people. By processes still not fully understood, what we may call copper-bottomed Protestants rapidly gained positions of influence and real power. In the House of Commons they made a kind of moral majority as early as Elizabeth's first parliament.

Most of the bishoprics, conveniently vacated by Mary's bishops, who had either died or refused to conform, went initially to Protestants who had spent Mary's reign in exile in Germany and Switzerland, not to so-called "Nicodemites" (Calvin's word for them), who, like Elizabeth herself, had compromised and conformed. (Matthew Parker, Archbishop of Canterbury from 1559 to 1575, was the exception to prove this rule.) Again, we do not know why and how, and we cannot say that they were necessarily her personal choices. It is thanks to these dedicated iconoclasts that in the whole country only one crucifix of the kind that stood on the rood beams of pre-Reformation parish churches survives.

The majority of the hereditary peers and their families were still at least small-c Catholics. But the Privy Council, in effect the government, was soon dominated by Protestants. William Cecil Lord Burghley was only a little less "forward" (in contemporary jargon) than Sir Francis Walsingham and the Queen's perennial favourite, the Earl of Leicester. Increasingly, the religious polarisation of the international scene favoured the adoption by "little England" of a self-consciously Protestant identity.

Locally, in the counties, market towns and parishes of Elizabethan England, the Reformation was being made piecemeal, especially in Essex and East Anglia, but also in the East Midlands and the West Country, and, above all, in that locality which was London, busily exporting its own culture to the rest of the nation.

The principal agency was Protestant preaching, as the patronage of "godly" gentlemen and townsmen replaced a generation of unreconstructed priests, inherited from the Henrician and Marian past, with a new kind of ministry, Protestant and university-educated. This did not happen on a significant scale until the 1570s, the decade when the Reformation really happened.

## The Elizabethan Settlement

The bare bones of the religious settlement were defined in 1559 by the Act of Supremacy and the Act of Uniformity, to which the Book of Common Prayer was legally a mere appendix, a piece of Erastianism never authorised by the clergy in Convocation.

The parliamentary process is poorly documented, but the ingenious hypothesis of the Elizabethan historian J. E. Neale that Elizabeth had not wanted to proceed immediately to the re-establishment of Protestantism by means of a re-enacted Edwardian Prayer Book (essentially the second Edwardian Book of 1552), but was nudged into it by a militant tendency in the House of Commons, is implausible. It is likely that she did intend the settlement more or less as it happened, but had to overcome traditionalist opposition in the Lords.

That Elizabeth took and bequeathed to her successors the title of "Supreme Governor" rather than "Supreme Head" was a concession in that direction. Small but significant changes were made to 1552, either to placate this opposition, or to cater for Elizabeth's own conservatism. These were the fusion of the words of administration from the earlier 1549 liturgy, "the body of Christ", to those of 1552, "take and eat this" (and what was "this"?), which accommodated anyone, perhaps including the Queen, still attached to belief in some sort of real presence; and the insertion of a rubric requiring the use of those church "ornaments" still retained in 1549, which meant especially liturgical vestments, the outward appearance of worship.

When in the summer of 1559 Elizabeth promulgated her Royal Injunctions for the Church, these included further steps in a conservative direction, including the requirement, which was inconsistent with what Parliament had just enacted, that communion be administered in unleavened wafers.

Such was the Elizabethan compromise. But Elizabeth's subjects were allowed to make their own compromises only in the privacy of their consciences and souls. So far as their bodies were concerned, the Act of

Arch anti-Puritan: Queen Elizabeth I, "odd sort of Protestant", at prayer: from Queen Elizabeth's Prayer Book (1569). *Photo © Lambeth Palace Library, London, UK/Bridgeman Art Library*

Of the period: a 17th-century font cover in St Clement's, Terrington. The font is reached through hinged doors whose inner faces are decorated with paintings of the Baptism and Temptation. *Photo © Paul Barker/Country Life Picture Library*

Prayer Book man: John Evelyn, the 17th-century diarist, by Robert Walker. *Photo © by courtesy of the National Portrait Gallery, London*

Uncontainable: Portrait of John Wesley by an unknown artist (1789). *Photo © by courtesy of the National Portrait Gallery, London*

Sermon-time: Dr King Preaching at the Old St Paul's before James I (by J. Stow). *Photo © Society of Antiquaries London, UK/Bridgeman Art Library*

Uniformity required them to fill the pews of their parish churches twice every Sunday and holy day, or pay a fine.

## Reform stops here

Whereas many Protestants assumed that this was merely the starting-point for further reforms, for the Queen it was where the process stopped. Anything not so far altered was to stay, an "anything" which ranged from baptism by midwives to bishops and the rest of the unreformed structure of the Church, including the courts, patronage, and tithes.

When Convocation met in conjunction with her second Parliament in 1563, a synod now headed by a house of Protestant bishops, attempts were made, with episcopal backing, to build and improve on the limited 1559 settlement with a whole basket of robust measures including, for example, the replacement of "all curious singing and playing of the organs" with metrical ("Geneva") psalms. But nothing came of this, beyond a kind of English Confession of Faith in the form of the Thirty-Nine Articles.

The Articles were acceptable to reformed Protestants, but only just, and their very limited applicability meant that the Church of England would never become a confessional Church on the model of its continental sisters: a recipe in the long term for Anglican latitude. Disappointed in Convocation, forward Protestants, who again included many of the bishops, hoped to make some progress in Parliament; but by 1572 it was clear that this was another blind alley.

Out of the consequent frustration a challenge was mounted to the half-reformed Church in the form of an organised movement of Nonconformity, Puritanism, which blamed the bishops for Elizabeth's inertia, and turned against them.

## Papists and Puritans

In the 19th century, the established Church held the high, privileged and middle ground, flanked on either side by substantial but marginal bodies of Catholic and Protestant dissent. Historians back-projected this scenario into the later 16th century, and described both Elizabethan Catholicism and Puritanism as minority deviations from the broad centre of established Anglicanism, which represented the norm and the future.

This was not a total distortion. Both Catholics and Puritan Nonconformists took exception to the Church of the Elizabethan Settlement. For Catholics it was simply a false Church, its adherents heretics or, at best, schismatics, and the hard core of Catholicism was defined by "recusancy", a conscientious refusal to have anything to do with what now went on in parish churches. The missionary and pastoral efforts of the Jesuits and other seminary-trained priests laid the foundations for the ongoing recusant Church which the Victorian cardinals Wiseman, Newman and Manning would inherit, the blood of the Catholic martyrs its seed-corn.

Puritans, for the most part, grudgingly accepted the validity of the Church and of its doctrine and sacraments, only a minority choosing the radical course of total separation from "Babylon"; but for them it was "but halfly reformed". Out of an initial rejection of what the hard men called "shells and chippings of popery", such as the surplice and the sign of the cross in baptism, emerged rejection of episcopal hierarchy as in itself popish, for the New Testament prescribed a ministry of pastors, doctors and elders: the Genevan model. This Presbyterian challenge was seen off by Archbishop Whitgift and his successor, Richard

Bancroft, but they could not have done it without the backing of the arch anti-Puritan, Queen Elizabeth herself.

### 'Church papistry'

However, Catholics and Puritans took even greater exception to each other, and sometimes it seemed that there was no middle ground. For those whose enemies nicknamed them Puritans, recusancy was but the tip of a large iceberg of covert "popery", and this was not all fantasy. We now recognise the continuing strength of "church papistry", the religion of closet Catholics who made their pragmatic terms with the legally enforced religion.

But in these matters perceptions are usually more important than facts. For Puritans, those who were not for them were against them, and that went for those many "cold statute Protestants" whose conformity was merely outward and suspect. We could say that when most people became Protestants, Protestants became Puritans, denounced as such not only by papists, but by the social majority which rejected their sectarian, sermon-gadding, alehouse-renouncing lifestyle.

When the Puritans were confronted by Whitgift and Bancroft and many other card-carrying establishmentarians, it was clear what was being opposed. But it was not so clear what it was that was being defended, other than the virtue of obedient conformity, until a new champion entered the lists: Richard Hooker.

## CHRONOLOGY

**1558** Accession of Elizabeth I
**1559** After Parliament of 1559, Prayer Book replaces Latin mass as only legal liturgy
**1563** First Convocation after Elizabethan Settlement sanctions the Thirty-Nine Articles
**1570** Pope Pius V excommunicates and deposes Elizabeth
**1570** Thomas Cartwright's Cambridge lectures advocating Presbyterianism
**1577** Archbishop Edmund Grindal is effectively removed from office
**1580-1581** Jesuits Edmund Campion and Robert Persons enter England; Campion executed
**1583** John Whitgift becomes Archbishop of Canterbury
**1584, 1586** Puritan campaign in Parliament reaches climax
**1587** Mary Queen of Scots executed at Fotheringhay
**1588-89** Marprelate Tracts
**1590-91** Trial of Puritan ministers in High Commission and Star Chamber
**1603** Death of Elizabeth
**1604** Death of Whitgift

# RICHARD HOOKER: ANGLICAN LOGIC

## *Rowan Williams*

If there is one person who might be thought to be the representative voice of historic Anglicanism, it is probably Richard Hooker. Yet in his lifetime he was certainly not seen in that light. Recent scholarship has tended to view him almost as the inventor of classical Anglicanism rather than its representative; and, while this is exaggerated, the point has some validity.

At a time when Anglican identity was a fiercely and violently contested matter, he drew out the logic of the Anglican position more carefully than any other 16th-century writer, effectively challenging his opponents to admit that the Church they wanted was a different kind of community located in a different kind of society.

Although much of the debate that prompted the composition of his great treatise *On the Laws of Ecclesiastical Polity* was aroused by attempts

Church of England apologist: portrait traditionally accepted to be Richard Hooker (artist unknown). *Photo © by courtesy of the National Portrait Gallery, London*

at state repression of religious dissidents in the 1590s, the quarrel between him and the incipient Puritan party was not about the right of the state to enforce religious uniformity. Both he and opponents like Thomas Cartwright assumed that Christian society was an undivided whole, in which the Christian prince had the right and duty to control expressions of faith. Cartwright, at one time a divinity professor at Cambridge, believed that the legal system of the Old Testament ought to be imposed by the law of the land.

The heart of the disagreement lay, you could say, in attitudes to history. For the Puritans represented by Cartwright, what was needed was a thoroughgoing reconstruction of Church and society on strictly and exclusively biblical principles.

This was believed to involve the rejection of most ecclesiastical ceremony, and a strictly negative evaluation of past and present Catholic practice as directly opposed to essential Christian doctrines about election and grace.

Hooker's response assumes that the reasoned judgements of human beings in history, their self-determinations and self-limitations, may be guided by God. Monarchy is not something that is absolutely given from heaven; it is the way in which human society agrees to limit itself and concentrate authority. Episcopacy is not explicitly laid down by Christ, but it is the way in which the Christian community agrees to concentrate its authority. Once these self-limiting decisions are made, it is idle to try to start again from scratch, in politics or church government.

But to root governmental structures in this way is also to say that their purpose and their rationale cannot be understood apart from the nature of the entire society that delegates authority in this way. The king is not above the law, but is the definitive voice of the law. This also means that, even if the king is the supreme authority in the life of the national Church, he cannot *create* law for the Church, but only administer the Church's laws as they are worked out in the light of revelation.

Behind all this argumentation is a profound and basic sense of law itself as the order of the universe. Natural law can never be set aside, because it is what human nature essentially is moulded to; and the point of natural law is to direct us to the eternal contemplation and enjoyment of God.

Hooker's theology has a strongly contemplative element, growing out of his deep appreciation of St Augustine, and indeed Aquinas. Specific laws made by any human community must be understood and evaluated according as they help us towards our eternal goal of loving and enjoying God. And this means that many specific laws, in the political and the ecclesiastical community, will need review and revision. They no longer serve the goal they once did. But there is nothing relativistic about this; human nature does not change, and what constitutes its central good and highest hope remains the same.

This allows Hooker to reject the idea that there could be a simple and God-given church discipline set down once for all in the Bible. God guides the decisions of the Church; once those decisions are made, they are not to be ignored or reversed, but they must still be distinguished from the law written into creation itself. But this interest in the slow growth of wise practice in history is related to his scepticism about the

## CHRONOLOGY

**1554** Richard Hooker born near Exeter

**1567-84** Student and Fellow of Corpus Christi College, Oxford

**1584-85** Rector of Drayton Beauchamp

**1585-91** Master of the Temple; controversy with Walter Travers on points of Calvinist theology and church practice; several influential sermons

**1588** Married to Joan Churchman

**1591-95** Subdean of Salisbury; Archbishop Whitgift institutes harsher measures against radical Puritans

**1592** Preface and first four books of *Laws of Ecclesiastical Polity*

**1595-1600** Rector of Bishopsbourne, Kent

**1596** Book V of the *Laws* published

**1599** Attacked by Calvinist opponents in *A Christian Letter of Certain English Protestants*

**1600** Death of Richard Hooker

**1648** Books VI and VIII of the *Laws* published

**1661** Book VII of the *Laws* published

kind of Calvinism that ignored growth, struggle and doubt in the Christian life. What he has to say about this, especially in some of his sermons, finds echoes in both John of the Cross and George Herbert.

His claim that Roman Catholics might be true members of the authentic Catholic Church, since they could possess genuine faith even in the midst of unclarity and even error, so long as they set their hearts on Christ, caused great scandal; but it fits not only with a general sympathy for patristic and high scholastic thought, but also with his doctrine of faith as something quite compatible with areas of immaturity, error and incompleteness in any individual believing subject. The basic condition is incorporation by faith into the life of the incarnate and glorified Son. There is no vagueness about his trinitarian and incarnational theology.

Though encouraged by Archbishop Whitgift to pursue his labours, he was never a completely "safe" voice; and his dense style produced problems of its own. But his remarkable mixture of pragmatic historical argument and intense theological and cosmological perceptions undoubtedly helped to give Anglicanism what was for a long time a very distinctive "orthodoxy": the firm defence of the Nicene faith, allied to a quiet but profound spirituality, and a conservative but not uncritical pragmatism about ecclesial and national government.

# THE SETTLEMENT THAT TOOK TIME TO SETTLE

*Judith Maltby*

*Historians differ about the means and the timescale of the reception of the Church of England's new position. Was liturgy as important a factor as preaching?*

There was a time when a textbook on the English Reformation could confidently draw to a close with the settlement of 1559, leaving us with the vision of a young, yet shrewd, queen on the throne, under whose supreme governorship the English Church was secure.

As at the end of a romantic novel, the reader could rest assured that, despite all the trials and tribulations catalogued in the preceding pages, a happy marriage lay ahead, and there was no need to go into the particulars.

Increasingly, however, historians of English Christianity speak of a "Long Reformation", and of a settlement that settled very little. England's reception of Protestantism is seen more and more as a drawn-out affair, initially imposed "from above", and trickling down to a hostile or, at least, unenthusiastic population.

One recent essay by Nicholas Tyacke on the concept of the Long Reformation provocatively pushes the reception of reformed Christianity to around 1800 — presumably just about in time for the English Church to be rescued from it by the Oxford Movement.

One of the reasons for this move from "fast" to "slow" has been the scholarly shift towards considering the religious landscape of England "from below" rather than "from above". Local studies of the Reformation have been one of the most important developments of the past few decades.

Broadly speaking, the result has been an emerging consensus that the reception of reform in the localities was in the end — in the words of the author of the recent magisterial biography of Thomas Cranmer, Diarmaid MacCulloch — "a howling success". None the less, it was a slow and bumpy road: much more a process of osmosis than one of conversion.

## Importance of liturgy

Nevertheless, *how* did it happen? Recent important work highlighting the vigour and vitality of late-medieval Christianity makes that question even more pressing and difficult.

"Generally necessary for salvation": baptism (*top*) and receiving communion in the 1570s, from Richard Day, *A Booke of Christian Prayers*, London 1578. *Photo © by permission of the SYNDICS of the Cambridge University Library*

On this point, historians of the period are much less of one mind. An emphasis on the influence of Protestant preaching has been fashionable: a view in which the people of England were, one might say, simply talked out of being Roman Catholics, and talked into being Protestants of however peculiar a kind. But that, surely, is to over-privilege the pulpit; and one has some sympathy with Bishop Lancelot Andrewes in his frequent criticism of some members of the established Church who, in his mind, reduced all religion to a sermon.

Increasingly, interest has turned to the less "intellectual" aspects of the post-settlement Church of England, focusing on the role and place of the liturgy, and specifically the Book of Common Prayer. Even one of the fiercest critics of the impact of the Reformation on lay piety, Eamon Duffy, has said in his highly important book *The Stripping of the Altars*, "Cranmer's sombrely magnificent prose, read week by week,

# Lancelot Andrewes

## *Kenneth Stevenson*

Lancelot Andrewes (1555-1626) is probably one of the most significant figures of the Stuart Church. Born in Barking, he was educated at Merchant Taylors' School, and thereafter at Pembroke Hall, Cambridge, where he attracted attention as a brilliant scholar, and as a preacher.

In addition to being Master of Pembroke, he was made Vicar of St Giles's, Cripplegate, London, and a Chaplain in Ordinary to the Queen in 1589, which meant that he began to preach before the Court. In 1601, he became Dean of Westminster: this office involved him in both the funeral of Elizabeth and the coronation of James.

Elizabeth had — it is alleged — offered him two diocesan bishoprics, but these Andrewes refused, because of the Queen's habit of taking her cut of episcopal revenues in such circumstances; Andrewes was good with money, as the Fellows of Pembroke knew well.

His relationship with James seems to have been a close one from the start. He was made Bishop of Chichester in 1605, moving to Ely in 1609, and finally to Winchester in 1619. In addition, he held the post of Lord High Almoner in 1605, which brought him into direct contact with the Court, as a regular preacher at the great festivals.

He had to surrender these responsibilities when he was made Dean of the Chapel Royal in 1619, after which his royal preachments continued, though at a less exalted scale. But his influence was still considerable enough for King Charles I to give instructions for a special collection of his 96 sermons to be published after Andrewes's death in 1626.

What kind of a thinker was Andrewes? There has been a tendency to paint him in romantic terms, even as a kind of Anglo-Catholic before his time. Nowadays he is seen in much more nuanced terms. The language of his sermons is rich. The texts for each occasion are characteristically thrown in every direction — at the end, usually calling the faithful to communion, and to look forward to the joys of heaven. Patristic quotations abound. Andrewes has a penchant for citing Augustine and John Chrysostom, just to show a balance between West and East.

His stance is often vocally against the more Puritan strand of the Church, which could over-emphasise individual experience. But he is always a loyal son of the Reformation, insisting on the illimitability of the grace of God, as he makes plain in a series of sermons on the Lord's Prayer published in 1611, the year when the Authorised Version of the Bible appeared, a project in which Andrewes played a prominent part.

Perhaps his lasting legacy lies in his *Preces Privatae* ("private prayers"), which he compiled for his own use. They have been translated several times from the Latin-Greek-Hebrew original in which he cast them, and their importance lies in their combination of biblical, patristic and Reformation piety, as well as their astonishingly frequent parallels with the sermons.

He has attracted a great deal of attention this century from people as different as T. S. Eliot, the poet, and Nicholas Lossky, the Russian Orthodox theologian.

entered and possessed [the laity's] minds, and became the fabric of their prayer, the utterance of their most solemn and vulnerable moments." This is a striking statement from a staunch critic of Cranmer and other proponents of the "new gospel".

It must be understood, however, that this discovery of the ability of liturgy to shape and inform religious consciousness is not a nostalgic endorsement of the literary qualities of the Prayer Book. T. S. Eliot warned his contemporaries that the Authorised Version of the Bible had such a profound effect on English letters not because figures like Herbert or Donne thought it was great literature, but because they believed it to be the word of God.

# George Herbert

Born of Welsh aristocratic stock, George Herbert (1593-1633) was educated at Westminster School, and at Trinity College, Cambridge, where he was made a Fellow in 1614. In 1620 he became the University's Public Orator, a post which brought him into the limelight on many state and ecclesiastical occasions there.

He seemed to be marked out for a career at Court, but for some reason — the death of King James in 1625, or a personal crisis of some kind — he underwent what we would nowadays call a career-change, and in the following year was appointed to Leighton Bromswold, near Huntingdon.

He had befriended Nicholas Ferrar, who was ordained in the same year, at nearby Little Gidding, where Ferrar founded a mixed religious community. The interior of Leighton Bromswold Church was reordered to Herbert's specifications, so that there were two twin ambos on opposite sides of the chancel, one for presiding at the offices and for prayer, the other for preaching.

Such an arrangement made the eloquent statement that worship was not just about coming to hear a sermon, but about praying as well, a theme that runs through the writings of others at the time, including Andrewes. Four years later, in 1630, Herbert moved to Salisbury to be Rector of Bemerton, a few miles from the Cathedral, where he was also Sub-Dean.

Herbert's time at Bemerton was short, but it bore great fruit. Two main publications have come down to us which were probably written, or at any rate completed, towards the end of his life.

The first is a collection of poems, *The Temple*, entrusted by him to Ferrar on his deathbed. This work is best-known today in three poems which are sung as hymns: "Teach me, my God and King", "The God of love my shepherd is", and "King of glory, King of peace".

Herbert's style is deceptively simple, as the numerous scholars who have studied him have pointed out. The influences (and possible sources) behind his work have come in for ever-closer scrutiny, notably by Elizabeth Clarke, who has shown how Herbert was aware of such Roman Catholic writers as Francis de Sales, but developed an approach to scripture as a living text in its own right.

Herbert has a genius for entering into the dark places of human experience, as well as for giving expression to great moments of joy. Many find in his poems (as in his dense eight-liner "Hope") an almost contemporary quest for faith as an acceptance of the reality of present life, without anaesthetics, in the face of a loving God who walks ahead of us.

Herbert's other main work, *The Country Parson*, which was not published until 1652, merits more attention than it has often received. In 37 pithy chapters, Herbert makes telling observations on the priestly life which, though sociologically distant from today, have a welcome profundity. They often echo poems in *The Temple*, as well as passages in the Prayer Book, such as in his treatment of baptism, for him a corporate celebration and an occasion for those present to "call to mind" their own baptism.

*Kenneth Stevenson*

Eliot's insight can fruitfully be applied to the Prayer Book: its influence was great precisely because English men and women believed they were worshipping God when they used it, not that they were in awe of its literary merits.

One of the great advantages of the Prayer Book over other means of inculcating reformed Christianity into the people of England is that it is a text which inhabited the worlds of the literate and the illiterate alike, because it is a text intended principally to be performed rather than read. Like death, it was a great equaliser. The Prayer Book provided an experience for all people, whatever their social class, gender or age — and in that sense provided truly *common* prayer — even if the response to the liturgy was informed by those categories.

Historians are coming to appreciate the significance of the liturgy's repetitive character, of the shape that it gave to the day, the week, and the year, and of its association with critical aspects of the life-cycle through the occasional offices. The claims of the self-defining and self-promoting "godly" (or "Puritans") to a monopoly on sincere reformed Christianity is at last receiving some long-overdue scrutiny and scepticism from scholars.

Ferrar's church: the Jacobean interior of St John's, Little Gidding. *Photo © Paul Barker/Country Life Library*

## Hostility to the BCP

There were those within the national Church who were hostile towards the lawful liturgy as the chief example, along with episcopacy, of remnants of popery. Or, in the words of one particularly insufferable Cheshire curate in the early 17th century: "I am perswaded that the reading of Common prayer hath beene the meanes of sending many souls into hell. That the booke of Common prayer doth stinke in the nostrails of god. That reading of Common prayers is as bad or worse than the mumbling of the masse upon beades."

He was not a member of the Prayer Book Society, one suspects, though he was indisputably a member of the Church of England. Yet, alongside such hostility, even contempt, there is evidence that, by the early years of the 17th century, the Prayer Book had indeed "entered and possessed [the laity's] minds and became the fabric of their prayer".

The evidence for such an assertion is largely not to be found in sermons or in formal theological works. Then, as now, such sources often tell us more about clerical and episcopal fantasies about the laity than about anything else.

Rather, we must turn and dig in parish and diocesan records: these are the sources that allow us to get the closest to the lives of the majority who make up "the Church" (not that one would know it from the way a great deal of church history is written): the laity.

A significant resource for the historian of the early Stuart Church are the records of the ecclesiastical courts, while we need to bear in mind that a court case means that relations in a parish have broken down to a considerable extent.

## Challenges to nonconformity

With that warning in mind, the records of the Church's courts open a window on lay support for the lawful liturgy of the Church of England against both "godliness" and simple negligence — indeed, it is often hard to tell which the clergyman is suffering from in the sources. Through this window we learn of ordinary parishioners who challenged their clergy's nonconformity. Take, for example, the complaints of the flock of the Manchester curate Ralph Kirk in 1604. Kirk failed to wear the surplice, use the sign of the cross in baptism, and administer com-

# William Laud

William Laud (1573-1645) is perhaps one of the most controversial figures of the Stuart Church. Born in Reading in 1573, he went up to St John's College, Oxford, in 1589, and became a Fellow, under the Presidency of John Buckeridge, who, as a bishop, preached at Andrewes's funeral, and collaborated with Laud in editing the 96 sermons published after his death.

Laud succeeded Buckeridge as President of St John's, and exercised strong discipline on the college. He was also made Dean of Gloucester in 1616, causing a storm when he insisted that the altar be fixed at the east end of the chancel, and decorated with an elaborate cloth and candlesticks. This was a custom favoured by the more advanced churchmen of the time; the more common practice, from the Elizabethan Church, was to keep the table at the east end when not in use, but to move it down into the chancel when the holy communion was celebrated.

In 1621, Laud was made Bishop of St Davids, a see he held until 1626, when he was moved to Bath & Wells; he then went to London in 1628. He was an avid supporter of the monarchy, and became close to Charles I, so that when the vacancy occurred at Canterbury in 1633, there was little doubt that Laud would become Archbishop.

In contrast to Andrewes's natural stature and comparative ease in persuasion, Laud was physically small and unimpressive, yet was an instinctive controversialist. He preached at the opening of Parliament before King Charles I, asserting the divine right of the monarchy, and took part enthusiastically in the Court of High Commission, which set about enforcing high-church liturgical practices that were unwelcome — and often anathema — to the moderate as well as the more definitely Puritan members of the Church. Those who got in his way were punished, sometimes with torture. In the growing confrontation between King and Parliament, Laud was imprisoned in the Tower of London in 1641. His trial did not take place until 1644, and he was beheaded for treason on 10 January 1645.

Unshakeable faith: William Laud, in a portrait by an unknown artist. *Photo © by courtesy of the National Portrait Gallery, London*

Laud's trial is well documented, and hardly qualifies as fair. He was accused of using wafer bread and incense, neither of which was true, although the more eirenic Andrewes managed to get away with both. He was also accused of having Christ the Good Shepherd engraved on chalices, a charge which he rebutted by quoting the third-century North African theologian Tertullian: "The shepherd will play the patron whom you depict on your chalice."

Laud compiled his own private devotions, for his daily use. They are simpler than Andrewes's, and they have the flavour of a man of simple but unshakeable faith. Among his theological works is the account of a public debate in 1622 with a Jesuit who took up the name of John Fisher. In it Laud defended the English Church as the "nearest of any Church now in being to the Primitive Church". When Laud died, his pet tortoise lived on at Lambeth Palace for another 108 years, until it was killed accidentally by a gardener.

*Kenneth Stevenson*

munion according to the canons and rubrics. Even more importantly, his parishioners complained that he attempted to curtail *their* participation in the liturgy itself.

"For the manner of morninge prayer whereas divers of the parishe, who have been used to helpe the parishe clarke, to readd verse for verse [i.e. to make the responses] with the Curate for fourtye yeares laste past and more. . . The sayde Ralph Kirke hath of late tymes not permitted them so to doe."

Even more emotionally charged, then as now, were the rituals associated with rites of passage. Parents and godparents were at times in conflict with "precise" clergy who scrupled at ceremonies such as the sign of the cross in baptism or baptising on a day other than Sunday. The latter instance could, and did, in a time of high infant mortality, result in children dying unbaptised — something which clearly added to parental feelings of loss and grief.

Improperly conducted funerals could be the straw that broke the laity's back with a godly or negligent minister, as was the case of the inhabitants of Ellington, Huntingdonshire, in 1602. Among the long list of abuses cited by the parishioners of one Anthony Armitage, the incident that prompted their court action was his tardiness for the funeral of one of their neighbours. Not only was Armitage late, he refused to meet the corpse at the churchyard gate or to read the appointed prayers. In the case of some funerals, the Vicar sent the parish clerk to do his job, as one witness remarked: "[Armitage] appointed the clerk of the parish to put them into the earth very undecently and undutifully, contrary to the order of the Book of Common Prayer."

## Different 'integrities'

Cases of this kind make the explosion on the eve of the Civil War of petitioning to Parliament for the Book of Common Prayer and episcopacy all the more explicable.

As petitioners from Cheshire remarked in late 1641: "Our pious, laudable, and ancient forme of Divine Service, composed by the holy Martyrs, and worthy Instruments of Reformation established by the prudent Sages of the State (your Religious Predecessors) honoured by the approbation of many learned forraign Divines, subscribed by the Ministry of the whole Kingdome, and with such generall content received by all the Laity, that scarse any Family or person that can reade, but are furnished with Bookes of Common Prayer: In the conscionable use whereof many Christian hearts have found unspeakable joy and comfort, wherein the famous Church of *England*, our deare Mother, hath just cause to glory; And may shee long flourish in the practisc of so blessed a *Lyturgy*."

This is the tradition that will be privileged and described retrospectively and anachronistically as "Anglicanism". It was not Anglicanism yet, but rather one considerable and, at times, spirited strand — one might even say "integrity" — existing and developing in relationship to others within the *Ecclesia Anglicana*.

## CHRONOLOGY

**1603** Death of Elizabeth I and accession of James VI of Scotland as James I of England; Millenary Petition produced outlining Puritan grievances with the Church of England

**1604** Hampton Court Conference called by James to address grievances in the established Church; Richard Bancroft, Bishop of London, consecrated Archbishop of Canterbury, and a new campaign against Nonconformity begins

**1605** Discovery of the Gunpowder Plot, and measures against Roman Catholic subjects intensify

**1607** Establishment of England's first permanent colony in Jamestown, Virginia

**1611** Publication of the Authorised Version of the Bible; George Abbot, Bishop of London, appointed Archbishop of Canterbury

**1625** Death of James I and accession of Charles I

**1629** Charles dissolves Parliament, and rules without the legislature for the next 11 years

**1633** William Laud, Bishop of London, appointed Archbishop of Canterbury; the Laudian party gains influence in the Church

**1640** After one abortive "Short Parliament", Charles calls the "Long Parliament" to meet his financial needs

**1641** Bills introduced to abolish episcopacy and the Courts of Star Chamber and High Commission

**1642** The King raises his standard at Nottingham, and the Civil War begins

THE SHEPHERDS ORACLES.

Hope

Charitie

Faith

Good workes.

Obedience

RELIGION

Written by Fran: Quarles.

London Printed for John Marriott and Richard Marriott &c. W.M sculp:

# HOW THE OLD CHURCH GREW ITS BACKBONE

*Judith Maltby*

*During the Common-wealth, English people felt the absence of the Christian year, the liturgy and the bishops who went with it, and their hearts grew fonder.*

Individual Anglicans have appealed to different periods of church history as underpinning their tradition. The Caroline divines of the 1630s, the Reformation, the Middle Ages, and the Patristic period are variously seen as definitive. The period chosen often, but not always, tells us something about the churchmanship of the apologist.

It is argued here that the persecutions and suppressions of the middle decades of the 17th century, a period usually passed over in embarrassment in confessional discourse, provided the experiences which helped to form a recognisable Anglican identity.

By the late 1640s, one of the central institutions of English society, its established Church, appeared to be the first significant victim of what would be called by some the English Revolution. Other institutions would follow its misfortune: the monarchy and the House of Lords, for example.

Through the 1640s, Parliament embarked on a series of items of legislation which achieved far more than taking away the Church of England's historic privileges and placing it on an equal footing with its emerging competitors in the religious marketplace.

It was not disestablishment that was achieved, but the abolition and the suppression of what were to many the established Church's most distinctive and best-loved features: the Book of Common Prayer, episcopacy, and the church year.

## Ban on feast days

The attack on the festivals of the Christian year was perhaps one of the Parliamentary government's greatest misreadings of the religious sensibilities of the English people.

It is worth remembering in current discussions about secularism that there was a debate in the 17th century, too, about how "religious" a festival Christmas was. Yet to many contemporaries, members of the clergy and laity alike, the government's continued observance of national "feast days" such as Armada Day or the discovery of the Gunpowder Plot, contained a bitter irony.

Church in danger: frontispiece of *The Shepherd's Oracles* by Francis Quarles (1646), depicting Charles I as defending the Church.
*Photo © by permission of the British Library*

The lay woman Elizabeth Newell provided a theological critique of this state of affairs in a series of poems she wrote in honour of the banned feast of Christmas from 1655 into the 1660s (this one was written for 1658):

> What! the messias born, and shall a day
> Bethought to much expensiveness to pay
> To that memorial; shall an Anniversie
> Be kept with ostentation to rehearse
> A mortal princes birthday, or defeat
> An Eighty Eight, or powder plots defeat[?] . . .
>
> And shall we venture to exterminate
> And starve at once the memory and date
> Of Christ incarnate, where in such a store
> Of joy to mortals lay, as never before
> The sun beheld, a Treasury of Bliss,
> The birth day of the world as well as his.

To Elizabeth Newell, her opponents lacked any proper understanding of Christology, or indeed a proper understanding of the relationship of the incarnation to salvation: "Ingrateful Man; It was for only thee/And for thy Restitution, that he/Did stoop to wear thy raggs . . . was content/Thus to affirme thy nature." It should be noted that her critique is clearly theological, not simply "spiritual".

## BCP goes underground

Despite the prolonged attack over several generations by elements within the established Church, the Book of Common Prayer proved harder to sink than might have been expected from the Puritan critique of it. Evidence for the liturgy's buoyancy abounds, and, despite its prohibited status, some English Christians continued to use it for worship.

The layman John Evelyn succeeded in finding churches in London itself which used the banned Prayer Book. On Christmas Day 1657, Evelyn and other devotees of the Prayer Book were attacked by Parliamentary troopers. He recorded in his famous diary: "I went with my wife &c: to Lond: to celebrate Christmas day. . . Sermon Ended, as [the minister] was giving us the holy Sacrament, The Chapell was surrounded with Souldiers: All the Communicants and Assembly surpriz'd & kept Prisoners by them. . . [They] examined me, why contrarie to an Ordinance made that none should any longer observe the superstitious time of the Nativity (so esteem'd by them) I durst offend, & particularly be at Common prayers, which they told me was but the Masse in English." Evelyn and his fellow communicants then proceeded to make their Christmas communions under testing circumstances.

"These wretched miscreants, held their muskets against us as we came up to receive the Sacred Elements, as if they would have shot us at the Altar, but yet suffering us to finish the Office of Communion, as perhaps [it was] not in their Instructions what they should do in case they found us in that Action."

In his diary, Evelyn provides numerous examples of both the use of the Book of Common Prayer and widespread observance of the holy days of the Prayer Book calendar — though, at certain times, government zeal was such that the Evelyn family had to make do with the private use of the Prayer Book at home.

## Clerics in the firing-line

Members of the clergy as well as of the laity could exhibit loyalty to the Book of Common Prayer, though their calling often put them, literally, in the direct line of fire.

To priests like John Hackett, who became Bishop of Coventry & Lichfield in 1661, faithfulness to the liturgy even in danger was a keystone. According to his contemporary biographer, Hackett coolly continued to read divine service even when a Parliamentary soldier of the Earl of Essex had a pistol pointed at him.

Hackett, and another future bishop, George Bull (consecrated Bishop of St Davids in 1705), each committed to memory the funeral service and the baptismal services respectively so that they could appear to be praying extempore. The ruse worked, as this account of a funeral of a prominent Puritan conducted by Hackett at the end of the Interregnum relates:

"There being a great concourse of men of the same fanatical principles [as the deceased], when the company heard all delivered by him [Hackett] without book, and, with free readiness, and profound gravity . . . they were strangely surprised and affected, professing that they had never heard a more suitable exhortation, or a more edifying exercise even from the very best and most precious men of their own persuasion!"

The assembled "godly" were aghast when Hackett revealed to them that not one syllable had been his own, and how "all was taken word for word out of the very office ordained for that purpose in the poor contemptible Book of Common Prayer." Examples of this type can be multiplied from around the country.

## Ejection of the clergy

Elizabeth Newell, John Evelyn and John Hackett are examples of

# Richard Baxter: Puritan who turned down a bishopric

## Kenneth Stevenson

Richard Baxter (1615-1691) was born in Rowton, in Shropshire, and attended Ludlow School. He tells of his confirmation by Bishop Thomas Morton, of Lichfield, in 1632; it took place "in a Churchyard and in the parish pathway; as the Bishop passed by, we knelt down, and laying his hands on every boy's head, he said a few words."

Baxter was not happy about the occasion. It did not mean much to him, and even if confirmation outside was a survival of medieval practice (not even the 1662 Prayer Book was to specify that the service should take place in church), Baxter's views were those associated with the Puritan strand of the English Church. If confirmation was to be retained, then it should be an occasion when the adult believer owned his or her faith before the local community.

Baxter soldiered on with the Church of England none the less, and was ordained in 1638, after an informal theological education, and served as an assistant at Bridgnorth. Here he encountered liturgical practices which he found alien: he disliked communion without a proper examination of those to receive, he did not wear the surplice, and he refused to make the sign of the cross at baptism (the only surviving such sign from the many in the medieval Catholic rites).

Other like-minded members of the clergy frequently acted in this way, some going further and refusing to kneel at communion or to use the ring at marriage, both of which customs Baxter was content to go along with.

He was soon to work at Kidderminster, but was

Puritan: Richard Baxter, in a portrait from the Sutherland Collection. *Photo © Ashmolean Museum, Oxford*

ejected by Royalist troops in 1642, whereupon he served as a chaplain in the Parliamentary army. He returned to Kidderminster in 1649.

Here he became an influential voice of such significance that two things happened at the Restoration. He was a delegate to the Savoy Conference, to deliberate Prayer Book revision, representing the Presbyterians. Second, he was offered — but he refused — the bishopric of Worcester. He was deprived of his post at Kidderminster, and spent the remaining years of life as a freelance Nonconformist preacher in London, often having to work clandestinely.

Baxter was a voluminous writer. He wrote a liturgical proposal for an alternative to the Prayer Book for the Savoy Conference. Though rich in imagery, it was too radical for the Conformists, and probably too rich for the Presbyterians.

Some of his hymns are still sung, such as "Ye holy angels bright" and "He wants not friends that hath thy love", both of them meditations on the communion of saints.

His devotional classic, however, is *The Saint's Everlasting Rest*, which was published in 1650. It breathes a Bible-based fervour, with recommendations for daily times of quiet, self-examination and meditation, though he realises that not everyone can fulfil this in the same way, because of age, duty, or way of life.

His *Reformed Pastor* appeared in 1656. This has been the basis of reflection for generations of clerics since, with its stress on pastoral care, and its emphasis on the preaching office of the clergy.

individuals who negotiated the new regime. Others did not. Figures are not certain, but between 2000 to 3000 clerics were ejected from their livings during this period by agencies such as Parliament's suitably named Committee for Scandalous Ministers. That could be a proportion as high as 25 per cent.

Clerics got the boot for a variety of offences, from royalism, the use of the Prayer Book, failure to preach, moral offences, or simply over-frequenting the ale house — or some fascinating combination of all these.

Although this does not diminish the ferocity with which roughly 1000 ministers were ejected at the Restoration for their failure to conform to a new Act of Uniformity, it does put it in some perspective, and goes part of the way, not to justify such actions, but to explain them.

Professor Ivan Roots's assessment of the political settlement is apposite for the Church as well: "There was only a smear of blood at the Restoration, but a whole streak of meanness."

## Parallels with recusancy

One of the striking things about the survival of features of the Old Church in this period is the lack of leadership provided by members of the episcopate.

Outlawed practices, such as the use of the Prayer Book or observation of holy days, survived in large part owing to the courage of members of the clergy and laity, not by any overt leadership provided by the bishops. In fact, the bishops in England ignored repeated requests from the exiled court in the 1650s to consecrate more of their order to make up for diminishing numbers.

In many ways, the history of "Anglicanism" in this period mirrors the story of recusancy under Elizabeth and the early Stuarts. There were no Church of England equivalents of the Jesuits, but there were plenty of obstructive and unco-operative clerics and lay people.

As with Roman Catholicism, the customs of the Old Church often endured in the household, sponsored by gentry who had the social standing to get away with it, and the finances to support sympathetic members of the clergy. The similarities to the experience of recusants are striking.

If bishops provided little public leadership to their flocks during this time of trouble, they did respond to requests for secret ordinations. A number of younger clerics, we do not know how many, often with no first-hand experience of episcopal government, sought out a second ordination from the hands of these "redundant" bishops. It was, in truth, a sort of top-up view of ordination, as these younger men continued to serve in the Interregnum Church.

## Jeremy Taylor: prisoner for the Prayer Book faith

Jeremy Taylor (1613-1667) is something of a contrast to Richard Baxter. He was born in Cambridge and studied at Gonville & Caius College, of which he was a Fellow in 1633.

Attracting the notice of Archbishop Laud, he was made a Fellow of All Souls College, Oxford, in 1635, and appointed Chaplain in Ordinary to King Charles I, who had him made a DD of Oxford for writing on episcopacy. He became Rector of Uppingham in 1638, but went to serve as a chaplain in the Royalist army in 1642.

He was imprisoned by the Parliamentarians, after which he spent some time in internal exile. From 1645 he was chaplain to the Earl of Charbery at Golden Grove, in Cardiganshire, but he was in London from 1655, officiating in St Gregory's Church, one of the very few places at which services according to the Book of Common Prayer were tolerated. Here Taylor befriended John Evelyn. He probably became too well known in this capacity for his own good. Cromwell imprisoned him for a time in the Tower of London, and in 1658 he went to Lisburn, near Belfast.

At the Restoration, he was made a bishop in the Church of Ireland. Scots Presbyterians had made their influence so strong that Taylor's episcopate, however pastorally distinguished, was marred by dissension.

Although Taylor's life stretches from the reigns of James I and Charles I until well into that of Charles II, it is without doubt during the Commonwealth that his main literary work was done, probably for the simple reason that he had the leisure to do it.

In 1649, the year of Charles I's execution, Taylor wrote *The Great Exemplar*, an extended life of Christ, the first of its kind. It weaves a narrative together from the Gospels, intercalated with "discourses" on various subjects, including a penetrating interpretation of the Lord's Prayer.

In 1650, Taylor's most popular work, *The Rules and Exercises of Holy Living*, was published, to be followed in the next year by *The Rules and Exercises of Holy Dying*. *Holy Living* opens with some sharp wisdom on the use of time, which reads as if it had been written for the Filofax culture of today. Taylor also wrote extensively about eucharistic theology, particularly in *Real Presence* (1654) and *The Worthy Communicant* (1660).

As Harry McAdoo has shown, these anticipate in many ways the work of Anglican-Roman Catholic International Commission for their unitive style, and for the way they approach the tricky area of eucharistic sacrifice by stressing the Lord's Supper as a dynamic memorial, and a pleading of the eternal offering in heaven.

But it is the short devotional book *Golden Grove* (1655) which expresses the depth of feeling among those who wanted to restore the old order of the Church of England, Prayer Book and all, set aside by Parliament.

*Kenneth Stevenson*

What motivated them to seek episcopal alternatives of this kind? Presumably it was a variety of factors, including a search for stability in a period of uncertainty and change in many areas of English life. Jeremy Taylor dryly observed of these youngsters that never had the excellency of episcopal government been so obvious now that it was lacking.

### Episcopalian identity

The period of England's brief (to date) experiment with religious localism and republicanism saw the suppression of the Book of Common Prayer, episcopal polity, and (perhaps most unpopular of all) of the reformed ritual year. These experiences of suppression helped to

# Simon Patrick: Royalist bishop-to-be, biding his time

Simon Patrick (1626-1707) was born in Gains-borough, Lincolnshire, and studied at Queens' College, Cambridge, where he became a Fellow on graduation. Although he was ordained as a Presbyterian in 1653 (there was no official alternative), he sought ordination from the aged Bishop Joseph Hall, formerly of Norwich, in the following year, a practice followed by others as well.

He served for a short time as Dean of Queens' Chapel, but he moved to London, to serve as domestic chaplain to Sir Walter St John, at Battersea Manor. In 1657, he became Vicar of St Mary's, Battersea, a church which appears to have survived some of the more drastic interior reforms necessitated by the Commonwealth.

Patrick's autobiography tells of careful preparation by the Vicar of the congregation for the reintroduction of the Prayer Book at the Restoration, for on 22 July 1660 he was able to use the Common Prayer service in full.

But Patrick was no Royalist pushover. When the Fellows of Queens' wanted him to be President, the King imposed Anthony Sparrow (later Bishop of Norwich) on them, an action which provoked Patrick to take the King to a court of law, in which he was unsuccessful. But other preferments came his way,

including the Rectory of St Paul's, Covent Garden, a canonry at Westminster, and the Deanery of Peterborough.

Patrick was one of the leading London clerics who opposed James II's policy towards Roman Catholics. He was rewarded by being made Bishop of Chichester in 1689, and was translated to Ely in 1691.

Although Patrick's writings blossomed at the Restoration, it was during the Commonwealth period that the main influences on his future ministry were exerted. He stands as something of a contrast to both Baxter and Taylor, as he survived the Commonwealth without great difficulty, and then went on to other posts in the following reigns.

His first two most important theological works were conceived during the Commonwealth. The first, *Aqua Genitalis*, published in 1658, concerns baptism.

Like the Prayer Book order for baptism, Patrick's work expounds a view of baptismal theology that is strong on regeneration. There are hints of the need to use the old fonts which used to stand at the back of the Church (not mobile basins). But, above all, baptism is where we enter sacramentally the covenant of grace, in which we are bound to God by mutual obligation. It is not an exclusive covenant, but it is owned at confirmation, a subject where Patrick takes a traditional view, though he does not mention bishops, since it is still 1658.

Patrick's second work appeared in 1660, entitled *Mensa Mystica*. It began a whole series of derivative and more popular books and sermons on the eucharist in the Restoration period. It is strong on the symbolic instrumentalism of the eucharist, as a memorial sacrifice, a means of renewing the covenant of grace, and a sacrament to be entered into frequently and with due preparation.

Ely: Simon Patrick became Bishop in 1691. *Photo © A. F. Kersting*

*Kenneth Stevenson*

## CHRONOLOGY

**1643** Solemn League and Covenant ratified in England
**1645** Parliament orders the abolition of the Book of Common Prayer and its replacement with the Directory of Public Worship
**1646** Parliament abolishes the episcopate
**1649** Charles I tried and executed
**1651** Charles II is defeated by Cromwell at Worcester and begins his Continental exile
**1653** *Instrument of Government* accepted, and Cromwell installed as Lord Protector
**1655** Cromwell allows the readmission of the Jews to England
**1658** Death of Cromwell; his son Richard succeeds as Lord Protector
**1660** Parliament dissolves itself and orders new elections; return and restoration of Charles II

form an "Anglican" identity, though even in this period it is a problematic word to use with any degree of historical and scholarly integrity. We must always remember that it was little used by contemporaries.

In fact, in many ways, "Episcopalian" is a better term, though ironically the bishops themselves were the least courageous champions of that cause. What we observe in the 1640s and 1650s is the hardening of certain religious traditions within the larger pre-Civil War Church of England, and their emergence as the Church of England.

The formation of this religious identity was greatly aided by the retrospective spin-doctors of the Restoration Church of England, the biographer Izaak Walton being both the most notable and engaging.

As one historian of the period, the Revd Professor John Morrill, has remarked: "Religious commitment is best observed in periods of persecution." Before the Civil War, religious identities invested in the liturgy, the calendar and episcopacy formed a flexible and considerable strand within the larger established Church. In Cromwell's England, the suppression of these things, not of the monarchy, helped paradoxically to create "Anglicanism".

# BECOMING HIGH AND MIGHTY

*Jonathan Clark*

*After the Restoration, Parliament drew a clear line between Churchmen, loyal to the 1662 Prayer Book, and Puritans — the new Nonconformists.*

The history of religion in England since the Reformation falls into three roughly equal parts.

In the first, almost all men assumed that there should be a single Church for all the English. That was what gave such urgency to their attempt to remake the Church in conformity with their own views on theology or ecclesiastical polity.

In the second phase, which began in 1660, Churchmen worked out over three decades a new regime in which a hegemonic established Church embraced the great majority of the population, leaving small groups of "Nonconformists" in separated denominations outside it. At first a temporary arrangement leaving Dissenters still persecuted, it eventually settled down into a system which Churchmen praised as "the Toleration": only a tolerant established Church could guarantee freedom of worship to Dissenters, and this system could be preserved only by denying Dissenters political power.

Beginning in 1828-32, a third regime was developed whose aim was to prevent conflict between denominations by granting to all of them equal civil liberties: a system which was to end as the "plural society".

The Restoration was a pivotal moment: not only was an episcopal and apostolic Church re-established against all the odds, but it began to move towards a *modus vivendi* with groups now outside it.

External challenges from "Rome" and "Geneva" continued, for Counter-Reformation Catholicism was still powerful, and revolutionary sectarianism ran on after 1660; but these threats were weathered. The more serious challenges came from within, in the persons of James II and William III; yet the Church was to survive even these.

The dominant form of English religion was to be both Catholic and statist; within a tradition defined by creeds, sacraments and apostolic succession, a hierarchical Church was identified with the secular structures of English society. Theologically, it was also the period in which the Church moved decisively away from the 16th-century influences of both Luther and Calvin.

Puritan: John Milton, after a bust attributed to Edward Pierce.
*Photo © by courtesy of the National Portrait Gallery, London*

## Restoration welcomed

None of this seemed likely in the 1650s. Even the Presbyterianism set up by the Long Parliament had been swamped by the bizarre array of beliefs which the Great Rebellion allowed to flourish. By 1660, the Church's episcopal structure was shattered, the lands of deans and chapters confiscated, thousands of livings held by the disaffected, the Book of Common Prayer formally banned and used only in secret, under threat of persecution.

What then occurred seemed to many a Providential deliverance. It began at parish level, as more and more ministers intruded under the

# The loser: John Milton, propagandist and poet of English Arianism

According to Milton (1608-74) in 1654, England had just witnessed "the most heroic and exemplary achievements since the foundation of the world". From 1649 to 1660 he was, in effect, the regime's press officer and chief propagandist. At the Restoration he went into hiding, was arrested, and narrowly escaped execution; perhaps his Royalist brother Christopher, or Andrew Marvell, lobbied sufficiently to avoid Milton's exemption from the Act of Indemnity.

Until 1660, Milton was famous as a leading writer of political and religious polemic, secondarily as a scholarly Latin and English poet. His greatest poetry came after defeat and retirement: *Paradise Lost* (1667), *Paradise Regained* and *Samson Agonistes* (1671). These poems owe much of their grandeur to Milton's agonised attempt to grapple with the defeat of a cause which he had vehemently believed to be providentially sanctioned: "The Lord has blasted them and spit in their faces," as Major-General Fleetwood had put it. Milton's task was to justify the ways of God to man.

He failed: it was the Church that pulled off this feat. His great poems also failed to be the Trojan horses for republicanism that he may have intended. The Stuart loyalist and Catholic John Dryden discovered *Paradise Lost*, and (with permission) even adapted it as an opera in 1674. When the publisher Tonson brought out a folio edition of Milton's poem in 1688, both the Whig jurist Somers and the Jacobite clergyman Atterbury promoted it. Milton the poet was absorbed into the national pantheon, and the story of mankind's fall and redemption was guarded primarily by the Church. It was the Church, not one of the sects, which buried Milton.

His most explosive legacy was suppressed: the manuscript of a work entitled *De Doctrina Christiana*, the theoretical foundation of *Paradise Lost*, which he entrusted to Daniel Skinner to publish after his death. Skinner offered it to the Amsterdam firm of Elzevir, but the English government intervened, and it ended in the State Paper Office, where it was discovered in 1823.

Published under the editorship of a future bishop, it revealed what like-minded thinkers had always suspected: Milton was an Arian, a supporter of free will and therefore anti-Calvinist, but heterodox on the doctrine of the Trinity, and therefore anti-Church, too.

"Some hatred", wrote Milton, "is a religious duty." He hated "tyranny and superstition", the English monarchy and Church.

English republicanism failed to find a middle ground, for it was militantly hostile to the Church on the grounds of ecclesiastical polity (it was anti-episcopal), and was offensive to Presbyterianism, too (it was often anti-Trinitarian).

Milton's prose works were therefore kept in print primarily by eager heterodox figures who could claim him as an exemplar, men like John Toland and Richard Baron: this was more of a handicap than a help. Despite the efforts of such figures, English republicanism and English Arianism equally failed. Milton was doubly a loser.

---

Commonwealth were forced out: popular Anglicanism more than top-down persecution created the parochial tone of the Restoration Church. The religious settlement was so durable because legislation met with an emphatic popular welcome.

Nevertheless, Laud largely failed: the formal structures of English religion as re-established were importantly different from what he had championed, and the laity were far more closely involved. JPs were to matter more than church courts, squires more than parsons. Nevertheless, Laud was rehabilitated, and the Caroline divines now enjoyed a spectacular retrospective victory.

# The winner: Gilbert Sheldon, champion of orthodoxy

Sheldon's background was humbler than Milton's: the son of a menial servant of the Earl of Shrewsbury, he became a key example of "sponsored mobility".

After he was sent to Trinity College, Oxford, his career as a don led to more worthwhile things, and soon to the chaplaincy to Lord Coventry, the Lord Keeper. Initially inclined against the Arminians (the anti-Calvinists), he soon joined them, and was associated with Lord Falkland's circle meeting at Great Tew. When he attended the King during the Civil War, it was as an associate of the constitutionalist Sir Edward Hyde rather than Archbishop Laud.

Sheldon (1598-1677) spent the years 1648-59 in retirement, but growing in stature among those who preserved the Church in adversity. At the Restoration he was at once made Dean of the Chapel Royal; the bishopric of London and a seat on the Privy Council followed quickly. He was the power behind the scenes at the Savoy Conference, which frustrated the Presbyterians' drive to shape the restored Church in their image; and it was Sheldon who was primarily responsible for defeating the policy known as "comprehension", the re-definition of Anglican formulae to include as many Protestants as possible.

Sheldon championed the Act of Uniformity, and his militant defence of it, once passed, blocked Clarendon's attempt to soften its impact. Though not a Laudian, Sheldon began the rehabilitation of Laud, arranging for the recovery of his papers, and putting in hand their publication.

When he succeeded to Canterbury in 1663, Sheldon's political involvement only grew. With Clarendon, he arranged for the clergy to give up their ancient right to tax themselves in Convocation: the English *ancien régime* developed through a close unity of Church and state rather than in legally defined estates. It was Sheldon who began the resistance to the royal claim to a right to dispense subjects from key statutes on religion, a defence that culminated in the decisive resistance of the Seven Bishops to James II in 1688.

Sheldon carried the main administrative burden of the repair and reinstatement of the Church of England. Gilbert Burnet claimed that Sheldon seemed "not to have a deep sense of religion, if any at all", treating religion "most commonly as . . . an engine of government and a matter of policy". This can probably be put down to political enmity. Samuel Parker, Sheldon's chaplain, wrote that the Archbishop, though "assiduous in prayers", nevertheless "was not such an admirer of them as some are", and "judiciously placed the sum of religion in good life".

Unmarried, Sheldon dispensed huge sums in charity, and gave a pastoral lead, remaining in London during the plague of 1665. He set the tone for the Church in the long 18th century before Tillotson (normally credited with it): a tone which combined political engagement, theological orthodoxy, and practical goodness.

Dissent took a different route, through political disengagement, increasing theological heterodoxy, and moral self-righteousness; but, thanks to Sheldon, Nonconformity was now outside the Church.

Anglican historians pinned the blame for civil war and regicide on "Presbyterianism". Anglican scholars from William Cave grounded the Church's present claims in Patristic studies. Anglican moral theology from Jeremy Taylor's *Holy Living and Holy Dying* and Richard Allestree's *Whole Duty of Man* explained social duties. Anglican catechisms, guides to the Book of Common Prayer, and handbooks to the doctrines and ceremonies of the Church flooded the market, and were reprinted in edition after edition even into the early 19th century.

All this was part of a single enterprise which linked John Pearson's

Anglican: portrait of Sheldon by Sir Peter Lely. *Photo © by courtesy of the National Portrait Gallery, London*

*On the Creed* (1659) and Joseph Butler's *Analogy of Religion* (1736) Dissent, and heterodoxy, had the worst of the argument.

Parochial practice and high theory reinforced each other. As Nonconformists roughly halved in numbers between 1660 and 1760, the Church strengthened its role in educating and catechising: despite the disruptions of the Rebellion, a Reformation (or, in other eyes, Counter-Reformation) project of popular piety reached its high-water mark by the early 18th century. This was a project in which all shades of opinion in the Church joined. A central part was even played by the Nonjurors: Robert Nelson's *Companion for the Festivals and Fasts of the Church of England* was a bestseller.

## Rebuilding the middle ground

The Church before the Civil War had defined itself as treading a *via media* between two extreme alternatives, Rome and Geneva, each claiming a right to judge and depose the "magistrate", that is, the civil power. After 1660 the Church's achievement was to rebuild a middle ground combining monarchy and law, conscience and orthodoxy, under the umbrella of the "ancient constitution". It was a middle ground which denied subjects a right of resistance and accorded them instead the duty of civil disobedience (in the phrases of the time, "passive obedience" or "non-resistance") in the face of unjust commands.

Where Filmer in the 1630s had implicitly rejected passive obedience, asserting that subjects must obey without reserve the orders of the rightful sovereign, Anglican clerics now argued the opposite: that a stable Christian polity could be based only on monarchical allegiance, tempered if necessary by civil disobedience, but stopping short of active resistance. Passive obedience became the hallmark of the centrist position around which opinion rallied after 1660.

All this rested on a programme of legislation, and with Charles II personally inclined to Protestant and Catholic Dissenters, its passage was no foregone conclusion. The Presbyterian-dominated Convention Parliament, which sat until March 1661, favoured a scheme for modified and limited episcopacy and "comprehension", the adaptation of Anglican formulae to include as many Protestants as possible. This changed with a Royalist landslide in the "Cavalier Parliament" which followed.

The political history of the 1660s and '70s was a subtle conflict in which the Commons was usually more Royalist, and more Anglican, than the king. Nevertheless, the Commons often got its way: the Corporation Act of 1661, the Act of Uniformity of 1662, and the Test Acts of 1673 and 1678 were landmarks. Their effect was twofold: to rule a clear line for the first time between Churchman and Protestant Dissenter, and formally to confine political power at central and local level to the first.

## 1662 Prayer Book

In 1662, a revised Book of Common Prayer implicitly rejected most of the Puritans' demands: it re-emphasised the distinction between the orders of priesthood, made clear the independent efficacy of the

Trial of strength: "the Seven Bishops" (Sancroft, Lloyd, Turner, Lake, Ken, White and Trelawney) being rowed to the Tower in May 1688, after they had resisted James II over his Declaration of Indulgence. James had underestimated their popularity; from a Dutch engraving. *Photo © British Museum*

sacrament of baptism, and located the firmly episcopal Church of England within "the whole Catholick Church of Christ".

In May 1662, the Act of Uniformity made assent to this revised Prayer Book and its doctrine necessary for holding office in the Church. An exodus of intruded Puritans followed: a Church more homogeneous than ever before now confronted separated groups which were soon organised as Nonconformist denominations, "gathered churches".

The object of this legislation was not just to persecute Dissenters, but to define a system. A social structure which successfully united Church and state was unusual in Europe, and had the potential to be immensely strong, as England's survival of the American and French Revolutions was to prove. In the short term, only one thing could effectively undermine it: a Roman Catholic monarch.

The accession of James II in 1685 inevitably reawakened memories of Mary I (1553-58). Debate continues over the extent of James's plans for the re-Catholicisation of England: did he seek only toleration for his co-religionists, or a full-scale Counter-Reformation conversion?

Encouraged by Whig and Tory anti-Catholicism, many Englishmen expected the second. Few intended a change of monarch, but when William of Orange seized an opportunity in 1688 to intervene in order to secure England's involvement in his crusade against France, James's power base collapsed. The Church largely refused to support him, and many men implicitly sided with their Church to restrain their monarch. Unexpectedly, William then seized the throne.

## Divisions after 1688

The Revolution of 1688 was in one way a triumph for the Anglican doctrine of passive obedience rather than for extreme Whig resistance theory: James II fell because many of his subjects did nothing to support him, not because many chose to resist him by force. The regime after 1689 could therefore continue to claim support from familiar Anglican teaching, and the monarchy continued to claim a Providential sanction. Into the early 19th century, the English state was to rest on an adapted version of the political theology of the Caroline divines; indeed, the Oxford Movement was triggered when that doctrine was violated in 1829.

In another way, the Restoration regrouping around a middle ground was fractured by the Revolution. Many argued that England's constitution in Church and state had been fundamentally changed in 1688.

On one wing, extreme Whigs and Dissenters contended that the Revolution had been a justified act of resistance, that the throne was thereby made elective, that the Church had only a parliamentary foundation, and that Nonconformity was therefore on a par with Anglicanism. On the opposite wing, some Tories and all Nonjurors agreed that 1688 had been an act of resistance, but an illegitimate one: the Williamite regime was of doubtful legality or plainly usurping, and the Church had fallen into schism. Some Nonjurors even denied the validity of the ministrations of the juring Church of England.

This rending schism was to preoccupy the English intelligentsia until the 1750s. Yet 1689 was not the prelude to "comprehension", for the bishops rapidly cooled towards their Dissenting allies after James's departure. As a rearguard action began, attempts in the Commons to repeal the Test and Corporation Acts failed. Growing acrimony produced a parliamentary compromise: the Whigs dropped their Comprehension Bill in return for Tory agreement to a Bill for "Indulgence", that is, toleration of those outside the Church.

Without "comprehension", this fell far short of Dissenters' hopes: the "Toleration Act" of 1689 did not contain the word "toleration" in its title or text. It did not abolish a national Church, nor set the stage for a plural society. The Church preserved a "holy alliance" with natural science that the sects could not match. Yet the Act made a difference: especially, it meant laymen could take advantage of it to attend no place of worship at all. Anglicanism's strength thereafter cannot be measured solely by the numbers in the pews.

## Points left undecided

Party conflict between Whig and Tory from the 1690s often revolved around still-contested religious issues, for where Dissenters insisted they had won toleration as a right, and that an extensive interpretation of the Revolution implied religious voluntaryism, Tories and High Churchmen adopted a minimalist interpretation, and continued to pursue uniformity.

William of Orange, a Dutch Calvinist Presbyterian, was no friend to High Church claims. After the failure of the Comprehension Bill, another Williamite attempt was made along Presbyterian lines to modify the Prayer Book and Canons, enforce "godly discipline" on the clergy, and perhaps to recognise the orders of foreign Protestant Churches; it was blocked by Convocation, its prolocutor, Dr Jane of Christ Church, declaring: "*Nolumus leges Angliae mutari*". "Church in danger!" was an alarmist cry, but it worked: Anglicanism defended itself against William, as it had against James.

At William's death in 1702, the outcome on some points of principle was undecided: it was this which characterised the Revolution "settlement". There was to be no resolution of the political position of Dissenters until the old order was recast in 1828-32, and Anne's reign saw a swing towards High Church ideals.

This was not fully to achieve its aims; but that it could have occurred at all identifies the Revolution of 1688 as a confirmation of the Restoration, not the inception of a novel Erastian, latitudinarian or worldly regime. England henceforward practised its virtues of moderation within a framework to a large degree set by High Churchmen, though not to the degree they wished.

In a conflict between clearly defined ecclesiastical alternatives, no side secured all that it sought. Yet the Church had survived its greatest trial.

## CHRONOLOGY

**1660** Restoration of Charles II and an episcopal Church
**1661** Corporation Act excludes Dissenters from local government
**1662** Revised Prayer Book; Act of Uniformity
**1673, 1678** Test Acts exclude Dissenters from central government
**1685** Accession of James II, already a Roman Catholic
**1688** Acquittal of the Seven Bishops shows strength of popular Churchmanship
**1688** William of Orange invades; James II deposed
**1689** "Toleration" Act grants limited sufferance to Dissenting worship
**1701** Act of Settlement provides for continuing Protestant monarchy
**1702** Death of William III

I am afraid of you, lest I have bestowed upon you labour in vain. Gal. 4.11

Wm Hogarth invt.

Cha Spooner fecit

THE SLEEPY CONGREGATION.

# THE MODERATE MEN IN CHARGE

*Stephen Taylor*

*In the 18th century, the Anglican clergy saw themselves as steering a wise course amid the dangers to Church and state of popery, deism, and enthusiasm.*

What was the main defining characteristic of the Church of England in the 18th century?

One answer was provided by *The Spectator*, that most influential of 18th-century periodicals. In a dream, Mr Spectator finds himself in the Great Hall of the Bank of England surrounded by the emblems of England's strength: "There, at the Upper-end of the Hall was the *Magna Charta*, with the Act of Uniformity on the right Hand, and the Act of Toleration on the left." He is shaken by spectres of discord, then relieved by the appearance of benign apparitions, a procession of couples who epitomise the factors which bring stability to English society. Well to the fore comes "Moderation leading in Religion".

Here, Joseph Addison provides an early and powerful invocation of the cult of moderation which was central to the character of 18th-century Anglicanism. It chimed well with another commonplace, that the Church of England was a *via media*.

This idea of the middle way had a long pedigree, but in this period it was invoked endlessly in a variety of formulations. In the *Spectator* article, the moderation of the Church offered a path between "Bigotry and Atheism". It was also claimed that the national Church occupied a median position between the competing ideals of religious unity and religious freedom. It maintained a middle way between the infallibilist authoritarianism of the Church of Rome and the excessive individualism of radical Protestantism. By distinguishing itself sharply from both deism and Methodism, it was charting a path between what Bishop Gibson described as the contrary evils of "lukewarmness" and "enthusiasm".

## What Anglicanism wasn't

One of the strengths of this idea was that it allowed Anglicanism to be defined negatively rather than positively. Churchmen were confident that the Church of England resembled more closely than any other visible Church the pattern of the primitive Church of the first four

Ministry of the word: William Hogarth's *The Sleeping Congregation*. The sermon dominated the liturgy.
*Photo © British Museum*

centuries. But apologists often concentrated on what the Church of England was not, rather than what it was.

The Anglican calendar in the 18th century encouraged this approach. The Prayer Book contained special services for 30 January, the commemoration of the martyrdom of Charles I, and 5 November, the anniversary of the Gunpowder Plot. Both were regularly observed, and popular with preachers. Sermons on 30 January often commented on the errors and iniquities of Protestant sectaries and enthusiasts, while 5 November provided an opportunity to reflect on Roman Catholic tyranny and superstition, and to celebrate the preservation of England from popery.

By conceptualising their Church in this way, Anglican divines avoided the problems inherent in defining the balance between the Catholic and reformed traditions. This twin inheritance of the Church of England had been divisive in the 17th century, as Laudians and Puritans contested its identity, and controversy was to resurface in the 19th century in the battle between Tractarians and Evangelicals.

## Limited toleration

By contrast, 18th-century Churchmen tried for the most part to distance themselves from the party conflicts of the preceding century. Moderation meant eirenicism and charity; and the Church's leaders deprecated and discouraged intra-Church controversies.

The ethos of moderation was easier to sustain because of the growing sense of security among Anglicans. By the mid-18th century, they were confident that the challenges from popery and Dissent, which had so dominated the clerical consciousness in the 17th century, had been overcome. Concern about Roman Catholics, who accounted for only two per cent of the population, faded after the failure of the '45 rebellion ended the last realistic hope of a Jacobite restoration.

Meanwhile, leading Nonconformists were lamenting "the decay of the Dissenting interest", as the size of their congregations declined. To many Churchmen it appeared that the Toleration Act, passed amid much controversy in 1689, had been a success. A policy of charity and tolerance was winning over Dissenters where persecution had failed. Indeed, by the 1730s the Toleration Act was commonly portrayed as one of the glories of both the Church and the constitution.

Moderation thus involved a commitment to religious toleration, but important limits were placed on it in the 18th century. Toleration certainly did not mean that all Christian denominations should be treated equally. Churchmen continued zealously to defend not only the idea of a church establishment, but also the maintenance of that establishment by means of a Test Act, which excluded non-Anglicans from government office.

# Churchman, but no party man: Secker

Very few people today have heard of Thomas Secker (1693–1768), who was Archbishop of Canterbury between 1758 and 1768. His contemporaries, however, would have found such obscurity remarkable. Many, indeed, regarded him as one of the most distinguished and influential bishops of the 18th century.

Secker's main claim to fame lay in his abilities as a preacher. Churches were crowded whenever he was delivering the sermon, and charities clamoured for his support at their anniversary meetings, knowing that an address from him would increase the collection.

One reason for his popularity lay in his ability to encapsulate the character of 18th-century Anglicanism. Secker personified the spirit of moderation. He defended the Church of England as a *via media* through scepticism, enthusiasm and popery. For him, faith was the rational outcome of an unprejudiced examination of the evidence for Christianity.

At the same time, while disapproving of the Methodists, he was critical of the failure of many Anglicans to preach "in a manner sufficiently evangelical", and tried to imbue his own sermons with a "discreet warmth".

Secker's churchmanship is thus very difficult to define. In his commitment to toleration and moderation, we see a Low Churchman; in his theology and teachings we can identify tinges of Evangelicalism; in his fierce defence of the rights and privileges of a Church there are the characteristics of a High Churchman. One reason why his reputation declined so rapidly from the 1820s may have something to do with the fact that none of the great parties of the Victorian Church could easily claim him as one of its own.

Secker was a vigorous pastoral bishop as well as a popular preacher. Here his influence was long-lasting. His *Instructions Given to Candidates for Orders* went through 50 editions in as many years. In the charges delivered at his episcopal visitations, he developed his advice to the clergy at greater length, examining topics such as preaching, study and holy communion. These were still being recommended as a pastoral handbook well into the 19th century.

Of humble birth: Secker (unknown artist, after Sir Joshua Reynolds). *Photo © by courtesy of the National Portrait Gallery, London*

In his preaching and pastoral work, Secker embodied the best traditions of the 18th-century episcopate. He was also representative of the Church in other, possibly less expected, ways. As the grandson of a Lincolnshire butcher, he provides evidence of the openness of the Church of England, in an age often thought to be dominated by an exclusive aristocracy, to men from modest backgrounds. Even more remarkably, his grandfather and father were Presbyterians, and the family had hoped that Secker would enter the Nonconformist ministry.

But Secker was in no way unusual. Many other 18th-century bishops, including Edmund Gibson and Richard Hurd, came from humble families. A number of others were brought up as Dissenters, including Secker's friend at Tewkesbury Academy, Joseph Butler, and John Potter, one of his predecessors as Archbishop of Canterbury. Through such men, the Nonconformist tradition, excluded from the Church in 1662, made a significant contribution to the character of 18th-century Anglicanism.

# When the mob turned on Dissent

In late February and early March 1710, a wave of riots spread through the cathedral cities and market towns of England. By far the most serious gripped London on the evening of Wednesday 1 March. It was the worst popular disturbance in the capital during the 18th century until the Gordon riots 70 years later; and, like the Gordon riots (directed against "popery"), the Sacheverell riots had their origins in the religious fears and concerns of London's middling and artisan classes.

The first target of the mob was the Dissenting meeting-house near Lincoln's Inn Fields, built five years earlier for the leading Presbyterian preacher Daniel Burgess. By the time that the rioters had been dispersed by troops in the early hours of the Thursday morning, six of the best-known Nonconformist chapels in London had been sacked and partly demolished.

While there was some plunder, the mob was not an undisciplined rabble. The rioters, many of whom had come equipped with the appropriate tools, methodically went about dismantling the interiors of the chapels. Pulpits, galleries, doors, floorboards, and other furniture were removed and carried to bonfires, which were sometimes built a considerable distance away where the flames would not damage nearby houses. Meanwhile, other rioters, such as William Watson, a bricklayer's apprentice, stripped the tiles from the roofs.

The occasion of these disturbances was the verdict given by the House of Lords in the trial of Henry Sacheverell, a fellow of Magdalen College, Oxford, and high-church clergyman. On 5 November 1709, the anniversary not only of the Gunpowder Plot but also of William of Orange's landing in 1688, he had preached a sermon in St Paul's Cathedral on *The Perils of False Brethren in both Church and State*.

This sermon was widely regarded as attacking the principles of the 1688 revolution, and Sacheverell was impeached by the Whig government, accused of "high crimes and misdemeanours" against the state. He was found guilty, but received only a token sentence, which was interpreted by his supporters as a moral victory.

Sacheverell was one of the most flamboyant and demagogic of high-church preachers during the reign of Queen Anne. He articulated perfectly the views of those Churchmen who were appalled by the revolution settlement of 1689. Such people condemned the Toleration Act for undermining the Church of England.

The threat from toleration appeared all the more menacing in London, as opulent Dissenting chapels sprang up across the city. Sacheverell also inveighed against the Whigs and their low-church allies.

These were the "false brethren", who, by their support for toleration, were destroying the Church from within.

The mobs of 1 March were, therefore, rioting in support not only of Sacheverell himself, but also of the Church of England. Their attention was directed against their hero's tormenters and the Church's enemies, the Dissenters and their supporters. Their slogans were "High Church and Sacheverell" and "God damn the Presbyterians and all that support them".

The Sacheverell riots reveal clearly the bitter party conflicts which characterised both religious and political life in the first decade of the 18th century. These divisions were to fade in the course of the next two decades. But the disturbances of 1710, like the Gordon riots later in the century, provide a striking reminder of the importance of religion in the popular culture of the 18th century.

Few believed that religious pluralism was desirable in itself, and they continued to support the ideal of religious uniformity. But they accepted that that goal could not be attained by coercion, and committed themselves to a purely pastoral strategy for the creation of a Christian, and more specifically Anglican, nation.

## Pastor and preacher

Eighteenth-century clerical handbooks and episcopal charges repeatedly emphasised the need for a vigorous pastoral ministry, which did not begin and end with the duty of Sunday services. The main task of the clergy, however, remained that of providing their congregations with a thorough Christian education, a goal which was to be achieved primarily though regular catechising of the young, and preaching.

Crucial to this task, as the Reformers of the 16th and 17th centuries had recognised, was the creation of an educated clergy. In this respect, if no other, the 18th-century Church can claim some success, as by the end of the period the vast majority of the English, if not the Welsh, clergy were university graduates.

The form of public worship offered by the Church, following that prescribed by the 1662 Book of Common Prayer, was more or less uniform throughout England, though in many Welsh parishes the liturgy was said in the native language. The morning service on Sundays consisted of matins and ante-communion (that is, the communion service to the end of the prayer for the Church), including a sermon. Evening prayer was said in the afternoon, usually without a sermon if one had been delivered in the morning, though sometimes the catechism was expounded.

The centrepiece of most services was the sermon, its role symbolised in many parish churches by the prominence of the pulpit. Sermons would have lasted for at least 15 minutes, and it was not uncommon for preachers to speak for up to an hour.

The emphasis on common prayer and preaching makes it clear that 18th-century Anglicanism was pre-eminently a religion of the word. This has often been seen as fostering a dry, intellectual piety which failed to engage the laity. Evidence for such an interpretation is not hard to come by, and ranges from Hogarth's *Sleeping Congregation* to payments to parish officers for "waking the sleepers".

But against this should be set the laments of many of the clergy about the reluctance of their parishioners to attend services when a sermon was not being offered, the evidence of sermon-gadding in urban areas, and the important part played by sermons in domestic piety. It was not uncommon for the head of a household to read a sermon to the assembled family on a Sunday evening.

This fact helps to explain the immense popularity of sermons as a literary form: more than 20,000 titles were published between 1700 and 1800, far more than were needed to provide the clergy with models.

## Infrequent communion

Holy communion, by contrast, was only an occasional event in the lives of most Anglicans. In the towns, monthly communion was often

"High Church and Sacheverell!": a contemporary depiction of the destruction of Burgess's Chapel in the Sacheverell riots in March 1710. *Photo © British Museum*

St Mary-le-Strand, in London: built in the reign of George I.
*Photo © Paul Parker/Country Life Picture Library*

offered; but in rural parishes the norm was three or four services a year, at the great festivals. On those Sundays and festivals when communion was celebrated, non-communicants generally left after the ante-communion, and the ideal envisaged was for those receiving the sacrament to move to the chancel for the rest of the service. Most Anglicans appear to have practised only annual reception.

This should not, however, be taken as evidence of a lack of piety. Fear of damnation through unworthy reception was commonly expressed as a reason for failure to partake of the sacrament, and some laymen clearly believed that hours of meditation and rigorous self-examination were essential by way of preparation.

## Challenge of deism

The emphasis so far in this examination of the defining characteristics of the 18th-century Church has been on moderation, the routines of the parochial ministry, and the familiar cadences of the liturgy. But perceptions of the period as one of calm, even indifference, can be very misleading.

There is much evidence of high levels of clerical anxiety throughout the century. One important aspect of this was concern about the spiritual and moral state of the nation. All around them, Churchmen saw evidence of the spread of "luxury", profaneness and immorality. The popularity of masquerades in the 1720s and 1730s, the craze for gin-drinking among the lower orders, the crime wave of the mid-century, the development in the capital of pleasure gardens like Vauxhall — all were denounced as evidence of the moral decay of the English nation.

These were matters on which the clergy were obliged to comment. Despite the impact of the new science and the Enlightenment, most people's understanding of the world was deeply providentialist. The clergy watched the "signs of the times" anxiously, interpreting them as evidence of God's intentions towards his chosen people. Military defeats in the early stages of the Seven Years War thus produced a flood of clerical jeremiads calling for repentance and reformation, among which the most famous is John Brown's *Estimate of the Manners and Principles of the Time*. God, it was claimed, was warning the English nation; and, if those warnings were not heeded, he would destroy it, just as he had once destroyed Nineveh.

Other threats came from outside, from deism and Methodism. Deism probably represented the most powerful intellectual challenge to Christianity in the first half of the 18th century, when its leading figures, men like John Toland and Matthew Tindal, rejected revelation, and developed a system of natural religion. Divines of the Church of England, such as John Conybeare, Bishop of Bristol, were at the forefront of the European response, and they found ready allies in Dissenting writers, such as John Leland.

Perhaps the most influential refutation of deism came from the pen of Joseph Butler, a Presbyterian who converted to Anglicanism and was eventually preferred to the bishopric of Durham. His *Analogy of Religion* (1736) was arguably the most important work of Anglican theology in the 18th century, remaining a set book in many divinity schools well into this century.

## Rise of Methodism

The deist threat in England was at its height in the 1730s, and without doubt helped to create the climate which gave birth to Methodism at the end of that decade. Methodism presented the clergy with a very different challenge, but one which many of them regarded with no less anxiety.

Methodist disregard for church order, the popularity of its field preachers, and its promotion of an intensely experiential spirituality revived among many Anglicans the fear of "enthusiasm". In 18th-century parlance, "enthusiasts" were those who claimed to experience the immediate guidance of the Holy Ghost, and it was a commonplace that such people — "sectaries" — had been responsible for the destruction of both Church and state in the 1640s and 1650s.

The knee-jerk hostility of many clergymen to the arrival of a Methodist preacher owed much to the belief that, less than 100 years after the restoration of the Anglican Church, such men were threatening once more to turn the world upside down.

Other debates and controversies tended to divide Churchmen among themselves. Indeed, during the first two decades of the century, Anglicans were bitterly divided into two parties which advanced competing views about the role of the Church in English society in the aftermath of the passage of the Toleration Act, which had extended the protection of the law to Dissenting congregations and their ministers.

High Churchmen campaigned for the limitation, even the reversal, of the act, and a return to the past when Church and state had been joined in a single authoritarian regime. Low Churchmen, by contrast, were happy to abandon the policy of intolerance and recognised, albeit sometimes reluctantly, that religious pluralism had come to stay.

## Decline of party differences

As we have seen, this issue soon faded from view, but others replaced it. Perhaps the most famous religious controversy of the 18th century was the Bangorian controversy, sparked off in 1717 by a sermon preached by Benjamin Hoadly, Bishop of Bangor, on the subject of the nature

## CHRONOLOGY

**1689** Act of Toleration
**1696** John Toland publishes the early deist work *Christianity Not Mysterious*
**1710** Sacheverell riots
**1717** Benjamin Hoadly publishes *The Kingdom of Christ Not of This World*; Convocation prorogued (does not meet again until 1852)
**1719** Repeal of Occasional Conformity and Schism Acts reinforces concessions granted to Dissenters in 1689
**1723** Edmund Gibson appointed Bishop of London
**1730** Matthew Tindal publishes the influential deist work *Christianity as Old as the Creation*
**1736** Joseph Butler publishes *The Analogy of Religion*
**1737** John Potter appointed Archbishop of Canterbury
**1738** Conversion of John Wesley — "birth" of Methodism
**1745** Jacobite rebellion
**1757** John Brown's *Estimate of the Manners and Principles of the Time*
**1758** Thomas Secker appointed Archbishop of Canterbury
**1778** First Catholic Relief Act
**1780** Gordon riots
**1781** Richard Hurd appointed Bishop of Worcester

and authority of the visible Church. It continued for longer than three years, and generated more than 1000 pamphlets.

After 1715, however, it becomes increasingly difficult to identify distinct "parties" within the Church of England. Different tendencies and schools of thought can be discerned — the weekly communion favoured by members of some religious societies was denounced by the Low Churchman Bishop Peploe as "popish" — but these divisions rarely acquired the depth or bitterness of the struggles between Laudians and Puritans in the 17th century or between Tractarians and Evangelicals in the 19th. One of the most important reasons for this is that the centripetal forces in 18th-century Anglicanism were stronger than the centrifugal ones. The deist and Methodist controversies in particular were powerful reminders to the clergy that what united them was far more important than what divided them.

To Anglicans on the eve of the 21st century, the 18th century may appear a dry and unexciting period. Its services would hold little appeal for today's churchgoers, and its history lacks the glamour and controversy of the periods on either side.

The claim of Mark Pattison in 1860, that "the genuine Anglican omits" the 18th century altogether from his history of the Church, probably still holds true today. Yet it is an assumption that demands re-appraisal. By helping to establish moderation as one of the defining characteristics of Anglicanism, 18th-century Churchmen did much to influence the identity of the Church of England right up to the present day.

# THE MAN THE CHURCH OF ENGLAND COULDN'T CONTAIN

*Henry Rack*

*John Wesley burst on to the 18th-century scene — and out of the Church of England. We chart his progress and assess his influence.*

Popular images of 18th-century England come in bewildering variety and capital letters: The Age of Reason, Bath and Beau Nash, Hogarth and Gin Lane, the Industrial Revolution. Through this panorama rides the incongruous figure of a small man in clerical dress, preaching to emotional crowds in the open air and to small groups in stuffy rooms.

His *Journal*, published in instalments, describes his travels and ministry, along with his often quirky views on scenery, religion, public affairs, strange phenomena, people and books. His following was one section of a chain of Evangelical revival movements stretching from central Europe to the American colonies. In Britain it emerged in different guises in Wales, Scotland and Ireland; and in England it included Evangelical Anglicans and Nonconformists.

How and why these movements originated remains something of a mystery. Evangelicals have often written off the contemporary Church of England as sub-Christian in theology, its parish organisation hopelessly inadequate to cater for changing patterns of population and industry, its clergy idle, ill-distributed and unevenly financed. What the rise of Methodism and other Evangelical groups suggests is that, while the Church satisfied the needs of the majority, a minority was looking for a very different style of religion.

"Wesley is a lean elderly man, fresh-coloured, his hair smoothly combed, but with a *soupçon* of curl at the end. Wondrous clean, but as evidently an actor as Garrick. He spoke his sermon but so fast, and with so little accent, that I am sure he has often uttered it, for it was like a lesson. There were parts and eloquence in it, but towards the end he exalted his voice, and acted very ugly enthusiasm; decried learning, and told stories, like Latimer, of the fool of his college who said, 'I *thanks* God for everything.'"

*Horace Walpole, describing Wesley in 1766*

"In his demeanour, there was a cheerfulness mixed with gravity; a sprightliness which was the result of an unusual flow of spirits, and was yet accompanied with every mark of the most serene tranquillity. . .

"In private life his manner was the reverse of cynical or forbidding.

"It presented a beautiful contrast to the austere deportment of many of his preachers and people who seemed to have ranked laughter among the mortal sins. It was impossible to be long in his company without partaking his hilarity."

*John Hampson, Memoirs of John Wesley (1791)*

## In pursuit of holiness

John Wesley seems an unlikely leader for such people. His parents, Samuel Wesley, the Rector of Epworth in Lincolnshire, and his formidable wife Susanna, were the children of Nonconforming ministers, but had become high-church Anglicans when young. Educated at Charterhouse and Oxford, John became a Fellow of Lincoln College in 1726.

From 1725 he began an ardent pursuit of inward and outward holiness. This he cultivated by a severe devotional discipline and ideas of "primitive Christianity", influenced by the extreme Nonjurors who had left the Church of England in 1688 in protest against the deposition of James II. From 1729 Wesley became a leader of the so-called "Holy Club", a network of small groups in the university who combined devotional concerns with charitable and educational work in the town. Oxford critics mocked them as "Methodists", a nickname later applied to Wesley's followers and other Evangelicals.

In 1735 Wesley voyaged to the new colony of Georgia as a missionary for the Society for the Propagation of the Gospel, ostensibly to convert native Americans. In reality, Wesley was more concerned to save his own soul, and spent most of his time trying to enforce his exacting disciplines on the unruly colonists. Their opposition and an abortive love-affair combined to drive him back to England in 1738.

In Georgia he had encountered Moravian immigrants, followers of Count Zinzendorf, who challenged Wesley with the idea that to become a real Christian one must cease to depend on one's own "works" and instead rely on God's grace through faith alone for salvation. In London on 24 May 1738 Wesley believed he had found this in an experience he described as having his "heart strangely warmed", so that he "did trust in Christ and Christ alone for salvation", and that Christ had "forgiven *my* sins, even *mine* and saved *me* from the law of sin and death".

Preaching his new-found faith, Wesley joined the electrifying revival preacher George Whitefield in Bristol in 1739. Whitefield persuaded Wesley to preach in the open air, with spectacular emotional results.

In 1740, however, Wesley broke with the Moravians over their "stillness" teaching — that one should wait passively for God to act rather than pursue salvation actively. The following year he also broke with Whitefield, because he rejected Calvinistic predestination in favour of the belief that all are open to salvation.

By 1751 Wesley had extended his mission from his bases in London, Bristol and Newcastle, by annual journeys to all parts of the British Isles, sometimes absorbing local revival groups.

## Methodism grows

Wesley's organisation grew piecemeal, with much borrowing and improvisation. It was more or less complete in substance by 1747, and he ruled it with ruthless autocracy. Local societies welcomed sincere seekers for salvation, regardless of denomination. Within the society smaller groups were developed, graded by spiritual progress. Societies were linked together in "Circuits" or "Rounds", overseen by travelling preachers posted for up to two years at a time. From 1744 Wesley summoned Conferences of the preachers, which soon became annual events for settling doctrine and discipline. In 1784 the Conference was legally defined as Methodism's governing body.

Having failed to attract almost any clerical helpers, Wesley was reluctantly forced to use lay preachers: Methodists who felt called to the work and became Wesley's indispensable aides. From the 1760s he even allowed women to preach discreetly. Both men and women were used extensively to lead local societies and devotional groups. As preaching houses were built, trustees were appointed; where possible they gave Wesley and his successors power to control the appointment of preachers. This was to avoid the organisation disintegrating into isolated societies under local control, like so much of English religious life at that time.

Wesley also provided for a varied diet of worship. Methodists were supposed to attend their parish churches and receive the sacraments there. Methodist worship was supposed merely to supplement this. In practice, many Methodists had little connection with, and less respect for, Anglican ministrations. Instead they had preaching services: the Covenant service for rededication; watch-nights to replace nights of dissipation; the love feast, a kind of folk sacrament of bread and water, and exchanges of religious experiences. These meetings were enlivened by extempore prayer and, above all, by hymns, especially those by Charles Wesley, which were vehicles not only for expressing religious feeling, but also for conveying theology.

## Wesley's system

What was the purpose of Wesley's system? It was more than a response to administrative necessity. The rules of the society and devotional groups (and Wesley was a compulsive composer of rules) suggest that the ideal Methodist was to be led from seeking for salvation to conversion, then to the cultivation of a holy life, and finally to the experience of Christian perfection.

What did this mean? Despite his apparently classic Evangelical conversion in 1738, Wesley was not a typical Evangelical. His old concern to achieve holiness was soon reasserted, and he became wary of seeing justification by faith as sufficient in itself for salvation. His

### Visionary experiences

*Vision of a young woman in Manchester (1748).* "I was sitting in the house while one read the passion hymn... On a sudden I saw our Saviour on the cross, as plain as if it had been with my bodily eyes, and felt it was *my* sins for which he died. I cried out and had no strength left in me... I could do nothing but weep and mourn day and night. This lasted till Monday in the afternoon. Then I saw as it were heaven open, and God sitting upon his throne in the midst of ten thousand of his saints, and I saw a large book in which my sins were written; and he blotted them all out, and my heart was filled with peace and joy and love, which I have never lost to this hour."

# Women preachers

*John Wesley's tactful advice to a Female Preacher (1769)*
I advise you . . . (1) Pray in private or public as much as you can. (2) Even in public you may properly enough intermix *short exhortations* with prayer, but keep as far as from what is called preaching as you can: therefore never take a text; never speak in a continued discourse without some break, about four or five minutes. Tell the people, "We shall have another *prayer-meeting* at such a time and place."

*Mary Bosanquet defends her preaching (1771)*
*Objection:* "The Apostle says, 'I suffer not a woman to speak in the church . . .'" "*I answer:* "'She is not to speak' here seems to me to imply no more than . . . she is not to meddle with church government."
*Objection:* "Nay, but it meant literally, not to speak by way of edification while in the church. . ." *Answer:* "Then why is it said, 'Let the woman prophesy with her head covered'; or can she prophesy without speaking? All I do is *lawful* I have no doubt, but is it expedient?"
*Objection:* "Will not some improper women follow your example?" *Answer:* "This I acknowledge . . . but the same might be said of (male) preachers. . . I do not believe every woman is called to speak publicly, no more than every man to be a Methodist preacher, yet some have an extraordinary call to it and woe be to them if they obey it not."

*Joseph Benson, a Methodist Preacher, condemns female preaching (c.1775)*
"Does not an inspired apostle expressly forbid a woman to speak in the church? Can you tell me why those who set aside this commandment of the Lord do not set aside all his other commandments? Can you tell me why those daring females, who seem to have stript themselves of the chief ornament of their sex, I mean chaste and humble modesty, and made themselves named to their shame, do not also commit fornication, and adultery, get drunk and swear?"

Appealing to women: a window from Wesley's Chapel, City Road, London. *Photo © Managing Trustees of Wesley's Chapel, London*

mature teaching suggested a process from repentance to justification and on to the total conquest of sin. In 1746 he declared: "Our main doctrines, which include all the rest, are three: that of repentance, of faith and of holiness. The first of these we account, as it were, the porch of religion; the next the door; the third religion itself."

Justification by faith, which for Luther and many Evangelicals was the very essence of salvation, was for Wesley rather the means to a greater end. "Perfection" was defined as perfect love, an uninterrupted communion between the believer and Christ and other people, conscious sin, at least, being overcome. This could be achieved by disciplined piety, but might be given in a moment in response to faith in Christ. Wesley saw the doctrine as a sovereign remedy against the risk of complacency after conversion, and he emphasised the importance of cultivating good works as well as constant dependence on divine grace.

The doctrine remains suspect for underestimating the power and subtlety of sin, and for running the risk of self-delusion. It is perhaps significant that Wesley himself never claimed the gift. He alienated many Evangelicals by attacking predestination and portraying salvation as something which could be as easily lost as gained. His perfection doctrine seemed to them dangerously optimistic, and suspiciously close to Roman Catholic notions of salvation by a mixture of grace and human effort.

## Power of experience

Wesley did indeed draw freely, though selectively and idiosyncratically, on devotional writings by the early Fathers, Catholics, High Churchmen and Puritans. He retained some of his high-church beliefs and practices, notably ideas of sacrifice and real presence in the eucharist. He preached "constant communion", and received communion several times a week whenever he could, a frequency that was rarely reached even by High Churchmen in his day.

Despite his use of lay preachers, he insisted that ordination was necessary for administering the sacraments. Yet he had also dropped many of his earlier High beliefs and practices: his irregularities and breaches of Anglican order were notorious. He denied apostolic succession; and in the 1780s he crowned his irregularities by ordaining men himself for America and Scotland.

There were other paradoxes, too, in Wesley's mentality. He liked to appeal to "men of reason and religion", had a keen interest in natural science and medicine, and increasingly followed the lessons of experience and experiment.

But the evidence of "experience" for him led to belief in the reality of witchcraft and demon-possession, and a strong sense of divine

# A conscientious Methodist

Thomas Willis, farmer and colliery owner (1744), reflected on how far he had obeyed Wesley's rules for the "band society". He does not follow all the directions, as he believes "one general rule for all sorts of people in all conditions of life cannot be performed without some exceptions". He obeys the rules as follows:

*Neither to buy nor sell anything at all on the Lord's Day:* "I do perform the rule exactly except selling milk on Sunday mornings which I believe is a work of necessity and mercy."

*To taste no spirituous liquors . . . unless prescribed by a physician:* He uses liquor only as a medicine in cases of necessity.

*To be at a word in buying and selling:* "I make very few words . . . and do always endeavour to speak truth. But in country business buying and selling cannot be at one word."

*To pawn nothing; no, not to save life:* "This rule I keep to perfection."

*Not to mention the faults of any behind their back:* "Here I confess I am guilty, but when I do mention the faults of another it is, as I think, for edification. . ."

*To wear no needless ornaments:* "This rule I can very easily keep."

Austere: the New Room, Bristol, built in 1739 by Wesley, still has his living quarters above the chapel.
*Photo © The New Room, Bristol*

*To use no needless self-indulgence, such as taking snuff or tobacco, unless prescribed by a physician:* "I do not know that I use any needless indulgence. I take no snuff. Sometimes I do smoke a little tobacco, the last thing going to bed . . . for an infirmity, and I find benefit in it."

He gives one-sixth of his profits to the poor; attends services and meetings, and conducts private and family prayers.

intervention in events and individual lives. He saw his mission as providentially guided in response to a divine call, and supernatural interventions were for him the answer to contemporary scepticism.

## Anglican Methodists

It is not surprising that Wesley's relationship with the Church of England was strained. He was never expelled, and always insisted that the Methodists were auxiliaries to that Church and should never leave it. Yet he also made it clear that he would rather be expelled than give up the irregularities which he believed to be necessary were Methodism to fulfil its mission. In reality, his organisation had evolved into an alternative and highly flexible system of evangelism and pastoral care which strongly contrasted with the static nature of contemporary Anglicanism. It is not surprising that, after Wesley's death in 1791, Methodism eventually separated from the Church of England, though by a piecemeal process which left "Church Methodists" continuing to depend partly on the Church of England, especially for sacraments.

## A radical Tory

Wesley was a man of many interests whose writings and activities extended beyond the narrowly religious to science, history and general culture. Given his busy life and relatively humble following, it is not surprising that he did not organise the kind of reforming campaigns associated with Wilberforce and the Clapham Sect.

He did, however, adapt a Quaker pamphlet against the slave-trade, and his last surviving letter eloquently urged Wilberforce on in his campaign. Wesley was an active philanthropist, begging for the poor and organising employment in times of distress. He ran a dispensary, and his bestselling *Primitive Physick* was a characteristic mixture of sensible advice on health and traditional folk-medicine. He was severely critical of the rich and, unlike many of his contemporaries, did not blame the poor for their misfortune. He even proposed a plan for a community of goods on the model of the Acts of the Apostles. His sermon on *The Use of Money* urged Methodists to "gain all you can" (by honest labour), and "save all you can" (avoiding conspicuous consumption), but only so as to "give all you can" beyond family needs.

In politics, Wesley called himself a Tory, defined as one who believes power descends from God, not from the people. He attacked radicals at home and the American rebels abroad. Methodism has been controversially credited with "helping to save England from revolution". This peculiar English immunity undoubtedly requires a more complex explanation, though it is less implausible to suggest that Methodism did unintentionally help to drill a section of the working classes in less violent methods of campaigning for reform.

Wesley once said that his aim was "not to create a new sect, but to revive the nation and especially the Church, and to spread scriptural holiness through the land". His achievement manifestly fell short of this. The 19th-century renewal of the Church of England arguably derived little directly from Methodism except the stimulus of opposition. Yet it seems reasonable to claim that Wesley captured a significant proportion of those neglected, alienated or uninspired by conventional religion. Methodism gave them faith, fellowship and scope for their frustrated talents such as few other religious groups of the time provided. And in the 19th century, the new Methodist family of churches eventually became part of the expanding Nonconformist world, which provoked far-reaching religious and social effects, still being explained and understood.

## CHRONOLOGY

**1703** Birth of John Wesley
**1729** Organisation of "Holy Club" at Oxford
**1738** "Evangelical conversion" of John and Charles Wesley
**1739** Wesley begins open-air preaching
**1744** First conference of Wesley's preachers
**1780** Hymns for the Use of Methodists
**1784** "Deed of Declaration" gives legal basis for the Methodist Conference. Wesley revises the Prayer Book and Articles for an American Methodist Church, and performs his first ordinations.
**1791** Death of John Wesley

# WHEN ONE REVIVAL LED TO ANOTHER

*Jeremy Morris*

By reasserting for Anglicans the importance of discipleship and ecclesiology, the Evangelicals and Tractarians utterly transformed the Church of England.

By the middle of the 19th century, the tide of reform was sweeping through the established Church. Reform was theological and devotional as well as institutional. Victorian Anglicanism was the product of a series of intellectual movements which, in the course of half a century, utterly transformed the life and ethos of the Church. By far the most important of these were the Evangelical and high-church "revivals".

Evangelicalism exercised a profound influence throughout the 19th century. It was a strikingly new form of religious expression. It saw itself as rooted firmly in the theology of the Anglican reformers, it is true, but its piety and its characteristic forms of expression were very much influenced by Methodism, and through that by Pietism and the Moravian Church.

## Clapham Sect

The leadership of early Evangelicalism was concentrated in the hands of a small group of affluent Anglicans, including the Wilberforces, the Venns, the Thorntons and the Macaulays — the "Clapham Sect". William Wilberforce's *Practical View of the Prevailing Religious System of Professed Christians* (1797) was a passionate and extremely popular appeal for the recovery of a due sense of the seriousness of sin, repentance, and Christian responsibility.

But Wilberforce is best known for his practical advocacy of Evangelical causes. Together with his friend Thomas Clarkson, he was instrumental in securing the abolition of the slave trade in 1807. (The abolition of slavery itself took another 26 years.) He was prominent in the development of missionary work overseas, including the foundation of the Church Missionary Society and the Bible Society.

Yet the Evangelical Revival was always much wider than the Clapham Sect. It had Anglican divines such as John Newton, who died in 1807, a "bridge" figure between the Wesleys and the Wilberforces. It had advocates such as Charles Simeon, the great Vicar of Holy Trinity Church, Cambridge, and Anthony Ashley Cooper, the 7th Earl

"Waterloo" church: St Ann's, Wandsworth, London.
*Photo © A. F. Kersting*

Campaigner: William Wilberforce, by Sir Thomas Lawrence (1828). *Photo © by courtesy of the National Portrait Gallery, London*

of Shaftesbury. It had champions of the new Sunday-school movement, such as Hannah More. Above all, Evangelicalism changed the pattern of Anglican devotion. Evangelicals re-emphasised well ordered worship, including regular communion, sought to improve the standard of Anglican preaching, built churches to accommodate the growing urban populations, and injected a new sense of responsibility and seriousness into pastoral practice.

They renewed the sense of religion as personal transformation. Conversion marked merely the beginning of Christian devotion, cultivated in personal prayer, in spiritual journals, in keeping Sunday as a day of rest and prayer, and in organising the family around a code of Christian morality and prayer. Victorian "respectability" was the creation of Evangelicalism as of nothing else.

## Oxford Movement

But it had unforeseen results. Some were alarmed by it, thinking that it

Leader: Edward Bouverie Pusey by George Richmond (1890).
*Photo © by permission of the Governing Body of Christ Church, Oxford*

underrated the Church and the importance of the sacraments. Others were influenced by its notion of holiness and disciplined devotion, and this included those who led the Oxford Movement.

This had its origins in the small, compact world of Oxford University, a stronghold of high-church orthodoxy which, unlike Cambridge, insisted its undergraduates subscribe to the Thirty-Nine Articles *before* beginning study.

Oxford seethed with resentment at Roman Catholic emancipation, and at political reform. In March 1833, John Keble preached his "Assize sermon", an attack on the Whig government's proposals to reform the Church of Ireland. John Henry Newman later wrote: "I have ever considered and kept the day, as the start of the religious movement of 1833."

Keble, Newman, Edward Bouverie Pusey and, until his death, Richard Hurrell Froude were the leaders of a vigorous movement of high-church assertiveness. If the Oxford Movement began in political reaction, it rapidly turned into a movement to revitalise the sacramental theology and practice of the Church as a whole.

Its leaders were able scholars and theologians, who used 17th-century Anglicanism and the works of the Church Fathers to bolster their claim that the Church had neglected its doctrinal and devotional heritage.

Their vision of an Anglicanism united to the Catholic Church by its possession of apostolic succession as well as common faith was compelling for many.

For six years, from 1833 to 1839, the movement appeared to carry all before it. These were years of intense literary activity for its leaders. But they were also years in which initial support gave way to suspicion, and then to outright hostility. Where was it all leading, contemporaries wondered. Could the new emphasis on the sacraments, on ritual, on church tradition and order lead, not to a "revived" Anglicanism, but to Rome?

Newman himself felt the dilemma. Increasingly he began to wonder at the gap between his vision of the Church, and the actual Church of England. His *Tract 90* argued that the Thirty-Nine Articles were consistent with Tridentine Catholicism.

The hostility he provoked shook him to the core, and four years of perplexity followed, leading to his secession to Roman Catholicism. The Oxford movement did not end with Newman's secession, though several hundred of the Anglican clergy eventually followed him.

The year 1845 marked the end of its Oxford phase, but it also marked the beginning of a new stage in the high-church revival, which eventually took its characteristic theology and devotion out into the parishes of the Church of England. And so appeared in time many familiar features of modern Anglicanism, including candles on altars, surpliced choirs, weekly communion, the religious orders, parish missions, and the revival of synodical government.

## A changed Church

Whatever the merits of the Georgian Church of England, by the middle of the 19th century Anglicanism was beginning to look quite different.

Evangelicalism and Tractarianism together had transformed its pastoral practice, its worship, and its theology. Successive waves of revival had revitalised the Church, and helped it to adapt to the rapidly changing conditions of the 19th century. Yet change had not brought internal peace: distinct church "parties" were coming into being, and with them the characteristic subdivisions of modern Anglicanism.

# A boom in ordinands that transformed parish life

## Frances Knight

The 19th century witnessed the last great age of Christian faith in Britain. For the vast majority of the population, some kind of distinctively Christian world-view was what shaped and gave meaning to many aspects of daily life.

The first half of the 19th century saw the flowering of several different types of Protestant Nonconformity, as well as the rapid expansion of Roman Catholicism. Thus, to a greater extent than previously, the established Church had to compete with the claims and attractions of other Christian denominations.

By the final third of the century, it had (in theory at least) learned to adjust to its altered status as one denomination, albeit still the largest one, among several, with equal status accorded to all. On the whole, the Church of England rose to these challenges with energy and vigour, although the tensions were real.

For most of the people of England and Wales, it was usually the established Church that baptised, married and buried them, particularly in the years before the passing of the Civil Registration Act (1836) and the Burial Act (1880). Sunday church-going was also practised by a significant proportion of the population, with about a quarter of the English and a fifth of the Welsh attending Anglican Sunday services in 1851.

No other institution could command the support and loyalty of so many people, and no other institution was so closely woven into the fabric of everyday life.

It might have been supposed that this state of affairs would have led to feelings of optimism, or even complacency; but the Victorians tended to concentrate on the negative side of church-attendance statistics, lamenting the numbers who stayed away, rather than rejoicing at the presence of the many.

Despite the fact that the Church remained one of the largest and most influential professions, for some of the clergy the mid-Victorian years were marked by a feeling of being beleaguered. The large number of young men who sought ordina-

tion from the 1820s to the 1880s led to an acute shortage of titles for orders, and, as time went on, to a shortage of incumbencies, too.

The crucially important 1838 Pluralities Act resulted in a shake-up for the parochial ministry by putting a gradual brake on the holding of more than one living (unless one was within ten miles of the other, and the populations and revenues of both were fairly small).

The Act affected incumbents, curates and lay people, although in very different ways. For the beneficed clergy, it meant the isolation of taking up residence in remote parishes where perhaps no clergyman had lived for years. For curates, it could mean being displaced from the parishes that they had been serving for years.

Thus the job of the curate changed from being (generally) in sole charge of a parish in the absence of a non-resident incumbent to being an assistant minister, working under the direction of a resident rector or vicar. Assistant curates were exempt from the legislation that governed the stipends of those in sole charge, and they were often paid very small sums from livings that could barely support one clergyman, let alone two.

Many were faced with an insecure, hand-to-mouth existence, and had to rely heavily on private means, or grants from the Additional Curates' Society or the Church Pastoral Aid Society. Unemployment became a real issue for curates, particularly for older ones.

From the perspective of lay Anglicans, the 1838 Act spelled the disappearance of the curate in sole charge, and the arrival of the resident incumbent, perhaps installed in a new or refurbished parsonage. Such a person would naturally determine the ethos of Anglicanism in his parish, and was more likely to make distinctions between his "church" people, who were increasingly regarded as the inner group of communicants, and the other parishioners, who, although they might continue to look to the Church for rites of passage, became gradually less closely identified with the Church of England.

# WHIGS AND REVOLUTIONARIES

## *Arthur Burns*

The experience of the American Revolution combined with the subsequent, closely observed spectacle of the French Revolution to leave the late Hanoverian political nation both shaken *and* stirred. Confidence in the providentially guaranteed invincibility of the Protestant state was undermined by defeat in America. The French Revolution suggested the fragility of the underpinnings of Christian civilisation. Moreover, the familiar threat to the élite Englishman's cherished inheritance of liberty, property and prosperity posed by the Catholic states of continental Europe was now superseded by a more sinister enemy, irreligion, a development marked by some commentators' ceasing to identify the Pope with the Antichrist, and their substituting Napoleon.

The new threat demanded a response. There was an efflorescence of lay activism, frequently in pan-denominational combinations, manifest in Sunday schools and home and foreign missions.

For high-church Anglicans, however, who perceived in Dissent the advance guard of the irreligious horde, the situation demanded a re-assertion of the state's exclusive commitment to the established Church. The postwar Tory administration indeed turned to the Church of England to bolster the religious underpinning of the social order. In 1818, government allocated £1 million for the building of additional Anglican churches; a further half-million followed in 1824.

## Limits to state loyalty

As a result of this largesse — the first state subvention for church extension since the reign of Queen Anne — London alone received an additional 38 capacious if architecturally utilitarian "Waterloo" churches by 1828.

By the early 1830s, however, many Churchmen believed the very existence of the Church of England to be in jeopardy. "The Church as it now stands, no human power can save," lamented the headmaster of Rugby, Thomas Arnold. Anxious to secure the loyalty both of Dissenters and — after the Act of Union of 1800-01 — Irish Roman Catholics, the government had demonstrated the limits of its commitment to the established Church by dismantling two cornerstones of the confessional state through the repeal of the Test and Corporation Acts in 1828, and Roman Catholic emancipation in 1829.

In 1832, the Great Reform Act increased the political leverage of the

Church's opponents, who now found new platforms for a strident assault both on the remaining privileges of the established Church and on the notion of establishment itself. Meanwhile, radicals who regarded the Church as the most vulnerable dimension of the nexus of aristocratic privilege they dubbed "old corruption" intensified their assault as bishops were prominent among the opponents of parliamentary reform.

All the Church's critics found plentiful ammunition in statistics which demonstrated both the failure of the Church's pastoral provision to keep pace with population growth, and the extent of "abuses" such as pluralism and disparities of clerical wealth. When a Whig government took office in 1830, the doomsday scenario was complete. It was not only the leaders of the Oxford Movement who perceived the beginning of the end in 1833 when the Whigs abolished several Irish bishoprics and considered transferring the revenues thus freed to non-denominational education.

## Recovery of morale

Yet, when the Great Exhibition opened in 1851, not only did the Church still stand, but, if there were no grounds for complacency, it had experienced a recovery of morale. This owed much to the impact of the Oxford Movement's assertion of an understanding of the Anglican Church less dependent on its relationship with the state, and which fostered clerical commitment and zeal. Yet it also owed more than later commentators allowed to two other factors.

First, there was a process of locally inspired and directed reform in the dioceses, originating long before 1833, and involving men of all parties. This produced more effective supervision of clerical activity and greater ecclesiastical *esprit de corps*.

Moreover, even under the control of the Whigs, the state proved more supportive of the Church — if as an institution defined more by its national character than its doctrinal particularity — than the Tractarians were prepared to recognise. There was reforming legislation, and with the creation of the permanent Ecclesiastical Commission in 1836 a mechanism was established for efficient management of the Church's resources, the internal redeployment of its revenues, and the recasting of its geography (including new sees at Ripon and Manchester).

The Commission both made a vital contribution to increasing the Church's pastoral effectiveness, and also enabled this process to occur insulated from the direct interference of the Church's parliamentary critics. If the alliance with the state was by no means as strong at the middle of the 19th century as it had appeared at its outset, it was still of vital importance to the fortunes of the Anglican Church.

## CHRONOLOGY

**1764** Ordination of John Newton
**1779** William Cowper and John Newton publish *Olney Hymns*
**1780** William Wilberforce enters Parliament
**1783** Charles Simeon becomes Vicar of Holy Trinity, Cambridge
**1793** Execution of the French king, Louis XVI
**1797** Publication of Wilberforce's *Practical View of the Prevailing Religious System of Professed Christians*
**1799** Church Missionary Society founded
**1803** Bible Society founded
**1805** Henry Martyn becomes missionary in Calcutta
**1807** Abolition of slave trade throughout British dominions
**1815** Battle of Waterloo
**1818** Parliament votes £1 million for church-building (further £½ million in 1824)
**1828** Abolition of Test and Corporation Acts
**1829** Catholic emancipation
**1832** Great Reform Act
**1833** Irish Church Temporalities Act; John Keble's Assize sermon
**1835** Establishment of Ecclesiastical Commission (permanent in 1836)
**1836** Death of Froude; civil registration of births, deaths and marriages
**1838** Pluralities Act; Froude's literary *Remains* published
**1841** John Henry Newman's *Tract 90*
**1845** Newman becomes Roman Catholic
**1852** Convocation of Canterbury summoned for the first time since 1717

# ALL THINGS THAT GIVE SOUND

*Richard Watson*

*Music in church: we survey its history, with special emphasis on hymns and recent challenges to their supremacy.*

Hymns are praise and prayer. They are also teaching, the exposition of holy scripture, theology and doctrine, poetry and music. They are greatly loved, too, for their ability to touch the heart. As George Herbert put it:

> A verse may find him, who a sermon flies,
> And turn delight into a sacrifice.

Herbert's verb is beautifully chosen: hymns at their best do not catch us, or bully us, but "find" us, giving expression to something that is our deepest self. Words and music unite in the praise of God, and that praise satisfies something within us that has been present in the human heart since the dawn of consciousness.

The Greeks sang hymns: so did the people of Israel, whose psalms have been an inspiration to worshippers since they were written. Calvin, who loved psalms, called them "the anatomy of all parts of the soul". Our Lord and his disciples sang a hymn after the Last Supper; and St Paul exhorted his followers to speak to one another in psalms and hymns and spiritual songs, "singing and making melody with your heart to the Lord".

"With your heart": St Paul's phrase captures the way in which hymns allow the heart to rejoice, as Mary did when she burst into poetry after the Annunciation, in the hymn that we know as the Magnificat.

## The earliest hymns

The early Church sang hymns: morning and evening hymns, later the Te Deum, supposedly by Ambrose, Bishop of Milan; it was the singing of an Ambrosian hymn at Milan that caught the ear of St Augustine in the garden, and led to his conversion. Celtic Christians, on the edge of the Roman Empire, sang their hymns by the northern seas, the most famous of which is "St Patrick's Breastplate". Latin hymns were an important part of the monastic tradition throughout the Middle Ages, but they disappeared, with the monasteries themselves, at the

Double meaning: "Sumer is icumen in" (anon. 13th century), early polyphony, with the alternative sacred text, *Perspice Christicola. Photo © by permission of the British Library*

Reformation. In their place, the Protestant exiles brought back from Geneva their custom of singing metrical psalms to strong tunes, such as the Old Hundredth:

> All people that on earth do dwell
> Sing to the Lord with cheerful voice. . .

These psalms and hymns played a part in the Reformation itself: Luther's hymns were sung through the length and breadth of Germany, and a Roman Catholic writer in England in 1616 reported that "there is nothing that hath drawne multitudes to be of their Sects so much as the singing of their psalmes, in such variable and delightfull tunes." The first challenge to the domination of the metrical psalms was George Wither's *Hymnes and Songs of the Church* (1623), which is notable not so much for its verse as for its music by Orlando Gibbons (some of which is still in use).

But this was also the great age of devotional poetry, when Donne, Herbert and Vaughan all produced poems that have been used as hymns. They were followed by divines such as Samuel Crossman, whose "My song is love unknown" was published in 1664, and Thomas Ken, whose "Morning Hymn" has opened successive editions of *Hymns Ancient and Modern* since its first printing. Hymns were also associated with Dissenting congregations, which used books by long-forgotten writers such as William Barton and Benjamin Keach.

From this Independent tradition came Isaac Watts. He is said to have complained about the quality of the hymns at the chapel in Southampton (probably Barton's), and to have been challenged by his father to do better. The timing was perfect: Watts was a man of his time, with philosophical interests and an enlightened understanding; but he was also the son of a man who had been to prison for his beliefs. He knew that religion was "duty and delight", but also that it had its demands:

> Love so amazing, so divine,
> Demands my soul, my life, my all.

His work has a dignity and clarity that is found in verses which have great strength, yet also have a sensitivity to the human condition:

> Time, like an ever-rolling stream,
>   Bears all its sons away;
> They fly forgotten, as a dream
>   Dies at the opening day.

Watts began the great century of hymn-writing: from Addison at the beginning to Cowper at the end, the 18th century produced a series of magnificent writers. They were often associated with Dissent, which produced Philip Doddridge and Anne Steele; and also with the Evangelical wing of the Church of England, in which writers such as Augustus Montague Toplady ("Rock of Ages, cleft for me"), John Newton ("Glorious things of thee are spoken") and William Cowper ("God moves in a mysterious way") celebrated the power of the blood of Christ to save sinners ("There is a fountain filled with blood").

The greatest of them, Charles Wesley, lived and died an Anglican priest, but became closely associated with his brother and the Methodists: his hymns dominate John Wesley's *Collection of Hymns for the use of the People called Methodists* of 1780. However, they have transcended all church barriers: "O thou who camest from above", "Love divine, all loves excelling", and others, such as "Hark, the herald angels sing", have become universally loved.

Wesley was deeply versed in the Bible, and his hymns ring with its phrases; but he also added his own particular excitement. It is instructive to compare his New Year hymn with Watts's "time/dream" verse above:

The arrow is flown,
The moment is gone;
The millennial year
Rushes on to our view, and eternity's here.

The last of the great Nonconformist writers was James Montgomery, whose "Angels from the realms of glory" is still widely sung; but in the 19th century the energy and the initiative passed to the Church of England.

## Anglicans enter the field

Three figures helped to make this possible, by making hymn-writing respectable, and by ridding it of the stigma of being a "party badge" (associated with the Nonconformists or Evangelicals): Reginald Heber, a bishop; Henry Hart Milman, a dean; and Henry Francis Lyte, a parish priest.

Their hymns, such as "Holy, holy, holy!" and "Ride on, ride on in majesty!", were examples of the way in which hymns could be adapted to the Church's year; and "Praise, my soul, the King of Heaven" could be used at any time.

This new interest in hymns was encouraged by the rediscovery of ancient and medieval texts, translated with great skill by John Mason

Translator: John Mason Neale (1818-1886). *The English Hymnal* used 72 of his pieces

Neale; and by the translations of German hymns by Catherine Winkworth and others.

The time was ripe for a good Church of England hymn book: and in 1861 appeared *Hymns Ancient and Modern*. It rapidly eclipsed all others, and completed the process of converting the mind of the Church of England to hymn-singing. It was subtitled "for use in the Services of the Church", and it had a profound effect on worship.

Edition followed edition for the rest of the century, each one adding its Anglican blockbuster hymns: "The Church's one foundation", "Thy hand, O God, has guided", "The day thou gavest, Lord, is ended", with unforgettable tunes by J. B. Dykes, S. S. Wesley, Arthur Sullivan, John Goss, John Stainer, and many others. William Henry Monk, the first musical editor for *A & M*, was a genius at finding the right tune for the words, and many of his "marriages" of music and text have become inseparable.

*Hymns Ancient and Modern* had its rivals and its detractors, but it was the supreme hymn book from 1861 to the beginning of the 20th century. Then came *The English Hymnal* of 1906, stamped with the genius of Ralph Vaughan Williams and the flair of Percy Dearmer. It swept away the Victorianism of *A & M*, putting some of its tunes in an Appendix (which Vaughan Williams called "the chamber of horrors"), and replacing them with fresh and lively ones, many taken from English folk melodies.

Even more lively and modern was Percy Dearmer's *Songs of Praise* (1925), a book which was full of unexpected treasures from English poetry (only some of which worked as hymns), but which was forward-looking and un-churchy. With its bright-blue cover, it looked cheerful; and a generation of children grew up singing from it.

That generation is now mostly elderly: and since the far-off days of *Songs of Praise* between the wars, much has happened in the world and in the Church. It is hard to predict how hymn-writing and worship will develop; what is certain, however, is that in traditional hymns there is a marvellous treasure-house of what might be called "inspirational doctrine" — the exposition of holy scripture linked with the understanding of human feeling — which has steadily accumulated over the centuries. It is a body of material which is often taken for granted, and sometimes derided; but it contains the work of writers who were poets as well as prophets, and who knew how to write a good line as well as search the soul.

The best hymns do both: in them, found and refound with each singing of a remembered and loved text, is a rich engagement with the truths of the Christian faith, written and rewritten in each generation, and centred on the human heart.

# THANKSGIVING AND SONG

## Ian Bradley

The hymn reigned supreme in English church worship for a little over 100 years — from the 1840s to the 1960s. The past 40 years have seen it challenged and in many places replaced by the worship song, generally having a shorter and less four-square metrical form, often though not always a more subjective theological perspective, and usually with a tune more suitable for accompaniment by instruments other than the organ.

Several factors lie behind the demise of the hymn and the rise of the worship song. The folk revival of the 1960s was undoubtedly an important musical and cultural catalyst. Perhaps its most brilliant and enduring exponent in the field of Christian song was Sydney Carter, whose "Lord of the Dance" and "One more step along the world I go" climbed rapidly into the nation's list of top ten favourite hymns, and remain among the most frequently used songs in primary-school assemblies.

The Charismatic movement was another extremely important influence behind the rise of the worship song. Its laureate, Graham Kendrick, a Baptist minister's son closely involved with the Ichthus Church, responsible for both the words and music of the enormously popular "Shine, Jesus, shine" and "The Servant King", represents the relatively modern phenomeon of the professional Christian singer/song-writer who earns his money by writing songs. By contrast, hymn-writing in its Victorian and early-20th-century heyday was a largely part-time and amateur activity engaged in by country clergymen and sickly spinsters.

The strength of interdenominational Evangelicalism has also helped to promote contemporary worship songs. *Mission Praise*, first published in 1983 and now the most widely used single hymn book in Britain, devotes more than 60 per cent of its contents to worship songs and choruses written in the past 30 years, many of them of American origin.

Annual gatherings like Spring Harvest and Greenbelt have also fuelled both the demand and the supply of contemporary worship songs.

Technological developments have also played an important part in changing the style and sound of what is sung and played in church. Synthesisers, keyboards and other instruments have gradually replaced pipe organs. Recording, amplification and mixing techniques have brought the pop-group sound into many churches. Increasingly, hymns and songs are seen as having a short shelf-life, and are projected on overheads rather than being enshrined between the covers of hymn books. By the end of the 20th century, several churches were beginning to ask whether the hymn, and the hymn book, had had its day.

Traditional hymn-writing is not dead. Anglican Evangelicals like Timothy Dudley-Smith, Michael Saward and Christopher Idle continue to produce hymns which are highly popular and recognisably in the idiom of Watts and Wesley. Popular taste, especially perhaps of the great unchurched majority, still favours traditional hymns over more modern worship songs and choruses. The most recent poll commissioned by the BBC's *Songs of Praise* at the end of last year revealed "How great thou art" to be the nation's favourite hymn, closely followed by two Victorian staples, "Dear Lord and Father of mankind" and "The day thou gavest, Lord, is ended".

The supplanting of hymns by worship songs betokens a bigger cultural shift in church music from participation to performance. In many ways we are witnessing a return to the pre-Victorian world of the gallery band, or the pre-Reformation world of the monastic choir after an all-too-brief reign of congregational hymnody. Yet not all contemporary worship songs are written for praise bands and semi-professional performance. John Bell, the Church of Scotland minister and leader of the Iona Community's Wild Goose Worship Group, who is one of the most innovative forces in contemporary church music, writes unashamedly for congregational singing, making much use of folk tunes and expressing a gritty and liberal incarnational theology.

Perhaps the wheel is turning full circle. Another notable feature of recent years has been a revival of interest in singing the psalms. Compact discs of Gregorian chant regularly top the classical bestseller charts; and the simple chants of the Taizé community have been widely taken up by churches of very different traditions and denominations.

Maybe the third millennium will see a balance struck between St Paul's three types of sacred song, with "psalms, hymns and spiritual songs" co-existing as equally valid ways to praise the Lord.

# EACH JUBILANT CHORD

## *Glyn Paflin*

We know very little about Christian music in England before St Augustine's mission in 597; and indeed before the 11th century, the date of the oldest surviving English musical manuscripts. Augustine would have known the chant used in Rome during the pontificate of Gregory the Great, though here the relationship between two surviving repertories, the Gregorian and Old Roman, remains a matter of widely differing academic conjecture.

Shortly after the Synod of Whitby (664), a teacher of chant was sent to England from Rome; and in 747 a council in Kent decreed chanting in accordance with a Roman sample. The Gregorian tradition, so-called, flows through England in the Middle Ages, with local variants surviving in manuscripts from great churches such as those at Sarum, Barking, York and Hereford.

## Rise of polyphony

Making verbal or musical additions to ("troping") the chant was a practice established before the Norman Conquest. New texts and new melodies would be added. But one of two manuscripts, the Winchester Troper (Winchester being a great centre, famous for its organ), is the earliest liturgical source of two-part organum — vertical elaboration of the chant in which, it has been suggested, lie the origins of the subsequent development of Western polyphony (music with a certain independence in simultaneous voices).

In the 13th century, influence from vernacular sources appears in Latin church music in England. The famous Reading *rota* (round), "*Sumer is icumen in*" (c. 1250), was also adapted to an ecclesiastical text, "*Perspice Christicola*".

The *cantus firmus* appears in England in the 13th/14th century: a plainsong melody in long values in the tenor part; and music develops richer rhythm and sonority. From the early 15th century survives the Old Hall manuscript, and the identities of some composers. John Dunstable (d. 1453) was named by the Fleming Tinctoris, *c.* 1474, as the chief musician in an England that had been the *fons et origo* of a "new art". English composers for a while were the rage in Europe. They may have been the first to organise a mass around one *cantus firmus*.

The closing years of the 15th century and the early part of the 16th were a golden age, with large forces used to exuberant effect. Massive, slow-moving harmonies are embellished by florid vocal lines. Between Robert Fayrfax (1464-?1521) and John Taverner (*c.* 1490-1545), preeminent figures of this period, and the great William Byrd (?1543-1623), is the transition to the late-Renaissance sound — the English version of the Palestrina style that, with its aptness to the Tridentine reforms, won lasting favour in Rome.

## 1549 and all that

The Reformation hits the generation of Tye, Tallis, Sheppard and Mundy amidships, blowing apart the world of church music, and scattering the musicians of the religious orders.

Tallis, like the recusant Byrd, enjoying royal favour, is able to mould a broadly international style to the changing liturgical requirements. Tye becomes a parson. We have only John Foxe's word that Taverner repented that he had ever "made Songes to Popish ditties"; but Geneva fever gripped John Merbecke (*c.* 1510-85), who gave special heed to Cranmer's opinion that in church "the song should not be full of notes, but as near as may be for every syllable a note". Caught out by the pace of liturgical change, his setting of the 1549 communion rite waited three centuries to be called out of obscurity by High Anglicans.

At the Reformation, the Service now takes over from the Mass as a liturgical form, mainly the morning and evening canticles. Anglican chant takes rather longer to oust the old psalm tones on which it is initially constructed. The anthem, though it waits till 1662 for the rubric about "Quires and places where they sing", is also allowed, and follows two patterns: "full" and (with solo sections) "verse".

Under the Jacobeans Tomkins, Wilbye, Weelkes and Gibbons, and the patronage of the Chapel Royal, these forms flourish. Sixteen years after Orlando Gibbons's death (1625), organs and cathedral music libraries are devastated by Cromwell's supporters, and English church music reaches its nadir.

## Blow and Purcell

The Restoration brings a boom in organ-building, and confirms theatrical influences on church-music style already audible before the Commonwealth. The climax of this tendency is found in the works of John Blow (1649-1708) and Henry Purcell (1659-95) — Chapel Royal eminences after whom the 18th century has usually been seen, in some respects unfairly, as a falling away. Its most distinguished figures, after Jeremiah Clarke shoots himself, are William Croft, Maurice Greene, and William Boyce. England takes Handel and the oratorio to its heart.

The 19th century sees a revival of cathedral music (which had never fully recovered from Cromwell), partly through the campaigning of John Jebb and Maria Hackett ("The Choristers' Friend"). The compositions of S. S. Wesley, also zealous for reform, display a new vigour. His Service in E becomes, in Kenneth Long's words, "a model which many copied but few equalled".

The foreigners Mendelssohn, Spohr and Gounod influence the characteristic sounds of a choral revival that spreads widely in churches with an impetus from High Churchmen, who reinstate the choral eucharist.

New and more efficient methods of musical education also help to see off the west-gallery minstrels.

## 1870 to today

With Charles Stanford's works, from the 1870s on, the symphonic idea resonates in Anglican chancels. Charles Wood, and later Edward Bairstow and Herbert Howells are among those who create the cathedral tradition we know today. The period also sees rising interest in the performance of plainsong, early music, and the works of J. S. Bach, and a fruitful overlap with the oratorio tradition. The cantata for performance in church finds its popular apogee in Stainer's *The Crucifixion* (1887).

The anti-Victorian reaction, increasingly now recognised as an over-reaction, brings in the 20th century a battle against allegedly "sentimental" music — a trend typified by the work of Sydney Nicholson and the early ethos of the Royal School of Church Music. Official efforts to curb choral domination of parochial worship in favour of "congregational" music are eventually superseded by a general decline in amateur singing.

By the end of the century, many chancels are choirless again, minstrels (or "music groups") are back in fashion, and the old monastic and cathedral repertoires may be less often experienced in worship than by forms of sound-reproduction.

## CHRONOLOGY

*c.* **339-97** Ambrose of Milan, who gives impetus to Latin hymnody

**597** Augustine arrives with Roman musical traditions

**7th-8 c.** English vernacular hymns; Synod of Whitby (664)

**10th-11th c.** Sequences introduced; Winchester Troper compiled

**12th c.** Giraldus Cambrensis writes of Welsh love of polyphony; hymns included in monastic offices

**13th c.** Vernacular influence in Latin church music in England

**early 15th c.** Old Hall MS

**1490s/1500s** Eton Choirbook: elaborate polyphony

*c.* **1505-85** Thomas Tallis

**?1543-1623** William Byrd

**1550** Merbecke's *Booke of Common Praier Noted*

**1557** Sternhold and Hopkins's "Old Version" (metrical psalter)

**1583-1625** Orlando Gibbons

**1640** Chapel Royal disbanded

**1654** Demolition of organs

**1660** Cathedral services reinstated

**1659-95** Henry Purcell

**1674-1748** Isaac Watts

*c.* **1700** Anglican chant emerging

**1711-79** William Boyce

**1738** John and Charles Wesley have "conversion" experience

**1741** Handel's *Messiah*

**1810-76** S. S. Wesley

**1827** Maria Hackett's *Brief Account of Cathedral and Collegiate Schools*

**1841** Leeds Parish Church Choir in surplices

**1852-1924** Charles Stanford

**1861** *Hymns A & M*

**1901-22** Solesmes monks (chant experts) resident on Isle of Wight

**1903** *The English Hymnal*

**1927** School of English Church Music (now RSCM) founded

**1963** "Lord of the Dance" by Sydney Carter (b. 1915)

**1973** "Series 3" language necessitates new music

**1983** *Mission Praise*

# WHEN THE FAITH WAS SET FREE

*Edward Norman*

*As the 19th century progressed, the state's grip on the people's religious life could not be sustained. We recall the mid-century census that showed how far things had gone.*

When Garibaldi, the great hero of Italian nationalism, came to England in 1864, there were incredible scenes of popular enthusiasm. The visit, it is true, was carefully managed by his English supporters, but their task was an easy one, for Garibaldi embodied two aspirations of English religion which lay at the heart of the 19th-century dynamism of Dissent.

The first was hatred of the papacy, and Garibaldi was the enemy of the States of the Church in Italy, the "Liberator", the Saviour of the *Risorgimento* — depicted in Christ-like guises in popular prints, a kind of surrogate English Protestant. The second was the ideal of "a free Church in a free state", the very centre of the Nonconformists' assault upon the existence of a religious establishment in England, the generator of "the dissidence of Dissent".

The anti-Catholic tradition was a striking cohesive, managing to unite the otherwise exceedingly particularist strands of English Protestantism. It was also multi-class. Leading figures of the ruling élite like Gladstone, and the stirrers of the *demos* like the numerous no-popery street orators, shared a common horror of the Roman Catholic Church — an institution which, so it seemed to them, enslaved the intellect and debased the people within its thrall.

English civil liberties were associated with the achievements of the Reformation; indeed, the Irish were frequently represented as a retarded nation principally because they were the victims of "priest-craft" and "popish superstition". A significant measure of English National Protestantism defined itself around antipathy to Rome, and the sentiment declined only with the decline of all religious sentiment, towards the end of the century.

## Attacks on establishment

It was therefore something of a paradox that the Church of England, the national repository of Protestant virtue, should itself be increasingly assailed by other Protestants. But the ideology of what contemporaries came to call "voluntaryism" — that authentic Christianity

Leading thinker: Millais's portrait of John Henry Newman, 1881.
*Photo © by courtesy of the National Portrait Gallery, London*

should be independent of state control (a "free trade in religion") — was one of the most forceful and effective movements of opinion in 19th-century society.

At the start of the century, it existed only in residual forms, among Baptists mostly; yet the extraordinary buoyancy of Dissent, as the decades passed, floated upon tides of hostility got up in opposition to the political exclusivity and privileges of the state Church. Great national bodies, like the Liberation Society, founded by Dissenters in 1853, and the temperance movement, the United Kingdom Alliance, became important dimensions of the Liberal Party and of subsequent popular political movements.

It is often said that English Labour politics owed more to Methodism than to Marx: it is not true, because the Methodists were actually among the more politically conservative of the Nonconformist Churches. But it is certainly the case that English popular politics in the 20th century are deeply indebted to the experience of organisation and the emotional investment in public issues which 19th-century Dissenting protests against the established Church generated.

The effectiveness of voluntaryism within English Nonconformity was remarkable. The country was covered with church and chapel buildings which paralleled the parish churches of the establishment; enormous amounts were donated for missionary and social work at home and overseas. Yet, oddly, little was spent on education — odd not only because Christianity has always regarded the enlightenment of the mind as an important aspect of its presence in the world, but because the Church of England and the Roman Catholics were simultaneously engaged in a massive extension of educational institutions.

The English Dissenters, from the very start of the century, restricted themselves to Sunday schools, and looked to the state to provide "non-denominational" education. Their attack upon government support of the denominational schools, in fact, became the greatest cause of bad feeling between Church and Dissent, and an issue which more than any other impelled the Nonconformists into the arms of the Liberal Party.

The established Church, in contrast, picked up an enduring reputation for being "the Tory Party at prayer" precisely because it was obliged to turn to the only sympathetic political presence which would protect its historic vocation to be the educator of the nation.

## Class differences

There was always a social-class edge to the relations of Church and Dissent, and that, too, helped to define Free Church identity. The establishment slipped from being the Church of the landed classes, but it never slipped further than being, as it still is, a bourgeois institution.

Nonconformists wanting to conform: Spurgeon's Metropolitan Tabernacle, London.
*Photo © Richard Watt*

Nonconformity was never, except in certain mining areas and among the "aristocracy of Labour", the Church of the poor, who in general did not go to church anywhere. The only Christian body with an authentic majority of proletarian members in the 19th century was the Roman Catholic Church; and that was due to the great Irish immigration, especially during the famine years of the 1840s.

The popular (rather Italianate) devotions introduced to English Roman Catholic practice during the century, by priests trained in Rome, were quite unlike the sober Prayer Book services of the establishment, yet curiously similar in some respects to Evangelical fervour, and so had resonances with English Protestant Dissent which few at the time, however, noticed.

Evangelicalism had divided all the Churches. The Protestant Dissenters were the first where large numbers of congregations went over to Evangelical devotional styles, so leaving behind, for a time, the Unitarians and the Independents (Congregationalists), who remained loyal to the formalism of the preceding century. The Low Church within the establishment came to adopt Evangelical worship, too.

That should in theory have provided a basis of sympathy to unite all Evangelicals regardless of denominational affiliation. In reality this did not happen: the sharp differences between Church and Dissent owed as much to social-class *mores* as they did to political conflict over education and state support for religion.

The doctrinal differences which divided the Churches theologically — and especially the doctrine of the Church itself, ecclesiology — simply did not enter Protestant consciousness, and when, in the 1830s, the leaders of the Oxford Movement began to canvass them, in a very elementary form, the bishops of the Church of England, as well as the Dissenting leadership, were quite unable to recognise what they were talking about.

## Towards emancipation

The great religious census of 1851 (the only one carried out by government in England) revealed, to general surprise, that the numbers of practising Churchmen and Dissenters were about equal.

This result gave an additional stimulus to the various political agitations of the Dissenters to secure their goal of "religious equality", and it also in some sense legitimised the case of those within the intelligentsia who were sceptical about the expediency of religious establishments in societies where they did not enjoy obvious numerical support. This meant the colonies overseas, where the Nonconformists' claims to equality elicited campaigns that echoed those in England and were often used as polemical ammunition by English Dissent. It also meant Ireland, with its sizeable Roman Catholic majority.

The second half of the 18th century had seen an accumulating growth of opinion in England that insisted that religious belief should not impede civil liberty. The first to benefit were the Protestant Dissenters. The repeal of the Test and Corporation Acts in 1828 was more a symbolical than an actual advance — it removed a badge of political inequality — since Dissenters had for many years taken part in government, both local and national, and had been protected from the formal penalties of the laws against them by the passage through parliament of annual Acts of Indemnity.

One of the most important consequences of the repeal of 1828, however, was the creation of a precedent for Catholic emancipation. The Protestant Constitution was no longer seen to be unalterable; the terms of political association could be broadened. Roman Catholicism, because of the vibrancy of the anti-Catholic tradition, and because of the fear of what the massed peasantry of Ireland could do if organised by a demagogue such as Daniel O'Connell (as many thought him) or by the craft of the Catholic priests, was another matter.

Yet by the end of the 1820s the case for emancipation was, as

New strand in Nonconformity: a Salvation Army meeting in 1880. *Photo © Salvation Army International Heritage Centre* politicians said at the time on the general issue of parliamentary reform, "irresistible". It had been promised at the time of the Act of Union between England and Ireland in 1800, and had remained on the agenda of politics ever since.

## Ultramontane influence

Emancipation itself was a question of changing the words of the oath required of those taking their seats in Parliament upon election: the existing oath described the Roman Catholic religion as "damnable" and "idolatrous", and could plainly not be subscribed to by conscientious Catholics. The delay in the passage of the legislation was due less to the English horror of Catholicism, which remained undiminished, than to divisions among Catholics themselves about how far they could consent to various rewordings of the oath. They acknowledged the need for continued securities for the Protestantism of the Constitution, but rejected any phrases which interfered with the purely spiritual jurisdiction of the Holy See.

On the governmental side there were problems because the Sovereign doubted if emancipation was compatible with the Coronation Oath, which obliged him to protect the established Church. This was not an arcane matter. The Church of England was subject to Erastian controls; its governing body was Parliament (Convocations having been in practical suspension since early in the 18th century), and the nature and composition of Parliament was therefore a matter of immediate concern to the Church.

Admitting Protestant Dissenters was acceptable, because in 1828 they had not yet begun their assault upon the political privileges of the establishment; but the admission of Roman Catholics created some serious anomalies. The English are used to political anomalies, however, and the Act of Emancipation was passed in 1829 amid fears of popular disturbances in Ireland if nothing was done.

English Catholicism showed astonishing resilience during the 19th century, and it was transformed in a number of ways. Since the Elizabethan settlement, the Catholics, under the threat of the penal laws, had retired to the periphery of public life: their strongholds were not very strong, and existed in the small towns and villages of the north and west, and wherever the local gentry could protect the small gatherings and maintain a priest.

The great Irish influx of the mid-century simply swamped this presence. The Irish were urban, working-class, and very public about their religion. The Catholic leadership continued to be drawn from among the old Catholic families, and, after the mid-century, from among the Anglican converts like Cardinal Manning. But the leaders were trained in Rome, and brought the confidence, authoritarianism and spiritual energy of Ultramontanism to England when they returned to take up their posts.

Despite a history of friction with the old Catholics, the Ultramontane clergy liberated themselves from the patronage of the gentry and inspired a revival of Catholicism which made it, in the 20th century, the most numerous and most successful of the English Free Churches. In Cardinal Newman it had the greatest English religious thinker of the 19th century.

## Victorian religiosity

Nineteenth-century revivalism in Christianity was thus a phenomenon which extended to all the denominations. "Denominationalism" itself, indeed, as a social concept, was one of its fruits — the idea that Christianity could be legitimately accepted as a series of parallel institutions, each entitled to equal recognition, and none claiming exclusive political privilege.

Yet it would be mistaken to exaggerate the Victorian boom in religion. It was largely restricted to the middle classes, and reflected their inventiveness and social ambition. For several decades — no more than that — the professional classes employed Christianity as the vehicle of their moral seriousness. A modest increase in public support for institutionalised religion resulted. It did not even keep pace with population increase, and has been in slow decline ever since.

The English, it might seem, are not by nature particularly drawn to religion when it makes demands on their time or their social position. "They gave no education at all as to any religion in their children," as the Benedictine Augustine Baker noticed in the 16th century, "but regard only in them a good moral external carriage." Nothing much has changed.

# FIGURES BEFORE SPIN

## *David Edwards*

On the last Sunday in March 1851, an attempt arranged by the government was made to count the people attending churches or chapels throughout England and Wales. For the Church of England in particular this was a turning-point, for the results showed that only about half of the worshippers chose the established Church, and less than half of the population went to any church. This contradicted the traditional claim to be England's Church.

The shock did a power of good. It stimulated the building or rebuilding of many thousands of churches which are still prominent, plus a great deal of evangelism and pastoral and social work, with more dramatic worship and more realistic preaching. It was only in the 1890s that people began to talk about a further crisis in church life, and only after the Great War that people began to think that the Victorian revival of religion had been among the casualties.

The year 1851 began the most successful half-century in the Church of England's history; and in Wales, where the census produced a victory of four to one for the Nonconformists, the Anglican response was to begin the slow process of becoming a Church recognisably Welsh.

Inevitably, the statistics were not totally accurate. Out of some 14,000, almost 1000 places of Anglican worship never filled in the form, and their support had to be guessed. The numbers based on completed forms were of attendances, not specifying whether individuals came once, twice or thrice; and it was not thought necessary to ask cathedrals, colleges, schools, work-houses, alms-houses, hospitals, asylums or prisons. But the broad picture which emerged was widely accepted.

Detailed analysis has confirmed the impression that the Church of England often fared better in rural than in urban areas; but the sweeping verdict that urbanisation has always meant secularisation has been modified. In small or genteel towns, or in leafy suburbs, matins could be fashionable. Even in the cities there could be a following in the working class — a collection of good wives and Sunday-school children, if not of men; of the respectable, if not of the underclass; of the poor needing handouts, if not of the devout; of a sizeable minority, if not of the typical.

Villages varied. In some there was no church, or the population was scattered; but in others the parson really cared about the welfare of the whole community — or, less nicely, a squire who went to church could be thought capable of making employees who did not go both jobless and homeless. So local historians, stressing local factors, have ploughed up generalisations.

Regions also differed. On a map, the Church of England's relative strength could be seen to lie within a triangle drawn from Canterbury to Plymouth, up to Carlisle and down again. The trouble was that this left the Nonconformists free to make the running in Cornwall, in the north and in much of the Midlands. In East Anglia, Anglicans and Nonconformists were neck-and-neck; in Liverpool, Roman Catholics led.

To map attendance by all denominations, the line enclosing strength had to be drawn from the Wash to Land's End and, miles lower down, back eastwards, avoiding both the Dickensian squalor of London and the backwardness of rural Surrey and the south-east. That left a considerable part of the population without much visible commitment to "the faith of our fathers". Total secularists were a small minority, but ominously articulate.

The census owed much to the Victorian energy of a single official, Horace Mann, who organised it and wrote the report. It has never been repeated on its full scale. Among the changes quantified in later studies have been the contraction of the Free Churches (44 per cent of those counted at worship in 1851) and the expansion of the Roman Catholics (then only four per cent). Anglicans have done better than the one group, worse than the other, and the secularists have done best of all, making rivalries between Churches look very Victorian.

## CHRONOLOGY

**1800** Act of Union between England and Ireland creates single established Church
**1826** Foundation of University College, London
**1828** Repeal of Test and Corporation Acts
**1829** Catholic Emancipation Act
**1836** Civil marriage legalised
**1843** Church of Scotland divides; a Free Church is set up
**1844** Dissenters' Chapels Act
**1845** John Henry Newman joins Roman Catholic Church
**1850** Restoration of Roman Catholic hierarchy in England
**1851** First religious census
**1858** Jews admitted to Parliament
**1865** Foundation of Salvation Army by William Booth
**1868** Church Rates abolished
**1869** Disestablishment of Church in Ireland
**1870** Forster's Education Act
**1871** University Test Act ends Anglican control of the ancient universities
**1880** Burials Act opens parish graveyards to Dissenters
**1920** Disestablishment of Church in Wales

# SCHOLARS, SLUMS AND SOCIALISTS

*Jeremy Morris*

*Biblical criticism, Darwinism and urbanisation were challenges to the Victorian Church. Recent research has changed our view of popular religion.*

By the 1850s, the Church of England had survived the storms of reform and radical criticism. It was slowly, but surely, revitalising its national structure and its parochial organisation. New dioceses were created for the first time since the Reformation. The building of new churches and the creation of new parishes was gathering pace. A new spirit of professionalism began to circulate through the clergy, as theological colleges were founded (the first was Chichester in 1839) and university reform got under way.

## Eminent lay people

In ruling circles, Anglicanism continued to exercise great influence. Prime Ministers took great pains over the exercise of church patronage — particularly the appointment of bishops. The Queen's own religious views — which tended towards sympathy with moderate Evangelicals and conservative Broad Churchmen — were not without influence, too.

This was an age of great Anglican lay people, of whom perhaps the most powerful was W. E. Gladstone, a staunch High Churchman whose immense energies were channelled as much into ecclesiastical causes as they were into politics. It was also an age of energetic, able church leaders, such as Samuel Wilberforce, the Bishop of Oxford, and Archbishops of Canterbury such as A. C. Tait, E. W. Benson, and Frederick Temple.

Yet institutional revival was masked by the conviction of failure. The 1851 census of churchgoing horrified the Victorians: the national character of the Church was imperilled. Disestablishment once more seemed imminent, and the prospect was kept alive by the disestablishment of the Irish Church in 1869.

The Victorian Church of England's material achievements were staggering. More than 4000 churches were built or enlarged in the half-century to 1875 alone. The number of active members of the clergy rose from 16,000 in 1851 to nearly 24,000 by the end of the century. Schools, mission churches and chapels, and charitable agencies were created at an unprecedented rate. Yet all of this enormous energy and

Built for Ritualism: St Augustine's, Kilburn, by J. L. Pearson.
*Photo © Paul Barker/Country Life Picture Library*

W. E. Gladstone by S. Priory Hall (date unknown). *Photo © by courtesy of the National Portrait Gallery, London*

achievement was driven by an underlying fear that the Church was also facing unprecedented challenges, and failing to rise to them.

## Intellectual challenges

By far the most perplexing intellectual challenge of the age was the development of biblical criticism. In reaction against allegorical and figurative modes of interpretation, reformed Christianity — Anglicans included — had, over the centuries, dangerously contracted the meaning of the Bible. If the Bible told a factual narrative, and its "facts" were of the same kind as those of the world of experience and science, how could the Bible's apparent contradictions and inconsistencies be explained?

The radical biblical criticism of German scholars such as F. C. Baur had little direct impact in Britain. But it was quite otherwise with J. W. Colenso, the Anglican Bishop of Natal, whose exposure of the mathematical absurdities in the Pentateuch was devastating. It horrified orthodox churchpeople in Britain, engineered a schism in the Church in South Africa, and prompted the calling of the first Lambeth Conference in 1867.

If the Bible was at issue, so too was church doctrine. By the middle of the 19th century, it was becoming difficult to sustain the claim that the teaching of the Church was simply identical to that of the Gospels. There were moral objections to the traditional doctrine of hell and its notion of irreversible judgement, and also to penal-substitutionary theories of atonement which had seemed to suggest that Christ deflected the anger of God by his death on the cross.

## Newman on development

But critical study of the Bible also opened up a gap between the Church of the New Testament texts and the Church of the 19th century. Could doctrine change? How could the growing knowledge of church history be reconciled with the Christian claim that the truth was absolutely unchanging?

The most creative answer came from John Henry Newman, whose *Essay on the Development of Christian Doctrine* (1845) was published on his secession to Rome. Newman's vision of an unfolding, magisterial authority in the Church contrasted with the insistence of his erstwhile Tractarian colleagues that the doctrinal standard was the faith of the early Church.

Yet Newman's notion of historical, evolutionary development takes us right into the heart of the conflict of science and religion. Theologians were struggling to absorb the impact of geological discovery long before Charles Darwin's *Origin of Species* (1859), and doing so with some success. But the importance of Darwin's book was undeniable. With one magnificently plausible sweep, its hypothesis of natural selection provided a framework for understanding the fossil evidence, and explained persuasively the emergence of the highest forms of life. It forced a revaluation of the factual content of Genesis.

Most of the clergy, within 20 or 30 years, concluded that the stark choice between Darwin and Genesis was too simplistic. Scientific "fact" was not of the same kind as religious truth: the "facts" of Genesis were not scientifically grounded, but religiously true.

## *Essays and Reviews*

By the end of the 19th century, a broad synthesis of historical method and symbolic interpretation was beginning to emerge. *Essays and Reviews* (1860), written by a group of Anglican clerics, startled and horrified orthodox Churchmen with its suggestion that the scriptures were open to free enquiry. The book started the mother of all modern ecclesiastical controversies, and drew synodical condemnation on its authors.

Nearly 30 years later, however, another volume of Anglican essays, *Lux Mundi* (1889), was produced by a group of hitherto "orthodox"

High Churchmen, led by Charles Gore. They, too, suggested a modification of the conventional view of biblical inspiration; they, too, provoked some controversy. But condemnation did not follow. The position marked out by *Lux Mundi* was already beginning to acquire the status of an orthodoxy itself. Science and history had forced a major revision of theology, but not overturned it.

## Social challenges

Yet the challenges of the age were not only intellectual. Most people, after all, probably knew little about the work of the scientists and biblical scholars. Much more immediate and more pressing were the challenges of social change.

There is immense controversy about the causes and the chronology of the Industrial Revolution. What is certain is that, from the end of the 18th century on, industrialisation brought in its wake social dislocation and rapid change.

The population of Britain swelled from nine million in 1801 to 33 million in 1901. Growth was even more dramatic in the towns, as labourers and their families left the countryside in search of work. The population of London doubled to 6.5 million between 1861 and 1901 alone.

More people required more churches. But sheer numbers were not the only problem. Society was becoming more stratified. Large, concentrated areas of working-class housing were created, often without adequate sanitation, with overcrowding, poverty and unemployment. The middle classes seized the more salubrious fringes of the great cities and towns.

The factory system transformed work habits and work discipline. To make matters worse, the working class seemed resistant to religion. This was not actually true, but Dissenters and Roman Catholics were certainly more successful in attracting working-class congregations. Establishment tainted Anglicanism with the values and attitudes of the social élite. And there were always critics ready to deny that the Churches had any significant role in the emergent modern society. When Friedrich Engels published his classic work of social observation and polemic *The Condition of the Working Class in England* (mostly a study of Manchester) in 1845, he scarcely bothered to mention the Churches.

## Mission churches

But the Churches were, in practice, remarkably adaptable. Even the Church of England was much more successful in urban mission than it dared to acknowledge at the time. The building of new churches and the creation of new parishes was evidence enough of this, especially since much of the money to support them had to be found from local sources. Victorian churches were the result of a long process of missionary endeavour, beginning with the building of a small mission hall or the hiring of a "tin tabernacle", a corrugated-iron church, supplied by mail-order. At every stage, local people were brought into the project. With churches went Sunday schools, day schools, charities, libraries, and even sports clubs.

So the religious response to social change was rooted in mission. The assumptions of Victorian Churchmen and -women about their society could not be expressed in the modern language of secularisation. Instead, they saw the appalling social conditions of their age as a symptom of religious indifference and moral decay. The reform of working-class life through temperance, churchgoing and self-improvement would help to engineer social improvement, so it was thought. Evangelism was a necessary precondition of social improvement.

## Slums and Ritualism

To some extent different church "parties" used different tactics. Evangelicals sometimes collaborated with Dissenters in supporting evangelistic initiatives such as the London City Mission. They were sometimes ready to use street evangelism, and to adopt the revivalist techniques favoured by the Methodists. They felt increasing dissatisfaction with the Prayer Book as a medium of worship, even after the Gorham Judgment of 1850 appeared to confirm that Evangelicals need not subscribe to the doctrine of baptismal regeneration formally embodied in the liturgy itself. They pioneered new forms of lay ministry, including the formation of the Church Army in 1882.

By the 1860s, a distinct type of High Churchmanship was evolving, namely Ritualism, which was temporarily curbed by Disraeli's infamous Public Worship Regulation Act. Ritualism expressed a new development in Anglican eucharistic practice, but it was also a vehicle for mission. Ritualists pioneered parochial missions, and developed processions and ceremonial as evangelistic media. Ritualist "slum priests" such as Charles Lowder in the East End gained respect for their commitment and self-sacrifice as much as for their theological opinions. They worked closely with the new religious orders that had emerged under the inspiration of the Oxford Movement.

Broad-church Anglicans, inspired in part by the legacy of the great headmaster of Rugby, Thomas Arnold, tended to concentrate on educational and social endeavour. They were particularly involved in the "settlement" movement, the placing of communities of schoolboys and undergraduates in poor areas of the great cities, in order to run religious and charitable agencies, to learn about the lives of the poor, and to lead others by their example.

## 'Christian Socialism'

The differences between the High, Low and Broad "parties" should not be exaggerated. They shared the common assumptions that poverty was in good measure a question of personal responsibility, that the role of government in combating poverty was limited, and that Christian faith entailed a commitment to voluntary work.

They also shared common assumptions about the hierarchical and deferential nature of society. A code of Christian "respectability" permeated their work. The poor could improve themselves by dint of discipline, moral and religious development, and sheer hard work. The rich had a duty to encourage the poor and to ease their burdens.

But there were, by the end of the Victorian period, a few Churchmen and -women who were beginning to question the conventional view. "Christian Socialism" was actually the creation of a small group of Anglicans in mid-century who included F. D. Maurice, Charles Kingsley, and J. M. Ludlow.

Maurice and Kingsley were not socialists in any modern sense, but Tory paternalists. They emphasised the corporate nature of faith, however, and saw social commitment as intrinsic to the incarnationalism of Christianity. They encouraged the co-operative movement, and though their practical achievements were negligible, except in the field of education, they were a major influence on the later Anglican tradition of Christian social thought.

## Workers in church

It has proved impossible to gauge precisely the Church's success in the Victorian age. By the end of the period, Victorian Anglicanism had managed to embed itself as much in the cities of Britain as in the countryside. There were working-class, urban Anglican congregations. The populations of the cities continued to seek baptism, marriage and burial in Anglican churches in huge numbers. They used the vast penumbra of Anglican charitable agencies with zeal. But the mission strategies of the period certainly did not succeed in turning the Church into an identifiably working-class institution. Evidently charity was not enough to solve society's ills: as that conviction grew, so too did the pressure for government action.

## Success or failure?

By the 1880s, church attendance was failing to keep pace with population growth. Outright decline was not to occur until the 20th century. But churchgoing was probably not a good index of popular religion, and counting attendances was in any case a characteristic product of the Victorians' own mania for statistics: as a definition of effective church membership, church attendance was new. So the perception of failure and eventual decline was as much a creation of the Victorian period as an accurate reading of its religious character.

In the end, certain incontestable facts remain. The Victorians vastly increased the physical presence of Anglicanism in the new towns, cities and suburbs of Britain. They increased the number of clergy, and improved their training. They reorganised the Church's administrative structures, revitalised the parish ministry, and began to reform the finances of the Church. They created the basis of the representative system of modern Anglicanism.

They rose to the intellectual challenges of the age, too. Anglicans played a leading part in recasting Christianity in order to adapt to new currents of critical thinking. This was nothing less than a new, a second Reformation. But it was achieved at the cost of permanent internal strife, and it left behind it a huge and, ultimately, unsustainable legacy of social activism and evangelistic ambition.

# GOOD NEIGIIBOURS AND PATRIOTS

## Hugh McLeod

Oral-history projects, and research into "popular religion", or what has come to be called "diffusive Christianity", have helped to change our view of Victorian working-class religion, showing that more working-class Victorians went to church than was previously realised, that churches and chapels often played a significant part in the lives of those who seldom attended services, and that non-churchgoers may have had their own strongly held religious beliefs.

As Sarah Williams argues in her new book on Southwark, working-class Londoners who seldom went to church were not necessarily less religious than middle-class people who went every Sunday — they were often religious in different ways.

They might be strongly attached to the church associated with family marriages, christenings or churchings. They might have a high regard for the vicar. A Bermondsey woman, for example, said that her mother "wasn't religious" (meaning that she did not go to church), but that "she practised religion." She worked all week on her sewing-machine — but never on Sundays. And, as she sewed, she sang hymns. When a neighbour died, she went to say the Lord's Prayer with the family.

## FROM THE MINING DISTRICTS.

### AN ATTEMPT AT CONVERTING THE NATIVES

*Assiduous Young Curate.* "WELL THEN, I DO HOPE I SHALL HAVE THE PLEASURE OF SEEING BOTH OF YOU NEXT SUNDAY!"

*Miner* "OI! THEE MAY'ST COAM IF 'E WULL. WE FOIGHT ON THE CROFT, AND OLD JOE TANNER BRINGS TH' BEER."

Historians have also been asking new questions about gender. In the 1980s the biggest historical growth area was the history of women. Historians began to realise that the religious life of women was often different from that of men. They began to take more notice of the mothers sitting by their children's bedside teaching them prayers, or playing the piano while their children (and often their husbands) sang hymns. They also began to document the emergence of women within the churches as preachers, Sunday-school teachers, missionaries, or members of crusading organisations, like the anti-drink campaigns.

Historians have been looking at nationalism, too. For many people, regardless of whether they ever went to church, Protestantism lay at the heart of what it meant to be British. Patriots claimed that Britain owed its greatness to the Protestant religion.

These new historical approaches all try to go beyond simply counting congregations, in order to look at the wider social influence of the churches and of religious belief.

Even in those areas where churchgoers were quite a small minority — for instance, the East End of London, or remote rural districts along the border with Scotland — religion and the churches were an inescapable part of most people's lives. Clergymen and district visitors were familiar figures. Churches had a central role in education and charity, and were important in providing leisure facilities. Ideas learnt in Sunday school could still influence the beliefs of adults who no longer attended church.

Religion could also be the ticket to a job. In Bristol, where jobs in the big cigarette factories were in high demand, "You had to be just so to get into places like Mardens or Wills. They wouldn't have just anybody in there." In particular, this meant that you needed a "Sunday-school character", and it helped if you belonged to Christian Endeavour as well. In Preston it was claimed that the only way to get a job at the station "was to say that you went to such a church".

Churches and chapels were powerful institutions, and as such they were resented as well as respected. Similarly with the clergy. Many were admired, and some were loved — especially those who were active visitors, and who were seen to treat parishioners of all classes alike. A Canning Town man remembered "Revd Varney" as an outstanding local personality, who was "kind", "gentle" and "treated everyone as an equal". And in neighbouring Poplar, Fr Bartlett "wasn't stuck up at all" — "he was for basic Christianity."

But it was all too easy for a clergyman to upset a large section of his parishioners. Working-class parishioners were on the look-out for snobs and hypocrites. A Preston factory worker complained that his vicar spent all his time in "the better-class areas", "where it wouldn't be beer, it would be wine and the rest of it." On the other hand, the upper

Priest and people: a *Punch* cartoon of 3 March 1855. *Photo © by permission of the British Library*

## CHRONOLOGY

**1836** Reconstitution of Ripon diocese
**1837** Accession of Queen Victoria
**1842** Peel's Church Building Act
**1847** Creation of diocese of Manchester, first new diocese since Reformation
**1851** National census of church attendance
**1854** Publication of census report
**1859** Charles Darwin's *Origin of Species*
**1860** *Essays and Reviews*
**1862** First volume of Colenso's work on Pentateuch
**1867** First Lambeth Conference
**1868** Abolition of Church Rate
**1869** Disestablishment of Church of Ireland
**1874** Public Worship Regulation Act
**1882** Foundation of Church Army
**1884** Establishment of Toynbee Hall, Whitechapel, first university settlement
**1889** *Lux Mundi*
**1899** Start of Boer War
**1901** Death of Queen Victoria

and upper-middle classes would despise a parson who was "not quite a gentleman". Protestants were scandalised by ceremonial, and, whatever the clergyman's politics were, one half of his parishioners would object.

Then, as always, plenty of people compartmentalised their lives. There were men of all classes who went to church with their wives and children on Sunday, but did not expect religion to interfere with their business or their pleasures. Zealous Evangelicals were often seen as ridiculous fanatics — as the novels of Charles Dickens show. Nonconformist politicians who tried to bring their moral principles into politics were dismissed as "faddists, pharisees and prowling prudes".

The tensions between religious profession and daily practice were well summed up by Samuel Butler in describing the Nottinghamshire farmers who were the mainstay of his father's congregation. They were "fat, very well-to-do folk" who "would have been equally horrified at hearing the Christian religion doubted and at seeing it practised".

So we need to move beyond the never-ending argument between "optimists" who highlight the achievements of Victorian Christianity, and "pessimists" who home in on the failures. The Victorian era was a time both of great religious vitality and also of secularisation. Both are part of the total picture. And this ambiguity was contained within the lives and thoughts of many individuals.

# IMPERIAL ENGLAND'S LONG HAND-OVER

*William Jacob*

*The spread of Anglicanism overseas was slow. The shift of power from expatriates to the indigenous peoples happened reluctantly, especially if they were black.*

Anglicanism has been a world-wide phenomenon since the 16th century. Anglicanism as a world Church, though, can only be described as a 20th-century phenomenon.

The 16th-century Anglican formularies allowed that its approach to reformation might not be merely English. Worship was permitted to be in the vernacular, and it was acknowledged that "Traditions and Ceremonies" might be changed according to times and places; also that "Every particular or national Church hath authority to ordain, change and abolish, ceremonies or rites of the Church ordained only by man's authority." The Bible and the Prayer Book were published in Welsh in 1567. Episcopal Churches related to, but not dependent on, the Church of England emerged in Scotland and Ireland.

Where Englishmen went they took their Church. A chaplain accompanied Frobisher to seek a North-West Passage in the 1570s; a chaplain circumnavigated the earth with Drake. From 1603 the East India Company appointed chaplains to its ships sailing to India and the Far East. A chaplain accompanied the first settlers to Virginia.

## Anglicanism in America

The first long-term overseas manifestation of Anglicanism was in North America. Successive Archbishops of Canterbury and Bishops of London, from the 1630s, endeavoured to secure bishops for the North American colonies. Endowments to provide incomes and expenses were the initial impediment, but by the early 18th century the Society for the Propagation of the Gospel in Foreign Parts (SPG) was raising funds. The New England colonies, however, where Congregationalists and Presbyterians were in a majority, opposed the appointment of bishops, and British governments were reluctant to antagonise them. A later fear was that in the southern colonies bishops might "go native" and become focuses for opposition and independence.

By the 1760s, having existed for 150 years without them, Anglican colonists could not muster much enthusiasm for bishops.

When independence was declared in 1776, clergy in the new United

States were forced to break their ordination oath of allegiance to the King and not to pray for him in the liturgy. About a third left for England or migrated north to Canada.

Anglicans in the newly independent states needed to establish a new form of ecclesiastical government, independent of England. William White, Rector of Christ Church and St Peter's, Philadelphia, proposed in 1782 that parishes be recognised as independent, and that each parish be invited to elect clergy and lay representatives to meet as a "convention" to elect a "superior order of ministers", whose tasks were limited to ordination and confirmation. They were to remain in charge of parishes, and thus needed no funding. Parishes were to appoint their own clergy.

The clergy of Connecticut acted independently, meeting in secret in 1783 to elect as bishop Samuel Seabury, who had been loyal to Britain during the war; and they petitioned the Archbishop of York, Canterbury being vacant, to consecrate him. As the states were now independent, he was unable to take the Oath of Allegiance, and this precluded his consecration by English bishops. Arrangements were made that he should obtain his episcopal Orders from Scotland, and he was duly consecrated at Aberdeen on 14 November 1784.

In 1784 a General Convention was held, with representatives of clergy and laity from seven states, Seabury and the Connecticut clergy declining to attend. It drew up a constitution for a Protestant Episcopal Church (PECUSA, now ECUSA), with a legislative body of representatives of clergy and laity in every state meeting together, but voting by houses, with a bishop. At the 1786 General Convention, two states having elected clergy for consecration as bishops, the United States minister in London, John Adams, was asked to request the Archbishop of Canterbury to consecrate them.

After consulting his fellow bishops, and obtaining an Act of Parliament permitting the consecration of non-British citizens without requiring them to take the oath of allegiance, the Archbishop consecrated the two American priests as Bishops of New York and Pennsylvania in February 1787. By 1789 a rapprochement was secured between Seabury and the General Convention; and in 1790 the English bishops consecrated another bishop, elected by the Church in Virginia, after which the Church in the USA had enough bishops to order its own succession. A framework had been created distinctively different from that of the Church of England.

## The other colonies

After the American War of Independence, the British Government's policy was to strengthen British institutions in colonies, and in 1786 they agreed a proposal by the Archbishop of Canterbury and the Bishop of London to establish a diocese in Nova Scotia. The bishop was regarded as being in partnership with the governor, and paid by a government grant. In 1793 a second Canadian diocese was established at Quebec.

In the first decade of the 19th century, under the influence of Archbishop Manners-Sutton, supported by a group of energetic high-church laymen and clergy known as the Hackney Phalanx, the SPG and the Society for Promoting Christian Knowledge (SPCK) were re-organised to provide better support for bishops and members of the clergy overseas. In 1812 one of their number, the Earl of Liverpool, became Prime Minister. He offered government funding to establish dioceses in India and the West Indies, as well as Canada.

Although bishops and governors were expected to work together to promote government policy, governors and colonial legislatures — and often chaplains — treated bishops with, at best, suspicion and, at worst, hostility. Governors failed to consult bishops when appointing chaplains; congregations sometimes resisted chaplains appointed by bishops.

Government funding for new overseas dioceses ceased in the 1830s, with the end of the Anglican hegemony of Church and state. A Parliament that, from 1828, included Nonconformists and, from 1829, Roman Catholics could not be expected to pay for Anglican bishops.

In 1841 Bishop Blomfield of London resolved the problem by establishing the Colonial Bishoprics Fund to endow new overseas bishoprics. Between 1841 and 1941, £900,000 was raised and expended to endow new dioceses. By 1872, 30 new dioceses had been wholly or partially endowed by the fund.

## Encouraging local leaders . . .

Except for the American Church and emancipated slaves in the West Indies, most Anglicans were colonists. Intentions to evangelise native Americans, and natives in South India in the 18th century, came to nothing, not least because SPCK and the SPG found it impossible to recruit English clerics to work overseas. In the 1720s, SPCK had to recruit Danish Lutherans as missionaries on its behalf in South India. The Evangelical founders of the Church Missionary Society (CMS) recruited German Lutherans to work among emancipated slaves in Sierra Leone, and in India. Between 1789 and 1858, only 559 Christian missionaries of any denomination served in India.

SPG put its missionaries at the disposal of bishops. CMS thought that, as it was recruiting and paying missionaries, it should deploy them. It also expected bishops to ordain candidates on its recommendation, and was annoyed when bishops insisted on examining candidates them-selves, and sometimes rejecting them.

From the 1830s, under Henry Venn, CMS's policy was to establish local churches as soon as possible, with vernacular liturgies, locally trained clergy, and under indigenous leadership.

In New Zealand, Bishop Selwyn endorsed its policy, and learned Maori on his way to New Zealand. He established a theological college in Auckland in 1844, though he insisted that Maori ordinands gain proficiency in New Testament Greek. The first Maori was not ordained until 1853, by which time 20 English candidates had been ordained.

Venn saw an opportunity to develop a local Church in the Niger Delta in West Africa in 1861. Although Anglican missionary activity had begun in 1752 on the Gold Coast, serious work did not begin until 1787, in Sierra Leone. In the late 1830s, CMS had initiated a project to persuade West African chiefs to abandon the slave trade and replace it with legitimate trade, thus creating a mercantile middle class of Africans to open up the country and promote Christianity.

But individual conversion from the tribal solidarity of traditional African religion had little impact. Tribal rulers regarded missionaries as subversive. The requirement that, to be baptised, polygamists abandon all but one wife was seen to undermine the basis of society and the economy.

Venn wanted an African, as bishop, to take charge of this work. He secured the consecration of Samuel Crowther, a Sierra Leonean missionary, as Bishop on the Niger in Canterbury Cathedral in 1864. Crowther had to finance himself by trading on the Niger, but instead of working among his fellow tribesmen in the Delta, as Venn expected, and despite his lack of languages, he undertook missionary journeys up the Niger.

## . . . and discouraging them

English missionaries, though, declined to accept Bishop Crowther's authority. Things were not improved by the influx of significant numbers of women and energetic young men from Oxbridge, attracted to the mission field in the latter part of the century. The idealistic new influx was scandalised by Crowther's trading to fund himself, and by what they regarded as lax practices among African converts. They concluded that Africans were not yet ready for leadership, and this became CMS policy. It contributed to a series of schisms among African Christians, causing them to form independent African-led Churches which maintained Anglican teaching, but regarded polygamy as acceptable (except for bishops) on scriptural precedent.

In Buganda, Central Africa, well beyond British influence, CMS missionaries began work in the 1880s. When they were expelled for two years, Christianity prospered, despite persecution, under aristocratic

Bugandan leadership. Under Evangelical pressure, the British Government established a protectorate over the whole of Uganda, and Bishop Tucker ordained four chiefs who had led the Church during the persecution. By 1899 there were 21 African clerics.

Once again, though, CMS missionaries resisted being incorporated into an African Church, even under a British bishop. Paternalism and reluctance to give authority to African laity and clergy had a stultifying effect on Anglicanism in Africa.

Similar attitudes were apparent in India. There was reluctance to give leadership to Indians, until V. S. Azariah was consecrated to the new diocese of Dornakal in 1912. In China, however, in the early 20th century, the clergy asked the bishops to establish a Chinese Anglican Church. With the support of CMS and SPG, a self-governing province was established in 1912. But in Hong Kong separate English and Chinese synods were established.

## Moves to self-government

Throughout the 1850s, attempts to secure parliamentary legislation granting freedom to colonial Churches to govern themselves were regularly defeated by alliances of Evangelicals and Nonconformists.

In spite of this, in the diocese of Toronto in 1853 a meeting of clergy and laity, chaired by the bishop, declared itself a synod, although opposed by Evangelicals in the diocese. The Bishop of Nova Scotia

Self-supporting (and un-supported): Bishop Samuel Crowther and his local clergy. Whites did not come under his jurisdiction. Taken from *The Black Bishop*, by Jesse Page, Hodder and Stoughton, 1908

For the first time: Anglican bishops on the steps of Lambeth Palace, for the 1867 Lambeth Conference. The use of a sub-committee for awkward matters proved a successful ploy. *Photo © USPG*

convened a synod in 1856. In 1857, the Canadian legislature, despite considerable Evangelical opposition, passed legislation giving legal standing to Anglican synods, and permitting dioceses to subdivide themselves. In 1861, the Bishop of Montreal called the first provincial synod.

In New Zealand, Bishop Selwyn subdivided his diocese to form a province. The constitution he drew up served as a model for many other provinces. In Australia, the Evangelical Bishop Barker of Sydney consistently opposed the establishment of a province, for fear of being out-voted by the country's high-church dioceses.

Many Anglican congregations and clergy wanted to remain English, and did not want to be part of a separate province, which might alter their Church of England customs and liturgy. Evangelical clergy in Cape Town were horrified when Bishop Gray wore a surplice, and were deeply suspicious of his attempt to form a synod.

One incumbent claimed the Bishop had seceded from the Church of England, and denied him authority to call a synod or exercise

discipline, appealing to the Privy Council when Gray attempted to discipline him. The Privy Council held that Gray's authority extended only to the clergy who recognised his authority.

In 1861 Bishop Colenso of Natal published books thought to be defective on the atonement and the sacraments, and which described the pseudonymous books of the Old Testament as "fiction" and "pious fraud". He was tried by Gray and all his fellow South African bishops, found guilty, and deposed. Colenso denied Gray's authority, and appealed to the Privy Council for an order to prevent Gray interfering in his right to exercise his office.

The Privy Council held Gray had no jurisdiction over Colenso. Gray still excommunicated Colenso.

## The Lambeth Conference

By 1865 there were 45 English overseas dioceses, and 34 American dioceses. There were five independent provinces with enough bishops to maintain their own succession.

Overseas dioceses were usually vast, and bishops laboured far apart from their neighbours. Lacking news, they had a deep sense of isolation, and were alarmed by rumours and misinformation about events in other dioceses and in England. From at least 1860 there were moves for a bishops' conference or synod.

In 1865, the Canadian bishops called for a meeting of Anglican bishops. The English bishops were unenthusiastic, fearing the overseas bishops might vote to overrule their cautious resolutions on Colenso. Archbishop Longley, however, was well disposed, though, unhappy about the Colenso affair, he stipulated that any conference would be a private meeting, and that Colenso should be kept off the agenda.

Only 24 bishops declined the invitation, including four from the province of York. There were significant divisions between High Churchmen, who wished Colenso's sentence to be endorsed, and Evangelicals and Broad Churchmen who wished it not to be discussed. There was much lobbying to stop Gray dividing the conference over Colenso.

They met for one week. Approval was given to the principle of synodical government in provinces and dioceses, and to the election of bishops by clergy and laity. Provincial synods were recommended to establish procedures for disciplining clergy and ordering the Church. Discussion of Colenso was confined to a sub-committee.

An encyclical was published. Greek and Latin translations were sent to the Orthodox patriarchs and the Vatican. Cardinal Manning noted it contained "nothing with which a Roman Catholic could disagree".

The conference successfully included the American bishops, although they resented the Oxbridge world of English and colonial bishops. A network of prayer and support was established. No one withdrew, and solidarity was maintained with the beleaguered Bishop Gray of Cape Town.

A pattern of ten-yearly meetings of bishops was established thereafter, under the presidency of the Archbishop of Canterbury. Their status as conferences, not councils, was always emphasised. Occasional attempts to inflate the Archbishop of Canterbury to a "patriarch" were opposed, usually by the American bishops. Attempts to create a secretariat were also resisted.

Many of the Lambeth Conferences' pronouncements have been bland, dull, and even unwise, but some were significant in promoting the development of Anglicanism and ecumenism, for example the Chicago/Lambeth Quadrilateral of 1888, the Appeal to All Christian People of 1920, and the eventual inclusion of Churches like South India, which had entered agreements of union with nonepiscopal Churches. The framework allowed disagreements to be contained.

## A world Communion

The second half of the 20th century saw dramatic developments in worldwide Anglicanism. As early as 1908, a Lambeth Conference approved seven principles of liturgical revision, to develop liturgies appropriate to local contexts, after consultation between Churches. The 1958 Conference gave renewed impetus to liturgical revision, urging a recovery of the worship of the primitive Church, the principle on which the Prayer Book was based, and endorsing the research of Dom Gregory Dix and the eucharistic liturgy of the Church of South India. The long-term result was to encourage liturgies appropriate to the context of local Churches, instead of the Prayer Book across the Communion.

In the 1950s, the Archbishop of Canterbury, Geoffrey Fisher, created a framework for Anglicanism as a world Church. Missionary work had languished after 1914. By 1950 little had been done to develop indigenous leadership in African dioceses. There were few Anglican theological colleges. There had not been a black diocesan bishop since Samuel Crowther's death in 1891.

Fisher took advantage of air travel to visit overseas dioceses, and

Church-making: Archbishop Fisher at the inauguration of the province of Central Africa, in Salisbury Cathedral, Southern Rhodesia, 8 May 1955. *Photo © Lambeth Palace Library*

## CHRONOLOGY

**1549** Act of Uniformity includes representative lay people in decision-making, and authorises a vernacular liturgy
**1567** Welsh translation of the Bible and the Prayer Book
**1603** East India Company appoints chaplains for ships to India and the Far East
**1606** Chaplain accompanies first settlers to Virginia
**1634** Bishop of London given jurisdiction over clergy and congregations overseas
**1638** Bishop proposed for New England
**1662** Bishop nominated for Virginia
**1698** Foundation of SPCK
**1701** Foundation of SPG
**1713** Fund established for endowing a diocese in American colonies
**1777** American Declaration of Independence
**1782** Publication of *The Case for a Protestant Episcopal Church in the USA*
**1784** Consecration of Samuel Seabury for Connecticut by the Scottish Bishops
**1787** Consecration of William White and Samuel Prevost as Bishops of Pennsylvania and New York by the Archbishop of Canterbury
**1787** Consecration of Charles Inglis for Nova Scotia
**1799** Foundation of CMS
**1814** Consecration of Thomas Middleton for Calcutta
**1841** Consecration of George Augustus Selwyn as Bishop of New Zealand
**1847** Consecration of Robert Gray for Cape Town
**1853** Consecration of J. W. Colenso as Bishop of Natal
**1861** Consecration of Samuel Crowther for the Niger
**1867** First Lambeth Conference
**1888** Chicago/ Lambeth Quadrilateral
**1920** "Appeal to All Christian People"
**1947** Church of South India
**1951** Province of West Africa

began to encourage devolution to autonomous provinces. He aimed to create an Anglicanism independent of the missionary societies from which many dioceses had originated.

In 1951, six Anglican dioceses in West Africa were formed into a new province. Fisher personally, in Freetown, Sierra Leone, released the bishops from their oaths of obedience to the Archbishop of Canterbury, and a new metropolitan was elected. This was seven years before Ghana gained independence from Britain.

In 1955, again well before political independence, the dioceses of Central Africa were formed into a new province. In 1960, a new province of East Africa followed; and the diocese of Uganda was divided into 11 new dioceses and became a province.

At the creation of the province of Uganda, the four Ugandan bishops Fisher had consecrated in Namirembe Cathedral in 1955 became diocesans, more than doubling the number of black African diocesan bishops.

Fisher established councils of bishops in South-East Asia and the Pacific, as a first step to creating provinces. He even managed to persuade the Australian dioceses to adopt a constitution as an autonomous province, which, however, left power in the hands of the dioceses.

By the 1958 Lambeth Conference, there was a significant number of non-Anglo-Saxon bishops, which affirmed the Communion as an international and multiracial fellowship of Churches, rather than an almost accidental imperial and missionary extension of the Church of England. The Anglican Communion remains united because each Church respects the rights of other Churches. This has been strained from time to time, but it has worked. Unity comes from a common faith, based on adherence to the Catholic faith contained in the scriptures, summed up in the Apostles' Creed, experienced in the sacraments of the gospel and in the rites of the primitive Church, and safeguarded by the historic threefold ministry.

Priest and poet: John Keble, by George Richmond (1863). *Photo © by courtesy of the National Portrait Gallery, London*

Sunday-school champion: Hannah More, by Henry W. Pickersgill (1822). *Photo © by courtesy of the National Portrait Gallery, London*

Strained relations: *Matrimonial infelicities or Mr State and his wife Church*, June 1829, possibly by Seymour. *Photo © British Museum*

Western influence: the gallery minstrels in *The Village Choir* by Thomas Webster (1800-1886); Webster used All Saints', Bow Brickhill, Bucks, as a model.
*Photo © V & A Picture Library*

Cousins: *Charles Darwin showing an ape how alike the pair of them are* (unnamed artist, 1874). *Photo © Mary Evans Picture Library*

Early pews: 16th-century, carved with sacred and domestic symbols, in St Nonna's, Altarnun, Cornwall. *Photo © Paul Barker/Country Life Picture Library*

Social conscience: William Temple, Archbishop of Canterbury, by Philip de Laszlo, 1934. *Photo © by kind permission of His Grace the Archbishop of Canterbury*

Recent history: women priested in England in 1994, Jane Hayward (*left*) and Sue Restall (*right*). *Photo © PA*

# LOOKING, LEARNING AND LEADING FROM THE PEWS

*Lay people play a key part in our Church's history. In the 20th century, a new dimension was added by mass communications — broadcast religion.*

*Nicholas Orme*

Augustine of Canterbury was not the first person to bring Christianity to the English, in 597. Or so says Bede. A few years earlier, King Æthelberht of Kent had married Bertha, a Christian Frankish princess, in return for giving her freedom to practise her faith. She brought a bishop to England with her, and they re-established worship in the old Roman church of St Martin, Canterbury. It was this marriage of lay people that opened the way for Pope Gregory the Great to send Augustine to England. Our first apostle was arguably not a bishop or priest, but a lay woman.

The point is worth making because, although the church history of England owes so much to the clergy, it is equally indebted to the laity, great and small. This is admirably illustrated in our churches, the primary route by which Christianity reaches the world. The generous provision of churches in our countryside, every couple of miles, is largely due to our Anglo-Saxon ancestors, particularly in the tenth and 11th centuries. Lords built churches for the tenants on their estates. Estates became parishes, different in size and intricate in boundaries. In the 19th century, wealthy Victorians contributed to a similar large-scale provision of churches in the new large towns.

A clergyman, however, has always cost more to maintain than a church. The provision of one to each church was possible only by laying the burden on the local population by a system of compulsory payments — tithes. Tithes took root in the tenth century and lasted until 1936. The laity thus bore the burden of sustaining the clergy, and also the church buildings, from very early times; and though the systems of doing so have changed, the principle has always been the same.

## Looking and learning

In the Middle Ages, Christianity reached people largely through services in church. These took place on Sundays, festivals and the main events of life — baptisms, confirmations, weddings and funerals. Services were in Latin up to the middle of the 16th century, because

Innocence: *My First Sermon* (1863) by J. E. Millais. *Photo (and Photo on facing page) © Guildhall Art Gallery, Corporation of London/Bridgeman Art Library*

Christianity in England was an offshoot of Roman Christianity and culture. Religion and learning in medieval Europe were alike in Latin.

English, until about the 15th century, was not sufficiently developed nor uniform for such purposes. This meant that services had to make their impact visually rather than aurally. At a baptism, for example, the priest read a series of psalms, lessons, and prayers, but the laity probably understood the service through its actions: the application of salt, saliva, and holy oil to the baby to exorcise it, leading to the three-fold total immersion of the infant in the font.

The emphasis on services also reflected educational factors. The medieval Church could not expect its parish clergy to do more than go to a school and learn enough Latin to read from the service books. Universities were expensive facilities for the few, and there were no theological colleges until the 19th century. Lay people, too, were not

Experience: *My Second Sermon* (1864) by J. E. Millais

envisaged as knowing more than the Lord's Prayer, Hail Mary and Apostles' Creed by heart in Latin. They were expected to say these only while they attended services or venerated images or shrines.

Gradually, however, during the later Middle Ages, the word made steady advances alongside the image. This antedated the invention of printing, which resulted from growing literacy and book production rather than creating them. In about 1200, the new orders of friars were founded, with a commitment to preach and therefore to study to equip themselves for the task. This duly encouraged the parish clergy, especially in towns, to do likewise.

An increasing number of literate lay people demanded religious literature. The book of hours appeared for their use in the 13th century, a Latin prayer book simpler than those of the clergy. Instructive works and saints' lives became available in French or

Prominent layman: detail of tomb of Sir William Lytton (d. 1705) in St Mary and St Thomas, Knebworth, Hertfordshire.
*Photo © Paul Barker*

English. By the 14th century, some of the aristocracy were reading the Bible in French, and an English Bible was produced by the Lollard followers of John Wycliffe in the 1390s. Tragically, this version was regarded as the work of heretics, and forbidden. Even so, some people read it surreptitiously up to the Reformation, and a few important ones like Richard III and Henry VII owned copies legitimately.

## Imposition of belief

But Christianity has not only communicated itself by clerical evangelism and voluntary lay support. When the rulers of the Roman Empire became Christian in the fourth century, they made Christianity the official religion of the Empire, and imposed it against paganism. The Church learnt to rely on the help of rulers to spread the gospel and establish Christian order. The English kings, once converted to Christianity, acted likewise to enforce the faith and its precepts on their people. England became a Church-state like Rome, and remained so until about the 1830s.

Living in a Church-state meant conforming to its religion. By the 11th and 12th centuries, every lay person had to be baptised, attend church, pay tithes, fast on appropriate days, and observe the Church's moral code. Those who were not amenable were dealt with by church courts and given penances or fines. Those not amenable to the courts could be arrested and imprisoned by the lay authorities. By about 1200, even the death penalty could be imposed for heresy, although this did not become a widespread practice until the persecution of the Lollards in the 15th century.

Chaucer sums up for us the various means which the medieval Church developed to reach the people. His parson ministers in a parish. His friar represents additional, voluntary evangelism, through preaching, parish visiting, and hearing confessions. His summoner hauls to the church courts those who have not toed the Church's line.

As we near the Reformation, we can sense the growing power of the Crown with regard to religious beliefs and practices. Even in the 14th century, the parish clergy were being told to organise prayers and processions for the king's success in his wars in France. When Lollardy appeared, it seemed to threaten Crown as well as Church, and Richard II, Henry IV, and Henry V all rallied to attack it.

## Quest for uniformity

The Reformation emphasised the power of the Crown and the important laity within the Church, though most of the power had always been there. It also emphasised uniformity: everyone believing and doing the same thing. Basic beliefs and practices had been uniform in the Middle Ages, but there had been much variety in what people chose to do. Church leaders in the 16th century craved greater uniformity. This was partly because of their religious confidence: we know what is right. It also reflected their fears about the survival of the English monarchy and state, and it was made possible by language and technology.

By the 16th century, the English language had come of age. Its grammar and spelling were more uniform, its vocabulary more sophisticated. Printing enabled it to be reproduced identically, quickly and cheaply. In 1539, an English Bible was at last placed in all churches. Ten years later, the Latin prayer books, with their regional variations, were replaced by one Book of Common Prayer in English. Bible and Prayer Book were the outcomes jointly of language, technology, and royal power. The written word was triumphant, a triumph sealed by the removal of images and of most visual ceremonies from worship.

In the long run, the uniformity of the 16th century was too ambitious to succeed. Church services were relatively easy to control. They took place in defined places, under the control of (mostly) biddable clerics. But services, once they were uniform, lost something of their appeal. Preaching attracted more interest, and the sermon became the great channel of communication between about 1600 and 1850, helped by the growth of a more learned clergy.

Preaching was harder to control, as was the circulation of religious literature in an increasingly literate population. In the end, uniformity could not be sustained, despite obedient clergy, Prayer Book services, and some censorship of books. Catholicism survived, Puritanism developed, and, by the 1640s, the Civil War allowed the emergence of Nonconforming sects. Since the Reformation, the Church of England has done much to proclaim its messages through worship, preaching, schooling, books, pamphlets, and eventually newspapers, radio and television. But it was already failing to stop other Christians doing the same by the reign of Elizabeth I.

## Power of the people

What has been said so far implies that church history is made at the top by clerics and important lay people, and handed down to the rest of the population. This is only half true. Church history is also made from below, by ordinary people. If the latter are in one sense a land to be conquered and colonised, they also determine, as land does, what is planted and built upon it.

In theory the clergy, backed by the lay authorities, had a great deal of religious power until it became fully possible to contract out of the Anglican Church during the 19th century. Up to the Reformation, the clergy had the power to hear confessions, give penances, and ex-communicate. The Reformation did away with compulsory confession, but penances and excommunications remained. The parish clergy even gained new powers under the Tudors, as their parishes became units of local government as well as of religion.

In practice, however, clergy power has never been absolute. As early as about 1400, the Shropshire canon John Myrc advised the parish clergy not to impose harsh penances on their parishioners, lest the penances be ignored. History is full of examples of clerics who made their own lives miseries because they did not temper their power with discretion. Take G. C. Gorham, hero of the famous Gorham case of 1847-50, when after three years of litigation and public controversy, he was finally inducted as Vicar of Brampford Speke in 1850.

His parish had experienced the sleepy reign of a Georgian pre-decessor for 57 years. Gorham set out to rebuild the church, install an organ, run the vestry properly, and bring the village inn to order. Within six years he had quarrelled with his churchwarden in church, been abused and assaulted at the inn, and suffered a mass boycott of the customary dinner for the tithe-paying farmers. He had been cited to the bishop's court, and had had his case against his assailant dismissed by local magistrates.

## Seats of influence

The laity, then, have always had a strong obstructing power within the

Church. But they have also promoted its development in positive ways. Critics of the Church have always liked to lay the blame for its alleged superstitions and defects on its clergy. From Chaucer to Cobbett and Dickens, writers have assumed that what they did not like, whether relics or images, pilgrimages or indulgences, and dull or formal services, were devised and run by the clergy from motives of power and greed.

In truth, such things have arisen just as much from popular demand. No fiats from above could have produced the large numbers of medieval pilgrims who visited shrines of saints, or of parish guilds that venerated images. Purgatory arose from popular fears about the after-life as much as from clerical speculations about it. Repetitive weekly services have survived for so long because many people like their predictability.

A good example of positive lay influence on religion is the intro-duction of uniform seating into churches. The question of how far people stood or sat in medieval services is an obscure one, and it would be unwise to assume that there were no seats. Important people probably had them, either fixed or portable, from early times. By the 15th and early 16th centuries, however, most parish churches possessed seating for all members of the congregation, in the form of rows of benches or pews.

This was primarily a matter of comfort, but it also promoted uni-formity. Once we sit or kneel within wooden restraints, we all have to do the same things. We cannot stand up or walk about without annoying our neighbours. In this way, church behaviour was coming to be uniform long before the church authorities required it to be so in 1549.

Indeed, the Prayer Book built on this development. Cranmer's static services married well with seated congregations, and would have been much harder to introduce if there had not been seats already. Yet, in another respect, the seats defeated him. His Prayer Book envisaged weekly communion services, like the old Latin mass, with the difference that communion would be given to the people, not only the priest. But the people were used to receiving communion solely at Easter, after long preparation by fasting and confession.

Within three years it was manifest that they were not willing to come out of their seats to receive it. There was a danger that priest-only communion would continue. Accordingly, the 1552 Prayer Book revision ordered that there should be "a good number" to communicate with the priest, with a quorum of at least three in a small parish. If not, there could be no communion. Communion services sank to being quarterly occasions, and remained largely so until the 19th century. The people effectively staged a "sit-in", deflecting the Reformation in one important respect.

## 'Family services'

Services have always been in part what people wanted rather than simply what they were given. When services, or at any rate their surroundings, became more ornate in the 19th century, with new church furnishings, windows, and flowers, that was because lay people liked such things and paid for them.

Even in the late 20th century, when new services and service books have again been handed down to churches by the church authorities, one of the greatest liturgical developments has been a popular, spontaneous one. Family services have appeared locally and unexpectedly, often on the initiative of untrained lay people, yet bringing in dozens and scores of supporters. It is the official Church that has had to react to this development by providing a framework for it, *A Service of the Word*, in 1994.

So modern parishioners, faced with parish reorganisations, clergy appointments and new liturgies, should not therefore suppose that the Church is run only from the top. Projects of leaders, like stewardship campaigns and the Decade of Evangelism, easily fail to strike roots in parishes. And the laity are capable of running ahead in ways that leave church leaders, like Gregory the Great, hurrying to catch up.

# CHURCH OF THE AIRWAVES

## *Ian Bradley*

The Church's attitude towards the main medium of mass communication in the 20th century has been distinctly ambivalent. Initially reluctant to embrace the evangelistic possibilities of broadcasting, it ended the century complaining at the lack of time and resources given to religious programmes on radio and television.

Thanks largely to one man, British broadcasting, and the BBC in particular, was given a distinctly Christian hue from its beginnings in the early 1920s. If their Latin is good enough, visitors to Broadcasting House in London can still get a flavour of the ethos which inspired the founder of the BBC by casting their eyes to the inscription above the lifts in the entrance hall. Translated, it reads: "This temple of the arts and muses is dedicated to Almighty God by the first governors of broadcasting in the year 1931, Sir John Reith being director-general. It is their prayer that good seed sown may bring forth a good harvest, that all things hostile to peace or purity may be banished from this house, and that the people, inclining their ears to whatsoever things are

beautiful and honest and of good report, may tread the paths of wisdom and righteousness."

Stern and unbending embodiment of the Presbyterian conscience that he was, Reith ran the BBC as though it was an extension of the Church, and took it for granted that it should be a strongly Christian organisation. The first question that he often put when interviewing prospective staff was "Do you accept the fundamental teaching of Jesus Christ?"

Characteristically, he complained that the Churches had failed to appreciate "how accidental and odd it was that, from the very beginning, and against indifference, ridicule and opposition, the Christian religion and the sabbath were given positions of privilege and protection in the broadcasting service, which — circumstances having been otherwise and as might have been expected — no protest or petition by the Churches could have secured for them."

He felt the Churches had lamentably failed to follow up the opportunities given to them. If they had, "there might have been a national revival on a scale hitherto unimagined."

The Churches initially saw the new medium of broadcasting as a

Sowing: Lord Reith, first director-general of the BBC, by Olive Edis. *Photo © by courtesy of the National Portrait Gallery, London* threat rather than a potential ally. In 1923, permission to relay the Armistice Day service and a royal wedding from Westminster Abbey was refused by the church authorities on the grounds that "the services would be received by a considerable number of persons in an irreverent manner, and might even be heard by persons in public houses with their hats on."

This kind of attitude persisted for a long time. Meanwhile, the BBC operated almost as a Church in its own right, creating highly popular devotional programmes, like the *Daily Service* and *Lift Up Your Hearts*, forerunner of *Thought for the Day* and described in the *Radio Times* as "early morning prayers, little services aiming only at converting each listener's home into a shrine for a moment or two before the day's work begins".

The gradual departure from the Reithian concept of religious broadcasting can be traced through the utterances of successive director-generals of the BBC. In 1948, Sir William Haley could still say: "We are citizens of a Christian country, and the BBC — an institution set up by the state — bases its policy upon a positive attitude towards the Christian values. It seeks to safeguard those values and to foster acceptance of them. The whole preponderant weight of its programme is directed to this end." Twenty-five years later, Sir Charles Curran talked rather of the moral neutrality of broadcasting in a "post-Christian era", and said: "It is not our job to adopt a particular morality and then to try to persuade everybody else to follow it."

From the 1960s onwards, religious broadcasting adopted a more pluralist tone, and shifted from evangelism to exposition and from proclamation to reflection. In 1977, the Annan Committee laid down clearly that "religious broadcasting should not be the religious equivalent of party political broadcasts." A document produced for the BBC's Central Religious Advisory Council in 1990 spelt out even more sharply the departure from the Reithian position: "It is no longer possible for the religious broadcasting department of a public service broadcasting authority to be the mouthpiece of the Churches or any other interest group. The BBC is not a Church. The *Daily Service* can no longer be introduced by a continuity announcer saying 'Our prayers are taken,' as if the whole BBC were at that moment on its knees."

Ironically, as overtly Christian programming fell out of favour with broadcasters, the Churches became ever more interested in the medium that they had once despised. The coming of local radio in the 1960s turned many of the clergy into radio presenters and led to Churches' setting up training schemes in broadcasting technique. The Church of England seconded members of the clergy to serve as religious producers on local radio stations.

In 1990, a new Broadcasting Act deregulated the airwaves and allowed Churches to run their own broadcasting stations both on local radio networks and on cable and satellite television channels. It also allowed advertising on radio and television by religious bodies, although with careful monitoring by the new Independent Television Commission. The first body to take advantage of religious advertising on radio in 1991 was the Church of England's Lichfield diocese, which took a series of spots on Beacon Radio on Good Friday to advertise Easter services.

Many in the Church of England opposed the liberalising measures in the 1990 Act, fearing that they would usher in American-style tele-evangelism, and end the restrained and balanced nature of religious broadcasting in Britain. The first daily British evangelistic programme, heavily based on a US original, *Victory with Morris Cerullo*, was launched on the Super Channel satellite station in 1991, going out for half an hour at 5.30 a.m. As yet there has been little evidence that tele-evangelism is gaining significant audiences or air time on British cable and satellite channels. The country's one national Christian radio station, Premier, has more than once been on the brink of bankruptcy.

The end of the 20th century saw an unprecedented attack by the Church of England on the BBC for marginalising religious broadcasting. This followed the limitation of the *Daily Service* to long wave, the shunting of the *Sunday* programme and main weekly worship service to earlier slots on Sunday morning, and the axeing of other programmes.

There is no doubt that religious programmes make up a much smaller proportion of the total than they once did. A glance at the *Radio Times* for Good Friday 1955 reveals that half of the five hours of television transmitted that day were devoted to Christian worship and reflection. Religious programmes now make up less than two per cent of the total output of BBC television. Yet the flagship programme *Songs of Praise* still regularly commands an audience of more than five million, and audience research reveals that more than 60 per cent of the population watches a religious television programme at least once a month.

## CHRONOLOGY

**590s** Arrival of Queen Bertha in Kent, and restoration of Christian worship in St Martin's, Canterbury

**900s** Proliferation of parish churches in England, and development of system of tithes to support a priest for every church

**1200s** Increasing emphasis on the word in churches, through sermons and lay prayer books

**1400s** Growth of uniform seating in churches

**1549** The Book of Common Prayer, enforcing identical static worship in all churches

**1828-35** Dismantling of the Church-state, leaving the Church of England largely a voluntary organisation

**1967-2000** New church liturgies and the rise of family services

# MARCHING FORTH WITH THE BANNER OF CHRIST UNFURLED

*John Wolffe*

*Between the archiepiscopates of the Temples, father and son, Church and nation were closely linked. But Church and state clashed over liturgy.*

The ready association of Christian commitment and patriotic loyalty found in the inscriptions of numerous war memorials may beg theological questions, but illustrates a historical climate that was central to the history of the Church of England in the first half of the 20th century.

Four years before the outbreak of the First World War, Archbishop Randall Davidson, in his address in May 1910 at the lying-in-state of Edward VII in Westminster Hall, articulated a seamless linking of national and religious vision. He called on both Houses of Parliament to pray that, "united by this great sorrow, we may be united for the tasks that lie before us, for the fight against all that is unworthy of our calling — as the Christian inheritors of a great Empire." The battles that lay ahead were to be of a far more literally brutal kind than Davidson or any of his hearers could have expected. However, while many comfortable Edwardian assumptions and institutions were swept away, the Church of England was to prove itself more resilient and adaptable than is often recognised.

## Rise in communicants

An appraisal of the Church's prospects at the turn of the 20th century leads to conflicting impressions. Overall attendances were falling, but communicant figures were rising, an indication of changing liturgical and devotional practice, and, arguably, suggesting that the congregations that remained were becoming more committed.

At Easter 1911, 6.74 per cent of the English population received communion in the Church of England. At first sight, that might seem a small proportion, but when one takes into account children, other non-communicants, and those unavoidably absent, one can postulate a substantially larger body of adherents. Anglicans made up rather less than half of English churchgoers, but they were still the largest denominational group.

Constitutionally, the Church's position had weakened substantially during the 19th century, but by 1900 pressure for disestablishment in

King-Emperor: Edward VII at his Coronation, 1902 (W. H. Margetson, from *The Coronation Book of Edward VII*). Photo © Dean & Chapter of Westminster

England had receded. The 1902 Education Act gave state support to church schools. Although this measure was bitterly opposed by many Nonconformists, in general they became more accepting of residual Anglican prestige.

In Wales, the minority Anglican Church had to accept the inevitability of disestablishment, only delayed as long as it was because of the First World War. However, the severance of ties with the state, and the freedom to develop a distinctively Welsh identity, contributed to a notable revival in the fortunes of the Church in Wales in the inter-war era.

Meanwhile, the Edwardian period saw the culmination of a trend whereby the Church, like the monarchy, although losing actual political influence, acquired increasing prominence in national symbolism and ceremonial. Architectural ambitions remained considerable, thus strengthening a very visible and physical presence: Liverpool Cathedral was begun in 1904, and Truro was finally completed in 1910.

The Church played a key part in focusing the waves of popular emotion that swept the country after the deaths of Queen Victoria in 1901, and Edward VII in 1910. The coronations of 1902 and 1911 saw the ceremonial reaffirmation of sacral links between Church, nation and monarchy.

## Marching as to war

During the decades before 1914, a widespread culture of Christian militarism helped to establish the preconditions for enthusiastic and somewhat naïve attitudes to war. When the clergy sang "Onward, Christian soldiers" or "For all the saints" they might well have had spiritual rather than material warfare in mind, but it is unlikely that congregations were so discriminating.

Among boys and young men, quasi-military religious organisations such as the Boys' Brigade and the Church Lads' Brigade reinforced the blending of patriotic and Christian inspiration. At St Nicholas's Church in Durham the war memorial lists 59 men who fell in the First World War, and notes that 28 of them had been members of the local Boys' Brigade. The inscription quotes Revelation 2.10, a text on Christian martyrdom, and expresses the prayer: "O God for England these strong souls have passed — grant we may make her worthy them at last."

During the war, the clergy were overwhelmingly supportive of the nation's cause. Not all went as far as Arthur Winnington-Ingram, Bishop of London, who preached up a sense of holy war, and revelled in being photographed in military uniform.

Winnington-Ingram might have been, as Asquith (Prime Minister

1908-16) put it, an "intensely silly bishop", but then as now it was "silly" bishops who were apt to capture the headlines, and there was no doubting his widespread popular appeal. And even the much more cautious Davidson thought the country was "fighting against what is veritably the work of the devil". Later in the war, however, he and other Anglican leaders spoke out against overly harsh treatment of conscientious objectors.

By raising the spiritual stakes in the war, the Church exposed itself to a significant cultural backlash in the face of the slaughter of the trenches. Poets such as Wilfrid Owen and Siegfried Sassoon probed the seemingly partial concept of God's purposes advanced by many of the clergy. While Stanley Spencer in his wall-painting at Burghclere in Hampshire (1928-32) visualised the resurrection of soldiers, most other artists presented a bleaker spiritual interpretation of war.

Among men who survived the battlefields of France and Flanders, nominal Christian faith was liable to be swept away by such experience. Despite the outstanding ministries of some army chaplains, such as Geoffrey Studdert-Kennedy ("Woodbine Willie"), the predominant experience of the clergy in the forces was described as one of "hens trying to lay eggs on moving staircases". At home, a National Mission, launched in 1916, brought only limited results.

## Inter-war controversies

Nevertheless, the return of peace was followed by a modest recovery in Anglican fortunes. Communicant figures touched a low point in 1917, but by the late 1920s had returned to pre-war levels. In 1924, the earliest electoral-roll figures showed that more than 3.5 million adults identified themselves as Anglicans. In 1931, the adult strength of the Church of England and the Church in Wales amounted to nearly ten per cent of total population. Thereafter, perceptible decline set in.

Meanwhile, the Enabling Act of 1919 had created the Church Assembly, which met for the first time in June 1920, and assumed legislative powers delegated by Parliament. Accordingly, the laity at last acquired an independent constitutional voice in the governance of the Church. The new structures were, though, to be severely tested in 1927 and 1928, when a revised Book of Common Prayer, overwhelmingly approved by all three Houses of the Church Assembly, was twice rejected by the Commons. The affair revealed the continuing force of Protestant sentiment, in opposition to the more Catholic tendency of the new book.

The ongoing potential for tension between Church and state was encapsulated in the career of Hensley Henson, an outstanding preacher and pastor, who held non-literal views of the virgin birth and the bodily resurrection. In 1917 his nomination to the see of Hereford

Anglican visibility: Truro Cathedral. *Photo © reproduced by kind permission of the Dean & Chapter, Truro Cathedral*

by Lloyd George (Prime Minister 1916-22) outraged conservative opinion. Translated to Durham in 1920, Henson was himself a powerful advocate of the continued national status of the Church of England, until the Prayer Book controversy led him, like some others, into a radical shift of position in favour of disestablishment.

The straightforward Christian piety of George V, given increased prominence by the commencement of the annual Christmas broadcasts in 1932, reinforced a sense of patriotic affinity between Crown and altar. In 1936, however, these links were rudely shaken by the attitudes of the new King, Edward VIII. In particular, his relationship with a divorcee, Wallis Simpson, offended traditional Christian morals, and led to his abdication. George VI (reigned 1936-52) restored the aura of non-demonstrative Anglicanism and idealised family life that had surrounded his father George V, and thereby did important service to both Church and monarchy.

During the 1930s, the rising tide of Nazism in Europe and the plight of Christians in Germany gave rise to increasing concern in England. George Bell, Bishop of Chichester from 1929, played a key part in drawing Anglican attention to the issues. Meanwhile, the Church as a whole, seeing the cause of peace as a Christian imperative, supported "appeasement", as pursued by Neville Chamberlain (Prime Minister 1937-40).

## A 'dedicated nation'

When war came in 1939, despite a sense that the moral issues were more clear-cut than they had been in 1914, the Church was much less ready to support a narrowly nationalistic stance.

William Temple acknowledged that no positive good could be done by force, and looked forward to the creation of a new world order. He saw Britain as a "dedicated nation" confronting the "deified nation" of the Nazis. It was left to Winston Churchill to equate the survival of "Christian civilisation" with victory in the Battle of Britain.

The war appears to have stimulated a rather more genuinely Christian response than the First World War had done. Days of public prayer drew large congregations, and in 1943 the Commander-in-Chief of the Home Fleet wrote that "it is my firm conviction that throughout the Service and on shore there is a deeper religious feeling and a greater longing to live a more Christian life than ever before in my lifetime."

Although there was now more space for Christian pacifism, acceptance of overt criticism of the war was still limited. When Bishop Bell condemned in the House of Lords the saturation bombing of German cities, he found himself an isolated figure. His courageous stance antagonised Churchill and the King, and may well have prevented

# After the Armistice

The events surrounding the interment of an unidentified soldier of the Great War just inside the west door of Westminster Abbey on 11 November 1920 well illustrate both the challenges and the opportunities facing the Church of England in the years after the Armistice.

Initially, the Government had envisaged an almost entirely secular ceremony for the unveiling of the Cenotaph in Whitehall. Acting on a suggestion from a former army chaplain, Herbert Ryle, the Dean of Westminster, proposed that after the unveiling a procession move on to a funeral service in the Abbey with a body brought from the battlefields.

After some initial hesitation, the King and the Cabinet accepted the idea. Meanwhile, Archbishop Davidson successfully argued for the singing of "O God, our help in ages past" and the saying of the Lord's Prayer at the Cenotaph. Hence a civil occasion assumed a strongly Anglican character.

It was, moreover, to be the grave in the Abbey rather than the Cenotaph that became the primary focus of pilgrimage by bereaved relatives during subsequent years. Sited at the transition between the secular space of the street and the ecclesiastical space of the Abbey, it was a powerful symbol of accommodation between the Church and secular nationalism. It can be contrasted with the wholly secular location of the French Unknown Warrior, underneath the Arc de Triomphe.

This ceremony in 1920 set the tone for subsequent Remembrance. Although until 1945 Armistice Day was marked on 11 November itself, rather than the nearest Sunday, there was still considerable scope for religious commemoration. War memorials were frequently erected inside churches as well as outside, and their language readily perpetuated the associations of Christianity and patriotism asserted during the war itself.

Hero's welcome: the coffin of the Unknown Warrior, draped in the Union flag, enters the north portal of Westminster Abbey on 11 November 1920. *Photo © The Illustrated London News Picture Library*

his being promoted to Canterbury, or at least London, after Temple's death.

As the war drew to a close, the 1944 Education Act led to a substantial reduction in the number of church schools, but safeguarded the maintenance of a minimal element of religious instruction in the curriculum. It was an appropriately ambiguous piece of legislation to be enacted at the end of a period that had seen very significant challenges to the Church of England, but also unexpected sources of strength and recovery.

# From Temple to Temple

A half-century was framed by a unique father-son succession of Archbishops of Canterbury, Frederick Temple (1896-1902) and William Temple (1942-44). Both had only short primacies — Frederick was already an old man when he moved to Lambeth, and William died suddenly and prematurely — but both made a profound impact on the Church of England.

In 1860, Frederick Temple had been one of the authors of *Essays and Reviews*, a publication bitterly attacked at the time for its perceived theological liberalism. His subsequent advancement to the sees of Exeter, London, and eventually Canterbury was a telling indication of the gradual accommodation between the late Victorian Church and modern thought. It was fitting that Temple, as a splendid survivor of the previous century, lived just long enough to crown Edward VII, and to make his last speech in the House of Lords advocating the Church's cause in relation to the 1902 Education Bill.

William Temple was a profound theological thinker, and also an advocate of a Christian social engagement that continued to shape both secular and church policy in the decades after his death. He was the major driving force behind the Conference on Christian Politics, Education and Citizenship held in 1924, while his *Christianity and Social Order* (1942) is widely seen as an important inspiration for the post-war creation of the welfare state. His hectic two years as wartime Archbishop of Canterbury were the coda to episcopates at Manchester (1921-29) and York (1929-42).

Nevertheless, although the brilliance of the two Temples brought a distinctive lustre to their primacies, the much longer period from 1903 to 1942 was divided between two men of very different qualities.

Randall Davidson (1903-28) was relatively lacking in prophetic vision, but his consummate skills as an ecclesiastical and political diplomat made him one of the most influential archbishops of modern times. He was the confidant and spiritual adviser of successive monarchs, an effective advocate of a strong Christian presence on state occasions, and a reconciler of tensions that, under a less adroit archbishop, could have split the Church.

Cosmo Gordon Lang (1928-42), who had been Archbishop of York from 1909 to 1928, was similarly well connected. His influence contributed to the increasing acceptance of Anglo-Catholicism in the inter-war period. He was the first archbishop to be able to make significant use of the new medium of radio to communicate directly with the population as a whole.

His political judgement was, however, more erratic than Davidson's, and while he was capable of inspiring many, he could also give inadvertent offence. His most serious error of this kind was in a disastrous radio address in the aftermath of Edward VIII's abdication, in which his judgemental tone towards the former King outraged many. He was also a shy and overly self-important man.

The contrast between him and the much more accessible and easy-going William Temple was well represented by the latter's quip to his fellow archbishop: "I have done something you will never do! I have stood in a queue for a bus outside Lambeth Palace!"

# THE UNAUTHORISED VERSION

*Michael Perham*

The Prayer Book controversy that we associate with the year 1928 was a long drawn-out affair, with its roots in the late-19th-century growth of Anglo-Catholicism. For Church of England Catholics, the provisions of the Prayer Book were liturgically inadequate, and they had few qualms about drawing on the ceremonies and the texts of the

Diplomat: Archbishop Randall Davidson, by Sir Leslie Ward, 1910. *Photo © by courtesy of the National Portrait Gallery, London*

Roman Church. They did not originally press for Prayer Book reform. Rather, it was the Bishops who wanted modest reform that would bring some of this practice within the law and make possible the restoration of liturgical order.

By the 1920s, there were other voices advocating Prayer Book reform, not least that of Bishop William Temple, and also the chaplains from the Great War; but until then the issue was more about containing a problem than providing a new liturgy for a changing Church and society.

The story is a complex one of draft reports, debates in the Church

**CHRONOLOGY**

**1901** Death of Queen Victoria
**1902** Education Act
**1910** Parliament Act crisis
**1914-1918** First World War
**1916** National Mission of Repentance and Hope
**1919** Enabling Act
**1920** Disestablishment of the Church in Wales
**1924** First Labour Government
**1927-28** Prayer Book controversy
**1933** Hitler comes to power
**1936** Abdication of Edward VIII
**1939-1945** Second World War
**1944** Education Act

Assembly, revisions and compromises. Alongside official proposals issued in 1922 there were a number of substantial unofficial alternatives: a Catholic draft known as the "Green Book", a series of pamphlets issued by the Life and Liberty Movement brought together as the "Grey Book", and then Bishop Walter Frere's proposals in the "Orange Book", which attempted to find a way through the competing material.

By the time the Assembly came to give its final approval in July 1927, it was clear that the sticking-points both related to the eucharistic rite: the limited provision for the reservation of the sacrament (which offended some Evangelicals), and the eucharistic prayer in the new rite, where the prayer for the Spirit (the epiclesis) followed the words of institution (which alienated Catholics).

When the Measure came to Parliament, it passed through the Lords, but the Commons rejected it (238 votes to 205). A majority of English members voted for it, so there was additional anger that it was members from other parts of Britain who had rejected a Prayer Book for the English Church.

In the light of the rejection of what had become known as the "Deposited Book", the Bishops went to work on a number of minor amendments, and then returned it to the Church Assembly, where it was again passed with a resounding vote in favour. Back it went to Parliament in June 1928, and this time the Commons threw it out by a slightly larger majority.

The Bishops reacted by issuing a statement that they would not "regard as inconsistent with loyalty to the principles of the Church of England" the use of the 1928 material. The book was published.

Much of its material, notably its pastoral offices (but not its eucharistic prayer), came into regular use, and copies were found in vicarage studies and clergy stalls, and even in the pews. Not until the authorisation of the Alternative Service Book 1980 did its influence wane. Legal or not, it was crucial to Anglican liturgy for half a century.

# ZEAL FOR REFORM AS NUMBERS SLIDE

*The post-war Church was not in the mood for radical renewal. Then came the '60s and three dramatic shifts in practice and attitudes.*

## David Edwards

After the war, for the Church of England life became a battle. That was the experience of all the Churches in England as the country became one of the most secular in the world, almost a Western China. But for Anglicans in England the experience was specially strange, since their Church remained established. By the end of the 1960s, the London-based media had become contemptuous, mocking an institution which seemed to be posh but no longer strong, conservative but no longer confident, dogmatic but no longer respected.

### Evangelism report shelved

In 1945, the report *Towards the Conversion of England* was realistic up to a point: inspired by two Evangelical bishops, it faced up to the fact that the country was no longer "Christian" in the sense that it had been between the reigns of Alfred and Victoria; but it trusted in the energetic proclamation of a traditional gospel for the recovery of a Church which needed to be modernised only superficially.

One of its recommendations was the establishment of a council which would promote evangelism, including an expensive advertising campaign. But the Archbishop of Canterbury (Dr Geoffrey Fisher) was sure that the council was not needed, and the Church Assembly (the General Synod's predecessor) was sure that the campaign could not be afforded. Their reactions were part of a widespread mood in the Church of the 1950s: what was needed was reconstruction, not a radical renewal. But the 1960s came, exposing the Church's status as a minority, statistically a sub-culture, spiritually a counter-culture.

From the 1960s onwards, the Church became liable to think that its chief task was its own survival. It did not often get martyred, but quite frequently its members had to endure a trial from which emergence as a hero was more difficult: the ordeal of uncertainty. The gods of the city or the tribe could seem far more successful than the God of the Church — so how important was the Church's survival? Openly or secretly, many people who persisted in belonging to the downsized Church grew depressed or at least very worried.

The heat of the conflict: Synod in session. *Photo © UPP*

It had not seemed obviously crazy for the enthusiasts of *Towards the Conversion of England* to think that advertisements in the papers (this was before TV) might have a great impact. The two world wars had been fought and won in defence either of "God and Empire" or of the vaguer "Christian values". Daily worship and fairly frequent religious instruction were legal requirements in the state's schools, and the Church maintained its own large network of state-subsidised schools and teacher-training colleges. The policy of the BBC was clear: family-based morality must be upheld, the Christian religion must be privileged.

But in the parishes, the Christmassy snow which still covered the reality of the public's growing alienation was beginning to melt even before the declining numbers began to be an avalanche.

## Worship and sacrament

The worship of God continued, partly in forms which were still familiar to some people, and therefore loved and defended by them as being beautiful and helpful, and partly in new forms. In past centuries, the distinguishing marks of the Church of England had been two: the supremacy in its life of the Crown or the Government, and the enforced uniformity of the "common prayer".

In the 20th century there were some traces of these traditions, but not many. Parliament (which was now not very interested) permitted the use of the Alternative Service Book of 1980. This was a modernisation of language and an enrichment of substance by drawing on spiritual discoveries made before and after the era of the Reformation. The ASB did not halt the pace of change, however: it was soon seen that the language needed further updating — and that liturgical uniformity needed a final push into its grave.

The renewed worship had two hearts which sometimes beat together and in time: the parish communion as the centre of Sunday for the faithful, and a hymn-and-chat session, it was hoped, for the younger or the less faithful. But in practice the eucharist became the only regular activity obviously open to the public in many churches. This was the fulfilment of the dreams of many Catholic-minded Anglicans in the past, although the style was now simple and congregational; but the triumph of the parish communion had its downside. It did not attract the vast majority of the public, who could make neither head nor tail of the talk about body and blood. The holy communion united and fed the Church — and kept it as a small minority.

Much the same was true about the new style in baptism. Words and actions made it clearer that this was a sacrament to incorporate the child or adult into the Church as the Body of Christ. But fewer parents now thought that it was socially necessary to have their baby christened.

## Zeal for reform

As always, the life of corporate worship and private prayer was the most important thing the Church did, because in it people glimpsed the reality and rule of God; but the part of the Church's life that could be quantified saw many changes in the attempt to make this institution more of a model and less of a scandal to the rest of society.

Much was achieved which was more relevant than the revision of canon law in 1947-69. The engines of church government were the General Synod as a kind of Parliament from the beginning of the 1970s, and the Archbishops' Council as a kind of Cabinet from the end of the 1990s.

The most important improvement in this sphere was the ordination of women. In comparison, the split caused was less significant.

But there was also a much needed reorganisation in the conditions of work for all the clergy. The more radical proposals were rejected, but big changes were made largely because the numbers of the ordained fell. Many villages no longer had "our own vicar"; in the cities and towns some churches were closed; over-large houses were sold off; stipends were both improved and equalised; while the parson's freehold and the patron's rights were retained in theory, in practice many parishes were now served by teams, groups or individual priests ("in charge") who were appointed for limited terms by the diocese; and the dioceses themselves were rationed in numbers of paid clerics.

The fall in these numbers did far less damage than would have been expected in the past. Not only did the numbers of honorary ("non-stipendiary") priests grow, but many functions hitherto reserved to the professionals were discharged by volunteers from the laity (some still called "Readers"). And the people in the pews gave more in cash and in time than ever before, enabling the Church Commissioners to concentrate endowments on the multiplying numbers of the clergy living longer on pensions.

## Zeal for ecumenism

Much energy went into the improvement of relationships with other Churches. Indeed, until 1982 there was hope (or fear) of a movement by stages into reunion with Methodism and the United Reformed Church. Those plans were vetoed by a conservative alliance, but what did take root was local ecumenism.

Some church buildings were shared; some local partnerships between denominations became close; friendships were often real; the rule that Anglicans should not receive communion from non-episcopalians was dropped in most consciences. After the Second Vatican Council, the Roman Catholic Church joined in this local ecumenism, as did many of the black-led congregations, but there were limits: under John Paul II the Vatican became more conservative, and the black-led congregations were, sociologically speaking, clubs.

Although itself sorely tempted to become an introverted club, the Church of England kept up a commentary on current affairs. It showed a concern for the nations struggling to escape from poverty and for an environment protesting against pollution. Racism was attacked by the thought that most of God's children do not have white skins, Thatcherism by the thought that most of them cannot be successful entrepreneurs.

Practical results of this prayer and talk could be impressive — the support for Christian Aid, for example, or for the Church Urban Fund. But the more theoretical commentary became weaker, partly because the mistake was made of dismantling the British Council of Churches, which had been a think-tank. Even on the moral problems in British society, the quality of the commentary diminished, partly because, with a few exceptions, the bishops became managerial rather than prophetic. Archbishops repeatedly called to the nation, but not many heard the call.

One of the difficult problems was how to respond to the revolution in sexual behaviour. Only gradually did a virtual consensus begin to emerge that contraception was positively desirable; that cohabitation with an eye to marriage, like homosexual activity, was neither ideal nor totally damnable; and that a marriage after divorce could be blessed by God. And many in the Church fought or hesitated at each step of the way to agreement. A clearer witness was given by lay Christians who in their own lives gave a firm no to practices which society no longer condemned with the old clarity — sleeping around, adultery, gambling as a habit, and the abuse of drugs, including alcohol.

## 'Biblical theology' and after

Above all, this period, 1945-2000, bequeathed to the future the need to deepen and clarify (twin necessities) the Church's teaching about God. Under Archbishop Fisher the teaching was mainly a semi-popularisation of "biblical" theology, involving a strong basis in the scriptures, but with a definite rejection of fundamentalism. Under Archbishop Ramsey the Church became more open to the questions about belief being asked in the world around it.

Under his three successors, because the radicals of the '60s had failed to suggest a religion which would work, the Evangelicals became the strongest movement in the Church. For the most part, they were not fundamentalists, not uninterested in the social and intellectual problems of the age, and not sectarian: being open to the Church and the world had been the choice made by most of them in the 1960s.

But they still struck most people, in an increasingly educated society, as being excessively simple-minded. This had been their downfall in the Victorian age.

# FROM OBLIGATION TO CONSUMPTION

*Grace Davie*

Surprisingly soon after the end of the Second World War, the predominant mood in the Churches became one of moderate com-

Crowned: Elizabeth II, supported (left) by Michael Ramsey, in 1953. *Photo © Hulton Getty Picture Collection*

placency. Given their relative success in rebuilding after the devastation (they did as well as anyone), this was understandable enough. It was a mood, moreover, which fitted the dominant conservatism of the 1950s — vividly symbolised in the coronation of Elizabeth II, a ceremony which brought together the Church of England, the monarchy and the nation in an impressive act of sacralisation, witnessed by a television audience numbered in millions.

The mood was not to last. As the '50s gave way to a far more turbulent decade, the world into which the Churches appeared to fit so well was challenged on every front. Nor have the post-war certainties been recovered since; they are gone forever, and not only for the Churches. The secular institutions of the post-war period (notably the political parties, the trades unions and large sections of the welfare

Mourned: pallbearers carry the late Diana, Princess of Wales. *Photo © PA*

state) — just as much as their ecclesiastical equivalents — are faced with the challenges of late modernity, as a world which turned on the idea of production gives way to a society dominated by consumption.

In many ways, their fates are similar: as the statistics of membership/attendance in all the mainstream Churches turn downwards, so do those from the trades unions, regular sporting fixtures, and certain forms of leisure pursuit.

Football and the cinema are particularly interesting, in that attendances fall rapidly from the early post-war decades to the 1990s, but then begin to turn up again, indicating the tapping of an alternative market. So why do these shifts take place?

From the point of view of the Churches, it seems that the reasons lie as much in the changing nature of society as in evidence of religious indifference — the latter, in fact, is as much a consequence as a cause of the change in churchgoing habits.

In terms of the indices of religiousness, a crucial element in the argument lies in the complex and disputed relationship between religious practice and religious belief. For many commentators, the relationship is assumed to be direct: as practice falls, so too will belief, though rather more slowly. From this point of view, the relatively high levels of belief at the turn of the millennium are simply vestigial, residues of a bygone age.

For others, including me, this relationship is as likely to be inverse as direct. As the British population, just like its European equivalents, loses its moorings in institutional religion, it becomes a nation of seekers as much as a nation of agnostics. What it does not become is a nation of secular rationalists.

Evidence for the continuation of religious sensibilities, albeit confused ones, is not difficult to find. Look at the Diana episode. Diana herself was a seeker, beginning and ending her life in the Church of England — like so many of her compatriots — but in between a personification of religious consumption as she tried first this and then that, ending her life in the company of a prominent Muslim.

Where would you place Diana in a table of statistics? And what of her mourners? They, too, displayed both independence from and reliance on the mainstream Churches, notably the Church of England, as they created individual acts of mourning, often in or near church buildings, and assumed — as day followed night — that the funeral would be held in the state church. The funeral, too, was typical of the 1990s: a mixed-economy affair for a family of divorcees, starting and ending conventionally, but with personalised, somewhat controversial elements in between. The television audience was numbered in billions.

Obligation has turned increasingly into consumption, a mood that the Churches would be wise to respect if not to endorse. At its best, an established Church can incorporate both tendencies; at its worst, it falls between all possible stools.

## Ordination of women

Within this framework, three shifts have taken place, all of which were unthinkable at the end of the war. All three reflect a changing social context alongside shifting theological perspectives.

Women played a significant role in the war effort, often replacing men (away on active service) in positions of public responsibility. It was unlikely that the return to "normality" would remain unquestioned for long. As the post-war decades passed, the position of women in Western societies began to change, and this time irrevocably. Increasingly, it was the professions that had no representation of women which had to justify their maintenance of the status quo, not the other way round.

The Churches responded, but in different ways. Both Roman Catholic and Orthodox Churches preserved the tradition as they had received it, the tradition endorsing an exclusively male priesthood.

Most Protestant Churches, on the hand, had little difficulty in incorporating women into their ministries, the Protestant minister being the representative of the people rather the representation of Christ.

The decision, finally (in 1992), of the Church of England — the mother Church of the Anglican Communion — to ordain women was a significant marker; it attracted huge public attention. A Church that is both Catholic and reformed voted democratically (and after much procrastination) to admit women to the priesthood. Accepted by large sections of the churchgoing public, this decision, understandably, has caused considerable difficulties for a sizeable number of Anglo-Catholics.

Much subtler has been the effect the debate has had on wider perceptions about churchgoing in general. Over-preoccupation with the presence, or otherwise, of women in the chancel has resulted not only in a lack of scrutiny concerning women in the pews, but in a failure to affirm their presence. Women outnumber men on almost any index of

Ecumenical partners: Bishop David Sheppard and the late Archbishop Derek Worlock. *Photo © Liverpool Daily Post* religiousness in Western Christianity, a discrepancy more often than not constructed as an under-representation of men.

## The ecumenical movement

When David Sheppard (already Bishop of Woolwich) was appointed Bishop of Liverpool in 1975, his first congratulatory telegram came from the then Roman Catholic Archbishop of Liverpool, George Andrew Beck. The gesture proved prophetic, as Bishop Sheppard's partnership with Beck's successor, Archbishop Derek Worlock, became nationally famous.

Liverpool is, and always has been, a special case, from which it is unwise to generalise. It is clear, none the less, that one factor among many which enabled such an outstanding Christian partnership in Liverpool was the transformation in the ecumenical climate in the country taken as a whole. For what was totally impossible in Liverpool in the immediate post-war period was almost impossible everywhere else.

The process by which this transformation took place is paradoxical. There has been more than one false start, notably the painful collapse of the Anglican-Methodist unity scheme in 1972. But almost as a reaction (and as the organisational schemes ceased to dominate the agenda), a gradual *rapprochement* of the various Christian Churches began to take place — so much so that what was unthinkable 50 years ago is now considered commonplace, a point worth remembering as the continuing efforts to formalise such gestures become from time to time acrimonious. The visit of John Paul II in 1982 was a memorable and hugely important public marker of the ecumenical process.

Religious pluralism now takes a different form in modern Britain, for just as the Christian Churches began to draw themselves back together, small but significant other-faith populations have established themselves in this country. The interfaith debate presents a new and somewhat different challenge.

## The European Union

The ecumenical movement is concerned with the rebuilding of Christendom. So, too, is the European Union. The nation state is a form of political organisation that received overwhelming endorsement at the time of the Reformation, and for very mixed motives; it is neither a necessary nor a "normal" model of political life. It is for this reason that the place of Britain in Europe forms, in the year 2000, a central, if controversial, item in the political agenda.

The implications for the Churches are considerable: should they emphasise the distinctiveness of their national role, not least the capacities of both the Church of England and the Church of Scotland to embody national identity? Or should they stress their commonalities with the Churches of continental Europe, embodied in the links made between Anglicans and Lutherans (at Meissen and Porvoo) and with the Roman Church in the ongoing deliberations of the Anglican Roman Catholic International Convention (ARCIC)?

Different people react differently to these suggestions. What is clear however, is the significance of the religious factor in the different parts of the United Kingdom (never mind the links with Europe), as the four nations that make up this shifting entity look for new forms of internal collaboration. And within this evolving entity, the position of the Church of England is unique: as the mother Church of the Anglican Communion, which, like the Commonwealth, is an effective global alliance, yet not in any way European.

## CHRONOLOGY

**1945** *Towards the Conversion of England* published
**1947** Report on Canon Law
**1948** Church Commissioners set up
**1953** Coronation of Elizabeth II
**1954** Billy Graham's first evangelistic "crusade" to Britain
**1961** Michael Ramsey succeeds Geoffrey Fisher as Archbishop of Canterbury
**1963** *Honest to God* by John Robinson, Bishop of Woolwich, provokes popular debate about orthodoxy
**1970** General Synod set up
**1972** Synod finally rejects Anglican-Methodist unity scheme
**1980** Alternative Service Book
**1982** Papal visit to UK
**1985** *Faith in the City* report reflects church consensus over Thatcherism
**1992** C of E's General Synod gives final approval to women priests
**1997** Death and funeral of Diana, Princess of Wales

# INTO THE NEW MILLENNIUM

*John Bowker*

*The Church should enter the new millennium with confidence, but it will need to unlearn the fatal mistake of the early centuries when it adopted a military model of leadership.*

Economists have been defined as people who tell you tomorrow why what they said yesterday didn't happen today. Unfair, no doubt, but if it's hard for them to predict the future, it's just as impossible for us — witness the triviality of astrology under the heading "Your Stars". None of us knows for sure what is going to happen in the next minute, let alone in the next thousand years.

And yet Christians do know all that matters. They know that the future belongs to God, whose *parousia*, or presence, fills every future with the completion of that work of rescue and renewal begun in Christ and continued in the Spirit. Biologists discovered in the last century that the future causes the past in decisively important ways, in what is known as downward causation. The future causes the present whenever Christians realise in the present the sovereignty of God which will in the future be manifest in all ways; and that means living always toward the horizon of hope — even when persecutions yet again assail them.

But none of that gives any detail about the "when" or the "how"; and, despite the speculations of the fringes, most Christians heed the advice of Jesus not to try to predict the dates and times of God's future. There may not be another thousand years, but we have to live both as though there may not be, and as though there could be. In the coming millennium, that will mean exactly what it has meant in the past two: that we realise ourselves in that Presence in those acts of perfect love and sorrow that we call prayer, penitence, worship and adoration, and that we seek to extend the practical meaning of that hope to those in need.

## Capitalism and poverty

The love of God and the love of our neighbour will not change. What may change is the way that human and other suffering occurs. In this new millennium, capitalism will be transformed.

Capitalism as the organisation of economies on the basis of the profit motive and the free play of market forces, resting on the human motivation to own and acquire wealth through competition, is not

Future factor: the need for humanitarian aid, as provided for these orphans in Sudan in 1998.
*Photo © PA*

"Doomed": the London Stock Exchange in the booming '80s. *Photo © PA*

going to disappear. But the ruthless and destructive forms of capitalism will be challenged, much as, in miniature, it is already recognised that the version implied by Thatcherism was a brutal error. Present-day capitalism delivers the goods, but it does not deliver the Good. There are about as many people now in slavery as there were at the height of the slave trade. Marxism (at least outside China) failed, but it did bring the poor to the centre of history. Christians will surely continue to be the agents of anger as well as of the meaning of mercy and of love, showing what it means in practice to give priority to the poor: the Jubilee 2000 campaign has been a promising start.

## The Internet

So the poor we will have always with us. But the opportunities to move from poverty to wealth will change completely. The immediate engine for change is the Internet. The price of access to the Internet is falling so fast, and the necessity for time-honoured institutions is disappearing so rapidly (chains of car dealers are as doomed as national stock-markets), that virtually all people will have the chance to become entre-preneurs.

Not all will succeed — to say the least. But many will try; and the problems of control against fraud will be far more formidable than the existing problems of control against the vicious evils to which the Internet gives freedom of expression — in, for example, child porn-ography, racial hatred, and revivals of anti-Semitism. The Internet will also accelerate the growth of new religions and alternative spiritualities, not least because religion is extremely big business, and open, as we see already in mainstream religions, to exploitation.

What will the Church of the Internet be like? It will give a new and exhilarating meaning to the Body of Christ, because it will connect us to each other in ways that will transform our experience and our ministry. The *ekklesia* of the Internet will be genuinely ecumenical: it will reach all people across the world without boundaries. Already religious communities provide resources for prayer on the Internet.

But while the Internet connects people in one sense, it also isolates them in another: it is certain that during the new millennium the faithful will be gathered on the Internet — probably, among much else, to celebrate the memorial of Christ. All the more important, therefore, for the Church to be the *ekklesia*, the calling of people out of their isolations into the presence of each other. The warmth as well as the worry of human fellowship will have to be given occasion, and it will be a major vocation of the Church in the new millennium to lead the way in providing those occasions of meeting. The isolations of the future will require a vastly different liturgical imagination from anything that has been exercised up till now.

## Christianity and conflict

But will there be a future, at least for human beings? This time the question arises, not from the fact that time and creation rest in the hand of God, but from the fact that humans are capable of great evil. I have spent a lifetime explaining why religions (or rather, people in religious systems) are likely to destroy human life as we now know it.

The invasion of Afghanistan in 1979 began what some regard as a third world war, in which the religious component is obvious. Religions are involved in virtually all the long-running and intransigent conflicts in the world. Many of them now have access to nuclear, biological and chemical weapons; all of them have access to the means of cyberwar — or cyberterrorism, depending on one's point of view.

It is imperative that the Church of the new millennium set itself against the destructive consequence of the fact that religions (including itself) have to be systems in order to survive. It is an imperative because this is God's creation, not ours. Even if (as Christian history suggests) Christians are not too worried about hating and destroying each other, they should remember the final words of the book of Jonah. It is an imperative also because it is the prayer of Christ that we should be one in a way that mirrors the unity of Christ and the Father.

## The ecumenical quest

To that end, the coming Church must begin again on the ecumenical quest, and that means taking a penitent look at its own boundary-maintaining structures. Yes, Edinburgh, 1910, set us on the way, but we are stuck because, in our ecumenical explorations, we never take seriously the necessity for religions, or for Churches, to be systems.

Churches are at least as much about the structures that enable them to continue through time as they are about doctrine, and it is those that need to be redeemed.

The ecumenical quest of the future will, if it is wise, be based on the value of diversity: it will seek to affirm the importance of diversity instead of seeking to achieve uniformity. One of the things we know for certain from creation is that God delights in diversity: every iris of every eye, every snowflake that falls, every tree in a beech wood, even every "identical" twin, is different. There is a God-created value in diversity constituting a greater whole.

It is that kind of diversity that the form of the future Church must affirm, far beyond the World Council of Churches, in a system of alliance that has so far seemed unimaginable. Only this will return to the Church the gospel that at present passes much of the world by, since to the world it is so obvious that the Churches prefer to despise (and seek converts from) each other.

## Religions

The ecumenical future is poised on an edge. If — a very large "if" — the Churches are able to affirm and endorse diversity in their own case, they may be able to extend that ecumenical quest to other human discernments of the reality of God, or to other human attainments of enlightenment — in other words, to other religions. They, too, are systems, and capable of huge destructions: quite apart from their threat, as systems, to future life on this planet, they have done immense harm to those whom they wish to control or of whom they disapprove: women, children, animals, each other.

Yet religions have also done immense good in protecting the transmission of information through which God, salvation and enlightenment have become true for billions of people. On religions, much that is enduringly good in human history and culture has depended. This is what I have called elsewhere "the paradox of religious urgency": religions are such bad news only because they are such good news. If religions had not protected and made available the stupendous ways in which life can be raised from death to life, from sin to salvation, they would have disappeared long ago; and they would not be so threatening now. The Church of the new millennium could well begin now to learn what it means to maximise the good and minimise the damage in its relations with other religions, without any compromise of truth.

## Sex and food

A serious problem for religions is that they are the earliest systems of which we have evidence that protected the birth of children and

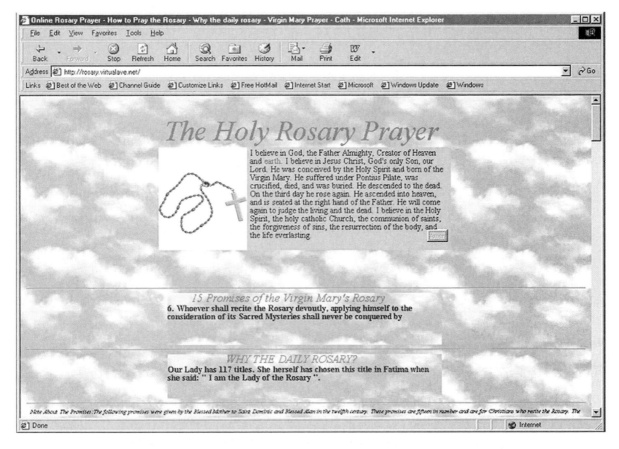

Internet religion: a page of an interactive rosary prayer site on the internet, www.rosary.virtualave.net

the sustenance of the extended family in which the upbringing of children was made more secure. In other words, religions have been, for millennia, systems for the protection of gene-replication and the nurture of children, long before anyone had any idea what those words meant.

That is why, for millennia, religions have been preoccupied with sex and food, and with regulating them. In the new millennium, that will not be so. Gene-replication no longer needs the protection of religious systems, and will increasingly go on outside them. The attempt of some parts of the Church to maintain that sex and reproduction (the unitive and the procreative functions of sex) cannot be separated is so obviously false in nature and experience that the Church of the new millennium will begin, here as elsewhere in ethics, to learn what it means to maximise the good and minimise the damage. It will also realise what this means in the case of homosexuality, but it may be another millennium before it acts.

Where sex (and women) are concerned, religions fight ferociously to keep their control, as a document like *Humanae Vitae* makes abundantly clear, but they will be increasingly unnecessary for those

Religious protest: Pakistanis burn the stars-and-stripes after US strikes on Afghanistan in 1998. *Photo © EPA*

purposes. They will remain concerned with birth and family (and these will change dramatically), but they will not be necessary for control. Religions will have other and equally important things to offer: the means of grace (an important word in all religions) and the hope of glory.

## The lifespan

The coming Church will be deeply involved in the problems that face the planet in terms of population and resources. In addition to the challenge of existing problems will come that of greatly prolonged life. For how long death can be postponed is completely unknown, but that it will be postponed for increasingly extended periods is certain: already the crucial link has just been established between a longer life and the body's resistance to oxidative stress. With much more life to lose, white-water rafting and bungee-jumping will begin not at 22, but at 122. What targets, then, for youthful adventure?

Even now, the fastest increase of Internet users in the United States is among the old. How will the Church of the new millennium evangelise older age, and bring to it the transfiguration of Christ as he prepared for his own exodus? Or how will the Church allow itself to be evangelised by older people? Allowing a few bishops to retire later than other clergy scarcely meets the point. The deepening of prayer in the very much longer opportunities of time will be a major miracle of the new millennium; and on this the new religious communities of the Internet will be founded.

## The brain

With equal certainty, education will be transformed, because it will rest more on the realisation of satisfactions in the brain than on designated ends. That will happen because the brain will be better understood. The brain itself will not change significantly in a natural way. The human genome is extremely stable, even according to the thousand-year rule of Wilson and Lumsden (the rule proposes that within a millennium, or fifty generations, genetic evolution can establish epigenetic bias over "virtually every category of cultural behaviour"). But the ways in which we can affect the brain's operations, and in which we can connect the electrical activity of the brain via microchips to the external world, will be immensely different.

As matters stand, we know extremely little about the brain, although we now have very detailed maps of the parts of the brain that are committed to the brain's many activities. We already have good maps of the emotional brain, and maps of the religious brain will not be long delayed.

None of this work is reductionist, though some, as always, will try to make it so. The new understanding of the brain demonstrates why God is necessary to account for what is going on in God-centred behaviour — and why, if God were not necessary, it would not be possible to invent him. In place of the old placard that proclaimed "Prepare to meet thy God", the new research holds up a placard saying, "Prepared to meet thy God" — prepared from the gene-protein process that builds our brains. The consequence of this research for the Church of the new millennium will be a profound increase in the sense of awe and gratitude and wonder — combined with a much sharper criticism of our institutions.

## The Bible

What will be the place of the Bible in all this? The Bible will remain fundamental in the network of constraints that control the lives of believers. The books of the Bible came into being in relation to events and words in which the self-revealing of God was recognised, at least by

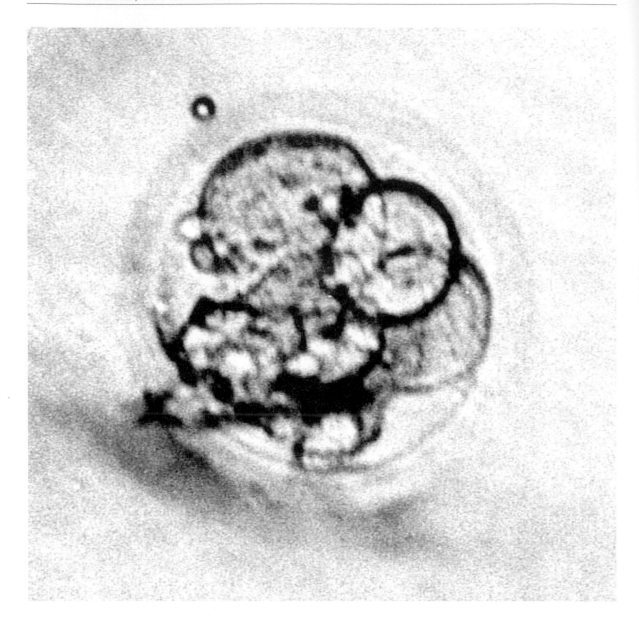

Future factor: genetic engineering, which produced these human cells, cloned in Korea the same year. *Photo © EPA*

some. It has not been possible for at least a century to think that the Bible came into being because God dictated it, since the production of those words and their designation as a canon were the consequence of a long process in which many more than some few original writers were involved. God who becomes incarnate and dies on a cross is unlikely to ignore and bypass history in creating scripture.

But that has not diminished the authority of the Bible. As we wrote in *The Complete Bible Handbook* (Dorling Kindersley, 1998), the crucial link here is between the two Latin words *auctor* and *auctoritas* — the link between the authority of God derived from God as Author.

But if we have learnt, with much pain, to abandon a dictation theory of the inspiration of the Bible, because it contradicts what God has done in Christ, the Church of the new millennium will have to learn — no doubt with equal pain — to abandon a dictation theory of how the Bible relates to our lives and decision-making now.

The instinct still of many is to look for texts that will dictate what we should do, or, in other words, that will act as warrants for our assertions. Read any encyclical. On the basis of that methodology, Jews have been murdered, "witches have been burned alive, homosexuals executed, children beaten, Africans shipped into slavery, women treated in law as children, animals regarded as human property, and wars justified in the name of the Prince of Peace" (*Complete Bible Handbook*). It will be a major liberation of the Holy Spirit if the coming Church no longer uses the Bible in that way.

Will that lead to anarchy in ethics? No. But the Bible will no longer be a substitute for the moral seriousness that Christ demanded of his followers. We have lost our way in the past decades because we have been bombarded with bizarre statements that the Enlightenment is the root of all evil: by making everything subject to reason, it is said to have introduced subjectivity into ethics, subjectivity being taken, absurdly, to mean that people decide for themselves what counts as right and wrong.

The Enlightenment was no doubt mistaken in supposing that reason can solve all our problems, but the alternative is even worse. As Jacob pointed out at the end of his book *The Possible and the Actual* (Washington University Press, 1981): "The enlightenment and the 19th century had the folly to consider reason to be not only necessary but sufficient for the solution of all problems. Today it would be still more foolish to decide, as some would like, that because reason is not sufficient, it is not necessary either."

Moral judgement arises because humans are aware that there is a future but have virtually no idea what is going to happen. Many of our judgements, therefore, involve evaluation: is this projected thought or projected action wise or foolish, prudential or careless, good or evil, right or wrong? No matter how much experience the human race builds up, and no matter how carefully we consult it (especially when it is embedded in revelation), we cannot always, in each particular case, be certain what is the right or the good thing to do.

Relativists in ethics do not say that, in consequence, we can never know for sure the difference between right and wrong, nor do subjectivists imply that morality has been privatised. They simply say that the outcome of evaluation is never dictated from the past, not even from revelation, and that morality is subjective only in the sense that we are all the responsible subjects of our own thoughts and agents of our own acts, much as the Church used to say about conscience.

Paradoxically, recent moral philosophy has realised that we do derive values from facts and "oughts" from "ises", but not with the same stringency of inference that used to be thought necessary if any true inference is to be made.

## Evil

Into that revolution the Church of the new millennium should enter with confidence. The Enlightenment established "a preferential option for options", and that is not easy for the Church to welcome. But the Church would be wise to endorse the option for options in the context always of maximising the good and minimising the damage, since that is clearly what Jesus did. On that basis, the contest against evil can be engaged with far greater confidence, because the battle is being fought, not under slogans, but under the grace of God.

And evils there will be. Joseph de Maistre looked back on the French Revolution, that well intentioned nightmare, and wrote: "From the tomb of a murdered monarchy has emerged an immense and formless monster, more terrible than any that has hitherto stunned and subjugated the imagination of mankind." From the tomb of a murdered Weimar republic, of collectivisation, of the Paris agreement in 1973, equally immense and formless monsters have emerged in our time (the Holocaust, the massacre of Kulaks and of Cambodians). In the future they will emerge again.

But the Church should not be afraid — provided it is not a part of the evil, as it has been too often in the past. The future of the Church's past (how we use the past for present purposes) is already a major challenge. To use it, as so many now do, to reinforce their malice is to deny the gift of the Holy Spirit.

## Authority in the Church

To serve the world and be the gospel, the Church will have to unlearn the fatal mistake of the early centuries when it was seduced by the Roman army. The metaphor of the Body, as Paul used it, slid almost imperceptibly into a metaphor of the Roman army, with its hierarchical chain of command. With Christ as Head, it is easy to see how it happened. The disaster has been that men (and it has been almost entirely men) have called themselves "church leaders", or "leaders of the Church", on a military model. The only people today who adorn themselves in clothes and decorations that state their power over others are the upper ranks of the military and the clergy.

Exemplary leadership is obvious in the New Testament, but what is claimed and exercised by the self-styled leaders of the Church today is far removed from what Jesus taught and lived about service. If the Church of the new millennium finally destroys the military metaphor, it will exhibit to the world a new style of authority — and that could be a consequence of the ordination of women. That the coming Church will at last welcome the giftedness of women is almost too much to hope for, given its record so far: it can at least be prayed for.

If the clergy do not own the Church, nor do theologians own theology. Theology has become an increasingly private game, played to its own rules and evaluated only by the players themselves. Perhaps in the new millennium there will be those who will reconnect theology with the world that is never anything other than God's creation.

Only then will that other essential connection be made between theology and the creative life of us all. Maybe the Church of the new millennium will found its own art schools. The Church knows well (because it knows it in the spiritual life) that constraint is the necessary condition of freedom. It would be a new form of patronage in the arts if it were to lead the way in recovering that truth for the arts.

## To the future

So, we who lived in the second millennium greet you who live in the third. May the sudden angels still come down and touch your world with new annunciations of old truth; may Holy Wisdom, who secures existence for you and for all things, persuade you into beauty and peace; and may we who live with you in the communion of all the saints be your companions in the completion of God's work, and in the adoration of the One who gives us life and love.

# FURTHER READING

**PREFACE**

Henry Chadwick, *Augustine*, Oxford University Press, 1986
Henry Chadwick (trans.), *Augustine, Confessions*, Oxford University Press, 1998
Henry Chadwick, *Boethius*, Oxford University Press, 1981
Henry Chadwick, *Early Christian Thought and the Classical Tradition: Studies in Justin, Clement and Origen*, Oxford University Press, 1984
Henry Chadwick, *The Early Church*, revised edn., Penguin Books, 1999
Henry Chadwick, *Heresy and Orthodoxy in the Early Church*, Variorum, 1991
Henry Chadwick, *History and Thought in the Early Church*, Variorum, 1982
Henry Chadwick, *Priscillian of Avila*, Oxford University Press, 1976

**CHAPTER ONE**

K. Cameron, *Place-Name Evidence for the Anglo-Saxon Invasion and Scandinavian Settlements: Eight Studies*, English Place-Name Society, 1987
P. Cavill, *Anglo-Saxon Christianity*, Fount, 1999
Norah Chadwick, *The Age of Saints in the Early Celtic Church Facsimile reprint*, Llanerch Publishers, 1960
B. Colgrave & R. A. B. Mynors (ed. and trans.), *Bede's Ecclesiastical History of the English People*, Clarendon Press, 1969
J. H. G. Grattan & C. Singer, *Anglo-Saxon Magic and Medicine*, Oxford University Press, 1952
C. Kennedy (trans.), *Beowulf: The Oldest English Epic*, Oxford University Press, 1940
F. Klaeber (ed.), *Beowulf and the Fight at Finnsburg*, 3rd edn., Heath, 1950
H. Mattingly (trans.), S. A. Handford (revised), *Tacitus: The Agricola and the Germania*, Penguin Books, 1979
Liam de Paor, *St Patrick's World — the Christian Culture of Ireland's Apostolic Age*, Four Courts Press, 1993
Richard Sharpe (trans.), *Adomnan of Iona's Life of St Columba*, Penguin Books, 1995
D. Wilson, *Anglo-Saxon Paganism*, Routledge, 1992
M. Winterbottom (ed. and trans.), *Gildas: The Ruin of Britain and Other Documents*, Arthurian Period Sources, vol. 7, Phillimore, 1978

**CHAPTER TWO**

J. Campbell, *The First Century of Christianity in England* in *Essays in Anglo-Saxon History*, Hambledon Press, 1986
B. Colgrave (ed. and trans.), *The Earliest Life of Gregory the Great*, The University of Kansas Press, 1968
B. Colgrave (ed. and trans.), *Two Lives of Saint Cuthbert*, Cambridge University Press, 1940
B. Colgrave & R. A. B. Mynors (ed. and trans.), *Bede's Ecclesiastical History of the English People*, Clarendon Press, 1969
D. Dales, *Light to the Isles: Missionary Theology in Celtic and Anglo-Saxon Britain*, Lutterworth Press, 1997
R. Fletcher, *The Conversion of Europe: From Paganism to Christianity 371-1386 AD*, HarperCollins, 1997

John Hines (ed.), *The Anglo-Saxons from the Migration Period to the Eighth Century: An Ethnographic Perspective*, Studies in Historical Archaeoethnology 2, Boydell Press, 1997

T. Hofstra, L. A. J. R. Houwen & A. A. MacDonald (eds.), *Pagans and Christians: The Interplay between Christian Latin and Traditional Germanic Cultures in Early Medieval Europe*, Germania Latina 2, Egbert Forsten, 1995

Henry Mayr-Harting, *The Coming of Christianity to Anglo-Saxon England*, 3rd edn., Batsford, 1991

B. Ward, *High King of Heaven: Aspects of Early English Spirituality*, Mowbray, 1999

D. Whitelock (ed. and trans.), *English Historical Documents I c. 500-1042*, 2nd edn., Oxford University Press, 1979

D. M. Wilson (ed.), *The Archaeology of Anglo-Saxon England*, Cambridge University Press, 1981

## CHAPTER THREE

C. W. Jones, *Bede, the Schools and the Computus*, Variorum, 1994

Henry Mayr-Harting, *The Coming of Christianity to Anglo-Saxon England*, 3rd edn., Batsford, 1991

W. M. Stevens, *Bede's Scientific Achievement*, St Paul's Church, Jarrow, 1985

W. M. Stevens, *Cycles of Time and Scientific Learning in Medieval Europe*, Variorum, 1995

F. Wallis (ed.), *Bede: The Reckoning of Time*, Liverpool University Press, 1999

## CHAPTER FOUR

N. Brooks, *The Early History of the Church of Canterbury*, Leicester University Press, 1986

J. Campbell (ed.), *The Anglo-Saxons*, Penguin Books, 1982

C. Cubitt, *Anglo-Saxon Church Councils*, Leicester University Press, 1995

S. Keynes & M. Lapidge (trans.), *Alfred the Great*, 13th edn., Penguin Books, 1999

P. Sawyer (ed.), *The Oxford Illustrated History of the Vikings*, Oxford University Press, 1997

## CHAPTER FIVE

J. Campbell (ed.), *The Anglo-Saxons*, Penguin Books, 1982

M. Lapidge with J. Blair, S. Keynes & D. Scragg (eds.), *The Blackwell Encyclopaedia of Anglo-Saxon England*, Blackwell Publishers, 1999

D. Scragg (ed.), *The Battle of Maldon AD 991*, Blackwell Publishers, 1991

D. Whitelock (ed.), *English Historical Documents c.500-1042*, English Historical Documents 1, 2nd edn., Routledge, 1979

## CHAPTER SIX

F. Barlow, *The English Church 1000-1066*, Longman, 1963

F. Barlow, *The English Church 1066-1154*, Longman, 1979

G. Bosanquet (trans.), Eadmer, *History of Recent Events in England*, Cresset Press, 1964

M. Chibnall (ed. and trans.), Orderic Vitalis, *The Ecclesiastical History, Volume II (of VI), Books III and IV*, Oxford Medieval Texts, Clarendon Press, 1969

R. R. Darlington, *Ecclesiastical Reform in the Late Old English Period*, English Historical Review, Vol. 51, 1936, pp.385-428

C. Johnson (ed. and trans.), Hugh the Chantor, *The History of the Church of York 1066-1127*, M. Brett, C. N. L. Brooke & M. Winterbottom (revised), Oxford Medieval Texts, Clarendon Press, 1990

E. Mason, *St Wulfstan of Worcester c.1008-1095*, Blackwell Publishers, 1990

V. Ortenberg, *The English Church and the Continent in the Tenth and Eleventh Centuries*, Oxford University Press, 1992

S. J. Ridyard, *Condigna Veneratio: Post-Conquest Attitudes to the Saints of the Anglo-Saxon*s in R. Allen Brown (ed.), *Anglo-Norman Studies IX, Proceedings of the Battle Conference 1986*, Boydell Press, 1987

R. W. Southern, *Saint Anselm: A Portrait in a Landscape*, Cambridge University Press, 1990

A. Williams, *The English and the Norman Conquest*, Boydell Press, 1995

## CHAPTER SEVEN

J. Blair & R. Sharpe, *Pastoral Care Before the Parish*, Leicester University Press, 1992

Janet Burton, *Monastic and Religious Orders in Britain 1000-1300*, Cambridge University Press, 1994

W. Davies, *Wales in the Early Middle Ages*, Leicester University Press, 1982

N. Edwards & A. Lane (eds.), *The Early Church in Wales and the West*, Oxbow Monograph 16, Oxbow Books, 1992

Rose Graham, *Gilbert of Sempringham and the Gilbertines*, Elliot Stock, 1901

Barbara Harvey, *Living and Dying in England 1100-1540: The Monastic Experience*, Oxford University Press, 1993

J. K. Knight, *The End of Antiquity*, Tempus Publishing, 1999

David Knowles, *The Monastic Order in England*, 2nd edn., Cambridge University Press, 1963

C. H. Lawrence, *Medieval Monasticism*, 2nd edn., Longman, 1989

R. W. Southern, *Saint Anselm: A Portrait in a Landscape*, Cambridge University Press, 1990

A. Squire, *Ailred of Rievaulx*, SPCK, 1969

G. Williams, *The Welsh Church from Conquest to Reformation*, University of Wales Press, 1962

## CHAPTER EIGHT

Frank Barlow, *Thomas Becket*, Weidenfeld and Nicolson, 1986

Brenda Bolton, *A Show with a Meaning: Innocent III's Approach to the Fourth Lateran Council, 1215* in eadem, *Innocent III: Studies on Papal Authority and Pastoral Care*, Variorum Collected Studies Series, CS 490, Ashgate, 1995

C. R. Cheney, *From Becket to Langton: English Church Government 1170-1213*, Manchester University Press, 1956

Stephen Church, *King John: New Interpretations*, Boydell & Brewer, 1999

Anne Duggan, *The Cult of St Thomas Becket in the Thirteenth Century* in Meryl Jancey (ed.), *St Thomas Cantilupe, Bishop of Hereford: Essays in his Honour*, The Friends of Hereford Cathedral, 1982

Charles Duggan, *From the Conquest to the Reign of John* in C. H. Lawrence (ed.), *The English Church and the Papacy in the Middle Ages*, Burns & Oates, 1965

Richard Eales, *The Political Setting of the Becket Translation of 1220* in D. Wood (ed.), *Martyrs and Martyrologies*, Studies in Church History 30, Blackwell Publishers, 1993

Ronald Finucane, *Miracles and Pilgrims: Popular Beliefs in Medieval England*, J M Dent & Sons, 1977

John Gillingham, *The Angevin Empire* in idem., *Richard Coeur de Lion*, Hambledon Press, 1994

John Gillingham, *Richard I*, Yale University Press, 1999

D. J. Hall, *English Medieval Pilgrimage*, Routledge & Kegan Paul, 1965

Henry Mayr-Harting (ed.) *St Hugh of Lincoln*, Oxford University Press, 1986

F. M. Powicke, *Stephen Langton*, Oxford University Press, 1928

Phyllis B. Roberts, *Selected Sermons of Stephen Langton*, Pontifical Institute of Medieval Studies, 1980

W. L. Warren, *Henry II*, Methuen, 1973

W. L. Warren, *King John*, London, 1961, reprinted with an introduction by D. A. Carpenter, Yale University Press, 1998

## CHAPTER NINE

T. S. R. Boase, *Castles and Churches of the Crusading Kingdom*, Oxford University Press, 1976

Jaroslav Folda, *The Art of the Crusaders in the Holy Land 1098-1187*, Cambridge University Press, 1995

Harry W. Hazard (ed.), *The Art and Architecture of the Crusader States, (A History of the Crusades, Volume IV)*, University of Wisconsin Press, 1977

C. Hillenbrand, *The Crusades: Islamic Perspectives*, Edinburgh University Press, 1999

S. Lloyd, *English Society and the Crusade 1216-1307*, Oxford University Press, 1988

J. S. C. Riley-Smith (ed.), *The Atlas of the Crusades*, Times Books/Facts on File, 1991

J. S. C. Riley-Smith, *The Crusades: A Short History*, Yale University Press, 1987

J. S. C. Riley-Smith (ed.), *The Oxford Illustrated History of the Crusades*, Oxford University Press, 1995 (reissued in paperback as *The Oxford History of the Crusades*, Oxford University Press, 1999)

C. Tyerman, *England and the Crusades 1095-1588*, University of Chicago Press, 1988

## CHAPTER TEN

W. A. Pantin, *The English Church in the Fourteenth Century*, Cambridge University Press, 1955

Richard Southern, *Robert Grosseteste: The Growth of an English Mind in Medieval Europe*, Clarendon Press, 1986

Robert N. Swanson, *Church and Society in Late Medieval England*, Blackwell Publishers, 1989

Norman Tanner, *The Church in Late Medieval Norwich 1370-1532*, Pontifical Institute of Medieval Studies, 1984

## CHAPTER ELEVEN

Marion Glasscoe, *English Medieval Mystics: Games of Faith*, Longman, 1993

Jonathan Hughes, *Pastors and Visionaries: Religion and Secular Life in Late Medieval Yorkshire*, Boydell Press, 1988

W. A. Pantin, *The English Church in the Fourteenth Century*, Cambridge University Press, 1955

R. N. Swanson, *Catholic England: Faith, Religion and Observance before the Reformation*, Manchester University Press, 1993

Modern English versions of writings of the principal mystics are available in the Penguin Classics editions.

## CHAPTER TWELVE

J. Bossy, *Christianity in the West 1400-1700*, Oxford University Press, 1985

E. Duffy, *The Stripping of the Altars: Traditional Religion in England 1400-1580*, Yale University Press, 1992

C. Harper-Bill, *The Pre-Reformation Church in England 1400-1530*, Longman, 1989

Simon Jenkins, *England's Thousand Best Churches*, Penguin Press, 1999

M. K. Jones & M. G. Underwood, *The King's Mother: Lady Margaret Beaufort, Countess of Richmond and Derby*, Cambridge University Press, 1992

R. N. Swanson, *Church and Society in Late Medieval England*, Blackwell Publishers, 1989

A. Hamilton Thompson, *The English Clergy and their Organisation in the Later Middle Ages*, Oxford University Press, 1947

B. A. Windeatt (trans.), *The Book of Margery Kempe*, Penguin Books, 1985

## CHAPTER THIRTEEN

Euan Cameron, *The European Reformation*, Oxford University Press, 1991

Mark Greengrass, *The Longman Companion to the European Reformation c.1500-1618*, Longman Companions to History, Longman, 1998

Hans J. Hillerbrand (ed.) *The Oxford Encyclopedia of the Reformation*, 4 vols., Oxford University Press, 1996

Carter Lindberg, *The European Reformations*, Blackwell Publishers, 1996

Carter Lindberg (ed.), *The European Reformations Sourcebook*, Blackwell Publishers, 2000

Andrew Pettegree (ed.), *The Early Reformation in Europe*, Cambridge University Press, 1992

Andrew Pettegree (ed.), *The Reformation World*, Routledge, 2000

## CHAPTER FOURTEEN

S. Brigden, *London and the Reformation*, Clarendon Press, 1989

Maria Dowling, *Fisher of Men: A Life of John Fisher 1469-1535*, Macmillan Publishers, 1999

E. Duffy, *The Stripping of the Altars: Traditional Religion in England 1400-1580*, Yale University Press, 1992

John Guy, *Thomas More*, Arnold, 2000

Christopher Haigh, *English Reformations: Religion, Politics and Society Under the Tudors*, Oxford University Press, 1993

C. Harper-Bill, *The Pre-Reformation Church in England 1400-1530*, Longman, 1989

D. MacCulloch, *Thomas Cranmer: A Life*, Yale University Press, 1996

J. J. Scarisbrick, *Henry VIII*, Yale University Press, 1968

## CHAPTER FIFTEEN

M. Aston, *England's Iconoclasts: 1. Laws against Images*, Clarendon Press, 1988

E. Duffy, *The Stripping of the Altars: Traditional Religion in England 1400-1580*, Yale University Press, 1992

D. M. Loades, *The Reign of Mary Tudor*, revised edn., Longman, 1991

D. MacCulloch, *Thomas Cranmer: A Life*, Yale University Press, 1996

D. MacCulloch, *Tudor Church Militant: Edward VI and the Protestant Reformation*, Penguin/Allen Lane, 1999

A. Pettegree, *Marian Protestantism: Six Studies*, Scolar Press, 1996

## CHAPTER SIXTEEN

Margaret Aston, *The King's Bedpost: Reformation and Iconography in a Tudor Group Portrait*, Cambridge University Press, 1993

Patrick Collinson, *Archbishop Grindal 1519-1583: The Struggle for a Reformation Church*, Jonathan Cape & University of California Press, 1979

Patrick Collinson, *The Elizabethan Puritan Movement*, Oxford University Press, 1990

Patrick Collinson, *The Religion of Protestants: The Church in English Society 1559-1625*, Oxford University Press, 1982

E. Duffy, *The Stripping of the Altars: Traditional Religion in England 1400-1580*, Yale University Press, 1992

Christopher Haigh, *English Reformations: Religion, Politics and Society Under the Tudors*, Oxford University Press, 1993

Peter Lake, *Anglicans and Puritans? Presbyterianism and English Conformist Thought from Whitgift to Hooker*, Unwin Hyman, 1988

Peter Lake, *Moderate Puritans and the Elizabethan Church*, Cambridge University Press, 1982

Diarmaid MacCulloch, *The Later Reformation in England 1547-1603*, Macmillan Publishers, 1990

Christopher Marsh, *Popular Religion in Sixteenth-Century England*, Macmillan Publishers, 1998

A. S. McGrade (ed.), *Richard Hooker and the Construction of Christian Community*, Medieval & Renaissance Texts and Studies, Arizona University, Tempe AZ, 1997

Michael C. Questier, *Conversion, Politics and Religion in England 1580-1625*, Cambridge University Press, 1996

Alexandra Walsham, *Church Papists: Catholicism, Conformity and Confessional Polemic in Early Modern England*, 2nd edition, Boydell Press, 1999

## CHAPTER SEVENTEEN

Elizabeth Clarke, *Theory and Theology in George Herbert's Poetry*, Oxford University Press, 1997

Kenneth Fincham (ed.), *The Early Stuart Church 1603-1642*, Macmillan, 1993

Judith Maltby, *Prayer Book and People in Elizabethan and Early Stuart England*, Cambridge University Press, 1998

Peter Marshall (ed.), *The Impact of the Reformation 1500-1640*, Arnold, 1997

H. R. McAdoo & Kenneth Stevenson, *The Mystery of the Eucharist in the Anglican Tradition*, Canterbury Press, 1995

Peter E. McCullough, *Sermons at Court: Politics and Religion in Elizabethan and Jacobean Preaching*, Oxford University Press, 1998

Kenneth Stevenson, *Covenant of Grace Renewed*, Darton Longman and Todd, 1994

Kenneth Stevenson, *The Mystery of Baptism in the Anglican Tradition*, Canterbury Press, 1998

## CHAPTER EIGHTEEN

H. R. McAdoo & Kenneth Stevenson, *The Mystery of the Eucharist in the Anglican Tradition*, Canterbury Press, 1995

John Morrill, *The Nature of the English Revolution*, Longman, 1993

W. A. Shaw, *A History of the English Church During the Civil War and Commonwealth 1640-1660*, 2 vols., Longman, 1900

John Spurr, *The Restoration Church of England*, Yale University Press, 1991

Kenneth Stevenson, *Covenant of Grace Renewed*, Darton Longman and Todd, 1994

Kenneth Stevenson, *The Mystery of Baptism in the Anglican Tradition*, Canterbury Press, 1998

David Underdown, *Revel, Riot and Rebellion: Popular Politics and Culture in England 1603-1660*, Oxford University Press, 1985

## CHAPTER NINETEEN

J. A. I. Champion, *The Pillars of Priestcraft Shaken: The Church of England and its Enemies 1660-1730*, Cambridge University Press, 1992

George Every, *The High Church Party 1688-1718*, SPCK, 1956

E. G. Rupp, *Religion in England 1688-1791*, Oxford University Press, 1986

W. M. Spellman, *The Latitudinarians and the Church of England 1660-1700*, University of Georgia Press, 1993

John Spurr, *The Restoration Church of England 1646-1689*, Yale University Press, 1991

John Walsh, Colin Haydon & Stephen Taylor (eds.), *The Church of England c.1689-c.1833: From Toleration to Tractarianism*, Cambridge University Press, 1993

## CHAPTER TWENTY

G. V. Bennett, *The Tory Crisis in Church and State 1688-1730: The career of Francis Atterbury, Bishop of Rochester*, Clarendon Press, 1975

Jeremy Gregory, *Restoration, Reformation and Reform 1660-1828: Archbishops of Canterbury and their diocese*, Oxford University Press, 2000

Colin Haydon, *Anti-popery in Eighteenth-century England c.1714-80: A political and social study*, Manchester University Press, 1993

Geoffrey Holmes, *The trial of Dr Sacheverell*, Eyre Methuen, 1973

W. M. Jacob, *Lay People and Religion in the Early Eighteenth Century*, Cambridge University Press, 1996

Norman Sykes, *Church and State in England in the Eighteenth Century*, Cambridge University Press, 1934

Norman Sykes, *From Sheldon to Secker: Aspects of English Church History 1660-1768*, Cambridge University Press, 1959

John Walsh, Colin Haydon & Stephen Taylor (eds.), *The Church of England c.1689 - c.1833: From Toleration to Tractarianism*, Cambridge University Press, 1993

## CHAPTER TWENTY ONE

F. Baker, *John Wesley and the Church of England*, Epworth Press, 1970

D. Bebbington, *Evangelicalism in Modern Britain: A History from the 1930s to the 1980s*, Routledge, 1989

Rupert E. Davies & others (eds.), *History of Methodism in Great Britain, volume 1*, Epworth Press, 1965

V. H. H. Green, *John Wesley*, Thomas Nelson & Sons, 1964

R. P. Heitzenrater, *Wesley and the People Called Methodists*, Abingdon Press, 1995

Christopher Idle (ed.), *Wesley's Journal* (abridged), Lion Publishing, 1986

Elisabeth Jay (ed.), *Wesley's Journal* (abridged), Oxford University Press, 1987

H. D. Rack, *Reasonable Enthusiast: John Wesley and the Rise of Methodism*, 2nd edn., Epworth Press, 1992

## CHAPTER TWENTY TWO

D. W. Bebbington, *Evangelicalism in Modern Britain: A History from the 1930s to the 1980s*, Routledge, 1989

G. F. A. Best, *Temporal Pillars: Queen Anne's Bounty, the Ecclesiastical Commissions, and the Church of England*, Cambridge University Press, 1964

R. Brent, *Liberal Anglican Politics: Whiggery, Religion and Reform 1830-1841*, Oxford University Press, 1987

O. Brose, *Church and Parliament: The Reshaping of the Church of England 1828-1860*, Oxford University Press, 1959

A. Burns, *The Diocesan Revival in the Church of England c.1800-1870*, Oxford University Press, 1999

O. Chadwick, *The Victorian Church*, 2 vols., SCM Press, 1987

R. Hole, *Pulpits, Politics and Public Order in England 1760-1832*, Cambridge University Press, 1989

Frances Knight, *The Nineteenth Century Church and English Society*, Cambridge University Press, 1995

G. I. T. Machin, *Politics and the Churches in Great Britain 1832 to 1868*, Oxford University Press, 1977

F. C. Mather, *High Church Prophet: Bishop Samuel Horsley 1783-1806 and the Caroline Tradition in the Later Georgian Church*, Clarendon Press, 1992

P. B. Nockles, *The Oxford Movement in Context: Anglican High Churchmanship 1760-1857*, Cambridge University Press, 1996

G. Parsons, J. R. Moore & J. Wolffe (eds.), *Religion in Victorian Britain*, 5 vols., Manchester University Press, 1988 & 1997

N. Yates, *Anglican Ritualism in Victorian Britain 1830-1910*, Clarendon Press, 1999

N. Yates, *Buildings, Faith and Worship: The Liturgical Arrangement of Anglican Churches 1600-1900*, Oxford University Press, 1991

## CHAPTER TWENTY THREE

Lionel Adey, *Class and Idol in the English Hymn*, University of British Columbia Press, 1988

Lionel Adey, *Hymns and the Christian 'Myth'*, University of British Columbia Press, 1986

Louis F. Benson, *The English Hymn*, George H Doran Co., 1915

Ian Bradley, *Abide With Me: The World of Victorian Hymns*, SCM Press, 1997

Brian Castle, *Sing a New Song to the Lord*, Darton Longman and Todd, 1993

Donald Davie, *Dissentient Voice*, University of Notre Dame Press, 1982

Donald Davie, *A Gathered Church*, Routledge & Kegan Paul, 1978

John Julian, *A Dictionary of Hymnology*, John Murray, 1892, revised 1907

Robin A. Leaver, *'Goostly Psalmes and Spiritual Songes', English and Dutch Metrical Psalms from Coverdale to Utenhove 1535-1566*, Clarendon Press, 1991

Erik Routley, *The Music of Christian Hymnody*, Independent Press, 1957

Nicholas Temperley, *The Music of the English Parish Church*, Cambridge University Press, 1979

J. R. Watson, *The English Hymn: An Historical and Critical Study*, Clarendon Press, 1997

Andrew Wilson-Dickson, *A Brief History of Christian Music*, Lion Publishing, 1992

## CHAPTER TWENTY FOUR

D. W. Bebbington, *Evangelicalism in Modern Britian: A History from the 1930s to the 1980s*, Routledge, 1989

H. McLeod, *Religion and Irreligion in Victorian England*, Headstart History, 1993

E. R. Norman, *The English Catholic Church in the Nineteenth Century*, Oxford University Press, 1984

D. G. Paz, *Popular Anti-Catholicism in Mid-Victorian England*, Stanford University Press, 1992

R. Swift & S. Gilley, *The Irish in Britain 1815-1939*, Pinter Publishers, 1989

## CHAPTER TWENTY FIVE

A. Burns, *The Diocesan Revival in the Church of England c.1800-1870*, Oxford University Press, 1999

O. Chadwick, *The Victorian Church*, 2 vols., SCM Press, 1987

Jeffrey Cox, *English Churches in a Secular Society: Lambeth 1870-1930*, Oxford University Press, 1982

Alan D. Gilbert, *Religion and Society in Industrial England 1740-1914*, Longman, 1976

H. McLeod (ed.), *European Religion in the Age of Great Cities: 1830-1930*, Routledge, 1994

H. Mcleod, *Piety and Poverty: Working Class Religion in Berlin, London and New York 1870-1914*, Holmes and Meier, 1996

H. Mcleod, *Religion and Society in England 1850-1914*, Macmillan Publishers, 1996

H. Mcleod, *Religion and the People of Western Europe 1789-1989*, Oxford University Press 1997

H. Mcleod, *Secularisation in Western Europe 1848-1914*, Macmillan Publishers, 2000

James Obelkevich, *Religion and Rural Society: South Lindsey 1825-1875*, Oxford University Press, 1976

G. Parsons, J. R. Moore & J. Wolffe (eds.), *Religion in Victorian Britain*, 5 vols., Manchester University Press, 1988 & 1997

Mark Smith, *Religion and Industrial Society: Oldham and Saddleworth 1740-1865*, Oxford University Press, 1995

S. C. Williams, *Religious Belief and Popular Culture in Southwark c.1880-1939*, Oxford University Press, 1999

John Wolffe, *God and Greater Britain: Religion and National Life in Britain and Ireland 1843-1945*, Routledge, 1994

## CHAPTER TWENTY SIX

Paul Avis, *Anglicanism and the Christian Church: Theological Resources in Historical Perspective*, T & T Clark, 1989

W. M. Jacob, *The Making of the Anglican Church Worldwide*, SPCK, 1997

William L. Sachs, *The Transformation of Anglicanism: From State Church to Global Communion*, Cambridge University Press, 1993

Brian Stanley, *The Bible and the Flag: Protestant Missionaries and British Imperialism in the nineteenth and twentieth centuries*, Apollos, 1990

Alan M. G. Stephenson, *Anglicanism and the Lambeth Conferences*, SPCK, 1978

Stephen W. Sykes (ed.), *Authority in the Anglican Communion*, Anglican Book Centre Toronto, 1987

## CHAPTER TWENTY SEVEN

John Blair (ed.), *Minsters and Parish Churches: The Local Church in Transition 950-1200*, University of Oxford Committee for Archaeology, 1988

Ian Bradley, *Marching to the Promised Land*, John Murray Publishers, 1992

Asa Briggs, *A History of Broadcasting in the UK*, 5 vols., Oxford University Press, 1995

O. Chadwick, *The Victorian Church*, 2 vols., SCM Press, 1987

B. Colgrave & R. A. B. Mynors (ed. and trans.), *Bede's Ecclesiastical History of the English People*, Clarendon Press, 1969

J. C. Cox, *Churchwardens' Accounts*, Methuen, 1913

Claire Cross, *Church and People 1450-1660: The Triumph of the Laity in the English Church*, Blackwell Publishers, 1976

Adrian Hastings, *A History of English Christianity 1920-1990*, 3rd edition, SCM Press, 1991

Nicholas Orme, *Exeter Cathedral As It Was 1050-1550*, Devon Books, 1986

Nicholas Orme (ed.), *Unity and Variety: A History of the Church in Devon and Cornwall*, University of Exeter Press, 1991

Susan Wright (ed.), *Parish, Church and People: Local Studies in Lay Religion 1350-1750*, Hutchinson, 1988

## CHAPTER TWENTY EIGHT

G. K. A. Bell, *Randall Davidson Archbishop of Canterbury*, 2 vols., Oxford University Press, 1935

Owen Chadwick, *Hensley Henson: A study in the friction between Church and State*, Oxford University Press, 1983; paperback edition Canterbury Press, 1994

G. J. Cuming, *The History of Anglican Liturgy*, Macmillan Publishers, 1969

Adrian Hastings, *A History of English Christianity 1920-1990*, 3rd edition, SCM Press, 1991

R. C. D. Jasper, *The Development of the Anglican Liturgy 1662-1980*, SPCK, 1989

John Kent, *William Temple: Church, state and society in Britain 1880-1950*, Cambridge University Press, 1992

Alan Wilkinson, *The Church of England and the First World War*, SPCK, 1978
John Wolffe, *God and Greater Britain: Religion and National Life in Britain and Ireland 1843-1945*, Routledge, 1994

## CHAPTER TWENTY NINE

S. Bruce, *Religion in Modern Britain*, Oxford University Press, 1995
Grace Davie, *Religion in Britain since 1945: Believing without belonging*, Blackwell Publishers, 1994
D. Martin, *A Sociology of English Religion*, SCM Press, 1967
G. Parsons (ed.), *The Growth of Religious Diversity: Britain from 1945, Volume 1 Traditions, Volume II Issues*, Routledge in association with the Open University, 1993
B. Wilson, *Religion in a Secular Society*, Penguin Books, 1966

## CHAPTER THIRTY

John Bowker, *The Complete Bible Handbook*, Dorling Kindersley, 1998
John Bowker, *Is God a Virus? Genes, Culture and Religion*, SPCK, 1995
John Bowker, *Licensed Insanities? Religions and Belief in God in the Contemporary World*, Darton Longman and Todd, 1987
John Bowker, *The Meanings of Death*, Cambridge University Press, 1991
John Bowker, *The Oxford Dictionary of World Religions*, 2nd revised edn., Oxford University Press, 1999
John Bowker, *Problems of Suffering in Religions of the World*, Cambridge University Press, 1990
John Bowker, *The Religious Imagination and the Sense of God*, Oxford University Press, 1978
John Bowker, *The Sense of God: Sociological, Anthropological and Psychological Approaches to the Origin of the Sense of God*, One World, 1995

# INDEX OF PROPER NAMES

Figures in italics refer to illustrations

Abbot, George, Archbishop of
  Canterbury 159
Abingdon 37, 43
Abraham, Bishop of St Davids 67
Act of Supremacy (1559) 146
Act of Uniformity (1559) 146-7, 172,
  174, 175, 179
Addison, Joseph 179, 205
Ælfheah, Bishop of Winchester 43
Ælfric, Archbishop of Canterbury
  43, 46
Ælfsige, Abbot of the New Minster,
  Winchester 43
Aelfweard, Abbot of Glastonbury 43
Æthelberht, King of Kent 15, 17, 18-
  19, 22, 23, 24, 41, 243
Æthelburgh 24
Æthelred the Unready, King of
  England 41, 44-6
Æthelwold 43, 46
Afghanistan 277, 280
Africa 236-7, 242
Agilbert 26, 27, 30
Agricola 15
Aidan 6, 16, 19, 21, 22, 24, 25, 26, 30
Ailred of Rievaulx 61, 62
Alaric 6
Alban 5, 10
Alcuin 33
Aldfrith 30
Aldhelm, Bishop of Malmesbury 21,
  30
Alexander II, Pope 51
Alfred, King 14, 15, 33-4, 36-7, 44
Alhfrith 26
Allestree, Richard 172
Alternative Service Book 262, 265,
  273
Ambrose, Bishop of Milan 203, 211
Andrewes, Lancelot, Bishop of
  Winchester 155, 158
Anglo-Saxon Chronicle 9, 23, 33, 44
Anne, Queen 182
Anselm, Archbishop of Canterbury
  6-7, 49, 51, 54, 57, 60-1, 70, 91
Aquinas, Thomas (see Thomas
  Aquinas)
Archbishops' Council 265
Arles 5, 6
Armagh 15
Armitage, Anthony 159

Arnold, Thomas 200, 227
Augsburg 120, 124
Augustine Gospels 21
Augustine of Canterbury 16, 17-18,
  21, 24, 25, 51, 62, 151, 208, 211,
  243
Augustine of Hippo 5-6, 8, 203
Authorised Version of the Bible 155,
  159
Aylesford, Kent 14
Azariah, V. S., Bishop of Dornakal
  237

Bach, J. S. 211
Bairstow, Edward 211
Baker, Augustine 219
Bancroft, Richard, Archbishop of
  Canterbury 148-9, 159
Barker, Frederic, Bishop of Sydney
  238
Barking 209
Barlow, Frank 52
Barton, John 107
Barton, William 204
Bath 43
Battle Abbey 62, 64
Baur, F. C. 224
Baxter, Richard 164, 167
BBC 250-3, 264
Beaufort, Margaret 108
Bec 60-1
Beck, George Andrew, Roman
  Catholic Archbishop of Liverpool
  272
Becket, Thomas, Archbishop of
  Canterbury 68, 69, 71-2, 73, 74-5
Bede 6, 9, 10, 15, 19, 20, 21, 23, 25-
  31 passim, 35, 39
Bell, George, Bishop of Chichester
  258-9
Bell, John 208
Benedict 58, 62
Benedict XII, Pope 64
Benedictines 58, 59, 62
Benson, E. W., Archbishop of
  Canterbury 223
Benson, Joseph 190
Beowulf 11
Bertha, Queen of Kent 243, 253
Beverley Minster 73

Bible Society 195, 201
Bilney, Thomas 128
Bishopsbourne 152
Blomfield, Charles James, Bishop of London 235
Boleyn, Anne 8, 129-30, 133
Bolton Percy 107
Boniface 6
Boniface VIII, Pope 74
Bonner, Edmund 139
Book of Common Prayer 137, 139, 146, 154-9, 162-8, 180, 183, 233, 241, 247, 249, 260-2
Booth, William 221
Bosanquet, Mary 190
Bristol 188, 231
British Council of Churches 266-7
Broadcasting Act (1990) 252-3
Brown, John 184, 186
Bucer, Martin 119-20
Buckeridge, John 158
Bull, George, Bishop of St Davids 163
Burgess, Daniel 182, *183*
Burghclere, Hants 257
Burnet, Gilbert 172
Butler, Joseph, Bishop of Durham 173, 181, 185, 186
Butler, Samuel 232
Byrd, William 209, 211
Byrhtferth 43-4

Cædwalla 19, 24
Calvin, John *117*, 119-20, 124, 169
Cambridge 111-12, 120, 125, 126, 130, 150
Campion, Edmund 149
Canada 235, 237-8, 240, 242
Canterbury 6, 17, 51, 56, 109, 253
Carter, Sydney 207, 211
Carthusians 62-3, 97
Cartwright, Thomas 150-1
Cave, William 172
Caxton, William 126
Cecil, William 145
Cedd 26
Cerdic 14
Chaldon, Surrey *91*, 92
Chamberlain, Neville 258
Champart, Robert, Archbishop of Canterbury 56
Charlemagne, Emperor 36-7
Charles I 155, 158, 159, *160*, 166, 168
Charles II 139, 168, 174, 177
Charles V, Holy Roman Emperor 116, 136
Chaucer, Geoffrey 7, 103, 247
Chester 97

Chesterfield 96
Chichele, Henry, Archbishop of Canterbury 90, 111
Christian Socialism 228
Christina of Markyate 63
Church Army 227
Church Assembly 261, 263
Church Missionary Society 195-6, 201, 235, 236-7, 242
Churchill, Winston 258
Churchman, Joan 152
Cistercians 61, 62-3, *66*, 74
Clanvowe, John 99
Clapham Sect 193, 195-6
Clarke, Elizabeth 156
Clarke, Jeremiah 210
Clarkson, Thomas, 195
Cluny 59, 62
Cnut, King 44, 47
Colchester 5, 14
Colenso, J. W., Bishop of Natal 224, 232, 239-40, 242
Colet, John 125-6, 129
Colman 25, 26, 28, 29, 50
Columba 13-16 *passim*, 29
Columbanus 14, 27, 30, 37
Confession of Augsburg (1530) 120
Constantinople 7, 76, 83-4
Conybeare, John, Bishop of Bristol 184-5
Cornwall 220
Corporation Act (1661) 174, 176, 177, 201, 217, 221
Council of Constance (1414-18) 90, 91
Coventry 93
Cowper, William 201, 205
Cranmer, Thomas, Archbishop of Canterbury 130, 131, 133, 134-42 *passim*, 154-5, 249
Croft, William 210
Cromwell, Thomas 107, 130-3, 135
Cromwell, Oliver 168
Crowland Abbey *40*, 39, 43
Crowther, Samuel, Bishop of the Niger 236, *237*, 241
Crusades 77-85
Curran, Charles 252
Cuthbert 22, 23, 33, 34, 56
Cynric 14

Darwin, Charles 225, 232
David *see Dewi*
Davidson, Randall, Archbishop of Canterbury 255, 257, 259, 260, *261*
de Maistre, Joseph 284
Dearmer, Percy 206
Denmark 118

Dewi (David) 65-7
Diana, Princess of Wales *269*, 270, 273
Dionysius Exiguus 28, 31
Dissenters 169, 174, 176, 181, 182, 185, 213-18, 227
Dissolution 64
Dix, Dom Gregory 241
Doddridge, Philip 205
Dominicans 116
Donne, John 155, 204
Dorchester 35
Drayton Beauchamp 152
Dryden, John 171
Dudley, Edmund 113
Dudley, John 135, 136-8, 141, 142
Dudley-Smith, Timothy 208
Duffy, Eamon 106, 139, 154-5
Duns Scotus, John 91
Dunstable, John 209
Dunstan 43, 46
Dunsthaughlin 15
Dunwich 34
Durham *20*, 34, *53*, 54, 56


Eadmer 50
Eanfrith, King 19
East Anglia 33, 93, 220
Ebbsfleet 14
Edgar, King 37, 42, 46
Edington 34
Edith 46
Edmund the Martyr 56
Education Act (1944) 259, 262
Edward I 80
Edward II 80, 103
Edward III 80, 103
Edward VI 135, 138, 139, 141, 142, 143
Edward VII *254*, 255, 256
Edward VIII 258, 260, 262
Edwin 18, 20, 22, 23, 24, 38
Eleanor of Castile *80*
Eliot, T. S. 155
Elizabeth I 8, 139, 140, 142, 144-9, 155, 159, 248
Elizabeth II 268, 273
Ellington, Hunts 159
Ely 43, 44, 167
Enabling Act (1919) 257, 262
Engels, Frederich 226
Erasmus 7, 105, 116, 119, 124, 125
Eton 110
Eugenius IV, Pope 7
Eusebius 14
Evangelicals 187, 191, 195, 205, 207, 227, 232, 238, 240
Evelyn, John 162-3, 165, 166

Fayrfax, Robert 209
Ferrar, Nicholas 156
Fin Barre 15
Finan 25
First World War 256-7, 258, 262
Fisher, Geoffrey, Archbishop of Canterbury 241-2, 263, 267, 273
Fisher, John, Bishop of Rochester 64, 108, 127, 129, 131, 133, 158
Forest, John 141
Fountains Abbey *62*, 64
Fourth Lateran Council (1215) 69, *70*, 90-1, 95, 100
Fox, Richard 126
Foxe, John 124, 141
Francis I, King of France 80
Froude, Richard Hurrell 197, 201
Fulk of Anjou, Count 80


Gardiner, Stephen, Bishop of Winchester *136*, 139-40, 141
Garibaldi, Guiseppe 213
Gaul 6, 17, 27
General Convention (1786) 234
General Synod 263, *264*, 265, 273
Geneva 120, 124, 136, 143
George V 258
George VI 258
Germany 6, 120, 122
Gibbons, Orlando 204, 210, 211
Gibson, Edmund, Bishop of London 181, 186
Gilbert of Sempringham 61
Gildas 9, 15
Gladstone, W. E. 223, *224*
Glastonbury 43
Gloucester *26*, 54
Goodmanham 23
Gore, Charles *226*
Gorham, G. C. 248
Gray, Robert, Bishop of Cape Town 238-40, 242
Great Missenden 132
Great Reform Act (1832) 200, 201
Greene, Maurice 210
Gregory the Great, Pope 15, 17, 18, 24, 36, 41, 47, 208, 243, 250
Grey, Jane 138, 141, 142
Grindal, Edmund, Archbishop of Canterbury 145
Grocyn, William 125
Grosseteste, Robert, Bishop of Lincoln 88
Guibert of Nogent 60
Guthrum 34


Hackett, John, Bishop of Coventry and Lichfield 163

Hackett, Maria 210, 211
Hadrian IV, Pope 89
Hall, Joseph, Bishop of Norwich 143, 167
Hampton Court 129, *131*
Handel, George Friederic 210
Hayley, William 252
Heber, Reginald, Bishop of Calcutta 205
Hebrides 25
Hengist 9, 14
Henry I 70
Henry II 70, 75, 80
Henry III 74, 80
Henry IV 80, 82, 105, 247
Henry V 64, 80, 113, 247
Henry VI *112*, 113
Henry VII 64, 105, 108, 113, 246
Henry VIII 7, 80, 107, 113, 125, 128-33, 135, 138-42
Henry, Earl of Lancaster 98
Henson, Hensley, Bishop of Durham 257-8
Herbert, George 143, 152, 155, 156, 203, 204
Hereford 93
Hexham 27, 34
High Churchmen 177, 188, 191, 210, 225-6, 227, 240
Hilda, Abbess of Whitby 19, 21, 24, 26, 38
Hilton, Walter 7, 98, 100, 103
Hinton St Mary 4
Hoadly, Benjamin, Bishop of Bangor 185-6
Hogarth, William *178*, 183
Holme 107
Hong Kong 237
Honorius III, Pope 74, 75
Hooker, Richard 149-52
Horsa 9, 14
Howard, Thomas 135
Howells, Herbert 211
Hurd, Richard, Bishop of Worcester 181, 186
Hus, Jan 117
Hygelac 14
*Hymns Ancient and Modern* 206, 211

Idle, Christopher 208
Ignatius Loyola 142
India 235, 237, 241, 242
Industrial Revolution 187, 226
Inglis, Charles, Bishop of Nova Scotia 242
Innocent III, Pope 69, 71-2
Innocent IV, Pope 88
Iona 6, 13-16 *passim*, 19, 24, 25, 208

Ireland 6, 12-15, 187, 213, 217-18, 221, 223, 233
Ivo 46

James II 167, 169, 175-6, 177
James VI of Scotland, I of England 159
Jarrow 19
Jebb, John 210
John of Avranches, Archbishop of Rouen 55
John of the Cross 152
John of Worcester 50
John Paul II, Pope 266, 272
John, King of England 70, 72-5, 80
Julian of Norwich 7, 98, 100-3
Justinian 7

Keach, Benjamin 204
Keble, John 197, 201
Kells 14, 15
Kempe, John 110
Kempe, Margery 93, 100, 103, 110
Ken, Thomas 204
Kendrick, Graham 207
Kidderminster 164
King, Dr *147*
King's College Chapel, Cambridge *104*
King's Lynn 110
Kingsley, Charles 228
Kirk, Ralph 157-9

Lambeth Conferences *238-9*, 240-2
Lanfranc, Archbishop of Canterbury 6-7, 51, 52, 53, 57, 60-1, 88
Lang, Cosmo Gordon, Archbishop of Canterbury 260
Langland, William 7, 99, 103
Langton, Stephen, Archbishop of Canterbury 69-70, 72-5
Latimer, Hugh 128
Laud, William, Archbishop of Canterbury 158, 159, 171, 172
Lavenham 107, *111*
Leicester 34, 35, 93
Leland, John 185
Leofric 55
Lewes Priory 62, 64
Lichfield 73, 253
Life and Liberty Movement 262
Linacre, Thomas 125
Lincoln 88, 97
Lindisfarne 6, 19, 24, 25, 29, 33, 34
Little Gidding 156, *157*
Liverpool 220, *256*, 272
Lollards 246-7

London 5, 92, 93, 220, 227, 229-31
London City Mission 227
Long Melford 107, 109
Longland, John, Bishop of Lincoln 127
Louis XVI, King of France 201
Louth 97
Lowder, Charles 227
Ludlow, J. M. 228
Lullingstone 4
Luther, Martin 105, *114*, 116-19, 123, 124, 126-8, 130, 139, 169, 191, 204
Lutherans 119, 120, 123, 235, 273
Lyndwood, W. 89
Lyte, Henry Francis 205
Lytton, William *246*

MacCulloch, D. 153
Maitland, F. 89
Malmesbury 21, 43
Mann, Horace 221
Manning, Henry Edward, Cardinal, Archbishop of Westminster 148, 218, 240
Marburg 119, 124
Martyn, Henry 201
Mary I 8, 138, 140-2, 175
Mary Queen of Scots 144, 149
Maurice, F. D. 228
McAdoo, Harry 166
Mercia 27, 33, 43
Methodists 186, 187-93, 227, 266, 272
Metropolitan Tabernacle, London *215*
Middleton, Thomas, Bishop of Calcutta 242
Midlands 93, 220
Milton, John *170*, 171
Monk, William Henry 206
Monkwearmouth 19
Montgomery, James 205
Moravia 120
More, Hannah 196
More, Thomas 112-13, 128, 131, 133
Morgenau, Bishop of St Davids 67
Morrill, John 168
Morton, Thomas, Bishop of Lichfield 164
Myrc, John 248

Neale, J. E. 146
Neale, John Mason 205-6
Nelson, Robert 174
New Room, Bristol *192*
New Zealand 236, 238
Newell, Elizabeth 162, 163, 165

Newman, John Henry, Cardinal, 143, 148, 197-8, 201, *212*, 219, 221, 225
New Minster, Winchester 44, 45
Newton, John 195, 201
Nicholson, Sydney 211
Nonconformists 169, 173, 175, 187, 205, 213-14, 235, 256
Northumbria 18, 19, 25, 27, 33
Norwich *58*, *86*, 92, 93, 100-2
N-Town 97
Nuremberg 130

O'Connell, Daniel 217
Orderic Vitalis 50, 52, 55
Osbern 50
Osric, King 19
Oswald 19, 24, 25, 43, 46, 56
Oswiu, King 24, 25, 26, 29, 38
Owen, Wilfrid 257
Oxford 7, 99, 111-12, 125, 126, 188
Oxford Movement 176, 196-8, 201, 217

Palladius 15
Parker, Matthew, Archbishop of Canterbury 128, 145
Parker, Samuel 172
Parker, Thomas 107
Patrick 13, 14
Patrick, Simon, Bishop of Ely 167
Pattison, Mark 186
Paul IV, Pope 140
Paul, Abbot of St Albans 52-3
Paulinus 20, 24, 25, 26
Pearson, John 172-3
Pecham, John, Archbishop of Canterbury 95, 99
Pelagianism 15
Pelagius 5-6
Penda, King 19, 24
Pershore 43
Persons, Robert 149
Peterborough 43, 50
Philip II, King of Spain 140, 142
Pius V, Pope 149
Pluralities Act (1838) 199, 201
Poland 120
Pole, Reginald 140, 142
Pollard, A. F. 144
Potter, John, Archbishop of Canterbury 181
Presbyterians 164, 166, 171, 177, 182, 251
Preston 231
Prevost, Samuel 242
Prosper of Aquitaine 14, 15

Public Worship Regulation Act (1874) 227, 232
Pugin, Augustus 107
Purcell, Henry 210, 211
Puritans 7-8, 148-9, 157, 163, 180, 186, 191
Pusey, Edward Bouverie 197

Rædwold 10
Ramsey 43, 46
Ramsey, Michael, Archbishop of Canterbury 267, 268, 273
Reformation 115-20, 124, 135, 153, 247, 248, 272
Reith, John 250-2
Repton 34
Rhigyfarch 66
Richard I 70, 71, 80, 85
Richard II 80, 103, 247
Richard III 110-11, 246
Ridley, Nicholas, Bishop of London 128
Ripon 27, 232
Robert II of Normandy 80
Robinson, John, Bishop of Woolwich 273
Rollason, D. 37
Rolle, Richard 7, 98, 103
Roman Empire 4, 6, 13
Roots, Ivan 165
Roper, William 128
Rule of St Benedict 39
Ryle, Herbert 259

Sacheverell, Henry 182, 183
St Albans 43, 53, 59, 73
St Anne's, Wandsworth 194
St Augustine's, Kilburn 222
St Botolph's, Colchester 64
St Davids (Menevia) 67
St George's Chapel Windsor 110
St Mary-le-Strand, London 184
St Mark's, Venice 76
St Mary's, Battersea 167
St Pancras Chapel 107
St Patrick's, Patrington 94
St Paul's Cathedral 109, 127, 182
Saladin 85
Salisbury 156, 209
Salvation Army 216
Sandwich 47
Sassoon, Siegfried 257
Savoy Conference 164, 172
Saward, Michael 208
Scotland 166, 187, 233
Seabury, Samuel 234, 242
Secker, Thomas, Archbishop of Canterbury 181, 186

Second Vatican Council 266
Second World War 258, 262, 267-8
Selwyn, George Augustus, Bishop of Lichfield 236, 238, 242
Sempringham 64
Sergius I, Pope 14
Shaftesbury 46
Shaftesbury, 7th Earl of (Anthony Ashley Cooper) 195-6
Sheldon, Gilbert, Archbishop of Canterbury 172, 173
Sheppard, David, Bishop of Liverpool 271, 272
Sigeberht 19
Sigeric, Archbishop of Canterbury 46
Silchester 4
Simeon, Charles 195, 201
Skinner, Daniel 171
Skirlaw, Walter, Bishop of Durham 107
Society for Promoting Christian Knowledge 235, 242
Society for the Propagation of the Gospel 188, 235, 237, 242
South Africa 238-9, 242
Southern, R. 56
Spencer, Stanley 257
Spurgeon, Charles Haddon 215
Stanford, Charles 210-11
Steele, Anne 205
Stephen, King 71
Stephen, priest of Ripon 25, 26, 31
Sternberg 115
Stigand, Archbishop of Canterbury 52
Stock Exchange 276
Strasburg 120
Stubbs, W. 89
Studdert-Kennedy, G. 257
Sussex 27
Sutton Hoo 10, 15, 22
Swein Forkbeard 47
Synod of Whitby 24, 25-31

Tacitus 11, 14
Tait, A. C., Archbishop of Canterbury 223
Taize 208
Tallis, Thomas 209-11
Taverner, John 209, 210
Taylor, Jeremy 166, 167, 172
Temple, Frederick, Archbishop of Canterbury 223, 260
Temple, William, Archbishop of Canterbury 258, 260, 261
Temple Church of St Mary, London 84
Tertullian 10

Test Acts (1673 and 1678) 174, 176, 177, 180, 201, 217, 221
Thirty-Nine Articles 7, 143, 148, 149
Thomas Aquinas 91, 151
Thomas, Archbishop of York 51
Thompson, A. H. 106
Thoresby, John, Archbishop of York 95, 99
Thorney 43
Tindal, Matthew 184, 186
Toland, John 184, 186
Toleration Act (1689) 176, 179, 180, 182, 185
Toplady, Augustus Montague 205
Tower of London 48, 175
Travers, Walter 152
Truro 256, 257
Tuda 29
Tunstall, Cuthbert 125, 127
Tyacke, N. 153
Tyndale, William 127, 128, 133

Ullerston, Richard 113
United Reform Church 266
United States of America 233-40
Urban II, Pope 82

van Parris, George 141
Vaughan Williams, Ralph 206
Vaughan, Henry 204
Venn, Henry 236
Victoria, Queen 232, 256, 262
Victorius of Aquitaine 28, 31
Vikings 32-7, 46, 47
Vortigern 9, 14

Wakefield 97
Wales 65-7, 187, 220, 221, 233, 242, 256, 262
Walsingham, Francis 145
Walter, Hubert 71-2
Walton, Isaak 168
Wartburg 118
Watson, William 182
Watts, Isaac 204, 211
Wearmouth-Jarrow 35, 38-9
Wenlock Priory 132
Wesley, Charles 193, 195, 205, 211
Wesley, John 186, 187-93, 205, 211
Wesley, S. S. 210, 211
Wesley, Samuel 188

Wesley, Susanna 188
Wesley's Chapel, London 190
Wessex 33, 36, 43
Westminster Abbey 56, 110, 259
Westminster Confession 7-8
Whitby 18, 19, 38, 39, 211
White, William 234, 242
Whitefield, George 188
Whitgift, John, Archbishop of Canterbury 143, 148-9, 152
Wilberforce, Samuel, Bishop of Oxford 223
Wilberforce, William 193, 195, 196, 201
Wilfrid 21, 25-30 passim, 35
William I 50, 51
William III 169, 177
William of Ockham 91-2
William of Orange 175-6, 177
William of Waynflete, Bishop of Winchester 111
William the Conqueror 67, 88
Williams, Sarah 229
Willibrord 6
Willis, Thomas, 192
Wilsnack 115
Winchester 136
Winkworth, Catherine 206
Winnington-Ingram, Arthur, Bishop of London 256-7
Wiseman, Nicholas, Cardinal, Archbishop of Westminster 148
Wither, George 204
Wolsey, Thomas, Cardinal 128-30, 131, 133
Wood, Charles 211
Worcester 36, 46, 56
Worlock, Derek, Archbishop of Liverpool 271, 272
Worms 116-17, 124
Wulfgar, Abbot 43
Wulfsige 43
Wulfstan, Archbishop of York 43-4, 47, 55
Wycliffe, John 7, 99, 103, 105, 126, 246

York 5, 92, 93, 97, 209
York Minster 92, 109, 110-11

Zurich 124
Zwingli, Huldrych 119-20, 121, 124